THE ALPINE JOURNAL

1990/91

1. *Old Man of Hoy, Orkney, 1985. Second pitch. Al Alvarez (top) and George Band.* (Chris Mikami) (From the President's Valedictory Exhibition) (p 1)

Frontispiece

THE ALPINE JOURNAL

1990/91

Incorporating the Journal of the Ladies' Alpine Club & Alpine Climbing

A record of mountain adventure and scientific observation

Volume 95 No 339

Edited by Ernst Sondheimer

Assistant Editors:
Johanna Merz, A V Saunders and Geoffrey Templeman

assisted by Marian Elmes

FREDERICK MULLER

in association with

The Alpine Club, London

IN ASSOCIATION WITH THE ALPINE CLUB

Volume 95 No 339
THE ALPINE JOURNAL 1990/91

Address all editorial communications to the Hon Editor direct at:
51 Cholmeley Crescent
London N6 5EX

Address all sales and distribution communications to
Victoria Adam
Random Century House,
20 Vauxhall Bridge Road,
London SW1V 2SA

Back numbers:
apply to the Alpine Club or, for 1969 to date, to
Cordee, 3a De Montfort Street, Leicester LE1 7HD

First published in 1990 by Frederick Muller in association with the Alpine Club
Frederick Muller is an imprint of Random Century House,
20 Vauxhall Bridge Road, London SW1V 2SA

Century Hutchinson Publishing Group (Australia) Pty Ltd
20 Alfred Street, Milsons Point, NSW 2061, Australia

Century Hutchinson Group (NZ) Ltd
PO Box 40–086, 32–34 View Road, Glenfield, Auckland 10

Century Hutchinson (SA) Pty Ltd
PO Box 337, Bergvlei 2012, South Africa

The Alpine Club, 118 Eaton Square, London SW1W 9AF

Photoset by Deltatype Limited, Ellesmere Port

Printed and bound in Great Britain by
Butler & Tanner Ltd, Frome and London

British Library Cataloguing in Publication Data

The Alpine Journal.
I. Mountaineering
796.522
ISBN 0 09 174318 4

Contents

Illustrations

Appearing between pages 182 and 183

Appearing between pages 214 and 215

Appearing between pages 246 and 247

Valedictory Address

GEORGE BAND

(*Read before the Alpine Club on 4 December 1989*)

(*Plates 1–8*)

Oreion

Oreion – my theme is of mountains and is drawn from the Greek title of James Wood's orchestral work which received its world premiere at the BBC Promenade Concert on 9 August 1989.

James Wood was born in 1953, a Cambridge man though regrettably never in the CUMC. 'Imagine yourself in a valley,' he said. 'You look up and see one outline of one mountain – one simple wind rhythm. Climb up the side of the valley and you see more. Gradually you get to the top, and you have this intoxicating view – a whole set of wind rhythms. The idea was to see how many layers of multiple rhythmic canons I could build up, yet still retain control.'

Reverting from music to mountaineering, the opening paragraphs of Chris Bonington's first book, *I Chose to Climb*, quoted a letter he received when he was a young management trainee with Van den Berghs. He had asked for six months off to join an expedition to the Towers of Paine in Southern Patagonia. He quotes from the letter;

> We regret we cannot accede to your suggestion. If you still want to pursue mountaineering to the point of long-term expeditions in distant parts of the world, then you must see it not as something which can be combined with your business career but as something which is incompatible with it. It was very much in our minds when you joined us after returning from an expedition to the Himalaya that it was your intention to settle down uninterruptedly to a business career, particularly as you were a few years older than most people who join us as management trainees. Put as plainly as possible, the time has come for you to make up your mind whether to leave mountaineering or Van den Berghs.

We all know the decision that Chris Bonington took!

Ironically, I received an almost identical letter after I had been working for Shell for some months in the small town of Midland in the plains of West Texas. This cattle and oil town was surrounded by 200 miles of semi-desert. It had great civic pride and a main business highway called Wall Street with a skyscraper 20 storeys high. I had met a friendly millionaire, William B Blakemore II who, out of the blue, had offered to help finance my next expedition. The opportunity came with permission to visit the Russian Pamir in

1962. When I wrote to Shell asking for time off I received a similar ultimatum in reply; the letter also suggested that my next oil-field assignment would be in Venezuela where, as far as my career was concerned, I most wanted to go. Like Chris, I had to resolve the conflict between a love of climbing and the need to find a worthwhile career. Unlike him, I chose to stay with Shell, so that the title of this address could well have been 'I Chose to Work'. However, that was rather dull, so I chose the more intriguing Greek word *oreion*: 'of mountains'.

Although I chose to work, it has not exactly been a humdrum life, as I hope you will appreciate from the personal exhibition of photographs which I have enjoyed assembling in the annexe with the assistance of Bob Lawford and Peter Ledeboer, for which I am grateful. The photos serve to illustrate the first part of my talk where I indulge in a series of reminiscences, as I believe did the irrepressible Tom Longstaff in his 1949 Valedictory Address. In the second part I wish to outline some of the important developments in the Club over the last three years, and in the third and final part I give some consideration to the future role of the Club.

Returning to my Texan benefactor, when I informed him of my withdrawal from the Pamir expedition I naturally expected him to withdraw his financial support from a team whose members, apart from myself, he had never even met. However, to his eternal credit he did not, as you will see confirmed on page 35 of Malcolm Slesser's book *Red Peak*. The Russians required a merger of the potentially separate Scottish Mountaineering Club party led by Slesser and the Alpine Club/Climbers' Club group led by John Hunt. With hindsight, it was perhaps an expedition to miss, as there was some difficulty in melding it all together and, sadly, there was the tragic accident when Wilfrid Noyce and Robin Smith fell 4000 feet to their deaths on Garmo on 24 July 1962.

Life in West Texas was more predictable, although I did very nearly tread on a rattlesnake while negotiating the rockfall forming the narrows of the Santa Elena canyon of the Rio Grande in the Big Bend country between Texas and Mexico. It was exciting to spin uncontrollably through the rapids in a little rubber dinghy, with the rock-walls of the canyon rising up at least 500 feet on either side. On another occasion, passing by the Tetons in Wyoming I was able to make the first ascent of the year of the Grand Teton under the leadership of Jake Breitenbach, who sadly came to grief in the Everest ice-fall the following year.

Venezuela in November 1961, after a brief leave in England, had its compensations. Our honorary member, Sir Douglas Busk, was British Ambassador in Caracas at the time, and our Shell personnel director was bemused when he received a request from the embassy for me – a young and very junior petroleum engineer – to dine with the Ambassador my first evening. Had I caught my connection for Maracibo as planned, I would have been on the first plane to be hijacked by dissidents from Castro's Cuba.

Sir Edwin Herbert (later Lord Tangley), who was the AC President during our Everest years, was passing through Caracas on business, and we had an impromptu AC Dinner hosted by the Ambassador. I was therefore summoned back again the following evening to discuss plans for a week in the Venezuelan Andes which Busk was busy organizing; it seemed my presence would be essential. I was delighted to fall in with his plans which he later recorded in the *Alpine Journal* (*AJ*67, 280–290, 1962). We managed several climbs including a first ascent of El Vertigo, a sharp subsidiary summit of Pico Bolivar and a delightful SW face route up El Abanico.

On a later occasion Busk managed to persuade Eric Shipton to stop over on his way to Patagonia. We immediately lured Shipton into an impromptu winter ascent of Pico Bolivar with a party of my fellow-engineers, some of whom had done very little climbing. I described this weekend dash from sea-level to nearly 5000m under the title 'A Physiological Experiment' in the *Climbers' Club Journal* of 1964. There is an exposed chimney near the top with a fixed rope. On the descent we were all rather cold and wet. I was anchorman lowering the others down. The heaviest, who is now the respected Inspector-General of the Dutch State Mines, was the last to be lowered – bouncing down the fixed rope in fine style – when suddenly its tired strands snapped. He jerked to a stop as the safety rope bit into my waist and took my breath away. I was thankful it broke with him because a moment later, with no protection from above, I would have been trusting the fixed rope myself.

From Venezuela we moved to what is now Bangladesh, as laconically described in a Shell telex: 'for the further development of Band'. In those days (1968) the country was called East Pakistan and we had to report to the Ministry of Natural Resources in Islamabad, West Pakistan, 1500 miles away. We were based in Chittagong, described in the latest 1953 edition of the *Bay of Bengal Pilot* as 'a pleasant coastal town consisting of low hills on which the Europeans live. In the hollows between there are native huts and fruit trees.' A fairly accurate description. Our company had found and were in the process of developing several gasfields, some of them in the tea-gardens of Sylhet. We also drilled the first offshore well in the Bay of Bengal with a rather ancient rig called the Sidewinder. It had to be completed in a hurry, in the interval between the two cyclone seasons.

The redeeming feature of our life was the Chittagong Hill Tracts where the Karnaphuli river had been dammed for a power project which had flooded the river system to create an extensive lake, bigger than Windermere, whose tentacles reached out to the borders with Assam and Burma. Whole villages had been flooded, but in the low-water season the top of the spire of the Chakma Rajah's palace at Rangamati still appeared above the water. The surrounding hills were sparsely populated by peaceful tribal people of Burmese extraction, a few wild elephants and the very occasional tiger. One was not allowed to penetrate far without a special permit which I eventually obtained for the purpose of oil exploration. At weekends we relaxed on simple houseboats on the lake and learned how to waterski.

On one short holiday we flew to Kathmandu, during the preparations for the wedding of the Crown Prince of Nepal. In the thronging crowds around the palace, two pairs of eyes suddenly met in instant recognition: it was Tashi, my personal Sherpa on Kangchenjunga 15 years earlier. As we embraced with joy, I remembered how he had carried to the last camp at 8200m, climbing one section with his oxygen inadvertently turned off so that, when I had exhausted my own supply and was trying to hack a small platform out of the 45 degree ice-slope for our tent, it was his remaining oxygen which had given me the strength to complete the job.

My next assignment was in the Sultanate of Oman, where we arrived at the end of 1970 just six months after the young Sandhurst-trained Sultan Qaboos bin Sa'id had ousted his father. Much to Wilfrid Thesiger's dismay, the Company had recently discovered oil on the edge of the Rub al Khali, where he and his two companions bin Khabina and bin Ghabaisha had nearly died of thirst in their epic first crossing of the Empty Quarter so vividly described in his book *Arabian Sands*. At a farewell party for my predecessor in much the same location, 20 years later, I felt rather ashamed to be tucking into sliced turkey and ham and French wines in our air-conditioned desert oilfield quarters.

One tends to think of the Middle East as sandy or gravel desert, but Oman was different. In the north the mountain range of the Jebel Akhdar rose to over 2400m and was seamed by immense gorges of Himalayan dimensions. In one of these, the Wadi Mayadin, the whole geological sequence through which we were drilling in the desert further south was exposed perfectly for examination and study. On the summit plateau there were scattered settlements, with cottage roses and terraces of grain and lucerne benefiting from the occasional rainfall which was denied to the desert below. Over one New Year weekend I made a memorable journey across the range in the company of Colonel John Cooper, who had been Stirling's first recruit to the SAS and was then in charge of the Sultan's officer-cadet training academy. It was his first return to the Jebel since 1958 when he had been in the SAS team, homeward bound from Malaya, who had responded to a call from the Sultan to oust the rebel Imam of Oman from his mountain-top hide-out. Although the SAS had surprised the rebels by scaling the Jebel at night, the enemy were able to escape by a secret route down to the desert where an escort of fast-riding camels was waiting to hurry them across the border to asylum in Saudi Arabia.

At the end of 1972, it was back to Europe and The Hague by way of Kenya, where we spent Christmas and I managed a quick jaunt up to Point Lenana of Mount Kenya with an Italian pharmacist.

The Netherlands are rather flat in many respects, so at weekends we sped to the Ardennes in Belgium where we wrestled up the tilted limestone slabs of Freyre beside the river Meuse. From the opposite bank, tourists gazed up at us in wonderment as they strolled around the formal gardens and fountains of the Château de Freyre. Susan took a soft-focus snap of me struggling with slings and karabiners on the overhanging *Toit du Monde*. Coming back an hour later she found me still in much the same position. At the superb Belgian Alpine Club campsite overlooking the river we fed well. For breakfast it was *pistolets*, the local crisp bread-rolls fresh from the baker, with smoked Ardennes ham, and in the evenings *truite almandine* with draughts of exceedingly strong Trappist beer.

The Dutch climbers were most friendly. One hard winter they introduced us and our house-guests, Mike and Sally Westmacott, to skating on the frozen canals. A photograph, 'The AC on ice', was the result!

In the long hot summer of 1976 we had our first taste, or should I say smell, of the maquis in Corsica before moving to London to help with the burgeoning Northern North Sea oil developments. During this period, in 1978, a dozen of us celebrated the 25th anniversary of Everest by trekking from Darjeeling, parallel to the Himalayan chain, past Kangchenjunga, to the Everest area; a journey I had always wanted to make. The first part had changed very little since the 1950s. It was only when one arrived at Lukhla, the airport below Namche Bazar, that one learnt that over 5000 trekkers per year were now making the journey up to the Everest Base Camp. Twenty miles from the mountain there was a little turf and stone croft which could have been in Ireland, with a sign proudly proclaiming 'Ama Dablam Hotel *and* Gourmet Restaurant'. Most of its stocks of Knäckebrot, saucisson and Tiger Rum were abandoned expedition stores brought down by Sherpas through the icefall from the Western Cwm.

My final overseas assignment was in Malaysia, 1980–83, looking after Shell's operations on the north-west coast of Borneo in Sabah and Sarawak; land of pirates, headhunters, orang-utans and hornbills, made famous by the nineteenth-century exploits of Rajah Sir James Brooke. One project I still have to complete is a climbing guide to the summit rocks of Mount Kinabalu, which is capped by a very recent granite. It is an intriguing area where the flora and fauna of Asia overlap with that from Australasia. The chestnut blackbird is unique and the *Nepenthes*, or pitcher plants, occurring at around 3000m on the mountain have their counterparts in Madagascar, Sri Lanka, New Guinea and the northern tip of Australia, providing botanical evidence for continental drift.

In the coastal town of Miri we worked with Malay Muslims, Christian Kelabits and Dayaks, Indian Hindus and the ubiquitous Chinese. Whenever their numerous feast days coincided to make an extra long weekend, I would take off for the Kelabit Highlands which form the border between Sarawak and Indonesian Kalimantan: thick jungle-covered hills mostly up to 900m, with the occasional peak of 2000m. Halfway there, behind Brunei, lies Mt Mulu, scene of the Royal Geographical Society's expedition in 1978. The caves there proved a magnet for Yorkshire potholers and led to the discovery in 1981 by Andy Eavis' and Ben Lyon's expedition of the world's biggest cave chamber. In the rain-forest lived the elusive Punans who exist on jungle fruits, fish and wild pig and the smaller animals they could kill with their blowpipes. One youngster showed us how to shin easily up a climbing rope by locking it between his prehensile toes.

The leading race in the Highlands was the very intelligent Kelabits, centred on the village of Bario. It used to take them up to three weeks on foot and by river to get down to the coast, but now they have a grass airstrip built by the British during the Second World War and so, when weather permits, light planes can make the journey in an hour. In many of their longhouses, skulls are stacked under the rafters; they are the cobweb-covered relics from head-hunting days.

One of the early British residents serving under the British Rajah – I think it was Charles Hose – encouraged the Kelabits to give up head-hunting and compete on the rivers instead. I am sure he must have been a Henley rowing man! So out of this 'Great Peacemaking' was born the Baram Regatta, held subsequently every few years. In 1982, after a long gap, it was an extra-special occasion. The Regatta coincided with the centenary of the river town of Marudi and was attended by the King of Malaysia. There were races for crews of five, ten and unlimited numbers in their longboats, carved from a single tree-trunk. The tribal people – Kelabits, Kayans, Kenyans and Ibans – came by river out of the jungle and down from the hills for several days of 'jollification' and feasting, providing me with a feast of photography.

Finally, back to the United Kingdom to enjoy a regular week each June in the far north-west of Scotland; occasional diversions like the Old Man of Hoy and Mt Aiguille in the Vercors; an initiation to ski-touring; joining in the activities of the Club; and serving on the British Mountaineering Council and the Mount Everest Foundation. Then, in 1986 you did me the great honour of electing me your President.

I suppose I took over formally from Denise Evans at midnight on New Year's Eve. I was actually staying at Brackenclose in Wasdale. A few hours earlier there had been a timid knock on the door and an attractive red-haired girl came in. Her husband Kevin had not returned from Scafell. It was a filthy night; he had no torch; what should she do? I guessed from her slight accent that she came from the Netherlands, so I felt I had to assume charge. The Lakeland mountain rescue were alerted. One member of the team had just been sitting down to Chicken à la King for his New Year's Eve dinner, but they all came willingly and with powerful pre-charged torches were off up the mountainside. They found Kevin soon after midnight. He had lost his way and had sensibly bedded down for the night, but was totally soaked through and chilled. Luckily he was a survivor, and I was impressed by the quiet efficiency of the rescue team.

I now turn to review briefly the highlights of the last three years of the Club. By far the most important event was the Committee's decision, endorsed by members in the special General Meeting on 20 September 1988, to surrender the lease here at South Audley Street which still had over 20 years to run until 2010. Then, if we had taken no further action, the Club would have been homeless and out in the cold. The deal was timed fortuitously close to the top of the recent London property boom, so we obtained a good price.

This sum, plus the appropriation set aside each year, together with a prudent proportion of the Club's carefully managed investments, would allow us to acquire premises on a much longer lease to house the assets of the Club and safeguard its future. Previous Committees had always assumed that premises would remain in the London area, preferably within the boundaries of London Transport's Inner Circle. However, there was a groundswell of opinion which noted that the centre of gravity for most British climbers was further north and that a case could be developed for premises closer to that centre, possibly in a mountain area. Accepting that the Committee members could have a natural bias towards London, I was keen that the debate should be opened to all members of the Club so that we could reach a clear majority decision which we would not ever regret. This was done first with a questionnaire and then with special notice at the General Meeting on 20 September 1988, followed by another informal meeting on 27 September in the Lake District.

The questionnaire generated a 60 per cent response in which a 77 per cent majority expressed a wish to remain in London; the same general conclusion was evident from the two meetings.

At the same time, the unique opportunity had arisen, if planning permission was forthcoming, to acquire a 125-year lease on a new building to our own specification in the garden of the Royal Geographical Society. If we could afford it, this seemed very much the preferred option. Our strong historical links with the RGS could be reinforced with a physical interconnection for our mutual advantage, but we would retain our independence. After several months of frustration, created by the usual interminable local authority delays, formal planning consent has at last been granted and negotiations with the developer on the form and detail of the construction and the associated price are well advanced. Before the end of the year I had certainly hoped to be able to deliver a firm contract to my successor, Tony Streather, with a view to actual occupation in 1992 towards the end of his three-year term. Efforts leading to a firm and prudent commitment may now take a little longer. There is no doubt that, thanks largely to the brilliant negotiations in 1956 by the then Honorary Secretary, Emlyn Jones, the Club has been living at South Audley Street since 1937 in a dream world, with the landlord paying rates and the art gallery providing a significant extra rental income. Wherever we might seek permanent premises in London, we would now have to pay substantial rates; gallery income is likely to be much less. These two factors alone will require us to fund an extra £20,000–£30,000 a year. However, after a careful look at the Club's finances and with the expectation of a tight construction budget and prudent subsequent housekeeping, your Committee felt that the opportunity to build new premises at the RGS should be pursued most strongly.

Meanwhile, for the interim period after we vacate South Audley Street (formally by 31 March 1990), the Club is concluding arrangements for temporary accommodation at the Ski Club of Great Britain in Eaton Square, with the use of the Council Room of the Royal Institute of Naval Architects just across the road for our General Meetings. In particular the Ski Club, with its attractive bar, should provide an excellent social base during this interim period, and I hope members will make full use of it. An enormous debt of thanks is due to all those who have worked on these arrangements, in particular our retiring Honorary Secretary, Steve Town, the retiring Vice-President, Sir Alan Pullinger who has led (and will, we hope, continue to lead) the Work Group on the future premises, Emlyn Jones for his financial negotiations, Stuart Beare for legal advice and the indefatigable Bob Lawford, amongst others, for his detailed planning of the move backed up by tiny scale models.

When we all 'chose to climb' we probably never envisaged getting quite so involved in administration, high finance and real-estate management in the name of mountaineering! However, we have to see all this through in order to preserve and build on all that is best for the Club and its present and future members.

Our other activities have been more in keeping with the traditional role of the Club; I mention but a few.

Mike Baker assisted in the updating and simplification of the Club rules, which at the same time brought Alpine Climbing Group members into full membership of the AC while remaining a distinguished group within it – an aspiration to which Emlyn Jones alluded in his Valedictory Address in 1982, and which is now achieved.

The *Alpine Journal* is maintaining its quality and steadily increasing in size under its editor, Ernst Sondheimer. Under a new agreement negotiated with Century Hutchinson, it is now published under their imprint Frederick Muller, in association with the Club, and marketed by Century Hutchinson worldwide. The Club benefits financially.

Two new guidebooks have also seen the light of day: the *Ecrins Massif* by John Brailsford and the *Dolomites* by Ron James. I was asked to take 30 copies of the former when I went out to the Dauphiné in the summer of 1988. Unfortunately on our first climb, owing to a misunderstanding, we didn't have a single copy with us!

Another success is the bringing on-stream of the computerized Himalayan Index comprising references to the *Alpine Journal*, *American Alpine Journal*, *Himalayan Journal* and *Mountain World* from the beginnings to 1987 for all expeditions to peaks between 6000m and 7000m in the Himalaya, Karakoram and China. This has been very much a personal contribution by Michael Westmacott, assisted by Anne Andrews, and has been in addition to Mike's major responsibility as Chairman of the AC Library. I am most grateful to him for continuing as Chairman during the critical period of the move. As Emlyn also mentioned in 1982, the importance of the library cannot be overemphasized. Its future is inextricably linked to the future of the Club.

Our meetings and lectures have been well attended and have generally kept a high standard. The annual symposia at Plas y Brenin are perhaps our most worthwhile indoor activity, stimulating the imagination of those present to visit the Greater Ranges, and providing a fertile recruiting ground. Subjects have been China, North America and the Indian Himalaya. The presentations have been given almost entirely by our own members, which illustrates the quality and extent of their mountaineering. However, like Colonel Strutt, AC President in the 1930s, I must express my astonishment at some of the modern trends of what I might term 'casual climbing'. I remember Andy Fanshawe describing the outstandingly successful traverse of Chogolisa, but showing one slide of his companions strung out individually and unroped along the heavily corniced ridge where Hermann Buhl had fallen alone to his death 30 years earlier. I recall my own experience on Rakaposhi in 1954 when a huge cornice broke. If we had not been roped up then, Ted Wrangham and Ali Dad would have gone the same way as Hermann Buhl.

At the other extreme there was an example of what one might call 'cold calculated climbing'. Alan Hinkes graphically described how he and Rick Allen, roped together, were teetering on thin ice high on Makalu. When Rick fell past him, Alan had the presence of mind quickly to unclip the rope from his own climbing harness as there was no possibility of holding him. Rick had a hard skull and survived, but, had there not been other parties on the mountain, Alan would probably never have been able to get Rick down alive.

I now turn to the third and final part of my address. Although the recent debate over the location of the Club's premises resulted in a clear preference for

London, it left many wider issues unresolved. Many of those who spoke or wrote in on both sides of the debate showed their genuine concern for the standing of the Club, the services and facilities it provides, and the continuing need to maintain the strength and quality of its membership.

I was particularly keen to make the Club more attractive to those members and prospective members living outside London. In January the Committee therefore agreed to appoint a small Study Group to examine the future role of the Club, looking ahead for the next 10–20 years. The last occasion of such a review was indeed 20 years ago, in 1969, under Charles Evans's presidency. I am most grateful to Mike Baker, our Vice-President Paul Nunn and Charles Clarke for agreeing to constitute this group under Mike Baker's chairmanship. They reported in October, and I wish to draw liberally from their conclusions and recommendations which have generated spirited discussion in our last two committee meetings. Since decisions about the move were in progress, it was necessary to assume these would result in the Club having a London base throughout the period under consideration.

The Club is not without its critics both from within and without. Indeed, for many of us within it seems an inevitable topic of conversation on the long walk up to Alpine huts or along Himalayan trails. The Alpine Club is seen by some to be exclusive in a bad sense, unknown in its own country and out of touch with the vast majority of young British climbers. The group's response was to state three matters of principle and make seven recommendations.

The first matter of principle was that, if the Club is to speak with authority and influence in the mountaineering world, then it must regain a membership which represents the best in British mountaineering.

Secondly, the Club should maintain its conscious shift of concentration from the Alpine to the Greater Ranges of the world (whose greater accessibility was a main theme of Roger Chorley's Valedictory Address in 1985).

Thirdly, the unique scientific, literary and historical role of the Club should be nurtured and widened.

I have no difficulty in accepting these principles myself and, after some tangential discussions, the Committee has also endorsed them. We must build on those strengths which distinguish us from other clubs.

The seven recommendations cover a fair range.

First, membership: while resisting any reduction in entrance qualification, the group recommends a conscious decision to double the numbers by the year 2000, ie a net increase of 100 members per year.

Second, the availability of cheap 'bunkhouse'-style accommodation in London could do more than anything to make the Club attractive to regional members. At the least, a register of London members willing to offer bed or floor space would be a start, and could be included in the next circular.

Third, a case is made for three public AC lectures each year, two outside London.

Fourth, the Committee could improve its efficiency – a fair criticism – and hold half its meetings outside London.

Fifth, the Club should strengthen its links with the British Mountaineering Council and with the UIAA, not to further the interests of the AC but for the benefit of British mountaineering.

Sixth, meets are recognized as playing an important part in a healthy Club and they merit greater support and encouragement.

Seventh, the Editor of the newly invigorated *Alpine Journal* is invited to consider commissioning articles grouped round the great issues of the day.

The Committee has not yet had time to give Mike Baker's report the full consideration it deserves. I would like to congratulate Tony Streather on his election as President and invite him, together with our hardworking new Secretary Mike Esten and the Committee, to continue the discussion next year and bring whatever they decide to fruition. Meanwhile, I have asked Mike to prepare a version of the report which can be mailed to all members together with the next circular, to invite their views and comments. On the vital question of membership, increased recruitment is essential to support the higher running costs that any new London base will incur. The Committee has agreed to the formation of a special task force to consider, taking expert advice, on how this can be achieved.

The Club lives or dies by its members. I would like in closing to pay tribute to all those who give their services freely and who have helped me during my term of office. I should also record the passing of two of our more memorable members who between them combined 140 years' membership of the Club. Last July died Wing-Commander Eric Bentley Beauman at the age of 98. He had climbed with Frank Smythe on Kamet and was also one of the country's early aviators, having trained under Louis Blériot. At the outbreak of the First World War, in a Caudron biplane with an unreliable 70hp Gnome engine, he was told that he was solely responsible for the air defence of London. Protesting mildly that his aircraft had neither observer nor armament, Beauman asked his commanding officer what tactics he was to employ, should a Zeppelin intrude into London's airspace. 'That I leave to you,' came the imperturbable reply.

The other was Professor Noel Odell, the last person to see Mallory and Irvine alive, who died in February 1987, aged 96. 'While his fame rests on his achievements on Everest and Nanda Devi in 1924 and 1936,' said Peter Lloyd in a letter to me, 'I believe that the AC will particularly honour and cherish his memory for his devotion and loyalty to the Club.' Only three days before he died, I had sat next to Odell at the Royal Geographical Society for the remarkable suite of lectures by Joe Brown, Nat Allen, Doug Scott and Chris Bonington in memory of Don Whillans.

I began this address in Greek; let me finish with a favourite quotation of Odell's expressing briefly and succinctly the credo of a mountaineer – the simple words of a Swiss savant of the Middle Ages which were found engraved on the summit of the Stockhorn:

δ τῶν σρῶν ερωζ αριστοζ

The love of the mountains is best

Rimo; Changing Fortunes

An Account of the 1989 Indo-British East Karakoram Expedition

NICK KEKUS

(*Plates 9–16*)

I first heard of the East Karakoram in the winter of 1986 when I teamed up with Jim Fotheringham on the first of many forays north of the border that winter. Jim was his usual enthusiastic self. 'You should really go for Rimo I, great objective.' He continued his tale: '. . . they were not far from the top'. He paused: 'and then Venables dropped his sac, they had to retreat, you can imagine their disappointment.' (See *AJ91*, 19–32, 1986. This article also contains a useful map of the Rimo area.)

I could, but I wondered how I would ever get there, given the political situation and the fact that the Indian Mountaineering Foundation were allowing only one foreign expedition in the area per season. I soon forgot about Rimo and the Siachen glacier but stored the memory away in the recesses of my mind, to be recalled when the time was right. It was another blank to fill in on my personal map of mountaineering.

Three years later I was all set for a rock-climbing holiday in North America; guaranteed sun and perfect rock were very tempting. A phone-call in the miserable depths of winter soon put paid to my relaxing summer vacation. 'Fancy coming to the East Karakoram, Youth': Doug's unmistakable drawl came over the line. I was easy prey and soon hooked. 'I'm going to Nepal in a few days, then on to Australia. Can you help organize things while I'm away?'

'Er . . . sure, Doug.'

'I'll keep in touch – see you in Delhi, end of May.' He rang off.

All right for some, I thought, as the reality of what I'd let myself in for sunk home.

27 May 1989 saw our team assembled at the IMF headquarters in Delhi. Doug, just in from Australia, met Stephen Sustad and me at the airport and helped us clear customs as we tried to look inconspicuous pushing 10 enormous Karrimor kitbags through the customs hall. The remainder of our (loosely speaking) British team arrived at the Indian Mountaineering Foundation building in New Delhi the same day: Rob and Laurie Wood from Canada, Robert Schauer from Austria, followed by Sharu Prabhu from Bombay.

As we were leaving Britain, reports of fighting on the Siachen glacier caused us concern. However, a telex from the Indians had allayed our fears, with its 'come as planned' message. But, once in Delhi, the real situation was explained to us. The permit for Apsarasas II had, we were told, been 'temporarily withheld'.

We knew then that Apsarasas was off and openly discussed alternative objectives. At the IMF we were also introduced to the Indian contingent of the expedition. While back in Britain we had been told the Indian leader would be Hukam Singh, who had led the successful first ascent of Rimo I with the Japanese in 1988. Last-minute problems had forced the IMF to change leaders to Sonam Palzor of the Indo-Tibetean Border Police (ITBP). Three climbers, also from the ITBP, were included: Tsewang Smanla, Kanhaiya Lal (KL) and Mohan Singh. They were all experienced: Sonam had reached the summit of Everest in 1984, Smanla and KL had climbed Rimo I with the Japanese in 1988.

The main group flew to Leh on 29 May, leaving Doug and Sonam to sort out the intricacies of Indian bureaucracy. It was three weeks before we finally received the go-ahead to leave Leh. During this time we spent several days exploring and acclimatizing in the Stok range, across the Indus valley from Leh. Doug and Sonam arrived on 9 June, bearing good news: our objective was Rimo III, in particular its SW buttress. An American group with permission for Rimo III had failed to raise a team, leaving the way open for our attempt. Doug had previously applied for Rimo III back in 1986 but had been turned down, and then again in 1988, when the American group had beaten him to the permit.

On 17 June we finally left Leh for Panamik, on the military road crossing the precarious Khardung La, to descend into the fertile Nubra valley. The problems with porters in the Nubra valley were well known: they often have far more lucrative work with the army and are naturally reluctant to carry for expeditions. We tried to overcome the difficulty by employing Nepalese porters in Leh, but the current poor relations between India and Nepal prohibited this. However, Sonam managed to engage eight young students from Leh. We looked questioningly at their designer jeans and flowery shirts, wondering if they were capable of the hard work required. The porter shortage and further delays in Panamik forced Robert Schauer to return to Austria; he had limited time, half of which had disappeared with the setbacks. Robert's departure was depressing: it focused our thoughts on the shortage of time and put undue strain on our dwindling morale.

With our small group of porters we left the Army Base Camp at the Siachen snout on 19 June, following the ever-shifting glacial moraine to reach the aptly named Dust Camp in the Terong valley. Dust Camp became a 'half-way house' as porters ferried loads up from Army BC and we started pushing up to Base Camp (4300m) at the junction of the North and South Terong glaciers. On 24 June the Leh boys left the expedition; they were unable to sustain the load-carrying and incited the Panamik porters to strike. Temporarily we carried heavy loads ourselves, sometimes up to 35kg, but soon managed to persuade 20 porters to continue, albeit with reduced loads of 15–20kg. By 28 June we had established and occupied Advanced Base Camp (4800m) on the North Terong glacier. Bad weather persisted and we only had fleeting glimpses of the Rimo peaks through the swirling cloud. Stephen and I were joined by the three Indians Mohan, KL and Smanla for a recce to the Ibex col (6000m), while Doug, Laurie and Sharu explored the cwm beneath Rimos I, II and III. It was at this time that Rob Wood developed worrying chest pains. He experienced great difficulty in acclimatizing and finally, on the advice of the expedition doctor, he returned to Canada.

Doug, Laurie and Sharu's exploration had revealed Rimo III's SW buttress to be out of condition as a constant stream of powder swept the wall. However, a fine ridge on Rimo II appeared to offer a reasonable and safe route. In view of our diminished time and the unsettled weather we plumped for this, Sonam agreeing to the additional peak and to a short extension of the permit time. We established Camp 1 (5400m) near the base of the W ridge of Rimo II and, with the help of our Indian friends, proceeded to carry supplies up to this camp. The intention was to join the Indian lads and make an ascent via the mountain's W and N ridges. However, the three Indians could not agree on this choice of route. They preferred the easier though more dangerous couloir to its left which gained the col between Rimo II and Rimo III some 400m below where the W ridge emerges on to the N ridge. We, for our part, could not agree to the couloir route, especially after Smanla had been struck by falling rocks while fixing ropes. Finally, the night before our departure for the mountain, we compromised. Just beyond where the W ridge joins the N ridge there is a prominent 'Notch'; it was agreed that we would follow our separate routes to meet here for the final climb to the summit.

On 10 July Stephen and I followed the winding footprints of Doug and the girls. They were just starting up the W ridge, roped together. We soon caught them and took the lead, happy to continue solo while the climbing was easy. After 600m of climbing we reached a change in direction as the ridge curved to a distant serac band, while the terrain turned rocky and steep. We roped up and I led the way, weaving around the steepest of the rock-walls, the snow softening as the sun rose on a glorious day. Gaining height, we could now look out across the Teram Shar ice-cap, seeing new vistas, an endless roll of sparkling peaks disappearing towards Pakistan. Above the rocky section the ridge opened out into a broad convex slope. The snow had turned to mush and, our progress extremely slow, we struggled from one rock island to another, often finding the rock easier to negotiate than the snow. Finally, crossing a slight narrowing of the ridge, we picked our way up the side of a serac wall to the spacious flat top which offered an ideal campsite. Steve and I soon settled into our cramped tent for an early night. Doug, Laurie and Sharu arrived just before sunset, very tired, Doug having led every pitch while the girls had jumared behind with heavy sacs.

Steve and I continued in the lead the following day, negotiating the steep buttress behind our camp on its right-hand side. The climbing now became interesting. At first steep ice led to the toe of the rocks, and we then took a devious line through the steep rock. A narrow icy groove, which saw us gain the top of a shattered tower, was followed by more mixed terrain which proved awkward and tenuous. Finally we arrived on the crest of the buttress from where we could see the more broken continuation leading to the N ridge, emerging close to the 'Notch' and our high-altitude rendezvous.

From above I could just hear the low chatter of voices. Instinctively I looked up, scouring the ridge for their source. I shouted out enthusiastically, knowing it must be our Indian friends on the ridge above. Soon three figures appeared, silhouetted against the bright sky. They waved and shouted excitedly. I assumed they must be at a bivouac site but, as communication was difficult, I could not be sure. Steve and I set off to join them, but we had not gone far when we noticed the Indian lads starting back down the N ridge. This was strange – what were they doing? We continued, hoping to shed some light on their actions. Once on the ridge we found fixed rope snaking down to the col and their tiny tent poised on its exposed crest. The three Indians could clearly be seen, milling around the tent and we shouted down, receiving a wave in return, but further communication was impossible over such a distance. We followed the fresh foot-prints in the snow to their end and over the next prow we were greeted by a string of colourful prayer-flags draped on outcrops spanning the narrow ridge. The remains of burnt juniper smouldered on an adjacent rock. This was the scene of a *puja* – a prayer ceremony. Were they coming back up or was it an offering for a safe retreat? Steve was at first reluctant to pitch our tent on this site: it just so happened that the only suitable tent platform was directly beneath the prayer-flags. He muttered something about bad Kharma and disturbing the spirits. I reassured him with the thought that after the *puja* it would probably be the safest place to camp and would undoubtedly bring good fortune for our final ascent to the summit.

Doug and the two girls had stopped some four rope-lengths beneath us on a small snowy platform and were busy pitching their tent. I told them of the Indians' descent, and Doug soon after shouted up with the news that their tent had disappeared. From where we were there were several blind spots on the ridge and we could not see this new development. We all concluded that the Indians must be coming back up to join us.

Steve and I relaxed, enjoying the last of the warm afternoon sun. It had been the fourth day of perfect weather – for how long could it continue? Tomorrow we would cut loose from the burden of our tent and equipment, going light for the summit. Doug and the girls would traverse beneath the ridge to gain the Notch while we would continue over the rocky crest to reach the same place. The final section of ridge looked steep and awkward; it would be no less demanding than our second day. The sun dipped low over the peaks across in Pakistan. I thought of all those soldiers compelled to fight over this breathtaking country, and the tragic waste of resources by two nations who can ill afford the terrible cost. Then of the lonely, often miserable, existence of the Indo-Tibetean Border Police, patrolling the bleak Depsang plains, sometimes away for three months at a time from their home and family. What a contrast to our brief recreational visit to this magnificent region. As the bitter cold crept upon us we slipped into the sanctuary of our tiny tent, concerned and perplexed at the antics of the three Indian climbers.

On the morning of 12 July Steve and I wrestled the frozen tent into its undersize sac. There was no sign of the Indian lads. Doug and the girls were similarly stirring below. We were just about to start climbing, so I thought I would make one last scan of the N ridge. Inadvertently I looked into the great snow bowl bounding the eastern side of the Rimo group, which forms the head of the S Rimo glacier. 'I'm sure that's a tent' – I pointed to the tiny black form on the glacier below. Further searching revealed three dark figures moving steadily up the SW flank of Rimo IV. They were indeed our Indian friends, already halfway up the mountain; we could only guess at the early hour they must have left camp. They had abandoned Rimo II. Later, when we questioned the Indians on the change of course, their answers varied between not having enough fuel and thinking we were against them using fixed rope!

Steve and I started up the ridge, at first taking a line on the left of the crest following steep snowy flutings. This proved desperate as we sank into the blank rock beneath. We quickly reverted to the rock again, climbing the black shaly crest with relative ease. After 10 pitches we reached the fore-summit from which we could see the snaking ridge leading more easily to the main top. We moved together, putting in the occasional ice-screw, anticipating another hour of climbing to the summit. At 2pm we reached the foot of an impending black tower which appeared to be composed of the worst kind of loose shale imaginable. Large unstable blocks perched at impossible angles convinced me that a frontal assault was out of the question. The steep snow on the eastern side offered the only practical way. Reluctantly I ventured on to this bottomless powder, digging away until the rock beneath revealed holds and a means of progress. This continued for 20m before, as I broke through the flowery cornice to straddle the rocky ridge at an airy notch, the W face of the mountain dropped before me; an icy air current rushing through the gap added to the drama. Beyond, Steve led an impressive wall composed of more perched blocks: he made it look so easy. I struggled to keep in contact with the rock, dispatching several monstrous blocks in the process.

The summit was close now and we could feel the tension mounting with every new rise gained. One last icy step and we were there. Collapsing in the soft summit snow, we shook hands and lay back to catch our breath, enjoying the warm sun of the brilliant day. Behind us, only 12m higher and temptingly close was Rimo I. I suggested it glibly to a 'laid-back' Steve, but it was 3.30pm and we both knew it was not possible; after all, we did not have permission. We were content with the first ascent of Rimo II. We surveyed the endless vista of peaks: to the north-west the familiar profile of K2 rose – and was that Nanga Parbat hazy on the far western horizon? To the south the Saser Kangri group stood out, left of the bleak sepia Depsang plains.

We started our descent, well aware of the time that had passed while we were on the summit. Moving together as much as possible and rappelling all the lower ridge, we seemed to make fast progress, but the light was going fast and urgency crept into our actions. Finally we cut two metres off our rope (our limited hardware depleted) to make the last abseil and gain the Notch an hour after dark.

During the next two days we all descended safely to Advanced Base Camp, Doug and the girls having turned back at the Notch. The Indians had also returned. They had completed their ascent of Rimo IV (the second ascent) and had returned via the Ibex col, covering almost 35km on glaciers and crossing two cols over 6000m. This was a fine piece of mountaineering of the type at which the Indians excel.

Our thoughts now turned to the future. The weather was set fair and conditions on the mountains were good, so Doug, Steve and I decided to attempt Rimo III, SW buttress. We had left all our food and equipment for the ascent at Camp 1 and planned for several days' rest before making the attempt. On 15 July our liaison officer, Rajeev Kakkar, arrived at ABC with a letter from

Sonam, calling off the expedition. We were surprised and angry. We had spoken to Sonam only the previous evening on the radio, and he had given no indication of his intentions. Steve left for Base Camp immediately to try and persuade Sonam to reconsider, but he was already too late. Sonam had left for Army Base Camp, and porters were evacuating equipment there. Fearing repercussions such as occurred on Peter Hillary's expedition, we had no option but to comply. Sonam could offer no satisfactory reason for his decision and later admitted that he had been hasty.

A few days later the weather broke: we had been climbing in a brief window of perfect weather. And so, despite the frustrations, delays and personal conflicts, Steve and I at least came back with a mountaineering success, but we were all left wondering about what might have been.

As Sonam said to Doug on the way out: 'We will never know why things turned out as they have – maybe it's for the best.' There was no arguing with that.

(*See also Doug Scott's Commentary in Area Notes (India), pp251–254 of this volume.*)

Chaos

A V SAUNDERS

(*Plates 18–23*)

And then again, it might have started in the pub. Most expeditions do. Maybe a chance mention of the mountain led to a beery response. Perhaps this led in turn to increasing enthusiasm, or a position from which it was difficult to back down. One never remembers the details. Suddenly there is an expedition. Expeditions are like the full frontal storms of recent years, no one really knows how or where they start. A South Pacific butterfly flaps its wings in a particular way and a month later the entire south coast of England is devastated. If the insect had slept two minutes longer, we would have had perfectly clear cold winters, and the best ice climbing this century.

There is a theory going the rounds of the popular science magazines which describes this sort of thing. It is all about instability, apparently. The theory calls itself Chaos Theory, and its proponents are known as chaologists. I find this highly descriptive of our expedition . . . Instability . . . Chaos. So, back to the pub, for Probability Theory suggests that it was a pub. The expedition was Mike Woolridge's idea. The team would not be a team, but four or five pairs of climbers. Base Camp was to be a shared facility: Snell's Field under Makalu. Should be cheap and cheerful, and the climbers would book enough routes on Makalu to keep everyone occupied without getting in each other's way. In the event this would cost us no more than if we had booked only one route on the mountain. In fact we arrived in Nepal armed with permission to attempt no fewer than five different lines on Makalu I and II.

The team consisted (in no discernible order, of course) of Gill Irvine (doctor), Hamish Irvine, Ulric Jessop, Andy Fanshawe, Rob Collister, Lindsay Griffin, Mike Woolridge (leader), Calvin Torrans, Stephen Sustad and myself.

We were also fortunate to gain the support and sponsorship of Blackspur Plc, a Mancunian printing concern. The Blackspur T-shirts became instantly popular in Kathmandu; when lost, one only needed to ask the shopkeeper which way the last batch of T-shirts had gone. Naturally, part of the sponsorship package involved taking the media with us. There was a video team, Kees t'Hooft and Annette Carmichael, and a film crew, Peter and Harriet Getzels. The Getzels brought their daughter Rachel, who in turn brought much joy to our Base Camp, and two assistants, Annie the Nannie, a staff photographer at the Architectural Association, and Tsering the Sherpani. In Kathmandu we picked up our Base Camp staff, a truly wonderful group of cooks and assistant cooks, a sirdar and our liaison officer, Mr Khanal of Interpol. All a normal part of the Nepalese conditions of granting permission.

So now there were 10 climbers, the seven media persons and the six Nepalese staff – and bureaucracy. Already we were feeling the gale from the butterfly wings. We needed food and supplies for two months at base, and then there was the fortnight walk-in each way: three months' total food. That made about 120 porter loads, but the porters themselves needed food, and the porters carrying the porters' food needed food too, and so on *ad infinitum*. Actually not *ad infinitum*, otherwise Zeno would have been right. But our final porter-load tally seemed almost as large . . . 180, though we never had more than 140 porters. Round one to Chaology.

Amongst the five routes booked on the Makalu massif, the prime objective was the traverse of Makalu. We never even got near to it: the early onset of the jet-stream and windslab high on the mountain saw to that.

Sustad, our Secret Weapon, had already once climbed to within metres of the summit by the nightmarish SE ridge (*AJ90*, 88–96, 1985). With Doug Scott and Jean Afanassieff, Steve had attempted a version of the SE ridge that involved dropping into the world's highest valley and, on retreat, trying to climb out of it again.

'It's like having to climb an 8000m peak just to get down', said Steve, who did not seem at all keen to repeat his 1984 experience. Nevertheless, he did agree to look at the possibility of a traverse in the opposite direction, from north to south. Always assuming, of course, that the weather allowed it and that we were sufficiently acclimatized.

Doug's 1984 expedition had acclimatized via a number of smaller peaks, including Baruntse and Chamlang. This plan had been highly successful, so we decided to emulate it; we, too, would acclimatize via a number of lower peaks on the outlying spurs of Makalu, climb Kangchuntse, then move on to Makalu.

Steve and I had completed the first part of our sports plan, including a new line on a 6400m peak on one of the southern ridges of Makalu, a climb we completed with Andy Fanshawe in a blizzard. Apparently we had looked into Tibet but I don't remember too much of that climb, what with the asthma, the altitude and the dysentery. A few days later, Andy and Ulric Jessop went on to climb a beautiful ridge to Point 6700m, a climb involving rock, mixed and ice climbing. Other members of the expedition climbed on the northern flanks of the Makalu massif and, in keeping with the original ambitions of the expedition, we finished up with 40 individual ascents of 17 peaks over 6000m.

So, by late September, when we had been acclimatizing for a month, Steve and I decided that we were ready for Part Two of the sports plan: the W face of Kangchuntse. Kangchuntse (7640m), sometimes called Makalu II, lies north of the Makalu La, and was first climbed in the autumn of 1954 by Jean Franco, Lionel Terray, Gyaltsen Norbu and Pa Norbu. The first ascensionists followed what was to become the normal route to Makalu I as far as the Makalu La, and then climbed the short S face of Kangchuntse directly to the summit ridge. Steve's researches revealed only one other route to the summit, the fine N ridge (S Nara and Lhapka Norbu, 1976), as well as a number of attempts at the W face which seem to have been repulsed by stonefall.

The W face of Kangchuntse was a natural secondary objective for the Blackspur Makalu Expedition. It looked like typical TD country, about 1000m high, with a central snow-field, a rim of summit cliffs, and granite slabs seamed with ice gullies in the lower half. The left side of the face had big black and red cliffs, from which we supposed the stone fall emanated. The right flank was guarded by a large serac. There was a possible line through the mixed ground, a faint depression slanting from the bottom right corner up to a narrow gully in the centre of the face. We had watched the face and noted that the sun reached the central section soon after 9am. We reasoned that, if we could pass the centre of the face before 9.30am, we should avoid the worst of any stonefall. That was about as much as Steve and I could agree on. Where to bivouac, how much gear to take, who would take the tent, whether to add bivibags to the sleeping-bags, what food and gas . . . all these things became so controversial that we gave up the idea of a so-called alpine-style ascent altogether. We would not take any of the gear. Just a water bottle each. Sort of Scottish-style, I suppose. Five Russian ice-screws, half a dozen pegs, a 9mm- and a 7mm-rope, a few slings. We would have a pretty good chance of returning to our tent the same day. Or so we thought.

It was the night of 26 September 1989, and I was sleeping alone at 6500m, just below the W face of Kangchuntse. Perhaps sleeping is the wrong word. I lay semi-comatose in our hopelessly tiny tent, wishing for my Blackspur umbrella to shed the snow-storms of ice rime that fell from the material with every snore. I should explain: Steve Sustad sleep-talks and I snore, or so I am told; I have never actually heard myself snoring. So, after a couple of experimental nights early in the expedition, we never shared the tent again. Next door Steve had installed himself in a comfortable Swiss tent, the Swiss Camp 2, on the normal route to Makalu I.

My alarm watch blittered dutifully at midnight; I turned it off and went back to sleep. An hour later, pricked by guilt, I wriggled out of the sleeping-bag, cursed the snow-storm of condensation and unzipped the entrance. It is a unique property of our tent that the entrance is designed for 18-inch dwarfs: anyone fractionally larger than a midget has to belly-crawl through the frozen soup and discarded noodles. The tents also have something called a valance, designed to catch snow and dump it down your neck as you emerge. This time the valance also grabbed my head-torch. It made me gargle with rage: neckfulls of snow, frozen soup, noodles, and somewhere in the icy mess was my torch . . . it was horrid. Funny name for a torture device, valance; it should be called a neck-trap. Outside, the sky was clear. It was sufficient excuse to abandon the tent. This was the moment of chaological instability. Had it not been for the neck-trap, a chaologist might argue, Steve and I would have slept peacefully till dawn, then walked down to base in time for lunch and an afternoon kip. Instead, by 1am that night, we were plodding up towards the bergschrund, following the track we had made the evening before. It was dark. There was no moon. Like an evil shadow, the W face blotted out the stars. The only noise was the shuffle of our snow shoes and my asthmatic wheezing as I struggled to keep up with Steve.

A fragile bridge crossed the bergschrund, above which we untied the ropes, trailing them behind. My rope only stuck among the rocks once, and Steve's only jammed when I trod on it. Immediately above the bergschrund the climbing was easy, low-angle ice ribbons weaving between granite outcrops. Our main problem was to pick the continuous line. This was done by switching off the torches and peering at the dark until the faintly luminescent ice appeared to glow around the buttresses. By 5am we reached the end of the ice ribbons, there were rock walls to negotiate, usually by steep ice bulges, or hidden ramps and grooves. Soon the climbing became quite technical: we needed to see to find the route, and runners, so we were pretty self-satisfied when, just when we needed it, the sky lightened. So far things were going to plan. Two pitches later we witnessed dawn flooding the Kangchung face of Everest and Lhotse Shar. A sea of cloud filled the Barun Valley below us, lapping against the islands of Chamlang, Baruntse and Tutse. In every climb there is a moment when it all seems worthwhile, and dawn on Kangchuntse was our moment. It lasted about 10 minutes. Then the constant front-pointing began to hurt. The ice was wintry, hard and glassy. Axes and points teetered on half-sunk placements, and it became important to gain that central gully before the stones came rattling down the face.

Steve led a pitch up and left out of the Spider, an Eiger-like feature we had identified during the process of writing our 'route description'. (We had spent the hours watching the face drawing out the features, estimating the pitches and time required, and setting down compass bearings for the descent. All of this was supposed to aid us in case of bad weather. Its real purpose was to divert our thoughts from the consequences of coming unstuck.) Down and to the left again lay the entry to the steep ice gully. It sported vertical steps, brittle stalactites capped with powdery cornices, so we climbed a buttress to the left; at least there we could get fine spike runners. By 1.30pm we reached the large central névé. Our difficulties should have been over, but the snow was thigh-deep and had been softened deep below the surface by raw, high-altitude sun. The original plan had been to climb to the main summit by a series of linked snow-fields, but now we could barely move. In one hour we plodded no more than 100m, so we chose a line that exited through the summit cliffs, to the right of the main summit. The perfect weather of the morning began to deteriorate through the afternoon. By 3pm we were only able to spot our route through intermittent clearings. We were aiming for a vertical chimney, blocked by a blank-looking boulder which appeared to lead on to a couple of pitches of slanting snow ramps. We reached the chimney pitch at 5pm. The next two pitches were the hardest of the day. First there was a little gentle rock-climbing, swinging about on a poorly frozen-in spike, then in order to avoid doing anything too intimate with the jammed boulder I followed a friendly-looking but deceitful corner filled with ice. The filling fell out about half-way up. Actually it wasn't much good anyway – the red rock grinned through, giving it an unsettling pink sort of colour, nor did the filling conceal any ledges or cracks. Not long after the ice fell out of the corner, I noted my last runner was too far away. The corner ended with a blank wall, and still no runner. There was another groove over to the right. It was a long stride. Wheezing a little, I watched a trembling leg stretch out towards the groove. The body, also trembling, followed the step, then a delicate traverse across thinly iced slabs and, thankfully, to a patch of snow. It was darkening quickly. Belaying took ages, the cracks were blind. The only usable flake was loose. I placed a couple of pegs behind the loose flake and dug a small stance.

When Steve followed, it was without a head-torch, groping for the ice. We thought we had cracked it. Only snow ramps above. But again we had been misled by the snow. Steve's pitch was a horror-show. It was on 60-degree granular powder, like a hill of salt. The snow was waist-deep generally, but would occasionally become much deeper, and then Steve had to struggle to make any kind of progress. He sank deeper with each effort to move up. The deepest powder lay below rock steps, which he had to mantle-shelf, having first cleared a vertical trench. There were no runners, of course. In the dark I saw none of this. All I knew was that I was shivering on the stance. I could not understand why Steve was taking so long. I shouted things I should not have shouted. But when my turn came, I understood why I had been left freezing for two hours.

A couple of slightly easier pitches led to the summit ridge. It was 9.30pm, pitch-black, and blowing a snow-storm. We had arrived at the point marked 7600m on the excellent Schneider map. A sort of South Summit. Turning left would, we knew – in so far as we knew anything – take us to the main summit. Turning right would take us down. We turned right. It cannot be said that we lost our way coming down; we never knew it. The map showed the Makalu La as being due south; it did not show the band of cliffs across the face. We had no idea of their existence until we almost fell over them. Heading due south, we moved roped together, first down a knife-edge with a cornice undercutting it, then a broad gully. Steve slipped down a powder-filled chimney which looked like an innocuous snow gully, but the snow fell away as he stepped into the chimney and left him dangling. Below the chimney slope was cut across by a blackness which swallowed the torch-light. In tiredness and despondency we turned to the left, and followed the edge of this thing – a long cliff or an enormous bergschrund. After a while we found ourselves confronted with a broad easy ice ramp which cut across the black thing and led us down to the plateau of the Makalu La.

The next part of our story is a little confused. We were tired and hungry and the water in our bottles had frozen. Ice berries formed in jangling bunches on our moustaches and, though irritating at first, later proved a useful source of water when licked. We needed to follow compass bearings. But facing into the storm, which blew from the south, was unpleasant. So we measured the wind direction and walked into it. But whenever I put the damn compass into my pocket the wind changed direction; it must have, because twice we checked our bearings, only to find we were heading north, away from the Makalu La. My brains had become quite addled. I remember saying to myself that I really did not want to go down Five Finger or the Steall Gully again, as I had done so often before. Trying hard, I managed to recall the consequences of descending the wrong way off the Makalu La. It would take us into Tibet, via the seracs of Chomo Lonzo. We would finish up on the Kangchung glacier.

After the second balls-up Steve turned to me and relieved himself of a great outpouring of spleen which, I would guess, consisted of mostly unprintable Americanisms, but the friendly gale took the words away before I could hear. I gave him the compass. We plodded on, knee-deep, thankful for the snow-shoes, the compass-bearer shouting directions to the trail-breaker, but all I could hear was the wind. By 2.30am Steve's toes had begun to freeze and he needed to loosen his boots. Also, we were a little lost. Perhaps dawn might bring new information. Our bivouac was a pair of holes in the snow. The idea had been to dig deep enough to get out of the wind, throw the rucksack into the bottom, and sit out the night; but the sack filled the hole and projected us into the weather. Steve slept well, his head thrown back, muttering peacefully. I spent the time shaking with cold and cursing the frozen water, while trying to melt the chips of ice by breathing into the neck of the bottle. 5am brought light, clouds and more snow, and that familiar conversation.

'Have you got the compass?'

'No, I gave it to you.'

'I don't think so . . .' We just looked at each other.

'Perhaps I put it down beside me . . .' Steve began to sift through the powder, but it was no use. An arm's depth of snow had fallen in the night.

'Let's wait.' We had no choice. 'Perhaps there will be a gap in the clouds.' There was no arguing with that.

After an hour a dim outline which we guessed to be Kangchuntse gave us a rough bearing. Keeping the full 50m of rope stretched out, we managed to steer a straightish line till we stumbled on the three empty tents of the Catalan Camp 3, and knew that we had joined the ordinary route again. That was the last we ever saw of the ordinary route. The tents were at 7500m; we had overshot the La. Somewhere below us were drifted-over tracks leading to fixed ropes and Camp 2. Stumbling and down-climbing, sensing that we were slowly losing height, we passed down buttresses, broad gullies and avalanche slopes. We became involved in a small avalanche; it took us 50m further on our way. Steve's only comment, brushing the snow-dust out of his hat, was, 'I hate avalanches . . .'

By late afternoon we began to recognize the contours of the seracs and the shape of the slots. It had taken all day to reach our tent; at first we could not see it. Standing 10 metres from it, I shouted to Steve that the tent had gone. Then I realized that the small pyramid of fresh snow was the tent. We had been away just 46 hours, and in that time over a metre of snow had fallen.

The next day, still dehydrated enough to produce dark brown pee, we packed the tent, sleeping bags, stove and our rubbish. The rucksacks were heavy, and the snow feathery. When we sat down we didn't stop till the sacks had dragged us beneath the surface.

The descent to 6000m should have taken an hour. It took five. In the blank whiteness, wheezing and gasping under the squeeze of the monstrous loads, we waited for clear patches to drift our way. Then one of the Catalan marker flags would appear briefly. To fix the direction before the flag disappeared, one of us would hurl a ski-stick in the right direction. It was a halting procession. In one place, where the way lay down the steep side of a serac, a hissing noise came out of the snow as I stepped on it. And then, as if a knife had been drawn across it, a slice opened across the slope. Shaking with fear I drew my foot back. I suddenly felt sick and sat down, forgetting about the feathery snow.

2. *Sherpa Tashi, who carried to Camp 6 (8200m) on Kangchenjunga in 1955.* (George Band) (From the President's Valedictory Exhibition) (p 1)

3. *Dawa Tenzing, Sherpa sirdar on Kangchenjunga in 1955, photographed in 1978 below Namche Bazar.* (George Band) (From the President's Valedictory Exhibition) (p 1)

4. *'Alpine Club on Ice', Reeuwijk, Netherlands, 1976. From L: Sally and Mike Westmacott, Jan Saltet, Rob Leopold, George Band.* (From the President's Valedictory Exhibition) (p 1)

5. *The South Face of Huagaruncho (5730m), Peru, 1956.* (George Band) (From the President's Valedictory Exhibition) (p 1)

6. *The North Ridge of Shkhara (5200m), Be ascent with Mike Harris, Derek Bull and An* (From the President's Valedictory Exhibitio

Caucasus, 1958. Third
Kustovski. (George Band)
1)

7. *Dave Atchinson and Hamish Nicol on the West Buttress of Coire Mhic Fhearchair, Beinn Eighe, Torridon, 1988.* (George Band) (From the President's Valedictory Exhibition) (p 1)

8. *George and Susan Band above Schladming, Austria. Christmas 1988.* (Rupert Band) (From the President's Valedictory Exhibition) (p 1)

'What's it like?' asked Steve, addressing a pair of boots sticking out of a hole in the snow. 'I think we might be stuck', I muttered, trying to clear my face and glasses of snow.

The problem was that the only way down was this slope. Bivouacking there was uninviting, and uphill retreat unthinkable. The solution was a small crevasse above the slope, and the job of belaying from inside the crevasse fell to me. I tied the two ropes together to lower Steve, whose job was to set off the avalanche by descending in the clumsiest way possible. He was up to the task and had soon set off a magnificent chest-deep slab which took the entire slope before it. Unfortunately he lost his way in the whiteness and had to traverse the vertical face of a serac, front-pointing his snow-shoes, to regain the avalanche cone. We had had enough of such novelties by the time we reached the deserted tented village of the ordinary route's Camp 1, at 6000m.

It took another full day to reach Base Camp, wading with snow-shoes through thigh-deep snow for six miles of broken glacier. But the weather had changed again. The skies were clear: a thin wisp, like a ragged prayer-flag, trailed from the summit of Makalu. The storm had ended and, like good amateur chaologists, Steve and I tried to make sense of it all.

'Easter Island,' suggested Steve.

'Pitcairn,' I countered.

'I bet it was Vairaatea.'

'No, no, no. Hereheretue, for sure.'

'Tongatapu?'

And then again, it might have started in the pub.

Kangchenjunga 1989

EDUARD MYSLOVSKI

(*Plate 24*)

The idea of a Second Himalayan Expedition came to our minds after the successful ascent of Mount Everest in spring 1982.

First we had to choose a mountain. Several possible objectives attracted us in the Nepal Himalaya: the Lhotse-Everest traverse, a traverse of the four summits of Kangchenjunga, the S wall of Lhotse, Makalu etc. There are enough mountaineers in the Soviet Union who are able to tackle such serious problems.

In reply to our enquiry, the Nepal Ministry of Tourism informed us that in 1989 the Kangchenjunga massif was available. This reply determined the objective of our expedition.

We started to study the literature thoroughly, in particular reports of previous expeditions to the Kangchenjunga region. Evans's book *Kangchenjunga: the Untrodden Peak*, which has had several Russian editions, was our main source of information. We also studied *Two Kangchenjungas* by P Molotetsky, published in Polish and Bulgarian. Valuable information was gained from the book *Holy Mountain of Sikkim*, and from the reports of the 1984 Japanese expedition. The most recent information on the route and on conditions for work on the face of the mountain was obtained from the Indian mountaineers who tried to climb the main summit in autumn 1988.

The USSR State Sports Committee supported our plan and agreed to finance the expedition. The Organizing Committee of the Second Himalayan Expedition was set up in November 1986. It was headed by A I Kolesov, Deputy Chairman of the USSR State Sports Committee. The systematic preparation of the expedition started from this moment. Candidates were selected from more than 60 of the best mountaineers of the Soviet Union. This was done during winter and spring 1987 at training meets in the mountains.

In spring of the same year we managed to make a reconnaissance trip to the Kangchenjunga area. The reconnaissance group consisted of six men: five prospective participants and coaches of the proposed expedition and also Eugeni Tamm, leader of our expedition 'Everest – 1982'. The group included Eduard Myslovski, its leader, Valentin Ivanov, Serguei Bershov, Serguei Efimov and Valery Khrichthaty. All of them had reached the summit of Everest in 1982. The reconnaissance route started from Taplidjung and went via Yamphodin to Base Camp near Pache's Grave (5300m). On our return to Kathmandu a preliminary agreement was concluded with the mediating agency.

During the summer meet in the Pamir, at the foot of the Peak of Communism (7495m), the main and reserve members of the expedition were selected. In winter 1988 we trained in Chimbulak near Alma-Ata city in the Tien Shan, gaining experience in making a traverse at lower heights in winter conditions. Here we partly checked the equipment of the expedition: tents, footwear, clothes, oxygen masks etc.

In the summer of 1988 we made a traverse of Peak Pobeda (Victory) (7439m) in the Tien Shan. It began from the Peak of Military Topographers and led to Peak Vazha Pschavela, a distance of about 10km at a height of 7000m. This traverse gave training in interaction tactics between groups of climbers. The final number of mountaineers in the expedition, both main and reserve, was fixed at 30.

In the autumn we visited Kathmandu where the final agreement with the mediating agency was concluded and various problems were resolved with the Nepal Ministries. In the same autumn, during a rest period on the Black Sea coast near Sukhumi, the members of the expedition and their coaches discussed the strategy and tactics of the planned traverse. There were long arguments about the starting-point: should it be Yalung Kang (the W peak) or the S summit? Many participants suggested a climb up from the side of the S summit, with an ascent of the main summit along the SW buttress, directly from the Yalung glacier. But this route is very difficult and makes it impossible to use Sherpas. We therefore finally decided to organize a camp on the plateau at 7200m, from there to establish six further camps in three directions, and then to make a traverse from the S summit. The plan was to set up two camps (4ju and 5ju) on the route to the S summit, two camps (4s and 5s) on the route to the col between the main and central summits and two camps (4ja and 5ja) on the route of the first ascent in 1955. The upper camps were to be placed at heights of 8100–8200m, to give maximum safety and to facilitate the traverse as much as possible.

The expedition started its work in February 1989. The first group flew to Kathmandu on 3 February. About 10 tons of baggage – accompanied by the expedition coach, Sergei Efimov – was taken to Calcutta by an IL-76 transport plane, and the rest of the party flew there on 9 February. Climbers and gear travelled from Calcutta to Biratnagar by buses and lorries. Difficulties arose when we reached the India-Nepal frontier at Djakbani (near Biratnagar). Only the baggage was allowed to cross; the climbers had to travel to Kakarbitta, where they were allowed to enter Nepal and move on to Biratnagar. Here the expedition bought provisions such as rice and vegetables. On buses and lorries the participants, Sherpas and 15 tons of gear were brought to Basantapur where the motorable road ended. Here we joined our film crew and 65 high-altitude porters recruited in Sola Khumbu.

The caravan of porters was organized in Basantapur; there were altogether more than 600 porters to carry the expedition's load. In order to avoid two difficult passes, covered at that time of the season with snow, we did not use the well-known route via Yamphodin. Instead we travelled along the Tamur river, then in the area of Hellok village along the Simbua Khola, and then from Torontan by the traditional route of all previous expeditions up to the Yalung glacier and the site of our Base Camp.

We experienced serious difficulties on the way from Hellok to Torontan.

There was no path there and we had to cut our way through the bamboo jungle. Some of our porters refused to work under such difficult conditions, but the strong porters hired for work on the glacier came to our help. Ramser became a temporary base for storing the loads. At this time of year the depth of snow was about 50cm. In order to cross the glacier, we set up two transit camps on it; they had big tents, kerosene kitchens and everything needed for the normal work of porters.

Base Camp was officially opened on 16 March, although loads continued to arrive. A study now started of the route from Base Camp to Camp 3. The height of the camps was as follows: Camp 1 – 6150m, Camp 2 – 6650m and Camp 3 on the plateau at about 7200m. Having put up these camps we started to establish intermediate camps. The greatest difficulties we experienced during organization of the camps were encountered in the southern direction. Here strong winds tore the tent. We had to change the tent of Camp 4 at a height of about 7650m and also change the site of the camp.

In the process of putting up Camp 5 several ascents were made. The main summit (8586m) was reached on 9 April at 4pm, by a new route from Camp 5s on the col between the main and central summits. The climbers were V Elagin (36, leader), E Klinezki (28), A Sheinov (31) and V Koroteev (33).

The S summit (8476m) was reached on 15 April at 3pm from Camp 5s. The climbers, who used a new route to the right of the Japanese and Polish routes, were M Turkevich (36), V Pastukh (32), R Khaibullin (28) and S Bershov (42, leader).

The central summit (8482m) was reached on 15 April at 5.30pm, by a new route from Camp 3. The members of this group, who did not use oxygen, were A Bukreev (31), V Khrichthaty (37, leader), V Balyberdin (39) and S Arsentiev (30).

The main summit (8586m) was reached by the normal route from Camp 4ja on 16 April at 5.30pm. The members of the group were L Troshchinenko (43, cameraman), V Suviga (35, without oxygen mask), J Moiseev (35, assistant cameraman, without oxygen mask), K Valiev (36, leader), A Glushkovsky (35, assistant cameraman), Z Khalitov (37, without oxygen mask), G Lunjakov (34, without oxygen mask) and V Dedii (29, without oxygen mask).

Another party repeated the route of S Bershov's group to the S summit, starting from Camp 5s on 17 April at 1.30pm. The members were V Karataev (34), M Mojaev (30), A Pogorelov (31) and E Vinigradsky (42, leader).

After their ascents all the members of the expedition came down to the Tseram area (about 3750m) to have a rest in the forest. Here we discussed the tactics of the intended traverse. As all of us were in good physical shape, we decided to make traverses from opposite directions by two groups, with five men in each.

The part of the traverse between the central and main summits was the most difficult and least known to us. It had been successfully carried out in two hours, but we realized that it was impossible to do the whole traverse quickly. We therefore decided to take two days over it. To provide safety for this undertaking it was necessary to supply Camp 5s between the central and main summits with everything necessary. This had to be done with the help of support parties.

The first support group climbed with oxygen up to Camp 5s. Starting at 9am, they reached the central summit at 11.20. The climbers were V Karataev, V Pastukh (leader) and M Mojaev. They then came down to the saddle where they were joined by S Bogomolov and R Khabibullin, and all five climbers reached the main summit at 2.20pm. After this ascent the group came down to Camp 3 at 8pm for a night's rest.

The traverse was started by the first group headed by S Bershov on 30 April. The members were S Bershov (leader), M Turkevich, A Pogorelov, E Vinogradsky and A Bukreev. Starting from Camp 5ja, this group climbed Yalung Kang (8505m) and returned to Camp 5 for a night's rest.

On the same day the second support group left Camp 4ja, brought oxygen up to Camp 5ja and climbed to the summit of Yalung Kang at 3pm. This group consisted of V Dedy, E Klinezky, S Arsentiev (leader), V Suviga, A Sheinov and V Khrichthaty, the last three without oxygen masks. After the ascent the group returned to Camp 4 at 7pm.

S Bershov's group continued the traverse on 1 May. It left Camp 5 at 8am, was on the main summit at 10, on the central summit at 12.40 and on the S summit at 2.45pm. Coming down from the S summit, this party removed Camps 5ju and 4ju and descended to Camp 3 at 7pm for a night's rest.

The second group selected to do the traverse consisted of V Elagin (leader), V Koroteev, Z Khalitov, G Lunjakov and V Balyberdin, the last three without oxygen masks. They left Camp 5ju at 9am on 1 May and reached the S summit at 12.30. During the rest of the traverse all the mountaineers went with oxygen masks. The two traverse parties met at 2.10pm on the saddle between the S and central summits. The second group was on the central summit at 3.50pm, on the main summit at 5.40pm, and came down to Camp 5ja at 8pm for a night's rest.

On the same day the second support group (with G Lunjakov instead of V Dedy and A Sheinov) left Camp 4ja and reached the main summit at 12. On the top they met the second party making the traverse, and they came down to Camp 5s at 7pm. Next day this group removed Camps 5s and 4s and came down to Camp 3.

The traversing party left Camp 5ja on 2 May, climbed Yalung Kang, and the same day came down to Camp 3.

So on 2 May the traverses to both ends of the Kangchenjunga massif were successfully completed. Only two camps, 4ja and 5ja, had not been removed. The third support group moved on 2 May to Camp 5ja, and the following ascended the main summit: Ang Babu Sherpa (22), S Efimov (45, leader) and N Cherni (51). Coming down they took off Camps 4ja and 5ja, completing the removal of the high-altitude camps.

In order to take off Camps 2 and 3 (Camp 1 had been removed in mid-April), we gathered together all Sherpas able to work at high altitude, climbed up to Camp 3 and, with the help of the Sherpas, carried all the load to Base Camp. In Tseram we set up a base for resting and started to organize the caravan for our return. By 7 May all members of the expedition and the film crew had come down to here. The return route was via Torontan – Yamphodin – Gopetar – Phidim – Ilam – Birtamod. From Gopetar, the load and part of the expedition were taken by lorries along the road which is now under construction. All of us arrived in Kathmandu in the evening of 18 May.

As the result of the work of the Soviet expedition 24 mountaineers out of 29, three out of five members of the film crew and one Sherpa had made ascents of summits of the Kangchenjunga massif. There were altogether 85 men/ascents on all four summits of Kangchenjunga.

Xixabangma 198

JERZY KUKUCZKA and JANUSZ

(Translated by Ingeborga Doubrawa

The first Polish expedition to the Tibetan Himalaya was organized by the Polish Alpine Association and the High Mountain Club in Katowice. Its main goal was to put a new route on Xixabangma (8046m) and to give Jerzy Kukuczka his fourteenth 8000m peak. (A short note on this expedition appeared in *AJ93*, 241, 1988/89. In the present article the height of Xixabangma has been left uncorrected at 8046m.)

Late in 1986, Kukuczka had talks with the President of the Association of Sport and Tourism of the Chinese People's Republic and a government minister, Mr Li Menghua. These were followed, in May 1987, by a week in Beijing during which Kukuczka and Majer had talks with the Chinese Mountaineering Association, led by its president Mr Zhanchua. Finally, in July of the same year, a delegation from the CMA, led by the general secretary Mr Wang Feng Tonga, visited Poland. As a result of all this activity, permission was eventually received to climb the W ridge of Xixabangma and the N wall.

The members of the expedition were: Jerzy Kukuczka (leader), Wanda Rutkiewicz, Artur Hajzer, Lech Korniszewski (expedition doctor), Janusz Majer and Ryszard Warecki, all from Poland; and from abroad: Elsa Avila and Carlos Carsolio (Mexico), Christine De Colombel and Malgorzata Bilczewska-Fromenty (France), Alan Hinkes (GB), Ramiro Navarrete (Ecuador) and Steve Untch (USA). The Chinese personnel were the liaison officer, the interpreter and the cook.

The expedition left Kathmandu on 16 August 1987 and by the evening of the following day we had reached Col Kodari on the Nepal-China border. Because of the condition of the road between Kathmandu, Kodari and Khasa (Zhangmu), parts of which had been destroyed, we were compelled to hire porters on both sides of the border. Transport was organized for us by the Chinese and, thanks to that, we were able to travel from Khasa via Nyalam and reach, very quickly, the point at about 5000m where the first conquerors of the peak had set up Base Camp in 1964.

Unfortunately, our speed in reaching such a high altitude so quickly had a bad effect on the health of some of the members of the expedition. On 20 August only part of the team was able to proceed with the yak caravan; Alan Hinkes and the two Mexicans had to be left behind at the Chinese Base Camp, looked after by the doctor. On 22 August, after three days' marching, we set up our Base Camp at about 5900m. On the same day, Janusz Majer developed symptoms of high-altitude sickness. During the night he became so ill that it was absolutely essential to get him down to Base Camp early the following morning.

s given oxygen and was carried on a makeshift stretcher made from skis pped together with pieces of rope. The transport team consisted of ukuczka, Hajzer, Navarrete and Untch. Rutkiewicz and some Tibetan porters carried down all the necessary bivouac gear. At the same time, Christine De Colombel hurried down to the Chinese Base Camp to report to the doctor. The next day, the transport team with their patient met Korniszewski at a place which we called 'sanatorium camp'. Thanks to this speedy and efficient rescue operation, Majer was soon out of danger, but his condition was still serious because of thrombosis in his leg.

During the next few days the expedition reassembled and on 28 August we started the climb. Hinkes, Warecki and Untch set up Camp 1 on the normal route at 6400m. The following day Kukuczka and Hajzer left Base Camp and, after bivouacking at 6400m, established Camp 2, also by the normal route, at 7000m, at the end of the so-called 'corridor'. On 31 August the same team reached the summit of a hitherto unclimbed peak, Yebokangal Ri (7365m) by way of the 'corridor' on the N side of the summit. Kukuczka and Hajzer then ski'd down to Base Camp.

Meanwhile, the other climbers were acclimatizing by spending the nights at either Camp 1A at 6800m or at Camp 2 at 7000m. On 5 September several teams left Base Camp aiming for the summit, but the weather deteriorated and by 7 September everyone had returned to Base Camp. Severe wind and snow prevented further action until 14 September, but on 15 September some further attempts were made on the summit. Several different teams set out at the same time. Hajzer and Kukuczka intended to climb the virgin W ridge. Avila, Colombel and Rutkiewicz, who were joined by Navarrete and Warecki, wanted to reach the summit by the normal route. Hinkes and Untch chose a more ambitious route – the unclimbed couloir of the N wall.

Hajzer, Kukuczka, Navarrete, Warecki, Avila and Rutkiewicz spent the night at Camp 1A (6800m) and Hinkes, Untch and Colombel at Camp 1 (6400m). The following day Hajzer and Kukuczka, accompanied by Warecki, reached the first pinnacle on the W ridge and spent the night at 7300m. Warecki returned to Camp 1A. Navarrete joined the ladies' team, Christine De Colombel having decided to give up her attempt on the summit. At Camp 2 they met Carsolio who had just come up from Base Camp. Hinkes and Untch reached Camp 1A. Majer and Korniszewski spent a few nights at Camps 1 and 1A and returned to Base Camp on 18 September.

By 17 September the final assault on the summit was taking place. Hajzer and Kukuczka bivouacked at 7900m after climbing the long W ridge; they had climbed all day on the S side of the W ridge in extremely strong winds blowing from the S of Nepal. Even after sunset, the winds did not stop and the temperature dropped to −35°C. The team on the normal route set up Camp 3 at 7400m. Warecki joined them in the evening, carrying one extra tent. Meanwhile Hinkes and Untch reached Camp 2.

On 18 September, at about 4pm, both teams (one coming from the W ridge and one from the normal route) met on the middle summit at about 8030m. Kukuczka and Hajzer had climbed that day on the W ridge, scaling rocky pinnacles of IV and V and sometimes abseiling off them. On their way, they reached the unclimbed W summit at 7980m. Between 5pm and 6pm all seven climbers reached the main summit of Xixabangma (8046m). Warecki carried Kukuczka's skis up the normal route and gave them to him on the summit. Both the weather and the views were superb and everyone filmed and photographed for a long time. Hajzer and Kukuczka bivouacked on the ridge between the summits while the 'normal route' team went down to Camp 3 (7400m) without any lights. The following morning Kukuczka started his descent on skis from the main summit and it took him all day to reach Base Camp. By the evening of 19 September everyone had returned except for Hinkes and Untch. They reached the summit on 19 September at about 6pm and very late that same evening they reached the tent at Camp 2 (7000m) which had been left for them. Their route through the couloir of the N wall had taken them two days to negotiate, with one bivouac at 7500m without a tent. The route traversed mixed terrain and a 50° snow and ice slope, joining that of Hajzer and Kukuczka on the ridge before the pinnacle of the W summit. During their climb through the couloir Steve Untch suffered frostbitten toes. He was wearing Koflach boots especially made for him but, unfortunately, they were too small.

On 24 September we left Base Camp and, soon afterwards, reached the Chinese Base Camp. Our caravan of yaks arrived on 26 September and by 28 September we were back in Kathmandu.

Despite the large number of members on our expedition – 13 in all – we climbed in 'alpine style' and were far from being a typical heavy Himalayan expedition. Each group within the team achieved its goals independently of the others, according to individual ambitions and potential. In this way, we achieved several notable successes: Kukuczka climbed, via a new route, his fourteenth 8000m peak; Kukuczka and Hajzer climbed two virgin peaks, Yebokangal Ri (7365m) and Xixabangma West (7980m). Hinkes and Untch made a first ascent of the central couloir of the N wall; and Hajzer and Kukuczka also made a new route up the W ridge. Avila became the first Latin-American woman to reach the summit of an 8000m peak – and at 23 one of the youngest women to do so. Ramiro Navarrete established a new altitude record for his country, Ecuador. (He died on Annapurna in 1988; see *AJ94*, 249, 1989/90, and Henry Todd's article in this volume.)

Out of the 13 members of our expedition, nine reached the summit of Xixabangma. What helped us to achieve such a successful outcome was the very pleasant atmosphere of cooperation which extended right through our international team.

A Tribute to Jerzy Kukuczka (1948–1989)

INGEBORGA DOUBRAWA-COCHLIN

Jerzy 'Jurek' Kukuczka died on 24 October 1989 when he fell near the summit of Lhotse (8516m) while attempting a first ascent of the S face. He was one of the greatest Himalayan climbers of all time and he placed the Polish flag on all fourteen 8000m peaks.

Kukuczka was born in Skoczow, Beskid Slaski, Poland, on 24 March 1948 and was educated in his local school. He became an electrical engineer and worked in the coalmining industry. In 1965 he started to climb in the Polish Tatra mountains and became a member of the Katowice High Mountain Club. He climbed the most difficult and demanding routes in the Tatra, both in summer and winter, and did some superb climbs. Then he went to the Alps, the Dolomites, the Hindu Kush, the Karakoram and Tibet. In recent years he climbed almost exclusively in the Himalaya. Kukuczka climbed all fourteen 8000m peaks, as did Reinhold Messner before him, but, unlike Messner, Kukuczka climbed all but one by new routes or in winter.

It had been Kukuczka's ambition to set up new routes on all fourteen eight-thousanders, either in summer or in winter. He climbed all but one of them without oxygen; it was only on Everest that oxygen was used for part of the way up to the South Summit. He achieved ten 8000m peaks by new routes, climbed Makalu solo, and made four first winter ascents. No other high-altitude climber has matched that record.

Kukuczka's stamina and strength at high altitudes were phenomenal. He acclimatized slowly but, once acclimatized, he was able to survive for very long periods at high altitude, if necessary without food or drink. An extremely strong climber, he reacted well to danger. He preferred to climb in 'alpine style', if possible by new routes or in winter, in a small team and without oxygen.

The most important first ascents made by Kukuczka were Everest by the South Pillar (1980); Makalu solo (1981); Gasherbrum 2 and 1 (1982) with Wojciech Kurtyka; Broad Peak – the first traverse of the massif of three peaks (1983), also with Kurtyka; Dhaulagiri and Cho Oyu (1985), first winter ascents and in the space of three weeks.

Kukuczka's ascent of Kangchenjunga in winter (1986) and then the first route on K2 via the South Wall were among his most remarkable climbs. In 1987 he finally completed all fourteen 8000m peaks. He himself once said that his favourite and most satisfying climbs were Makalu and K2. When he reached the summits of these mountains, beside leaving the Polish flag, he often left little mascots or souvenirs from his two sons.

In 1988, with Artur Hajzer, Kukuczka established yet another route on

Jerzy Kukuczka's 8000m Peaks

(This is a revised version of the list in AJ93, 258, 1988/89.*)*

1	*Lhotse*	*8516m*	4.10.1979	*Normal route. (On 24.10.1989 Jerzy Kukuczka died in a fall near the summit of Lhotse while attempting the unclimbed South Face.)*
2	*Everest*	*8848m*	19.05.1980	*New route, S Pillar. (Using oxygen only to the South Summit.)*
3	*Makalu*	*8463m*	15.10.81	*New route – Flank from Barun glacier and NW ridge. Solo.*
4	*Gasherbrum 2*	*8035m*	1.07.1983	*New route, SE Flank, via virgin peak 7772m.*
5	*Gasherbrum 1*	*8068m*	23.07.1983	*New route, SW wall.*
6	*Broad Peak*	*8047m*	17.07.1984	*New route, Traverse of the Massif of 3 Peaks 7538m, 8016m, 8047m. (In 1982 Jerzy Kukuczka climbed Broad Peak via the normal route.)*
7	*Dhaulagiri*	*8167m*	21.01.1985	*1st Winter Ascent, normal route.*
8	*Cho Oyu*	*8201m*	15.02.1985	*1st Winter Ascent (as a second team), new route, SE pillar.*
9	*Nanga Parbat*	*8125m*	13.07.1985	*New route, SE pillar.*
10	*Kangchenjunga*	*8586m*	11.01.1986	*1st Winter Ascent, normal route.*
11	*K2*	*8611m*	8.07.1986	*New route, S wall.*
12	*Manaslu*	*8163m*	10.11.1986	*New route, NE wall.*
13	*Annapurna*	*8091m*	3.02.1987	*1st Winter Ascent, normal route. (On 14.10.1988 Jerzy Kukuczka established a new route via the E buttress of the S face.)*
14	*Xixabangma*	*8027m*	18.09.1987	*New route, W ridge.*

Annapurna, via the almost 2000m-high right E buttress of the S face. Over the years, he made several outstanding climbs with his close friend and longest-serving partner, Wojciech Kurtyka. He also climbed with Czok, Pawlowski, Wielicki, Heinrich, Piotrowski and Hajzer.

Kukuczka received several gold medals in Poland for achieving outstanding results abroad in sport. In 1987 he was made 'Man of the Year' in Poland after completing the 8000m peaks. He also received a crystal trophy from the Polish Foreign Minister 'for making the name of Poland famous throughout the mountaineering world'. In 1988 he was awarded an honorary Olympic silver medal by the Winter Olympic Committee in Calgary.

Kukuczka was a wonderful husband and father of two sons. He was a quiet, modest and sensitive man, religious, dependable, a considerate friend and tolerant in his opinions of other climbers. His magnetic personality was an inspiration to all around him. His loss is a severe blow to his family, to Poland and to international mountaineering. His eternal bivouac is high among his beloved Himalayan peaks, and his memory will remain for ever with those who climb mountains.

Annapurna Test 88

(Dedicated to the memory of Jerzy Kukuczka)

HENRY TODD

Mountaineering is an extremely hazardous sport and only the lucky should involve themselves. Too many first-rate climbers perish in the mountains for there to be any doubts about the inherent risks. Almost all climbers have epic tales to tell about friends who have lost their lives in pursuit of the ecstasy and elation that accompany success on high peaks.

The story of our expedition to Annapurna I South Face in 1988 is just one more in the list of epics. My motive in writing about it, however, is that expeditioning raises important questions of morality and ethics in climbing. On Annapurna I found myself faced with an extraordinary dilemma, when I had to decide between my instincts and my unspoken but ever-present obligations towards the other members of the expedition.

It could be said that such a conflict is rare, since rescue or assistance above 7000m are unusual and not to be relied upon, but on Annapurna I was faced with what I regarded briefly as an impossible choice. Alone and unprepared, I went to the aid of members of a summit team and faced what I felt would be probable death. What was proposed seemed, frankly, suicidal. The alternative was to obey my strong instincts for self-preservation and decline to help, offering absolutely any excuse for escape down. If I had done this I would never have been able to face my colleagues again, and certainly my expeditioning career would have been at an end. I would have saved myself, but would have lost my self-esteem. In the event there was no choice and I held on to my dignity, but I feel very fortunate to have survived the experience.

14 October, Camp 1, 5800m, Annapurna I South Face

I emerged from my tent at 6.30am to watch the world's premier mountaineer, Jerzy Kukuczka ('Jurek'), the expedition 'director', and his Polish compatriot Artur Hajzer ('Elephant'), climbing the S face to the E ridge, on their new route to the E summit of Annapurna I. It was a beautifully clear sunny morning as they made their ascent, which required the utmost commitment and high technical expertise. Despite the difficulty, they were progressing well.

We had previously seen the bottom section of this new route on the extreme right of the S face; it was guarded by enormous hanging ice-cliffs deluged by an avalanche. This had led the rest of the expedition to choose an alternative route to the E ridge which ascended the W flank of Tarke Kang (Glacier Dome, 7142m). We then planned to join the Loretan route to the west of the summit of Tarke Kang, where the ridge descended before joining Annapurna I below Roc Noir (7500m).

Later that day Janusz Majer, the expedition 'leader', Phil Butler ('Lobby') and I climbed from Camp 1 to Camp 2 (6700m), in order to establish the alternative route. On reaching Camp 2 we could see that Jurek and Elephant were almost at the E ridge. There had been a storm since our last visit and we spent the day digging out the battered tent and attempting to fix the broken poles. At this altitude such exertions took their toll and the next day we decided to rest, allowing the three behind to catch up. We therefore worked on the site until the arrival of our Californian friend Steve Untch ('Lunch without the L, sir'), Francisco Espinoza ('Pancho') of Ecuador – an extremely gifted and experienced Andean climber on his first Himalayan expedition – and Ramiro Navarrete, Ecuador's leading mountaineer who had been promised a new house if he succeeded in climbing yet another 8000m peak. They pitched another tent and, after a long discussion, it was decided that Janusz would join them and proceed the next day to Camp 3, leaving Lobby and me to descend to Camp 1, ostensibly to pick up more gear and then, hopefully, to follow the others up after a couple of days, at least as far as Roc Noir.

Around midday we heard the good news on our radio that Jurek and Elephant had reached the E summit and were on their way down.

Next morning Lobby and I slept in while the others prepared for departure. It was again clear and sunny, but extremely cold, and inside the tents we were registering −25°C. At 7am we got up to photograph the other four as they left, and we then began leisurely preparations for our descent. This took longer than usual as Lobby was feeling tired and ill. Before our departure, however, we were amazed to see Steve, the strongest member of the ascent group, returning. He told us that the stumps of a couple of his toes, amputated after his ascent of Xixabangma (8027m) in 1987, were starting to freeze, and he had felt it prudent to return. The three of us therefore proceeded down to Camp 1 where we all spent the night before Steve continued disconsolately to Base Camp – his climbing ended, he thought, for this expedition.

Later that morning Lobby explained reluctantly that he felt his condition precluded any further ascent, and he would therefore have to follow Steve. After he had departed I spent the day in Camp 1, contemplating my options and waiting for Jurek and Elephant to come down from their successful ascent. By the time they reached Camp 1, I had decided to stay up. I informed them of my decision before they continued down, and they were pleased. Everyone other than the three going for the summit would otherwise have been in Base Camp. Although we had radio communication, my descent would have left the three very vulnerable so high on the hill.

The second team was not expected back in Camp 1 for a couple of days, and my thoughts therefore turned to soloing Tarke Kang. I was glad to have the Annapurna Sanctuary ostensibly to myself. It was on Fluted Peak, dominating that part of the area, that my friends Jane Richmond and Trevor Pilling had last been seen 10 months earlier. It was as if I was in their presence, and this feeling was accentuated by the incredible beauty of the place. I felt a sense of elation at my solitude and spent much of the next two days in idle absorption.

Once back in Camp 2, on my way up to Tarke Kang, I heard on the radio that Ramiro had reached the E summit and that Janusz had got within 10m before being beaten back by a fierce wind. Pancho was 100m behind and had been similarly defeated.

In Camp 2 I spent a sleepless night and then rose early next morning to prepare for my ascent. It was again a beautifully clear and calm morning with perfect visibility. Once outside the tent, therefore, I was not too surprised to hear distinct but unintelligible shouting. It did not sound distressed and I was excited at the prospect of meeting Janusz, Pancho and Ramiro later in the day. Since their summit call we had had no radio contact, but it was assumed that this was because of a frozen battery.

In order to return from the Tarke Kang summit in time for their arrival at Camp 2, I set out as briskly as 6800m would allow. The higher I climbed, the more I could see of their descent route, and I expected to see them soon. An hour after leaving I managed to raise a typically hung-over response from Base Camp on the radio and briefed them on my plans. Two hours later I was still climbing in beautifully clear conditions, although the wind had started to rise very slightly and, as had been the daily pattern, a few clouds were coming up from the Modi Kola. I was beginning to wonder why I had not seen the others descending to my left. I could see almost all of their descent route and it was obvious that they were not on it, nor could I see any tracks in the snow. I continued to climb. After another hour I reached the first of the three summits and, deciding that the middle summit was the highest, I climbed it. The view was stupendous: Tibet and China to the north, India and Pakistan to the south and west, and the mountains of Nepal stretching to the east. I felt tremendous.

Once I had descended out of the wind, the entire route from Camp 3 to Camp 2 was visible. But there was no sign of life. Suddenly full of apprehension, I got out the radio and called Base Camp. Elephant answered. He suggested that something must be amiss and that maybe I should go across to Camp 3 and check things out. To me this seemed a suicidal idea. I reminded him that he had thought the ridge between Tarke Kang and Roc Noir, below which Camp 3 was situated, was one of the more treacherous parts of the route – and he had crossed it roped up with Jurek. He was now suggesting that I should solo it despite the dangers which, as I had already pointed out, were heightened by fresh avalanche tracks across my path. He became more urgent and suggested that I had certain responsibilities. Jurek then broke in, speaking passionately. He pointed out that I was one and they were three, and he wanted to know who had spent the previous night in Camp 3. I conceded and closed the radio down. I was absolutely horrified. How could I have agreed to probable self-destruction? Even if I reached the other side I had no gear for survival, and I would be too exhausted to return to Camp 2 that day. The wind was now definitely rising. I called and asked to speak to Lobby, but I realized that there was nothing he could say. How could anyone help with such a dilemma? I just had to go.

I set out full of apprehension, a feeling that was strengthened when I soon came upon a double cornice, my first serious objective hazard. I couldn't work out its configuration but started to cross gingerly. Suddenly I fell through the crust, up to my armpits. I thrashed around trying to get an axe in. It refused to bite, pulling instead through the crust to the soft snow beneath which kept collapsing around me. After a terrifying 10 minutes of frantic effort, I eventually managed to extricate myself. Once out, I lay beside the huge hole gasping for breath, taking another 10 minutes to pull myself together. I called Base Camp again and informed them of my terrible fright, telling them that I would be calling every 10 minutes from now on. If something happened there was nothing they could do, but I wanted them to know where I was. Without really thinking about it, however, I immediately adopted a more aggressive approach to what had previously terrified me. The ridge which I had to cross required a traverse along a 100m line, about 10m below its summit. The rising strength of the wind helped to press me towards the slope, making it a little easier, and I ignored the 1000m of air directly beneath me. An hour later the worst was over.

Once on the other side I began to look for Camp 3, which was partly hidden by some very nasty-looking seracs. I eventually spotted the blue Gemini and, as I approached, I saw the amazing sight of my friend Janusz sitting in the doorway, grinning delightedly but with blood all over his face. He just sat there looking very pleased as I approached the tent.

We exchanged greetings. (The Poles love greetings!) Inside the tent, as I knelt down, I could see a body in a sleeping-bag. It was breathing irregularly. 'Who's that?' I asked. 'Pancho,' Janusz replied. 'Oh,' I said, 'How is he?'

'He's had an accident,' said Janusz. I had already guessed that. By now I could see his badly swollen face and could smell a strong, disturbing, odour. I asked Janusz if he was unconscious. He said no – he was only sleeping, as they had been forced to bivi out the night before, high on the summit ridge.

My thoughts naturally turned to Ramiro. Janusz said that he was almost certainly dead, but did not explain exactly what had happened. In what could only have been in hallucination, Janusz had been convinced that he had seen me or Jurek, he wasn't sure, beckoning him down the summit ridge. He had followed with Pancho behind him. Ramiro, however, had chosen not to be directed in this manner and had decided on an alternative line. Janusz, on reaching the spot where he had seen the apparition, found the beginning of the fixed rope.

Once Janusz's face had been wiped clean I discovered that the blood was coming from his gums. They had been lacerated from eating ice and had bled into his beard, which he had then rubbed on to his face to make a grotesque mask. I called Base Camp. I had not reported back since my scare on the cornice well over an hour before, and they were understandably relieved to hear from me. I explained the situation and Jurek asked to speak to Janusz. After they had spoken for five minutes in impenetrable Polish, Janusz announced that we were to go down immediately. This utter lunacy was more than I could countenance. I took the radio and forcefully explained that there was no possibility whatsoever of returning across the ridge that day and keeping them both alive, let alone myself. An afternoon storm was brewing and it was already snowing lightly. There would have been absolutely no chance of reaching Camp 2. I explained that I did not think Janusz was fully *compos mentis* and that Pancho was in no state to move. They believed that moving down would improve Pancho's chances of survival, but I disagreed and told them that he would never survive a descent that afternoon. They had to accept this. Janusz then asked me for gas cylinders. It transpired that the early-morning shouting had been to request more gas and sleeping-bags, as well as some food. Of course, this had been completely lost on me. I had been climbing solo in the expectation of returning to Camp 2, and I had travelled as lightly as possible. We therefore had only two sleeping-bags between three, and less than half a cylinder of gas – a woefully inadequate amount, especially as we were all badly dehydrated.

By now Pancho was awake and talking rapidly in Spanish. I examined him as best I could. His hands were badly frostbitten and he had no use of his fingers or thumbs. He had also lost his spectacles though, on closer examination, his facial injuries were fairly superficial. He complained of internal pains, but there was nothing that I could do. He had apparently fallen 30m down a slope, missing gaping crevasses on either side, miraculously bouncing the right way each time. From the first-aid kit that Jane Richmond had given me the previous year I took a temgisic tablet (a strong analgesic) and told Pancho with exaggerated mime (he spoke no English) to put it under his tongue and not to swallow it. Despite the language barrier he continued to talk volubly and, to my consternation, immediately swallowed the tablet. I then gave Janusz – still sitting there looking bemused – some painkillers which made him feel better. He soon cheered up and started brewing a small, inadequate drink. It was the most we could afford under the circumstances. We knew that in our position a serious, prolonged change in the weather spelt certain death, and we had to be frugal with our paltry gas supply. Later, and with great difficulty, I succeeded in getting Pancho properly into his sleeping-bag, only to have him fighting to get out again in order to have a pee. He struggled to the door of the tent which I unzipped for him, and he then unceremoniously urinated all over Janusz's rucksack.

It was an extremely uncomfortable night with the three of us squashed into what I would regard as a comfortable one-man tent. An inch of hoar-frost on the inside meant that any movement was met with a shower of ice particles. Having no sleeping-bag I spent the night sitting up, rubbing my steadily freezing toes while the other two slept fitfully. My new Asolo expedition boots had let me down. Next morning was hell. I had to put on Pancho's boots and crampons for him, and he was the only member of the expedition who had ancient strapped ones. It took me ages and my hands froze.

We travelled as lightly as possible, leaving behind all unnecessary equipment including the ropes. Pancho asked about roping-up and I pointed out that each of us stood a better chance unroped. The climbing was risky enough without being dragged off by a probable fall by one of the other two. My intention was to cut big steps and holes for ice-axe shafts, back across the ridge. As we were earlier than on the previous day, the ice was crisper, though it was still a time-consuming and exhausting task. But it was the only method which gave the other two a chance. To my great relief, Pancho was able to hold his axes in the palms of his hands without requiring his fingers, and he followed me closely, always waiting 10 or 15m behind each time I stopped.

Eventually, and with great relief, Pancho and I reached relative safety. Janusz, however, was in difficulty; he seemed exhausted and he had stopped moving. After shouting to him I decided to proceed with Pancho, and we left good tracks behind us. It was a good hour before Janusz caught up and I was very relieved at his sudden reappearance. But then he always was a wily old man of the mountains. Our descent was painfully slow. The storm the previous evening had completely obliterated all tracks, and a new way had to be found down to Camp 2. The seracs below, which could not be seen until we were almost upon them, posed the main difficulty. These great ice-cliffs dropped suddenly from a fairly gentle slope, and finding our way through them proved time-consuming and difficult.

In search of safer ground, I started to descend an ice-cliff towards what looked like a snow-bridge crossing a crevasse at the cliff base. I climbed down, facing towards the slope, using both my axes. On reaching the snow-bridge, still facing inwards, I tentatively prodded behind me with one crampon. Slowly I put more weight on the bridge. It held. I then put my other foot down, slowly placing even more weight on the snow, straightening my arms to hang full-length on my axes. Suddenly, the bridge collapsed. One of my axes pulled and for a brief second I held on one axe only. That then pulled as well as I plunged down into the crevasse beneath me. I dropped about six metres down a vertical ice-wall before my fall was broken by a downward-sloping ledge. My plunge then continued down the ledge, but more slowly. I swung my axe and eventually arrested my fall after another six metres. Large amounts of fine snow cascaded down on top of me and choked me. The axe still held but my rucksack, which I had undone around the waist because of avalanche danger, was now trying to strangle me too. I methodically sorted myself out, terrified that more snow would come down. I could find no footing. Everything I touched with my crampons collapsed into the void, and I did not want to move too abruptly for fear of losing my grip altogether. Eventually, after moments of sheer terror, I managed to find a tentative footing by bridging across the crevasse. I was virtually doing the splits between the two ice-walls, but I could see my position as the clouds of falling snow cleared and there was now more light. Laboriously I started to climb up. In order to avoid the serac above, I needed to emerge from the crevasse on the downhill side, and this started to worry me. I was able to get some leverage on the poor snow above and, to my extreme relief, I eventually escaped on the safe side. I was in an exhausted state and collapsed on the snow, panting, retching and shaking.

Once I had recovered I looked for Pancho and Janusz. To my astonishment I could see them some way off. They had obviously given up on me and were on their way down. I just couldn't believe it. Logic would have told me that there was nothing they could do for me, and that they had no other choice but to press on if they were to survive. At that moment, though, it was difficult to understand, and I was completely dumbfounded. Soon I had caught them up. Exhaustion precluded discussion and we continued onwards. We were making very slow progress and the day was racing past. The terrain was still awkward and dangerous and Janusz twice fell into small crevasses, one of which I had pointed out to him. He attempted to jump across but disappeared up to his waist, frantically swinging his axe before arresting his fall and then painfully pulling himself out. We continued down and eventually used our diminishing battery to call Camp 1 and ask for general directions. Steve and Elephant had left Base Camp immediately it had become apparent that there was an emergency, and had reached Camp 1 by climbing through the night in record time. Elephant told us that Steve, in a great feat of determination, had continued and powered his way up to Camp 2.

Elephant was unable to help with directions, however, and although visibility was still good we just did not know where we were in relation to Camp 2. Then, suddenly, we heard a voice and could see that it was coming from a tiny red figure way down to our left. We started towards him and I could soon tell it was Steve. After 20 minutes we could make out his shouted directions, but as we got closer a change of wind direction took his voice away and we were left on a very nasty slope with distinct slab-avalanche potential. As we went across the snow was cracking around us, and it was with considerable relief that we reached more substantial ground from where we could see Camp 2 quite close by.

Steve greeted us on our arrival at the camp but, on hearing that we had no sleeping-bags, he explained that he had to go back down immediately, as there were only two in the tent. He had been unable to bring anything up with him, but there was gas and food and we would be OK until the next day. Within minutes he was gone. Our rescue seemed to be retreating in front of us.

The three of us were exhausted. Pancho's fingers looked terrible; the blisters of the frostbite had more than doubled in size. He also seemed very disorientated and it was difficult to communicate with him. Janusz seemed relatively all right physically. He was very tired but could rely on the depth of resources at his disposal. I was relieved to see that he was now fully *compos mentis* and set on survival. For myself, I was exhausted. The incident in the crevasse had forced me to dig very deeply into my own reserves. I was also extremely dehydrated and couldn't feel my toes in my right foot. No amount of massaging brought back any sensation. We put Pancho in a sleeping-bag and I climbed into the other, giving Janusz my bivi-sack and duvet. He was quite content to eat my treasured stash of marzipan and brew. Then, after taking one of my Tremalzipan, he slept soundly.

Next morning had us rested. Pancho seemed more distant but was apparently still able to understand what I required of him, and he had stopped asking about Ramiro. I put on his boots and crampons again and tried to explain that I would help him down the fixed ropes. I couldn't quite think how I was going to do this, as parts of the ropes hung almost free. My fears soon proved unfounded, however, as again he seemed to retain all his technical ability and was able to use the palms of his hands to grip the rope after I had attached his descendeur. The problem came at the bottom of the first stretch of rope. A deep crevasse required a very athletic leap which in our state was obviously impossible. I had tied some spare rope on to the bottom of the fixed rope, and this enabled us to cross the crevasse with some degree of security. But, when Pancho reached the knot joining the two ropes, everything halted. How on earth could he take off his descendeur and reattach it without the use of his fingers? He worked it out, though. He pulled up the end of the rope and with his almost useless hands threaded it through his figure-of-eight descendeur. It was simplicity itself, yet his mind seemed a million miles away. We then worked our way down slowly. Even though we were descending, we had to stop and rest frequently, sometimes after only six strides or so. Eventually, however, we could see Steve in the distance on a plateau. He had brought the medical oxygen cylinder with him and had set it up. We still had to get to him, as he needed to conserve his own strength and could not approach us. After a tremendous effort we finally reached him, and at last I felt that I could hand over responsibility for Pancho to his friend Steve.

With the others following behind more slowly, I then continued down to Camp 1 where I met Elephant who told me that we were to proceed straight down to Advanced Base to see the doctor, Lech. As it would soon be dark, I departed again immediately the others arrived at Camp 1, hoping to get through a dangerous section before nightfall. I succeeded in this, only to be faced with the badly crevassed glacier which had changed out of all recognition since I had crossed it almost two weeks earlier. After getting lost several times, I eventually arrived at Advanced Base, Lech's head-torch having guided me on the last stretch. Several hours later the others arrived, and next morning we continued down to Base Camp. Unsurprisingly, I felt badly in need of a rest, although no more so than Pancho. However, the next day the porters arrived and we broke camp. It took us five days to reach Kathmandu, stopping only to eat and sleep. Pancho was able to walk only on the first day and it became apparent that he would have to be carried. Two extra porters were hired to take it in turns to carry him down in a specially-constructed basket which they carried on their backs.

From the time I set off from Camp 1 to Tarke Kang I had not had a single rest-day until reaching Kathmandu 10 days later, but I felt tremendous.

Janusz was met on the walk out by Sofia, his beautiful wife, and his condition then improved exponentially.

Pancho's Hands?

But Ramiro was never seen again. The last photograph which I took as we recrossed the ridge descending from Camp 3 shows Pancho tired and resting behind me. In the background rises the E ridge of Annapurna I and a small blue shape marks Camp 3. Below this, an indistinct red dot can just be discerned. It may be a blotch on the film, but Ramiro was dressed in red and it might be him.

On the way down, I became aware that all the radio conversations had been recorded by a Polish television crew making a film about Jurek. This disturbed me more than a little, as I wondered just how studied the responses had been from Base Camp in our radio conversations. I have yet to hear the tape, but it will certainly be fascinating to hear myself *in extremis*.

This is my story of the expedition – my epic. Every member has his own story, though. When Jurek was asked by his Swiss publisher, Juliusz Komarnicki, about me, his answer was: 'Henry. Oh, he just climbed as high as he was able, and then climbed down again.'

Six weeks after returning to Europe, Janusz asked me if I would like to join him and Elephant in trying a new route on the W face of Everest. This time I hesitated before saying yes.

A Single Yellow Headlight

MAL DUFF

(*Plate 17*)

I was wet. Very wet. I had in fact reached that level of saturation where further soakings had ceased to be a matter of concern. Rivulets flowed unheeded down the cleft of my buttocks, mixing with the swirling puddle in which I sat. The puddle swirled because we were both, me and the puddle, located on the roof of a lurching bus.

The rain of the last five hours had transformed my previously acquired thick coating of dust into a rich ochre pigment. This had gradually spread to all parts of my body. My watch spluttering under the deluge registered 3am.

After 21 hours I was bruised, battered and could quite easily have become bored. Life was temporarily so unpleasant that it was a perverse pleasure, a matter of stubborn pride, to remain unnumbed and alert.

The bus was of a variety and vintage long since deceased in all but the most exotic backwaters of the Asian continent. This particular specimen was of such remarkable decrepitude that it inspired awe for its unfortunate but exceptionally talented mechanic. Our passage through the night was illuminated by a solo headlight, the beam of which staggered ahead of us, bathing the sheeting rain in a sickly amber light.

The single-track road on which we travelled switchbacked high above the valley, cliffs fell vertically for 250m below us, terminating in a river of obvious malevolence. This, along with the absence of windscreen wipers, and the bus trundling on abstractly bald tyres, accounted for the palpably nervous atmosphere generated by our complement of passengers.

By contrast three goats and several baskets of chickens destined for the pot in Kathmandu didn't give a damn. One of the goats – a belligerent billy, showing remarkable presence of mind under the circumstances – devised an oddly symbolic pre-emptive revenge by biting a large chunk from the back of my partner's expensive fleece jacket.

Of course, being on the roof I was lucky. Inside was a hell which can only be imagined. Nepali hillpeople are unusually susceptible to motion sickness. Despite my good fortune I could only reflect on how different things had appeared when we started out nearly a day before.

For all expeditions (Asian bus journeys surely qualify for this exalted title) planning, preparation and reconnaissance are essential for success. Like true professionals, we had held a tactical discussion the night before our proposed departure. We felt confident of our Third-World body-swerving abilities.

Nepalese buses are all scheduled (at least this is the illusion portrayed) to depart at 6am, a manoeuvre performed with much gusto, horn-blowing, revving (black smoke is vital for effect at this point) and dog-barking, all underpinned by a chorus of cocks crowing in the nippy, soft light of dawn. Bus departures are exciting. Most of the villagers, babes in arms through to ancient crones, thrill to the symphonic ritual.

In the resulting mêlée a Caucasian with an imperfect mastery of the Nepali tongue is quite likely to get on the wrong bus, perhaps one which will never leave, trampled underfoot, or – worse – as pulling remorselessly away he notices that all the equipment so carefully stowed on the roof is now a swiftly diminishing and forlorn-looking pile residing at the side of the village street.

We had concluded that by entering the bus (illegally or otherwise) at dead of night, when all Nepal sleeps, and by lashing our baggage on the roof and occupying the prime seats, those in the glass cage beside the driver, we would – when eventually discovered – be able to announce a *fait accompli* and ignore all and every effort to displace us. This we achieved in the stealthy time before dawn, holding our places firmly as an endless struggle of passengers boarded. Our plan, founded on hard-won experience, looked good.

An hour later the bus started, stopped, took on water, fired up again (a complicated procedure, this), backed up to get oil, collected a repaired but dubious-looking tyre, throughout all of which we were involved in a fierce ritual battle repelling boarders from our comfortable and privileged positions. When the driver felt that he had caught the attention of a sufficient percentage of the population, we (the bus) – with a positive swagger of our overloaded suspension – departed for Kathmandu. Our collective sigh of relief was barely exhaled when we pulled up outside a particularly noxious teahouse, into which the driver and brakeman disappeared for breakfast. (When things go wrong, as they frequently do, the brakeman jumps off the bus and thrusts a huge wooden wedge under the wheels. A tyresome (sic) job with few prospects.) Having established their positions, the mobile pecking order if you will, the passengers disembarked (an extrusion which looked impossible to reverse), and following our driver's example took a light meal. Boiled rice and pepper tea have little fascination for me as breakfast, but as no alternative seemed likely I tucked in, with a reluctant grace. We kept an eagle eye on the driver at all times as, once he has finished, the bus leaves, often with no warning. It is prudent to eat swiftly on these occasions.

Progress was uneventful for some time after breakfast, although our defences slipped somewhat, allowing an extremely pretty girl, wonderfully built, to enter our privileged position. Our doctor, fresh from repelling boarders at the window ('Now chaps, just LET GO,' emphasized by a ski-stick jab to the throat) was all courtesy and grace, even trying but failing to come to his feet. For an ex-member of the Rhodesian SAS, the very thought was of the highest order of gallantry.

Six hours into the drive circumstances changed for the worse. Exiting from a narrow gorge, we noticed that an obviously vital bridge was missing, along with 90m of road. The river was of a type described as fearsome in the best travel literature, and on the opposite bank lurked an ancient bus, showing the scavenging tendencies of a vulture. Our SAS member, trained in quickness of thought, realized that, as another overcrowded bus was only a few metres behind us, speed was of the essence in this daunting situation. Several factors caused concern. Our equipment was of tremendous variety and volume and, because of our initial tactics, was now buried at the bottom of an enormous scrummage of humanity. The Doc was elected to resolve this problem. Meanwhile, Andy, master of diplomatic relationships, started offering outrageous terms to all and sundry, hoping to corner the porter market, whilst I was to ford the river and secure sufficient space on the other bus.

As we slowed, a turbulent sea of humanity surged from the bus and foamed into the river. Scrambling and tumbling to reach the far shore the main pack, comprising the young and fit, picked up speed and with considerable tactical jostling swept ashore and pounded up the far hillside. An elongated tail of pregnant mothers, ancients, the lame and the sick, trailed behind. A microcosm of the human race!

Arriving a close second, I had only a moment to co-opt the roof area; this was the most logical option, being easily defended. I clambered up, shook off a strong grip on my left ankle and turned, ski-stick at the ready. In the far distance I could dimly perceive, through the rising dust of our recent charge, a commanding figure marshalling a stream of porters towards me. If I could hang on for a further few minutes, relief would be at hand.

A short while later, our gear on board, this relic – twice overflowing – chugged off towards Kathmandu. The roof, filled beyond possibility, shed passengers at every bump and corner until equilibrium was reached and the survivors, myself included, could get a grip. Some hours later it started to rain, monsoon-style, in lumps.

My reflections ceased abruptly as the bus lurched violently, clipped a house-wall, entered a sharp bend on the wrong side of the road, and collided with and partially demolished an ambulance going in the opposite direction. Violent altercations swiftly erupted. The goats, whose erstwhile owner had been a roof-falling casualty, took their chance and headed for the distant hills. When shortly thereafter a platoon of soldiers and numerous policemen appeared – for we had entered the outskirts of Kathmandu – it seemed politic to salvage our battered equipment and retire. As it became apparent that the surviving passengers were being arrested for 'necessary interrogation', this idea was implemented with some urgency.

The general confusion being considerable and the night tropically dark, our strategic withdrawal was accomplished with ease. The equipment was deposited in a nearby house, whose reluctant owner succumbed to Andy's financial approach. Thus unencumbered we stole away, crossing several acres of flooded paddy. Wading through knee-deep mud like an extra from a cheap Vietnam war movie can on occasion make one feel slightly foolish. This was one of those occasions. The Doc's SAS training was obviously a bit rusty: he demonstrated this by stepping into a metre-deep fishpond *en route*.

As the first glimmer of dawn lit the sky we clambered over the protective gate of our hotel, heartily congratulating ourselves on such a successful expedition.

Jaonli: A Ridge Too Far

MIKE BANKS

(*Plates* 28, 29)

Starting to draw the old-age pension is such a landmark that I half expected everything to change. Of course it didn't. The great thing about the ageing process is that the old enthusiasms endure but clearly the pensioner mountaineer has trickier problems than, say, a grower of roses. I wondered about the Himalaya.

A problem shared is a problem halved, so I wrote to Joss Lynam, only a year my junior and the doyen of Irish climbing. One more throw of the dice, I suggested to him, one last big mountain? How about it? To my great joy, Joss readily agreed and we were in business. He even had a ready-made objective to suggest.

In 1947 Joss Lynam was serving in the Indian Army – and there is no room here to explain why a citizen of the Republic of Ireland was doing that! Anyway, from his camp in north India he could see the Garhwal peaks and planned to climb one particularly attractive mountain: Jaonli (6632m). However, before he could make his attempt he was demobilized. My invitation therefore gave him the chance to fulfil a 40-year-old dream.

In the intervening years Jaonli had been climbed from the west; these climbs included the first British ascent in 1988, by Chuck Evans. But the east side via the Khatling glacier was untried and virtually unknown. This would provide a superb challenge.

Following the military axiom that 'time spent in reconnaissance is seldom wasted', I nipped out to India in the autumn of 1988, trekked for five days towards our mountain and was able to get a clear view of the east side from a distance of some eight kilometres. The impressive E ridge ran down towards me, a mixture of snow and rock; it looked steep and would certainly be no push-over. The S ridge looked an easier proposition but it was an awful long way away.

Imprinted on the snow of a glacier I saw a trail of footprints which I cannot explain. It was a glacier leading from nowhere to nowhere, and I could not work out why a yeti, animal or man would want to pass that way. Anyway, if they turned out to be yetis and I met them the following year, I resolved to comfort them with the reassurance that Bonington, the Yeti Hunter, was no more than a benign English myth!

Back home, we started to plan our Anglo-Irish expedition with the assistance of liberal potions of Jamieson's Irish whiskey. In a moment of inspiration I approached Saga, the travel company for the over-sixties. After all, I reasoned, we were certainly going to travel and we were over 60! Saga, or more precisely *Saga Magazine*, took pity and most generously agreed to sponsor us. In fact they spoilt us outrageously – a most enjoyable sensation.

Joss and I each recruited a relative 'youngster' to strengthen the team: experienced mountaineers in their mid-fifties. I approached Alan Blackshaw (55), a past editor of this journal. I hope he has forgiven my gaffe in introducing him on one occasion as 'the author of the thickest book on mountaineering technique'! From Ireland came Paddy O'Leary (54), director of the Tiglin Adventure Centre in the Wicklow Hills. In fact all four of us had previous expedition experience. When a non-mountaineering Dublin bookseller, Don Roberts, inexplicably volunteered for the thankless job of Base Camp manager, we immediately foisted on him the chore of procuring our high-altitude rations, a job we had all studiously avoided. Don instantly bombarded us with interminable sheets of computerized food lists which effectively silenced us, until we found ourselves living on a diet consisting of chocolate and toffee bars, when we became more vocal. But by then it was too late and I came home 10kg lighter.

In Delhi we were joined by our Indian liaison officer, Ravichandra, and a Ladakhi-Tibetan cook-porter, Chewang Thundup, a delightful man and a master chapatti maker. Assisted by 25 local porters, we trekked for five days up the lovely and unspoilt valley of the Bhilanganga and reached our Base Camp at about 4100m on 19 May 1989. Winter seemed to be lingering and it was a snowy camp.

We had timed our arrival for mid-May to benefit from the theoretical calm before the onset of the monsoon. The theory didn't work. Almost every day we had snow by noon. Do we blame the Greenhouse Effect?

The 600m Khatling icefall barred our approach to Jaonli. We tried to puzzle a way through its maze of crevasses, but by mid-morning the snow of the crevasse bridges was turning to slush. The route was a write-off. I made the prophetic remark: 'Getting to this mountain is going to be more hassle than climbing it.'

After a good deal of searching we found a route which bypassed the icefall on the land side, but our further progress was blocked by a rock-step which, from a distance, I rashly predicted to be climbable. Ravichandra almost instantly proved me wrong by trying to climb it and falling off. He started up a steep crack which led to a wet and slippery overhang, then pulled up on to a sloping ledge and, teetering on the edge of balance, reached above the overhang for a vital and urgent hold. Unluckily it was loose and broke. He shot backwards into the air and plummeted down. Luckily he had placed a chock in a crack just below the overhang – the first one he had ever used! When he had fallen about three metres the rope twanged tight, the chock held and he was spared a very nasty fall all the way down to the glacier. No one else fancied a try.

To get past the rock-step we had to make an unwelcome climb over a 400m hill and down the other side. We then crossed the glacier with little difficulty. Alan and I made a reconnaissance of the E ridge and were particularly deterred by a beetling, snow-spattered rock-band half-way up. Time was now running short, so we decided on a quick attempt on the snowy S ridge. A further day's climb landed us at the foot of a steep 600m snow-face leading up to the crest of the ridge. It seemed to us that, if we could get a camp established on the ridge, the route to the summit would be open.

First Alan, Paddy and I made a depot of three days' food and some equipment in a notch on the ridge. The climb was steep and took us well above 5800m. Despite our ages we coped with the altitude with little difficulty. From here we enjoyed a clear view of the SW fork of the Khatling glacier, the Samgli Bamak. It was ringed with attractive peaks, unnamed and unclimbed, of just under 6000m.

Next day we climbed the snow slope again, with heavier rucksacks, and attained the crest of the ridge higher up. It was too narrow for a campsite, so we descended some way and set about clearing away the surface snow and hacking a tent platform in the ice beneath. As we were walloping away with our ice-axes, tendrils of cloud crept up the mountainside, snow began to fall and there was a sharper edge to the wind. A blizzard developed and we found ourselves in a dour race against time.

As we were unfolding the tent one of the poles rattled down the mountainside. Eventually we pitched the misshapen tent on its cramped platform. Unbeknown to us, we were going to have to survive the next four nights in the wildly flapping, semi-collapsed tent.

Our situation was precarious. A snow slide from above could sweep us 600m down the face into the bergschrund. We therefore hammered in ice pitons from which we led safety ropes into the tent which we kept connected to our safety harness day and night. We even dangled on a safety rope over the drop when we went to the toilet. To make matters worse, Alan developed dysentery, poor chap. To facilitate his frequent and urgent exits, he slept next to the door and was therefore lumbered with the cooking.

The storm went on for three days and by the time the weather cleared our food was expended, Despite this, Paddy and I decided to grasp our only opportunity of snatching the summit. It was a forlorn bid but, if we had not tried, we would for ever have reproached ourselves. Alan was far too weakened by his dysentery to join us. He had not uttered a word of complaint about all the cooking and had supported us stoically throughout. We had found the most unselfish of companions.

Deep new snow lay everywhere and the avalanche danger was obvious. We roped up and climbed cautiously, making painfully slow progress. We passed a rock outcrop, clawed our way up a steep wall of mixed snow and rock and edged along a crinkly, corniced ridge. Paddy, who had emerged as the expedition strong man, ground to a halt. He turned back to me and called: 'I'm coming back.' We had attained a height of just under 6000m. With the heat of the day building up and the avalanche hazard increasing, it was a wise decision. Even so, it was a poignant moment when all our dreams of the last year turned to ashes.

By the time we got back to the tent the snow was too dangerous to descend any further. We continued down next dawn, in a fair state of anxiety. Hoping that lightning does not strike twice, we followed old avalanche tracks where a swathe of new snow had been stripped off. It was the most nerve-racking three hours of the whole expedition.

Back at base good news awaited us. Joss Lynam and Ravichandra had climbed a mixed snow and rock peak of 5450m. Starting at dawn on 10 June, they had followed a series of steep snow gullies to the upper snow-fields. At 10.30 they trod the summit snow and, as a gesture of gratitude to our sponsors, called the peak 'Saga Parbat'. It was a sterling effort by the 65-year-old Joss, who had recently undergone triple heart bypass surgery!

There was now no time left for a second summit attempt, so it all ended with one failure and one consolation prize. At least we could comfort ourselves with the thought that our failure on Jaonli could be blamed on the weather rather than the burden of age. There was one less obvious bonus: it had been one of the most harmonious expeditions I have ever been on. Perhaps in our mature years we are more tolerant and less hell-bent on proving something.

Schoolboys on Kolahoi

A brief account of the climbing exploits of a group from Glenalmond College, Scotland, in Kashmir in 1987

DAVE COMINS

(*Plates* 30, 31)

Everything was fine until the goat's-liver curry at Lidderwat. From then on we all moved up the valley keeping an eye open for likely spots just in case we needed to dash for cover. But this did not detract from the delightful walk up the Lidder valley right to the snout of the Kolahoi glacier. Here we joined Neil MacDonald, who had walked up the day before to select a suitable site for our Base Camp. This was to be on the last level bit of grass before the snout, and about 40 minutes' walk below it.

Instead of unpacking our kit and establishing base we sat on the mound of donkey-bags gazing at our intended peak, Kolahoi, which protruded menacingly above the ridge to the south. How on earth could a party of schoolboys scale this 5000m peak? The answer, as we knew from our researches in the Alpine Club Library, lay in the south side, which we could not see from our Base Camp. Still, the view engendered a sense of commitment to our purpose.

Kolahoi, at 5425m, was first climbed by Dr E F Neve in 1912, up a snow couloir to the E ridge. John Hunt climbed the S face in 1935, as a 'warm down' from a trip to the Karakoram. However, we had a more personal link with the mountain: a recently retired chemistry master from our school had climbed a route on it during the closing stages of the Second World War. Arnott Russell, who seconded Kellett on the first (summer) ascent of Route Two on Carn Dearg, Ben Nevis, was able to encourage us, though Richard Gilbert warned us off the mountain; he thought it dangerously loose when he climbed it with a small party of boys from Ampleforth. We hoped to climb Kolahoi before the snow became soft and the loose rocks began hurling down the face.

We had a recce up the 'Twin Rocky Peaks' at the corner of the valley. From this vantage point we selected a route bypassing the horrendous icefall and gaining the plateau, across which we would need to travel to reach the hidden S face. Our original plans were thoroughly wrecked by the after-effects of the liver curry and, when one group set off with kit and food to establish an ice camp high up on the plateau, they took a wrong turning and returned to Base Camp tired and a lot wiser.

Meanwhile, as the expedition leader, I was confined to Base Camp with the local equivalent of the 'Delhi belly', living off Rehydrat and reading up about all the gastro-intestinal nasties in Wilkerson's *Medicine for Mountaineering*. Needless to say, this light reading did nothing to hasten my recovery! However, within a few days there was nothing left inside to come out, so I gathered what strength I had and set off with Patrick and Simon up on to the ice plateau to establish our high camp on 27 July. My High School French suggested that 'plateau' would indicate an element of flatness. However, it was definitely uphill the way we were going, and I might have turned back if it hadn't seemed to be uphill that way too!

After a lot of trail-breaking from Simon and even more encouragement from Patrick, we slumped down in the snow, staring up at the 1000m S face we hoped to climb the next day. Neve's couloir looked unsafe, with a heavy accumulation of unconsolidated snow at mid-height. The face had much more snow on it than we remembered from the pictures we had pored over in Scotland. Just to the right (east) of Hunt's route was a snow couloir which led directly to the top. This looked a likely bet for us, as we were accustomed to steep snow and it seemed preferable to loose rock. First we had to hack out a flat ledge for our tent and cook a meal before snatching a few hours' rest. We aimed to leave the tent by 1am, and we weren't far out. The cold air initially sharpened our minds, then almost numbed them as we trudged across the glacier to the snow cone beneath the face. Front-pointing up the bottom third of the face was done on rock-hard snow, causing our calf muscles to make their presence felt. We zig-zagged a little to relieve the strain on our legs. I was definitely flagging; my lack of energy was an obvious consequence of having no significant food intake for several days. Patrick and Simon provided sustenance in a way that non-climbers find hard to understand and, as the sun's rays slowly worked down the mountain towards us, so we climbed even more slowly up to meet them. Despite the extra weight I was glad to be carrying a camera, as this gave me reason to stop and capture the fantastic views of Nun Kun being revealed behind us. We had hoped to be on our way down by now, and here we were still plodding up. A major effort was needed to finish off the climb. Just after 10am an elated and desperately tired trio flopped into the snow which caps the summit pyramid. Across in Pakistan we could see Nanga Parbat and, looking back across the S face, we picked out K2 and the Karakoram mountains in the far distance.

The summit of Kolahoi at 5425m set a new 'record' for our school mountaineers. In 1981 we had made the first ascent of Quipucamayoc, at just over 5000m, in the Peruvian Andes, but Kolahoi was not only higher, it was also infinitely more spectacular. Our thoughts were more on a safe descent than on making inconsequential record books as we headed briefly down the E ridge to a point from which we could abseil in six or seven rope-lengths on to more reasonably-angled snow on the S face. The consistency of this snow was reminiscent of Scotland at its worst, though we felt the life draining back into our tired frames as we lost height. Our tiny tent, hundreds of metres below, looked inviting if a little sad as it sagged in the soft snow. We finished our descent by down-climbing the bottom section of Hunt's route to regain our starting point, and were soon priming the stove to melt snow for a longed-fot drink.

We left the tent for use on a second attempt by Donald, Charlie and Neil. Rajinder, our liaison officer, with one or two friends, tried a line further west on the S face, and both parties moved parallel up the face to the summit on 30 July

1987. Rajinder's group suffered a terrible shock when they saw a light cartwheeling down the full length of the S face, right where our second summit party was climbing. This was fortunately no more than Donald's head-torch, which pinged off his helmet. (He collected the torch from the bottom of the face some eight hours later, still working, and proceeded to use it with the same battery throughout the rest of our seven weeks in India!)

All had been successful in reaching the summit and we now had a day or two to bask in the Kashmiri sun before striking camp and returning to Srinagar, where we reprovisioned. Our next objective lay in Ladakh, and this necessitated the two-day journey via the Zoji La and Kargil to Leh. A group of trekkers had walked from Pahalgam to Pannicker, then hopefully on to Leh, and we were due to meet them there before stage two of our enterprise commenced.

For us this meant an attempt on Stok Kangri (6121m), which presented a completely different challenge. Base Camp was to be at about 5000m; we found this was too high. Minor cuts did not heal, and we just deteriorated throughout our stay there. Simon, Donald and I scaled Gulap Kangri (6000m) on 9 August, to give further acclimatization, while Charlie and Neil carried a tent up to the foot of the huge E face of Stok Kangri, returning to Base Camp the same day. The first group to try for the summit comprised Rajinder, Neil and Charlie; they intended to climb all the way from Base Camp to the top and back in a day. Donald, Simon and I decided to move up and try the face after a night in the tent. We arrived in time to see Rajinder, Neil and Charlie picking their way laboriously down the lower snow slopes. Rajinder was dog-tired when he reached the tent, but all three continued on to Base Camp, completing the round trip in 19½ hours. Charlie had thus reached his second Himalayan peak before his 16th birthday!

Rajinder's group had been tempted by the E ridge and they advised us against it, so we took the direct route straight up the 1000m snow-field, across a short rocky band and on up the last snows to reach the summit in under 5½ hours from the tent. The controlled descent took 35 minutes! Back at the tent I waited for Patrick, who had been ill and hoped to recover in time to have a shot at Stok Kangri the next day. He came up to join me and we departed at midnight in poor conditions to put our last climbing member on the top. Unfortunately the snowfall became heavier and, a mere 200m below the summit, we retreated down to the tent which was by now buried in soft snow.

As we walked out through the incredible moon-like scenery, we felt happy that our modest school trip had been so successful. We felt we had chosen our peaks well, as both had given us considerable challenge and much enjoyment. Back in Srinagar we beat Rajinder's school at water-polo and drew a torrid football match in front of a very partisan crowd. We finished our trip with a couple of days on the Dal Lake, a trip to Jaipur and then on to the Taj Mahal – none of this spoilt by the continuing effects of that goat's-liver curry.

Members of the Expedition

Dave Comins
Donald Ballance ('old boy' of Glenalmond College)
Neil MacDonald
Simon Mills
Patrick Robinson
Charlie Russell
} (boys at Glenalmond College)
Rajinder Kaul (liaison officer, and teacher at the Tyndale Biscoe School, Srinagar)

REFERENCES

AJ 21, 185–189, 1902–03; 26, 407–409, 1912; 39, 79–86, 1927.
HJ 8, 103–106, 1936; 9, 173–174, 1937; 16, 112–119, 1950–51.
D Comins (ed), *Glenalmond Peru 1981 Report.* Glenalmond College, Perth, Scotland. (In AC Library.)
D Comins (ed), *Glenalmond Kashmir 1987 Report.* Glenalmond College, Perth, Scotland. (In AC Library.)
J A Wilkerson (ed), *Medicine for Mountaineering* (3rd ed). The Mountaineers, Seattle, 1985.

9. *Rimo group. L to R Rimo III, Rimo II (appearing as a shoulder), and Rimo I.* (Nick Kekus) (p 11)

10. *Teram Shehr ice plateau, from Pt 6660, Rimo II.* (Doug Scott) (p 11)

11. K2 from Pt 6660, Rimo II. (Doug Scott) (p 11)

12. *Stephen Sustad on the summit of Rimo II (7373m).* (Nick Kekus) (p 11)

13. Rimo III, SW buttress. (Nick Kekus) (p 11)

14. *Rimo III. Climbing to the N ridge on the second day.* (Nick Kekus) (p 11)

15. Rimo III. Above the final pinnacle on the summit day. (Nick Kekus) (p 11)

16. *Rimo IV. Indian ascent (2nd) L of rocks in centre.* (Doug Scott) (p 11)

17. *'The Bus'.* (Mal Duff) (p 43)

Saser Kangri 1987

IVAR HELLBERG

(*Plates* 32–35)

'Saser Kangri' literally means 'Yellow Mountain'; it derives its name from the bright yellow granite rock which can clearly be seen on the summit ridges. The Survey of India lists the mountain as K22 at 7672m. Situated in the eastern Karakoram range in the district of Ladakh of Jammu and Kashmir State, it is the highest peak amongst a group of 7000m peaks which constitute the Saser range. This range is bounded by the Nubra river to the west and the Shyok river to the east and south (see sketch map). The mountain itself is surrounded by seven main glaciers and defended by precipitous rock and ice faces. The area, often referred to as 'Little Tibet', is particularly rugged and has developed a culture of its own as a result of being cut off from the rest of the world for most of the year by high passes and heavy snowfalls. Early reconnaissance expeditions considered the peak to be impregnable.

The first person to have recorded the mountain was Arthur Neve who, in 1899, climbed a peak near Panamik and photographed the Saser range. Dr Tom Longstaff (the first man to climb Trisul in the Garhwal Himalaya) led an expedition to the area in 1908 and reached a height of 5486m on the Phukpoche glacier to the west of Saser I. He recorded the difficulties of a western approach in an article for the *Geographical Journal* published in June 1910. Other visitors to the area were the Vissers who mapped the area in 1929, and Lieutenant Colonel Jimmy Roberts who made the first attempt on the mountain in 1946. Although the attempt was unsuccessful, Jimmy Roberts's thorough reconnaissance of the western approaches added immeasurably to our knowledge of the mountain. Another attempt from the west was made by an Indian team led by Major N D Jayal. This team counted no fewer than 20 avalanches hurtling down the W face of Saser I in one day. Again they could find no way up. Another Indian expedition attempted the west side of Saser I in 1970. It was led by the late Major Bahaguna (who died on the ill-fated 1971 International Expedition to Everest). With Captain Alok Chandola, he directed the main effort towards an approach via the N Phukpoche glacier and up the NW ridge of Saser IV (7310m). Again, the sustained difficulty of the route turned the climbers back after they had reached a high point of approximately 6600m. No other serious attempt was made from the west and attention turned to an easterly approach (advocated by Jimmy Roberts). In 1973 the mountain was at last climbed from the east by a team led by Commander Jogindar Singh, after an epic approach march via the E Shyok river and the N Kunchang glacier. The western side of the mountain remained unvanquished.

The 1987 expedition was a joint British-Indian Army Expedition, sponsored by the Army Mountaineering Association in conjunction with the Royal Geographical Society, with the aim of climbing the unclimbed W ridge of Saser I (7672m) and the unclimbed Saser Kangri IV (7310m), between 4 April and 3 July 1987. It should be noted at the start that Saser Kangri is in a disputed area which belongs to India but is claimed by both China and Pakistan. In consequence the area is subject to constant border skirmishes which in the past have prevented foreign expeditions from visiting the region. We were privileged to be allowed to climb in the area on a joint basis with the Indian Army.

The expedition was to consist of 19 British Service climbers and a similar number, with a support team, provided by the Indian Army. It was led jointly by myself and Colonel Dashan Khullar, an experienced Indian mountaineer with many successful expeditions to his credit, including Everest in 1984 (when the first Indian lady achieved the summit). From the British team's point of view there were two important supplementary aims: firstly to help select a team for the British Services Everest Expedition 1988, and secondly to record the ecology and environment of this seldom-visited part of the world.

The expedition flew to Leh on board a giant Soviet-built Ilyushin 76 transport plane on 4 April 1987. The British team needed time to acclimatize and also to get to know their Indian counterparts and to climb together. The ancient city of Leh is at a height of 3300m and we chose the mountains of Zanskar to the south for our work-up training. It was during this training period that some members of the team were privileged not only to see but also to photograph three beautiful snow leopards, a mother and two fully-grown cubs. It was the first time that these elusive creatures had been photographed in the wild in India.

We were much delayed from leaving Leh at the start of the expedition by heavy snowfalls on the Khardung La (at 5600m the highest motorable pass in the world) which prevented any movement north into the Nubra valley. We were not able to cross the pass until 1 May, some two weeks late. The Khardung La road is a masterpiece of Indian engineering which zig-zags for miles up the steep snow-sides of the pass and at one point actually cuts through a glacier to allow the trucks to pass. It is the supply line for the Indian Army stationed on the Siachen glacier to the north of Nubra: a narrow road with very few passing points which has to be cleared at the start of each day by a snow-plough. When a truck breaks down it is sometimes easier to push the truck over the edge rather than hold up a convoy of hundreds of vehicles! The evidence of a number of such broken-down trucks can easily be seen in the valley below. The journey over the pass and into the Nubra valley took about 20 hours, and was the roughest journey in a truck that I can remember.

The scenery of the Nubra is on a vast scale and is almost completely devoid of vegetation, as the mountains of Zanskar to the south block off the passage of the summer monsoons in this remote region of the eastern Karakoram. The valley base was established at Panamik in the Nubra, at approximately 3200m. The route to Base Camp followed the line of the precipitous gorge of the turbulent Phukpoche Nullah. The intention had been to use a large number of locally recruited porters to help shift the 30-odd tons of

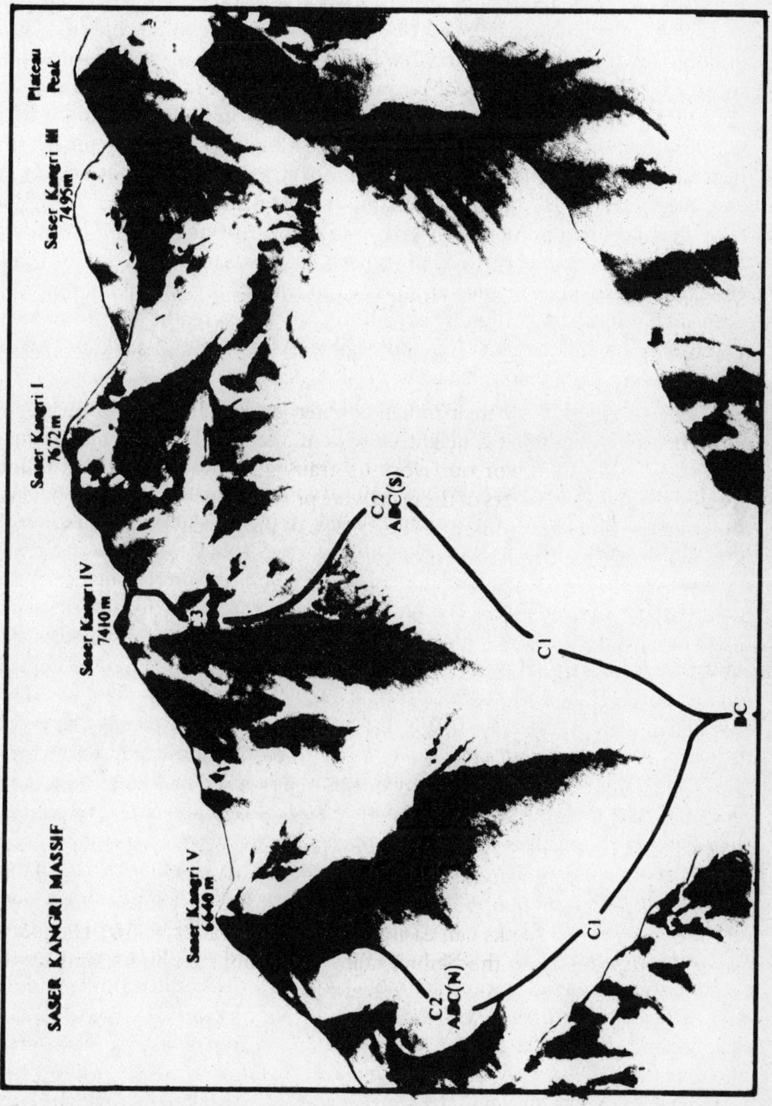
SASER KANGRI MASSIF
Saser Kangri V
6640m
Saser Kangri IV
7410m
Saser Kangri I
7672m
Saser Kangri III
7495m
Plateau
Peak
C2
ABC(N)
C1
BC
C1
C2
ABC(S)

expedition supplies and equipment over the two-day march from Panamik to Base Camp. However, very few porters could be recruited from amongst the local people, as most of the able-bodied men were ploughing the fields with oxen and planting seed. For the most part, therefore, expedition climbers had to carry 20kg loads every day for about two weeks, with one day's rest in three. This caused a good deal of anguish for some who felt that they were expending needless energy and wearing themselves out for the climb. In reality they were undergoing rigorous acclimatization! The nullah was a magnificent route, secured by ropes in the more dangerous places, leading to an intermediate camp established on uncomfortable boulders at about 4300m. Base Camp was only another three hours' march beyond this point, and as people acclimatized it became possible to make the whole journey from Panamik to Base Camp in one day. Base Camp was fully operational by 11 May, and by this time the Indian team members had miraculously grown in number from 19 to 36! It was also readily apparent to the relatively inexperienced British team that their Indian colleagues were super-fit and extremely experienced Himalayan mountaineers, with anything up to 12 major expeditions to their credit. With only a few exceptions the Indians came from hill regiments – Gurkhas, Ladakhis, Dogras, Garhwalis etc – and therefore had been born at altitudes of at least 3000m. This gave them miraculous speed in the mountains, causing admiration, incredulity and depression amongst the British team.

On 12 May, with Captain Steve Bell and Rana, I departed for a recce of the mountain on skis. We hoped to determine the best route on to Saser IV and also to find a suitable place for Advanced Base Camp. The skis worked well in the deep fresh snows which exist early in the year. Rana, who was a cheerful optimist with a Terry Thomas smile, provided endless entertainment with his commitment to downhill speed and unbelievable stopping techniques which involved 'yetiing', as the impact area resembled the legendary impact of this mysterious creature. The recce confirmed that the SW ridge of Saser Kangri IV was a feasible if somewhat difficult route. However, it failed to show whether it was possible to get on to the NW ridge from the direction of the N Phukpoche glacier. Clearly this route needed to be explored further from the northerly glaciers as, once the NW ridge which started at a huge 'notch' on the col had been reached, the route looked good. It was decided to detach a team to the N Phukpoche for a proper recce while a concerted start was made on the SW ridge. The start of the SW ridge was gained by 300m of 70° ice climbing on which fixed rope was installed. Morale was shattered when the Indian deputy leader, Major Gash Gill, and Steve Bell jumared up to the start of the ridge in a state of considerable exhaustion, where they found the legendary ND Sherpa eating his lunch in a very relaxed mood, having walked up from the other side in mukluks!

The northern team was led by Major Kit Spencer, the British deputy leader, and, like all teams on the mountain, it had a joint Indian-British membership. They set up their own Advanced Base Camp at 5800m at the head of the N Phukpoche glacier under another significant peak of 6640m which was named Saser Kangri V. Fixed rope was put in place up a steep snow-field which led on to a col under Saser V where Camp 3 was established. On 31 May the summit of Saser V was reached by Kit Spencer and Surgeon Lieutenant Andy

Hughes, together with Lobsang and Mahavir. However, the summit party reported back that the route to the NW ridge of Saser IV would be long and difficult and was definitely not such a favourable proposition as the SW ridge.

On 2 June Captain Ashok Abbey of the Indian Army became critically ill with pulmonary oedema and nearly died at Camp 3. Ashok was carefully lowered on a stretcher down 600m of fixed rope by Kit Spencer's joint team with Andy Hughes, the team's doctor, in attendance, administering life-saving oxygen. It was fortunate that Sergeant Pete Kay, Royal Marines, had noticed the state of his team-mate as early as he did while in his sleeping-bag early that morning. Ashok was delirious and almost comatose at times; the speedy action of the team in getting him off the mountain undoubtedly saved his life. The final evacuation was completed by remarkably skilful flying by an Indian Army pilot on board a Cheetah (supercharged Alouette) helicopter which landed in cross winds in appalling visibility at 5800m on the N Phukpoche glacier – a notable achievement. This episode concluded the activities of Kit's team on the northern side of the mountain.

On 10 June I returned to Advanced Base Camp (North) with a selected team of some of the less experienced mountaineers. In an initial abortive attempt I got benighted in the broken tents of Camp 3 in a blizzard, with Captain Sarah Dennis and Lieutenant Lincoln Rowe (our artist). After retreating from our first attempt I returned with Sarah on 15 June, and we successfully scaled the summit of Saser V. The weather, although rather blustery and cloudy, cleared to allow us to get good views. We arrived back at Advanced Base Camp (North) at 6pm after a 14-hour climb. As far as we know, Sarah was the first service lady to have climbed a Himalayan peak above 6000m.

Early progress on the southern side of the mountain was good, although the scale and technical difficulty of the climb were daunting. Camp 3 (6800m) was established on the top of the SW shoulder of Saser IV on 23 May, after 1000m of very steep snow and ice climbing, culminating in a gripping and loose rock-band before safety could be found. On 6 June success was achieved on Saser IV (7410m) when Captain Martin Bazire RAOC and Sergeant Dave Howie RAF reached the virgin summit, followed by Nb Sub Thakur Dass, Hav Devi Singh and Nk Lalit Kumar who reached the top about an hour later. The following day Staff Sergeant Dave Orange APTC, Gunner Dave Torrington and Captain Jo Singh Dhillon also reached the summit.

At the same time the route along the difficult and exposed NW ridge of Saser I was fixed by Magan Bissa's team of four Indian supermen. Magan was unusual in that he came from the Indian plains rather than the Himalayan massif. It was a fantastic effort which we watched with fascination through the Zeiss telescope. Sadly, the weather prevented them from going any further than the S summit of Saser I, at a height of about 7600m. All seemed set for successful assaults on the main summit on the ensuing day. On 8 June ND Sherpa with Sonam, Dorgeh and IB Gurung made a determined bid for the summit but were again defeated by the weather after having reached the S summit at 10am. The weather began to deteriorate, and some of the worst continuous weather I have seen in the mountains prevented any further attempts for 16 days. Three times teams returned to Camp 3, only to be driven back down the mountain in the face of high winds, blizzards and low temperatures.

It seemed that the Yellow Goddess of the Eastern Karakoram was calling on the weather god to come to her aid, as every day the clouds and wind came racing in to her protection. Time was running out for the British team, who had a plane to catch at Delhi to return to the UK. On 22 June I accompanied the last of the British team down from Advanced Base Camp, believing that the weather would never change. Steve Bell and Simon Lowe arrived back at Panamik, tired and dejected, knowing that their last chance for the summit had finally gone. However, the Indian team with Colonel Dashan Khullar decided to hold out for a few more days, as they did not have our deadline.

On 24 June the weather cleared again and allowed Lobsang's team to return to Camp 3. On 25 June the weather was perfect and by 4am Lobsang and his team of L/Nk T Sonam, L/Nk T Wangdus, L/Nk P Angchuk, Hav Devi Singh, Hav Tashi and Hav Umed Singh started to reopen the route up the NW ridge of Saser I, forcing their way through very deep snow and with great difficulty digging out the fixed rope which was frozen under up to two metres of fresh snow. At approximately 10am Lobsang and his team reached the S summit of Saser I, and by 10.40am they stood on the main summit, having conquered the western approach for the first time. At the same time that Lobsang and his team were forging up the western ridge, another drama was unfolding. The back-up team consisting of ND Sherpa, Magan Bissa and Sonam, who were positioned at Advanced Base, asked permission to tackle Saser IV direct – a very daring and challenging enterprise which was only possible because of the colossal strength of these three climbers. Permission was granted, and by 9am these men reached the col between Saser IV and Saser I. After a short pause they asked permission to have a crack at Saser I rather than Saser IV, and once again this was agreed. They then shot up the tracks of Lobsang's group at an unbelievable speed, considering the height, the wind and the absence of oxygen. They reached the summit of Saser I at approximately 12.30pm, having covered a distance of about five kilometres and gained a height of over 1800m in 9½ hours. They returned before dark to a triumphant welcome at Camp 1. This must surely be a Himalayan record – as a European I am left in awe and wonderment at the power of these mountain people. They have slender frames and meagre rations, yet they have seemingly endless powers of speed and endurance.

The expedition was also a wonderful opportunity to meet the patient, gracious people of Ladakh with their timeless culture, Buddhist philosophy, generous and cheerful outlook. Their life is a hard one, eked out of the cold and unforgiving soil with adze and oxen; it was a medieval scene with no sign of mechanization. What they had they shared without complaint, and they expected nothing in return except friendship. They are a very honest people who strongly adhere to the spirit and strengths of family life. Pressure of time has not reached them; watches and clocks seem irrelevant. It was a refreshing lesson for those of us who had forgotten, or had never known, the joy of bowing to the force of nature and occasionally stopping to consider the beauty of the whole of God's creation.

The wildlife of the region was more prolific than I had expected, bearing in mind the barren desolation of a huge region with very little rainfall (5cm per annum in the Nubra). Of particular note were the Burrel (Blue Sheep) which seemed to be neither goat nor sheep but something in between. The large wolves of the area who hunted, not in packs but in ones and twos, leaving huge paw-marks the size of a tennis ball, will not be forgotten. I had to admire the mighty birds of prey, the lammergeyer and the Himalayan golden eagle, that reside in the precipitous cliffs of the area. However, without doubt, the most lasting memory was the excitement of seeing and photographing the magnificent snow leopard: a privilege none of us will ever forget.

The expedition was blessed with good fortune. We achieved almost all our goals without accident or loss of life. Saser I was climbed by a challenging new route from the west. Saser IV and Saser V were climbed for the first time. We saw the lovely people of Ladakh and were privileged to see the snow leopard. What more could we have asked? From the British point of view it was sad that time prevented any British serviceman from standing on the summit of Saser I with our Indian friends. Considering the difference of culture between the British and Indian teams, the expedition was remarkably successful as a joint venture; the teams mixed well together and learned a lot from each other. Ther is no doubt that the common heritage and traditions of the two armies plus a common language were a great help.

The aim of helping to choose a team for Everest was certainly achieved, as Saser Kangri provided an unusually tough apprenticeship in Himalayan climbing. Saser, the Yellow Goddess, is an irresistibly beautiful mountain with three main sister peaks all over 7300m high, and many others approaching that height. The landscape is on a vast scale and there is a timeless quality about the arid desolation of the region; indeed the whole area is inundated with high unclimbed peaks, offering a mountaineering dream! We were very fortunate to be allowed by the Indian government to climb in this remote yet politically sensitive area. We remain deeply grateful to our Indian hosts for their generous hospitality and in particular to the Indian Army who unstintingly provided all the administrative support we needed. It was a most successful joint operation.

Shani, South-East Face

PETER LEEMING

(*Plates* 36–38)

From our bivouac, we watched the orange flashes lighting a western part of the August night sky . . . the result of a Mujahidin rocket attack on Kabul. Over the summer of 1989 the Mujahidin were maintaining a quota of such attacks in order to ensure their supply of weapons from the United States via Pakistan. Wherever our sympathies lie, innocent civilians, as ever, were getting hurt.

Duncan Francis, Martin Oakes and I were perched on a rocky ledge, half-way up the unclimbed 2000m SE face of Shani (5800m) in the Naltar valley, West Karakoram. It was midnight on our first night on the face. We had been climbing since noon, and now we awaited daylight to tackle a rock tower which barred access to the second, main icefield which we hoped would take us to the summit ridge . . .

Shani, Urdu for 'flower garden', is a particularly impressive peak which came to my attention late in 1986, after the first ascent by Roger Everett and Guy Muhlemann by the W ridge (*AJ*92, 220, 1987). I immediately thought that it would be wonderful to spend five or six days traversing the mountain.

Early in 1989 we contacted the various British climbers who had visited Shani since 1984. We learned that the Naltar valley hosted a variety of wildlife and unclimbed peaks, or peaks with only one ascent; that Shani's SE face had repulsed some strong attempts; and that the 1000m N face was virgin. By the time we left England, the expedition had swelled to 13 people: three climbers, a medic and nine trekkers.

We arrived in Naltar on 28 July, after a dusty three-hour drive by jeep from Gilgit. While waiting for the jeep to be repaired near Nomal, some of us were entertained by a large and handsome family who welcomed us into their largest room. We sat on cushions on a beautiful rug while the head of the family led the songs and dancing. Their spirits were high as they awaited a wedding later that afternoon.

I was struck by the similarity between the Naltar valley and the Swiss Alps, with snow-clad peaks rising from alpine meadows and larch forests.

Next day the expedition lumbered in a disparate fashion up to the Naltar Lakes (3200m). We spent the late afternoon and evening relaxing with the porters, investigating the crystal-clear, trout-filled lakes, and wandering through the ancient birch woodland which hosted a variety of birds such as rose-finches and whistling thrushes.

In Naltar we had hired 30 porters who lived in different villages in the valley. This gave us a glimpse into the philosophies of the Muslim religion, as the porters were composed of Sunni, Shia and Ismaili Muslims. Our relations with them were excellent, and for me one of the best things about the entire expedition was the friendliness and co-operation of the porters and all the Pakistani people we met.

At about 3pm on the following day we reached our Base Camp, situated at 3700m, at the side of the moraine above the Shani glacier and just above Lower Shani, a summer shieling for goats, sheep and cattle. The cloud was down and it was pouring with rain. Nine out of the 21 days we spent at Base Camp were destined to be like this, and in fact the weather across the whole Karakoram had been bad since May.

After a few days' rest in Base Camp, Ginny Crowther and I climbed to a bivouac at about 4500m on Snow Dome (5030m), an obvious mountain similar to Mont Blanc. I left the bivouac at 3.30am and reached the summit, alone, about three hours later. I found this an intensely satisfying experience, and was rewarded by clear views of the Batura massif to the north, a storm-struck Rakaposhi to the east and the majestic twin peaks of Shani across the valley. This seems to have been the second ascent of Snow Dome, and Duncan, Martin and others followed a few days later.

Duncan and I also made a number of parapente descents from a ridge about 600m above Base Camp, while we waited for Shani to come into condition. We quickly realized that we would never get the five or six days of good weather needed to attempt a traverse, and the massive amounts of snow on the N side precluded any thoughts of climbing there. We turned our attention to the SE face which dominated the scene from Base Camp. After the periods of bad weather, avalanches poured down the complex ridges and buttresses of the face. Despite this, Duncan and I agreed that our best chance of success would be a rapid ascent of the icefields on the left side of the face. We decided to forgo sleeping-bags, karrimats and spare clothes: we would climb at night and rest during the heat of the day. After a false start, when an intestinal problem kept Duncan at Base Camp, a few of us spent a day carrying the climbing gear across the glacier to the bottom of the route. A tributary glacier below the face, which we had to ascend, was in a very dangerous state – I fell through a snow-bridge at one point – and then the weather broke as we scuttled back to Base Camp.

Duncan, Martin and I left Base Camp early on 11 August in very good weather. We said farewell to our friends who were departing on a trek, quickly crossed the Shani glacier and soon arrived at our gear dump. As I toiled up the loose scree towards the initial rock-spur in the midday heat, our approach felt anything but lightweight.

The rock-spur was an unknown quantity, and we couldn't really assess its true angle from Base Camp. After a few pitches we were surprised at the quality of the climbing and the rock, good granite, and it began to feel like a pleasant day out in the Alps. The hardest pitches were 4c, with pleasant, airy belay ledges decorated by wild flowers. Shani was living up to its name.

We found ibex hoofprints all the way up the spur and, until we had passed a line of prints half-way up the first icefield, ibex had been higher on the face than any mountaineer! Perhaps it is only here that these beautifully adapted animals feel safe, despite the ban on hunting since 1970.

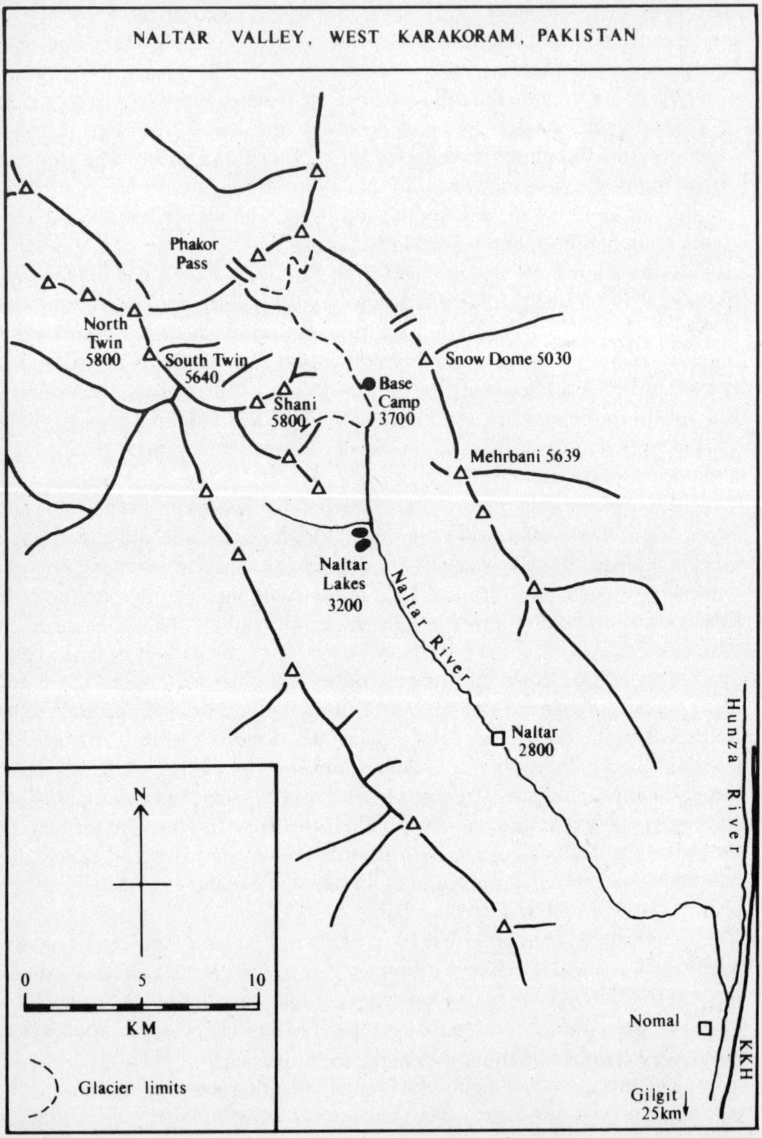

Based on U.S. Army map NJ 43-14; R.Everett, HJ 43, 1985-86; and A.McNae, British Shani South Face 1988 Expedition Report

By 4.30pm we had climbed the spur and were at the bottom of the first icefield. We rested on the large ledge, made tea and prepared some food. At 6.30pm we moved on to the ice. The angle was easy and we climbed unroped, keeping to the left to avoid the two to three-metre deep avalanche runnels in the centre. As daylight faded, we could see the lights moving around at Base Camp where our friends settled down to supper with Niaz Khan and Safarullah Khan, our cooks from Hunza.

Each of us climbed at his own pace in his private world of ice and torchlight. We occasionally took turns at breaking trail but, apart from asking each other how we felt, we didn't really communicate at all. The icefield narrowed towards its top and it felt like climbing in a couloir with rock buttresses on either side. There was no moonlight and our head-torches didn't illuminate much in the distance. We simply followed the icefield, hoping it would take us up to the ridge bounding the left side of the face. At about 9.30pm we found a few sloping rocks to perch upon for a rest. Duncan had recovered and Martin's ankle, injured in a parapente mishap, was holding up OK, so the climb seemed to be going to schedule.

The temperature had fallen quite quickly to about −5°C as the daylight disappeared, but it never seemed to get any colder than this. Higher up the ice steepened and became more brittle. We climbed through one awkward section and then sensed the ridge was not too far away. Shortly after this we found Duncan sitting on the ridge, the large rock-tower looming above him. It was obviously impossible to climb it in the dark. We could only sit tight and puzzle at the orange flashes in the west until dawn.

The sunrise over Snow Dome and Mehrbani was as spectacular as our position. The second icefield looked reasonable, once we had established ourselves on it. Duncan led off, taking a chance that a vague and broken traverse line around the tower would lead us to the icefield. Five pitches and one abseil later, we found ourselves on the ice and, with some relief, saw a straightforward ice-slope leading up to the ridge to the right of the tower. We had bypassed one of the main worries of the climb and within an hour we had climbed the ice-slope, still unroped, to a ledge on the ridge.

We spent the day dozing and eating, and gazing up at the second icefield. After some discussion we opted to follow the right-hand of three ice couloirs which we hoped would take us through the summit buttresses to the summit ridge. From our perch, we watched impotently as storm clouds visited each neighbouring peak in turn. Shani and ourselves received three squalls of hail, never very serious but enough to make me apprehensive. Soon the summit of Shani was cloaked in a grey cloud. I remembered that we hadn't come equipped for a long stay on the face . . .

At 5.30pm we moved off again, but the snow was still very soft. We came back to the ledge and waited for an hour. There was no improvement but Duncan's impatience drove him to break trail diagonally rightwards across the icefield. Again the angle wasn't extreme, but crossing the deep avalanche runnels with the constant surge of hail and spindrift down the ice made the climbing quite unpleasant. At around 8pm Duncan and I cut out a ledge in the ice, and when Martin appeared we rested for half an hour.

We continued up the icefield, soon climbing up into the cloud and losing sight of the lights of Base Camp, 1200m below. A difficult traverse across ice-glazed slabs took us to a sloping ledge, where we made some tea in a very exposed position. After this we roped up and I led a rising traverse into the ice couloir. We spent the rest of the night climbing steep, brittle ice, wondering when the angle was going to relent. The details are a blur now, as the pitches seemed to merge into each other. Even though we were weaving between rocks protruding from the ice, we could never really find any secure belays or runners as the rock was so compact and smooth.

Duncan and I alternated leads: the two climbers following would climb simultaneously, but I was still conscious of how our progress had slowed. I tried to encourage the others to climb as quickly as possible, but it was not the type of climbing that you could rush. Belays were usually a combination of a snarg and a peg or wire – with two people hanging on them! Duncan cursed my rope, which by now had frozen solid and was quite unmanageable in the belay devices. All in all it was quite stressful climbing: Shani was beginning to show its teeth.

At around 7.30am we could detect that the gloom was lightening, and by 9am it was bright enough to survey the terrain through which we had climbed the previous night, and also to get our bearings. Looking down the ice couloir, we saw all sorts of ghostly buttresses and pinnacles, covered in fresh snow, appearing out of the mist. The ice was still as brittle as ever, and safe belays as sparse, but daylight brought a psychological relief.

We sensed rather than saw the summit ridge, and the higher we climbed the greater the depth of fresh snow. I led an awkward pitch through loose rock before running out of rope and being forced to belay on ice axes just below the ridge. Duncan led through and we anxiously asked him what he could see as he reached the crest.

'We really are up the creek without a paddle,' was the alarming reply.

Duncan elaborated by describing the hollow snow, the wafer-thin ridge and the double cornices. The summit – if it was the summit – appeared to be about 200m away to the west, and not much higher than where we were. The idea of descending from here if we couldn't traverse the ridge was unthinkable, so I set off on the next pitch with an aggressively patient approach.

Within seconds I was totally engrossed in the climbing, clearing snow to find runners, carefully arranging the ropes, testing ice-axe placements and finding the safest way along the ridge. My concentration was great and I felt completely detached from the others. Sometimes an arm or a foot would meet with less resistance than expected, and I would be gazing into the 1000m depths of the N face. Having led three pitches along the ridge I began to feel more hopeful. Duncan led through to tackle a very unstable snow bulge which demanded a lot of energy. We had now been climbing for 17 hours continuously on our third day on the face, and it was a real effort to keep going.

I took over from Duncan again and led up an easier snow-slope to another bulge. The rope trailed uselessly behind me as I worked out how to tackle this obstacle. Martin and Duncan were two shapes in the mist, 40m below. It was easier on the right, but I realized that this formed part of the cornice over the N face. Further on the left the ground was more stable but more difficult, as it was undercut. Eventually I half vaulted over and half squirmed through the bulge, and hauled out over the top on to the flat snow above. As I lay gasping, I felt that I might still be on top of a cornice, so I crawled further back from the bulge. I knelt up and looked around, and realized that I was on the summit of Shani. The other two soon joined me; it was 11.30am on 13 August 1989.

The mist was as thick as ever and, although Roger Everett had described the W ridge to us, we felt anxious about finding it. After resting for an hour we left the summit, Duncan leading Martin and me downwards. I had a tremendous sense of foreboding about the descent but was so tired that I just followed Duncan without thinking.

About 200m below the summit we found ourselves on a steep snow-slope, lashed by a sudden, violent squall of hail and snow. Duncan disappeared in the mist and we followed his prints, jumping the occasional bergschrund and gradually losing height. We descended diagonally leftwards towards some rocks which we thought might protect us from a possible avalanche. While stopping for a rest as the mist cleared slightly, we glanced back up the mountain to see our tracks skirting the huge icefall that Roger had mentioned.

We continued downwards, our crampons balling up with the wet snow at every step. Suddenly we dropped out of the mist into brilliant sunshine and blue sky. Down below us it seemed that the snow-slope we were on led easily to the Upper Shani glacier which we had to reach. We could see the Twins (5800m) across the glacier in front of us, and we were all relieved that we were in the right place.

However, 20 minutes later we found we had descended into the jaws of a very steep and frightening icefall. Each of us scuttled back and forth across the edge of an icecliff, but the only way out was to reascend the snow-slope in order to skirt the icefall higher up. All three of us were hit by a tremendous lassitude at the thought of this and were soon fast asleep on our rucksacks, only being woken up by the stove boiling over.

Two hours later we were down on the glacier, but the descent had caused Martin's ankle to flare up, and he was now limping badly and often falling in the deep snow. We were still roped together as I led the way down the glacier to the point where we had to climb over a subsidiary ridge to gain the main Shani glacier. Duncan, as ever, broke trail strongly up the 150m ice-slope. On the col we had supper and prepared our bivouac: a small trench scraped out of the snow, lined with ropes and rucksacks. As we had no real bivouac gear, once again we shivered the night away as it began to snow. At 3am the mountains resounded to my bloodcurdling yells as I emerged from a nightmare.

The dawn was misty and grey, and it was very difficult to judge distance and make sense of the glacier's contours. I was perhaps more apprehensive now than at any time during the last three days. The glacier was still blanketed by snow from earlier in the summer, concealing every crevasse. We came to the edge of a 50m icecliff which stretched virtually the whole way across the glacier. Again we had to reascend to avoid this on the west bank. The mist cleared, and very soon it was uncomfortably hot. Duncan and I knew that we should get off the glacier as quickly as possible, and we tried to encourage Martin to keep up a good pace, although by now he was in considerable pain.

At 9.30am we reached the moraine below the Phakor Pass and knew at last that we were safe. We were all sunburnt and very dehydrated, and after a long drink from some meltwater we scrambled slowly up the appalling moraine above the glacier. At the top I left Duncan to help Martin down to Base Camp. I was keen to be alone with my feelings as I descended the upper part of the Naltar valley. My mind seemed more receptive than before to the beauty of the valley, and I stopped frequently to watch the river chats and leaf warblers.

My lasting memory is of the shepherd giving me a bunch of a beautifully fragrant meadow cranesbill, asking me where I had come from and, seeing me struggling, offering to carry my rucksack. This was really the epitome of the Pakistani people's friendliness: a touching end to a fine adventure.

Summer and Winter in the North-West Karakoram

LINDSAY GRIFFIN

(*Plates* 39, 40)

It was with some trepidation and not a little discomfort that I arrived in Rawalpindi towards the middle of June 1988. Illness and injury had dogged the previous two months and had left a certain feeling of disappointment. Also it was hot. Temperatures were at a maximum since Partition, and Lahore had been subjected to almost 50°C. There, a night sitting under the cold-water tap in a fourth-class station hotel made more practical sense than attempting sleep in a supersaturated atmosphere.

Phil Bartlett, fresh from an unseasonably fine British climate, arrived at 1am. Baggy cotton trousers, acquired nearly 10 years ago in Delhi, were beginning to look a trifle threadbare but this was offset, not uncharacteristically, by a huge floppy hat over-patterned with garish green daisies. His organizational strategy was simple but effective. Trailing in his wake I could only offer money and a little enthusiasm, but at 5am the following morning we were on the road north to our destination of Moorkhun on the Karakoram Highway.

This neck of the woods lies north of the Shimshal valley, enticingly close to forbidden Chinese territory, and access to it had not been freely available to the modern traveller until 1986 when foreign tourists, previously allowed no further on the KKH than the delightfully situated oasis of Passu, were granted permission to cross the Kunjerab Pass as a means of entering the Chinese province of Xinjiang.

Prior to the construction of the new track into the austere confines of the lower Shimshal gorge, upper villages were traditionally reached via an ascent of the Moorkhun valley and a crossing of the 4873m Karun Pir Pass. This is an arduous and largely waterless journey at the best of times, and it was no surprise to find that Shimshal village had originally been created as a convict colony for misdemeanants from the Hunza mirdoms. This journey was reversed by Shipton in 1937 at the termination of his explorations of the Shaksgam, and had possibly seen no British traffic since those times.

Tucked away at the head of the valley, hidden from view on westerly approaches, lies the fine snowy pyramid of Karun Koh (7350m). Reserved for the Pakistan Alpine Club and thus open only to joint expeditions, it was first attempted in 1983 by a small Austrian team led by Robert Schauer. Although little height was gained, the way was now paved for first British (Bonington and Rouse) and second Austrian (led by Harry Grun) teams in June 1984. Very bad weather and lack of time led to an early retreat by the British pair but the Austrians, persevering for another month, reached the summit on 31 July. Later, Bonington was to remark on the wealth of particularly attractive 6000m peaks further down the valley: '. . . we had a superb view of them from our Base Camp and they were a perpetual temptation to divert our energies from the main objective.'

In 1987 a Sheffield team made the first ascent of Tupopdan (6125m), the highest of the southern group, via the NNE ridge. This proved an easy climb, hampered by very poor snow conditions – a phenomenon, alas, all too common at these altitudes during the early summer months. The summit was reached on 4 July by Cave and Stevenson. Grun returned in September; for three years the vision of Tupopdan had obviously featured prominently in his mind's eye and despite the disappointment of being pipped at the post, his Austrian team made the second ascent.

It was in February 1988 that Phil pushed a photograph of the neighbouring JurJur Khona Sar under my nose. 'What d'you think of that?' he asked, pointing at the fine sweeping arêtes leading up to a spire of acute sharpness.

The village of Moorkhun lies several miles south of Sost, the last checkpost on the KKH beyond which, officialdom would have us believe, one can only travel with a Chinese visa. Inhabitants here have their origins inside the Wakhan corridor and until the construction of the road these Ismailis, whose spiritual leader is the Aga Khan, lived in isolated mirdoms. A journey to Gilgit, now four harrowing, precarious hours above the turbulent Hunza river, took seven days. In the last year, their stone and mud huts have received the blessing of hydro-electricity; yet these simple folk are as hospitable, honest and generous as any mountain dweller that I have met. But for how long, in their ever-increasing exposure to tourism, remains an unanswerable question.

Recent parties, however, have not failed to mention a certain lack of motivation amongst the porters, and this was borne out by our three-day march to Base Camp. They were 'splendid chaps' and excellent company throughout the journey, but daily stages were indeed short. When later we packed up our base prematurely and crawled out with loads that weighed a crippling 40kg, we still managed to reach the KKH in seven hours despite movement that, on my part at least, was almost imperceptible.

Base Camp was, characteristically, up the wrong valley, though we convinced ourselves that we could be excused for not realizing it at the time. Perhaps more significant was the temperature. Clear skies prevailed, but at 4250m we were finding it a trifle uncomfortable getting inside our sleeping-bags at night.

A number of attempts were made on the N face of JurJur. We could see that attaining its attractive 6000m summit would be lengthy and far from straightforward. An approach couloir, flanked by rotten rocky walls, led to a shoulder at 4900m; Bartlett stormed up this carrying the usual embarrassingly monstrous rucksack. Most mortals find this performance impossible to match, and the knowledge acquired from 15 years of climbing together allowed me to congratulate myself that, by just keeping in visual contact, I could conclude that

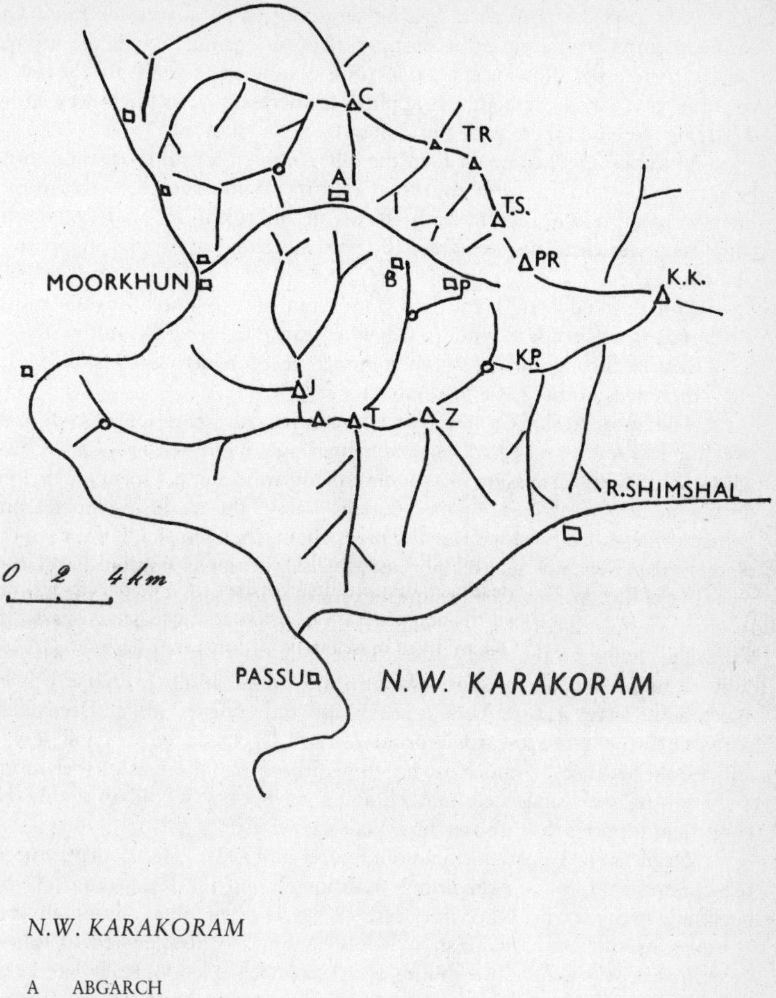

N.W. KARAKORAM

A	ABGARCH
B	BOEBAR
C	CHIT (5474m)
J	JURJUR KHONA SAR (c6000m)
K.K.	KARUN KOH (c7350m)
K.P.	KARUN PIR PASS (4873m)
P	PARIER
PR.	PREGAR (c6200m)
T.	TUPOPDAN (6125m)
TR.	TRICH GACH (c5700m)
T.S.	TAPADAN SAR (c6000m)
Z.	ZARTGARBIN (c5850m)

my health and fitness must at last be returning to an acceptable level! On occasion, and for a pathetically short period of time around dawn, the surface would crisp a little, allowing enjoyable frontpointing up 55° névé. For the rest of the time the same movement was applied, unsuccessfully, to thigh-deep snow overlying ice. Then there were the stones!

Once we spent three days on the hill, climbing for no more than three hours each day and sitting out the rest at a site free from stonefall. As if to mock, the sun beat down remorselessly from an unbroken azure. The logical conclusion was clear, but we agreed to spend more time at base in anticipation of a change.

Phil cracked first; I still had possession of 120 unread pages and a Walkman. It was ironic to withdraw in what transpired to be the only period of good weather throughout the summer, but we were forced to swallow the bitter pill – there was nothing else to climb.

Tilman once said, 'time spent in reconnaissance is never wasted', and over the last few years I had become increasingly interested in a Himalayan winter visit. With permission from India still unforthcoming, I spent much time during the next week quizzing locals on the state of the art during this season. Lying further north and west of the main chain, the Shimshal/Batura region tends to experience better weather and, overall, less precipitation than other parts of the Karakoram. Clandestine ibex hunters in Passu, who use the Batura to this effect, talked of a snowline no lower than Guchisham (3500m). Shimshalis living on the shady side of their valley at 3600m were at variance, some opting for a foot of snow and others for none at all. Everyone was in agreement, however, that the first heavy snowfall occurred in late December, with one or two more towards February/March. This reduced snowfall, it was felt, would be offset by much lower temperatures than in areas further south and east (it was suggested that climbing at 6000m would probably be equivalent to more than 7000m in a Nepalese winter).

Nazir Sabir, Pakistan's top mountaineer and a local Hunza man, voiced the opinion that, while expeditions traditionally left the Karakoram by the beginning of September when heavy snows would often fall at alarmingly low altitudes, by mid-October this snow would have largely disappeared. October, he enthused, was generally a month of unparalleled splendour. He had been liaison officer to Hasagawa during an October attempt on the Rupal face of Nanga Parbat, where snow conditions had proved better than at any other time of year. Defeat in November had been solely due to strong winds.

Choice of venue would be crucial to success in the short time available to us, and realistically dictated prior knowledge. Ease of access and escape was of prime importance – the thought of being stuck in some remote corner until the April thaw had little appeal! A big open S face would do nicely, but there was still the lure of JurJur which, if nothing else, would be safe from stonefall.

Mike Woolridge was an obvious choice of companion. He had covered much of the approach on the K2 expedition in trainers during early December, before the soul-destroying experience of being promptly helicoptered from Base Camp with acute appendicitis after a surprisingly short exposure to the Polish diet. We enlisted Pete Cox, a larger-than-life (in every sense of the word) character and ex crime-squad officer in the Metropolitan Police. Four years ago he simultaneously took up climbing and dieting and, from being 6′ 3″ and 20 stone, he now has a pulse rate of 38, runs London marathons and climbs Scottish 5. Though short on big mountain experience, the physique was mighty powerful and made more plausible a number of anecdotes in which his figurative assailant 'failed to survive the arrest'. Phil was unable to join us as was Nazir, though we appreciated the latter's loan of Base Camp equipment – baggage allowance being a trifle inadequate for the extra gear required in winter. Well attired in the latest collection of Karrimor clothing, so generously donated by Mike Parsons, we flew from Heathrow in November.

I have now travelled the KKH eight times, and each journey seems worse than the one before. Transport now motors much faster, careers closer to the edge, overtakes with alarming frequency on blind bends and stops far more regularly to show you the upturned wreckage of yet another vehicle hundreds of feet down in the Indus gorge. In contrast, it was a joy to snuggle into a down sleeping-bag in Gilgit, where normally one would be sweating naked under the raucous whirring of fan blades.

Our arrival at Moorkhun in the early afternoon was bathed in sunshine. Hemmed between steep flanks of neighbouring peaks, overshadowed by giant scree slopes, I had expected little or no sun. We had underestimated its zenith at this latitude and now realized, with some optimism, that a carefully selected base in the bed of the Moorkhun valley would receive three to four hours sunshine a day.

In effect the choice was made for us. Heavy and unseasonally early winter snow in late October lay down to 3500m, and beyond this our porters would not go. Neither, apparently, had their motivation improved for, while ferrying loads down the valley on our way home, we walked back up the second day's stage, admittedly unladen, in 35 minutes! A group of shepherds' huts at Boebar became our spacious Base Camp and, with dead wood in abundance, our stay would not be uncomfortable. Night-time temperatures only fell to −6°C, though they barely struggled to 0°C during the sunny daylight hours.

Inevitably, reaching the southern group became out of the question. Even below 4000m we were up to the waist in a substance that would have delighted the Colorado 'Powder-Hogs' but provoked mutiny amongst our team. Approach couloirs, if they could indeed be reached, would be impossibly avalanche-prone and it was estimated that our summer Base Camp lay under two to three metres of unconsolidated soap-flakes. However, since the first day all eyes had been constantly drawn to an elegant 6000m snow crest to the west of Karun Koh, referred to by our porters as Tapadan Sar. A vast snowy face composed of ribs, shelves and gullies rose for nearly 2000m above the northern scree slopes. I had always considered this route a possibility since my first sighting in the summer, and under its newly found winter garb it appeared doubly attractive. Closer inspection confirmed this.

Four days after our arrival at Boebar, and after a subsequent battle with a colony of hungry mice rudely awoken from peaceful hibernation, we set off well laden and reached the summit after five days of climbing. Our route took a blunt rib, interspersed with rocky outcrops and towers, towards the left side of the face. This led to a snow-field at two-thirds height that we dubbed the 'Great Shelf'. Access to this involved crossing a complicated section of crenellations which Pete, having recently consumed a large diet of modern Himalayan accounts, christened 'The Pinnacles'. The weather was crystal clear and in the sun movement was far from unpleasant provided the E flank, where some consolidation had taken place, was followed. Camp 2, atop the first pinnacle at 5100m, afforded some gorgeous views across the Shimshal to the stupendous N faces of Lupghar and Distaghil Sar. The night was reasonably calm, with a temperature of –17°C; this was fortunate, as sleep had proved difficult at Camp 1 where strong winds had completely destroyed the flysheet.

Next morning we were away early carrying light sacks, despite the lengthy struggle to cocoon the feet with, first, polypropylene socks, followed by vapour barrier socks, woolly socks (two pairs in my case), aveolite inners, plastic outers and finally cumbersome neoprene overboots. By midday we were approaching the top of the 'Great Shelf', which in reality had become a 40° snow-slope and a purgatory indeed. Round to the right a gully system – the only means of reaching the summit slopes – broke through the large rock barrier above our heads. So far we had climbed largely unroped, apart from several sections on the flanks of the pinnacles, but now I was delighted to be able to lead the four pitches in the 'Bottleneck' (Pete again!) on good ice, with an exit up a steep mixed corner which in retrospect was no harder than Scottish 2.

The summit looked a long way off, and twilight was but a few hours away. Above a steeper section of poor snow overlying ice, which seemed a bit dubious at the time, the going improved and at 4.20pm we were there. I say 'there', but in fact the highest point, a cornice projecting a good 10m towards China, was left untouched. The anticipated panorama northwards was thus concealed, save for an unexpectedly huge pyramid that appeared mysteriously higher than anything designated on the map.

Up till now one-piece thermal underwear, shirt, fibre-pile jacket, salopettes with windproof covering, and a pair of insulated overgloves had been quite adequate. As the night-time temperatures dropped to –24°C on the upper slopes, we donned down suits, adding balaclava helmets and more gloves. A stiff breeze accompanied our descent and nipped hands and feet as we carefully reversed the 'Bottleneck', trying to get the weight on to the heels at stances to restore circulation to the toes. Pete's fingertips remained tender for several weeks. 21 hours after leaving its comfort, I was ensconced in the tent, vainly trying to make a brew while fighting off the sleep that had overcome the others.

Despite my protestations, born out of laziness, Woolridge whipped us into action after only a few hours and we descended, albeit slowly in my case, to reach base later that night.

It had been a great experience. We had made it to the top and, perhaps of more importance, wit and rapport had been at a premium. We had worked well together, enjoyed each others' company and looked after one another consistently on the hill. Summits are important, but so are personal relationships. As we turned for home we were already talking about next year.

Sandy Allan, Topping Out

ANDREW GREIG

From Base Camp to the stream there is a path now
and the grass is yellow at the centre of the path.

So began to lead the last of the Tower
Quite hard   more bold than difficult
tough ice   loose snow   but soon my brain
began to play the game   My points investigated
stabbed good placements to be had
among loose choss   Crucified by altitude
I bridged a steepish rockwall   Good
value that   I remember everything
like ice-slivers in my windsuit's creases   Camp 4
a thousand feet beneath my heels   Climbing
into my shadow the sun
flashed off my axe
Jon he was somewhere
giving good rope and no advice   the ideal second
but me I was gone

Nice work when you can get it
the hardest   the best   hours passed
till I wanted a think and a rest
so thumped in an ice-screw and hung out awhile –

Like I cannot spell, speak porter-talk
but who does not who's lived like me
with oil roughnecks and a French girl?
One look in her eyes, I know.
One straight hit, I find good ice.
Climbing's not so much, my life's more in
the way I eat my food, the man I rise above,
the roads I drive to friends,
these suit –

Re-engaged myself and winkled on
with patient pickers unlocked the crux
set my axes well and at full stretch
pulled over the top and saw into China

head was mute

felt ok   felt well
à cheval across the summit
K2 in the distance looking good
suspicion of moisture behind my shades

Made a belay and took in the ropes
as Jon came up. So how's it going?

Oh, wasted youth . . .

Tasmanian Overland

J G R HARDING

(*Plates* 41–44)

As Earth's wild places contract, so have lands once reviled become our new adventure playgrounds. Such has been the experience of Tasmania, which first intruded upon the European consciousness with Abel Tasman's discovery in 1642 – 128 years before Captain Cook's Australian landfall. Christened by Tasman Van Diemen's Land, its geography remained a mystery until Flinders' circumnavigation in 1799 which established it as an island rather than an appendage of the mainland. Four years later the first settlers arrived and starved. For the next 50 years of the 19th century, Van Diemen's Land became notorious as the principal penal settlement for Britain's transported convicts. In convict lore this was the Fatal Shore, the land of white slavery, and 'to plough Van Diemen's Land' argot for a convict's life of retribution. When transportation was finally abolished in 1853 and the name Tasmania substituted for Van Diemen's Land, the systemized brutality which had characterized the white man's life-style had been transmitted into a campaign of genocide against the Aborigines. Within 45 years of British settlement, the dreamtime had turned nightmare and primitive man had been exterminated from the land he had inhabited for millennia.

For many years, little was written or read of Tasmania's 19th-century history; but as time shades and perceptions change, the convict stain has been expunged and to modern visitors the reputation of Victorian Tasmania would be incomprehensible. In the island continent of Australia, the flattest and driest on earth, whose predominant physical characteristic is inconspicuousness, this offshore isle with abundant rainfall, forests and mountains is almost unique in its display of genuinely dramatic scenery. Western Tasmania's Wilderness National Park – one of the globe's last temperate rain forests – has taken its place in a World Heritage List that includes Mount Everest and the Grand Canyon. The Macquarie Estuary, confluence of Australia's wildest and grandest rivers, the Franklin and Gordon – once a dreadful penal settlement reserved for the hardest recidivists – has become a rallying point for conservation international. Tasmania is pre-eminently Australia's holiday state, occupying top position in the Great Outdoor Experience of bush walking, climbing, caving, rafting and kayaking. A place intended for the damned has been transformed by the wand of wilderness.

But if Tasmania has been rehabilitated, its true character remains enigmatic. Travel cliché compares it with Scotland or 'England Down Under'. Trollope described it as 'more English than is England herself' and Betjeman as 'the heart-shaped island of content'. These cosy analogies are misleading.

Tasmania's flora and fauna are quintessentially Australasian. Its land forms and scenery have no European equivalents and defy the tired game of topography snap. Its dank jungles of primeval fern tree and archaic palm are vegetal relics of the primordial super-continent of Gondwanaland, now dispersed through the southern hemisphere by continental drift. Its discomforting bush – spiny, prickly and spiky – achieves the ultimate in impenetrability in the form of a vigorous creeper whose scientific name *anodopetalum biglandulosum* is as convoluted as the shapes it assumes. This is the infamous 'horizontal bush' growing as a matted mesh suspended several metres above the ground. Tasmania remains a land where nature is hostile and where, in the unfamiliarity of its dark silent forests, the ghosts of old Van Diemen's Land – convicts, cannibals, bush-rangers and aboriginal spooks – still dwell.

What's in a latitude? For Tasmania, just about everything. Our northern hemisphere's equivalent might be Spain's verdant Atlantic coast. But Tasmania, lying at a similar latitude between 40°S and 44°S, is slap-bang in the path of the Roaring Forties, low pressure systems that move inexorably west to east throughout the year, and the waves of the Southern Ocean that have had half the circumference of the world to gather the climactic strength which explodes on Tasmania's wild west coast. Tasmania's 'temperate maritime' climate is a misnomer for 200 inches of rain, sleet and snow dumped annually on its western heights; high winds and snow-storms that blow out of Antarctica at any time of year, and a summer that can either desiccate by drought or incinerate by bush-fire.

In October 1988, my wife Georgina and I stopped over in Tasmania on a round-the-world tour. What to see of this intemperate Nether England which a lifetime of sabbaticals would not exhaust in a mere 10 days? Australia rejoices in travel hype. In addition to routine kangaroos and bandicoots, wallabies and wombats, Trapdoor and Redback spiders, Tasmania has platypus and echidna, Tiger snakes, Tasmanian devils and Tasmanian Wolves – the virtually extinct thylacine. For new boys, disconcerting tales of the Tasmanian bush are stock-in-trade, but before leaving England I had quizzed mountain guru Rupert Hoare on baggables. His assorted list included Mount Anne, Frenchman's Cap, Federation Peak and the remote ranges of the SW. These offer rare prizes, but ventures to such parts must be measured in weeks even with aerial drops. On reflection, I reckoned that Tasmania's most famous bush-whack, the Overland Track traversing the Cradle Mountain National Park, was about our mark.

The Cradle Mountain National Park, conceived in the late 19th century, became a reality through the enthusiasm of an Austrian *émigré*, Gustav Weindorfer. A Scenic Area was created in 1922 and the present boundaries of the 1300 square kilometre Park drawn in 1947. The Park's landscape was sculptured 20,000 years ago by an ice-cap 65km in diameter, crowning mountain ranges that were then part of the mainland. The park takes in most of the island's highest peaks, including seven that exceed 1500m and Mount Ossa, the highest at 1617m. Mountain tarns, glacial lakes and moraines; gorges, ravines and waterfalls; arêtes, cirques and head-walls are all remnants of Tasmania's ice age. But the Park's most striking feature is its rock architecture of igneous red dolerite. Plugs and pinnacles, columnar and hexagonal pillars, fluted cliffs and porcupine ridges offer some of Australia's best rock-climbing and most spectacular scenery.

The Overland Track traces a fragile thread through the heart of the Park, linking rain-forest and swamp to hummocky sedgelands, button-grass moors of soggy peat to an alpine tundra of rare cushion plants. Above this floral wonderland lies the climbers' world of rock, snow and ice. The Track was completed in 1935 and opened two years later to unguided parties. A guiding tradition survives to this day, and tour operators vie to take you through the heart of Tasmania in summer at £450 a throw. We were to discover for ourselves why winter tours are less popular. The 85km Track is usually walked north to south from Cradle Valley to Cynthia Bay at the southern end of Lake St Clair. Thanks to a line of huts which are maintained by the National Parks and Wildlife Service and sited within an easy day of each other, the traverse should be completed comfortably within a week.

I had originally banked on a party of six but, as it turned out, only two of us boarded the Tasbus that left Hobart for Queenstown on 19 October 1988 at 8.30am. We had spent the previous two days sightseeing a snow-topped Mount Wellington, trekking out to Cape Hauy's spectacular sea stacks on the Tasman Peninsula; buying food, maps and guidebooks and ingratiating ourselves with local bush-whackers. At Derwent Bridge, our roadhead, it was cold and spitting with rain. Through scudding clouds and lowering skies, snow-covered hills occasionally emerged. The scene was thoroughly un-Australian, yet we were heartened by the sight of two young trampers who had disembarked with us and were, we assumed, also bound for the Overland Track. We exchanged greetings. They prophesied a 'monster low' and moved off down the road in the opposite direction; we never saw them again. At the Ranger's Office at Cynthia Bay we signed in, paid a $10 Park fee and crouched under a verandah to escape the rain. Our last hot meal for days was spoilt by hassling, hungry crows and yellow wattle birds grotesque with their pendulous jowls. Elbowing through a mob of domesticated wallabies, we took the plunge into the rain-forest at exactly 2.45pm to begin the Overland Track.

For its first 15km, the Track hugs the contours of the western shore of Lake St Clair. This, the deepest lake in the Australian continent, occupies a trough scoured out by what was once Tasmania's greatest glacier. The forest merges into the very waters of the lake and the track, running just above it, tunnels through an opaque and overwhelming vegetable mass. Gigantic eucalypts such as Stringy Bark (*eucalyptus obliqua*) and Alpine Ash (*E delagentensis*) vie with the Antarctic Beech or Myrtle whose uppermost branches, 80m above, form a canopy that creates eternal twilight. In clearings grow Sassafras, Leatherwood and Tasmanian Laurel and below them ferns, archaic palms and scrub. On the ground itself, the carcasses of rotting boles are hosts to a riot of multi-hued mosses, fungi, lichen and other parasitic growths.

On that gloomy wintry afternoon our destination was the Echo Point hut, three hours away according to the guidebook but four for us. They say that Tasmania has 200 different bird species but, apart from brief sightings of wombat and wallaby sidling silent through the bush, we neither heard nor saw a living thing. Incessant rain left us sopping wet because of, or in spite of, Goretex suits. Happily, each hut in the park is improbably equipped with coal bunkers. Echo Point is supplied by boat; others by helicopter. The standard issue pot-bellied stoves take some figuring when fuel is wet, but by our third attempt we had created a cosy fug.

Our Sportplan, such as existed, was to bag the odd peak en track with Olympus and Ossa as a pair, with Cradle Mountain the final flourish. But if Olympus and Ossa, why not Pelion? The Park obliges with not one but two Pelions – East and West – and its other mountains represent a thesaurus of classical nomenclature. Opposite Echo Point rose Mount Ida; behind Mount Ida, the mountains of Jupiter; at the head of the lake, beyond Narcissus Bay and dotted about the Du Cane range were the Parthenon, Acropolis, Geryon, Hyperion and Eros. Why this profusion of classical allusion in a land where the myths of its original peoples have been comprehensively destroyed? The apostle of Tasmanian classical romanticism was a 19th-century scholar, Surveyor-General George Frankland, who initiated a vogue that later cartographers have unswervingly imitated.

Olympus (1447m) was high on our list for, as Tasmanian mountains go, it appeared relatively accessible. I even had a preview of what it looked like from Piguenit's classic 'Mount Olympus', painted from Lake St Clair in 1875. Piguenit, the first Australian-born professional painter of standing, knew this hard country as a surveyor with the Tasmanian Survey Department. The burgeoning glacis of his dank Olympus emerges from the lake covered by forests skirts to culminate in a triumphant crown of mist-shrouded dolerite pillars. The mountain was first climbed by Frankland in 1835, but our Park guidebook made no mention of any route up it.

After a night of torrential rain, morning brought clear skies and sunshine to transform the gloom of the previous day. The waters of the lake now sparkled and the hilltops glinted white with new snow. Back in Hobart, Gloria Barnes, queen of local bush-whackers, had conspiratorially advised us to leave the Track and strike inland some 30 minutes beyond the hut at an 'obvious' stream. Our 1:100,000 Tasmap indicated that the source of this stream was Lake Oenone, named after the nymph whose gift of prophecy would have helped on this occasion, for the map gave nothing away in identifying our stream from countless others which cascaded into the lake. 40 minutes out we struck off west at right angles and climbed steeply through groves of enormous Antarctic Myrtles. Initially, the eye of faith might have discerned a path but this quickly vanished and our guide became the torrent that cascaded down a series of rock steps which we climbed with the aid of lianas and fixed roots.

In the upper forest we made first contact with the 'bovver boy' of the bush, *richea pandanifolia* or pandanni. This triffid-like grass tree is a cross between a giant groundsel and a superannuated palm. Richea grows up to 12m high, retaining a straggly ruff of old leaves up the length of its trunk as insulation against the cold. Its smaller relative *scoparia*, growing at body height, is a vegetable pincushion. Both types sprout serrated fronds that can gash your hand at a touch: by the time we had reached the snow line at 1050m both mine were lacerated. As the forest thinned out, we began to see something of Tasmania for the first time. The eye strayed from the deep pool of Lake St Clair

– now 400m below at the bottom of the dense forest through which we had struggled – to Mount Ida. Yesterday, this sharp pyramid had dominated Lake St Clair's eastern shore to provide us with a marker; but from this height it was dwarfed by a succession of purple tiers rising above and beyond to the snow-capped Mountains of Jupiter. High-stepping through the snow's breakable crust – first calf-deep, then knee-deep and ultimately thigh-deep – which overlaid button-grass, scrub and boulders, we eventually got level with the source of our stream, Lake Oenone, suspended in a hollow between the shoulders of Mount Olympus, its waters uncompromisingly black.

The route now led round and into a broad summit couloir choked with titanic blocks of red dolerite. Exactly five hours after starting from Echo Point, the couloir debouched us on to the flattened summit of the Seven Apostles of Olympus. It was 1pm and the secret heartland of Tasmania was spread before us. To the north and east, beyond the dark blue troughs marking forested wilderness, an immense white tableland stretched out to every horizon. Its bleak uniformity was broken only by a succession of black rock outcrops, pillared turrets and, away in the north-west, the unmistakable scarp of Frenchman's Cap protruding like the thumb's top digit. The sun was shining but without warmth, and a snow-chilled wind hastened our descent. Reversing our tracks through the snow, we were back at the idyllic Echo Point hut within nine hours of setting out. That evening, as we were relaxing by the lakeside, a lone walker hurried past in the dusk. His name was Didier Monselesan, his nationality Swiss and he was bound for the Narcissus hut. Over the next six days, Didier was to become a part of our life.

The storm that night presaged the end of good weather. Grudgingly, we left the romantic Echo Point hut with the aim of reaching Pine Valley in the Du Cane range that same day. Our route lay via Narcissus hut and Cephissus Creek. Arcadian names, but yesterday's elation was quickly leached away in the rain. One bird at least was active – the currawong, whose raucous cry is the harbinger of bad weather. The Track tunnelled remorselessly through dripping ferns under enormous trees whose roots criss-crossed the path and whose upper branches were invisible in the cloud. Without a maintained path, the Overland Track in winter would be a trial by mire and water. First you tend to patronize the Track's boardwalks (constructions of mind-boggling labour), but before long you wonder how you could possibly manage without them: Harrison's Crossing, the causeway across the Narcissus Creek delta, alone avoided 400m of swimming.

The Narcissus hut was empty but, according to the hut book, a large school party had left a few hours ahead of us for Pine Valley. Narcissus Creek, some two hours north of the hut, was just about fordable, thigh-deep; but Cephissus Creek, the next obstacle, was fast filling up the valley floor. After wading waist-high for 50m we shied at the main stream which had grown into a metre-high bore that powered over 80m of boardwalk like a miniature Niagara. You don't hang around in these parts to dry off, for the bush is alive with leeches always alert for a meal on the hoof. Retreating to the main track we eventually reached Windy Ridge hut that evening, cold and wet, eight hours after leaving Echo Point. Much later, we learned that the schoolgirls did make it to Pine

Valley but were there cut off for days and eventually helicoptered out. It was good to see Didier busy with the pot-bellied stove but the real proprietors of the hut were an uncurious pair, employed on hut maintenance, who had taken over most of its occupiable area and whiled away the night smoking pot. Alone in this strange company and alien land, Didier was experiencing a crisis of confidence: to continue or turn back? His equipment – standard Oz impermeable parka, combi suitcase/sac and second-hand boots – was against him, but he was young, Swiss-Army trained and carried a larder of food. We needed each other and agreed to join forces.

The carrot offered by the next day's 15km Windy Ridge to Pelion huts stage was Tasmania's highest peak, Mount Ossa (1617m), by way of a three-hour detour from a pass, the Pelion Gap (1130m). In theory, no problem. But as we climbed higher the weather deteriorated. Some 4½ hours out we broke cover from another Jabberwocky forest to emerge on to a bleak open moorland where snow overlaid a glutinous bog ribboned with deep trenches that disguised fast-flowing becks. As we struggled upwards towards the pass, unsighted by stinging snow, Georgina slipped and fell waist-deep into a torrent. I lunged just before the water ripped her legs from under her and landed her on a bank of muddied snow. The scene was set for a hypothermia epic but, as we approached the Pelion Gap through a fire-scarred forest of skeletal pines, the weather momentarily relented and the veil of cloud was rent to reveal storm-banners streaming from the snow-wreathed ridges of a now unattainable Ossa. Once across the gap and down into the windless forest, the crisis was past, and so we stumbled on to the Pelion hut to be greeted by snow-encrusted wallabies outside and Didier within tending his pot-bellied stove. That night we blockaded the door against a pack of possums.

Yesterday's march was eight hours' worth. Today's, 23 October, was much the same length and mixture. It rained or sleeted in the forest and snowed or hailed on the moor. We were soaked within 30 minutes of leaving the hut and for the rest of the day waded through the stream that had now become the track itself. Pelion West (1554m), an 18km 830m day rating 10 hours in good conditions, had once seemed within our grasp. Now a mere diversion to see the Hardnett waterfalls was beyond us. At the Windermere hut a genuine guide, John Boden of Tasmanian Highland Tours, short-shorted over longjohns, was in residence with his Roman client Sylvia. Once past the formalities of ritual Pom bashing, John admitted to an earlier manifestation. He too had been a Pom – a schoolmaster converted to the Lucky Country and now running a nice line in mountain travel. As our relationship blossomed, so were we indoctrinated into higher bush lore – using tea-tree leaves as billy scourers and plastic bags as antidotes to bush foot. That night the cold was such that Boden relit the stove at 4am and again an hour later. Next morning, through eyelids glued together with coal-dust, we looked out on a landscape transformed by a blizzard which had plastered everything in a metre of new snow. In this alpine scene Didier was at last beginning to feel at home.

Not one stage of the Overland Track rates as anything but a walk. But over the past six days the constant attrition of rain, sleet and snow and endless wading through creeks, streams, bog and mire had left us with bush feet lacerated at heel and toe. Georgina had a strained muscle and septic toe; all three of us had colds and 'smoky eye' from the coal-dust. Much later than intended, John and Sylvia set forth for the Cirque hut via Lake Will. We stayed firmly put, making the only serious excursions of the day to the patent composting lavatory sited the statutory 150m from the hut, past a miserable mob of marsupials seeking shelter from the snow. This shrine to Oz hygiene had one drawback. Notices inside the throne room warned that one puff of a fag would detonate the works and make mockery of minimal-impact bushwalking. Lunch was the gastronomic event of the entire tour, with Didier's fondue hewn from the nugget of cheese he had humped around these past six days.

Each of us now pledged to bring down the curtain on the Overland Track. Cirque hut was only six kilometres away and Cradle Valley, journey's end, 17km. At 7.50am we locked the door of the Windermere hut and marched out, straight into a blanket of sleet blowing steadily in from the west. The track was obliterated by knee-deep snow and the marker poles were barely visible. The map indicated that somewhere ahead there was a ridge but, at this of all times, the marker poles ran out on us. After meandering around for 2½ hours, I reckoned that we had made only a quarter of our distance and were getting nowhere, so sounded a retreat to the hut. We were wet, cold and dispirited, but the prospect of another night at Windermere steeled common resolve and, second time out, on fixed compass bearings, we hit off the key to the passage – a shallow col that marked the transition from forest to moorland. In weather reminiscent of a bad day in the Western Highlands, we ploughed on across the moor with spirits rising. Just above a confluence of streams, where scrubby undergrowth overlaid a morass of slush and knee-deep water, we reached the Cirque hut. Later, we were mollified to learn that the day's weather had also doubled the guidebook time for John and Sylvia.

A lone Brit, Richard Bryan, was lying comatose in his sleeping-bag next to the stove. Thus had he stayed for the past two days, despairing of the weather, his Overland Track abandoned. Next day, 28 October, the four of us left for Cradle Valley or bust. As we climbed through the thinning eucalypt forest out of Waterfall Valley towards Cradle Cirque, a miracle occurred. The clouds rolled back, the great dolerite plug of Barn Bluff revealed itself, and, for the first time in a week, the sun appeared. Two hours on, at Kitchen hut, we rounded on Cradle Mountain (1545m), Australia's most photographed peak. The red dolerite was warm to the touch and rough to the hold and the scramble to the summit achieved in an hour. On that marvellous morning, with the northern sun on our backs and the south side of the mountain still plastered in snow, the complete traverse of Cradle Mountain's two-kilometre ridge – an Austrian first in 1914 – would have been a worthy objective. As it was, we were well satisfied just to have reached the top. Cradle Mountain was first climbed by the surveyor Henry Hellyer in 1831 and from its summit Gustav Weindorfer, the park's spiritual founder, declared '. . . this must be a national park for all time. It is magnificent.' Now at last, looking back across the ground which had been our penance for the past week, we could share something of that enthusiasm. Beyond the moorlands streaked with snow where streams and waterfalls now flashed silver, the snow-capped ranges of Pelion and Ossa were luminescent in the sun.

Yet, even as we started our descent, the weather reverted to type with an armada of clouds, pitching and dipping, racing in from the west. On the steep track down to Lake Dove, prodigious gusts of wind hurled us to the ground and spectacularly reversed the flight of waterfalls, blown upwards in billowing fountains of spray. Dove Lake, blue and welcoming on first sight, had turned grey with white-topped waves. Barely had we reached Cradle Lodge when the storm which had already blighted the west coast broke about us. There was no room at the Lodge but a man with a knowing look, sporting a snakeskin-banded felt hat with kangaroo device, offered us a lift to Devonport in a government truck. A few miles short of that town he exchanged this vehicle for one of his own marque bearing the device 'Proud to be Tasmanian' and, at the Formby Hotel, relieved each of us of $25 by way of surcharge. This brush with a genuine Van Diemonian left as sharp a taste as had the Overland Track. Although we had seen tantalizingly little of this unusual country, it had stirred our imagination and its wildness will always challenge the instinct to explore.

The Alps in the 1950s

HAMISH NICOL

(*Plates 45–48*)

When I first saw the Alps in July 1949, I nearly fell off the train with excitement. We were on the little rack railway which goes from St Gervais to Chamonix on the last stage of a two-day journey from London. Suddenly the train turned a corner at Les Houches and the whole North face of Mont Blanc came into view, so close that you could almost touch it. The seracs of the Bossons glacier seemed to tumble and sparkle in the sun. I had never seen anything like it before. I jumped from coach to coach on the rattling train, shouted for joy, tried to climb on the roof to get a better look, and couldn't understand why all the other passengers were not doing the same. I was just 20 years old.

Malcolm Slesser and I had travelled slowly by train to Newhaven, by boat to Dieppe, and then overnight across France, sitting bolt upright all the way, on the hard seats of the SNCF. Dan Stewart met us in Chamonix where we spent a frenzied hour buying food and a little equipment, not forgetting that candle lanterns were required on alpine glaciers at night. It does seem incredible that little aluminium candle lanterns were still being sold to gullible alpinists in 1949, long after the invention of the electric torch. The way into the mountains, then as now, was by way of the Montenvers rack railway. This was a coal-fired steam train pushing little carriages, very like the Snowdon mountain railway.

At 4.30am the next day the three of us set off to climb the Grands Charmoz. We reached the summit at 3pm in our tricouni-nailed boots and with our hemp ropes, not returning to Montenvers till about 6pm. I was completely exhausted by my first alpine climb. For the next two weeks we rushed about all over the Chamonix Alps, climbing non-stop but attempting only the easiest routes, such as the Géant by its fixed ropes. There did not seem to be any English people about, but one American spoke to us; he was attached to a guide. Every so often we would descend to Chamonix to buy food and, perhaps, to eat a decent meal. You could eat in Chamonix for 650 (old) francs, which was about 13 shillings (65p). This was pretty expensive by our standards. As a National Service second lieutenant in the Army, I received 13 shillings a day.

My first season in the Alps had been an enormous success for me, though by present-day standards it was not impressive. We were intensely parochial and had no idea about what, if anything, other British climbers were doing. There were then no monthly climbing glossies full of advertisements. In 1949 there were in fact only two shops in the United Kingdom which specialized in mountaineering equipment: Robert Lawrie in London, and Brighams in Manchester.

At this period, continental climbers were years ahead of us. The 1950 *Climbers' Club Journal* contained a description by Bernard Pierre of his second ascent of the W face of the Aiguille Noire de Peuterey, with the guide Gaston Rébuffat, in 1949. The first ascent had been made in 1939 by the Italian climbers Ratti and Vitali. Bernard Pierre was a top French amateur who spoke good English and was often seen in London. His lectures to the Alpine Club in the post-war period must have been partly responsible for the surge in British activity which took place from 1950 onwards.

Tom Bourdillon would have heard these lectures, and it was he who took up the challenge. He ran the Oxford University Mountaineering Club meet at the Wayfarer's hut RLH in Langdale in December 1949, and this is where we first climbed together. As meet leader he was responsible for the food, which consisted of a very good supply of porridge and jam, purchased in the grocer's shop at Chapel Stile which, I am happy to say, is still in business. To my surprise and delight, he invited me to climb with him in the Alps in 1950. We teamed up with Dick Viney and John Saxby, who were old friends of Tom's.

At that time nobody in England knew anything about artificial climbing using pitons and rope ladders, or, if they did, we had not met them. The official Alpine Club view was that such activities were not really sporting or 'British', and Colonel Strutt in his editorials in the *Alpine Journal* in the 1930s had roundly condemned them. High-standard rock climbing had been going on in the Dolomites for many years, and Cassin had climbed the N face of the Cima Ovest de Lavaredo in 1935. But Tom and I had to teach ourselves how to do it from square one, and we learned the techniques by practising on a tree in his garden in Quainton, Bucks. Tom had inserted wrought-iron bars at suitable intervals into the tree's trunk, and from these we suspended our rudimentary ladders, or étriers. It was rather fun.

Tom and I left Oxford on 10 July 1950, and arrived in Chamonix two days later, by train. That night we walked up to the Albert Premier hut, groaning under enormous rucksacks full of pitons and food. Tom had decided that our first climb would be the W face of the Aiguille Purtscheller, by the Rébuffat route, 200m, *Très Difficile*. This was almost certainly the first TD climb done by a British party in the Western Alps. It had two or three very hard pitches, of which two were artificial pitches for our pitons and ladders. We got up in 4½ hours, and down again by abseiling, in a hailstorm, back to the hut. Two days later Viney and Saxby arrived at Montenvers. At first the weather was poor. By 21 July it cleared, and we went up to the Envers des Aiguilles hut to climb the Ryan-Lochmatter ridge of the Plan on the next day. This amazing route had been climbed by Ryan with his guides in 1906. It was my first big alpine lead, and it was magnificent. There are many pitches of grades 3, 4 and 5, and the bergschrund at the start of the climb can be quite difficult to cross. It is interesting that the Oxford climbers John Hoyland and Paul Wand planned to climb this route in their 1934 season. These two climbers, two of the best from Oxford University in the 1930s, climbed the Mer de Glace face of the Grépon as their first alpine climb, but a few days later they were both killed on their way to the Innominata ridge of Mont Blanc. It is possible that this accident delayed the development of British alpinism for many years.

18. *Makalu S face.* (A V Saunders) (p 17)

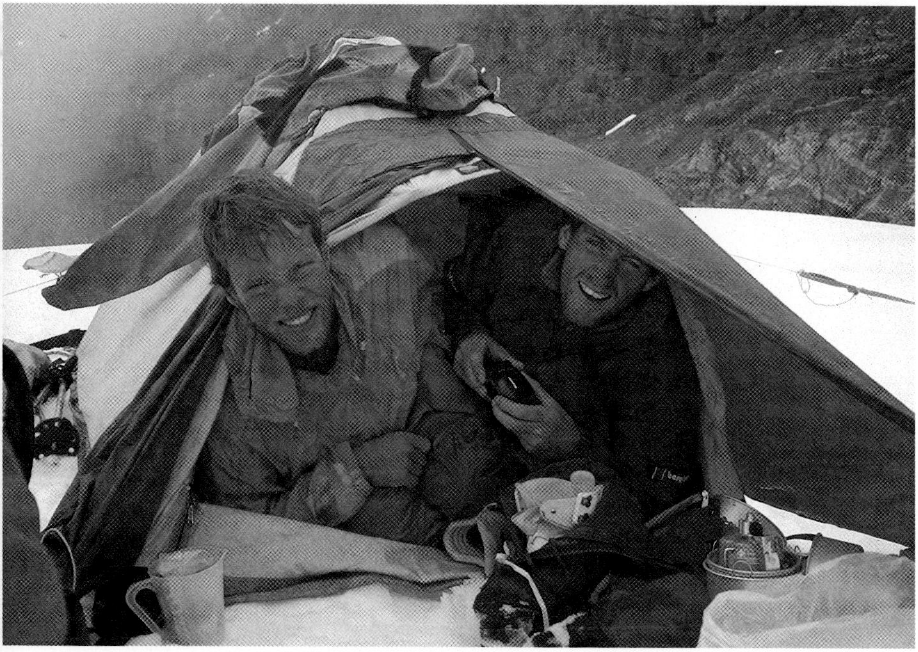

19. *Stephen Sustad and Andy Fanshawe.* (A V Saunders) (p 17)

20. *Victor Saunders on Yaupa, 6433m.* (Andy Fanshawe) (p 17)

21. *Chamlang, 7319m, Camp 1 – ordinary r*

V Saunders) (p 17)

22. *Stephen Sustad on Kangchuntse (Makalu 2), 7640m.* (A V Saunders) (p 17)

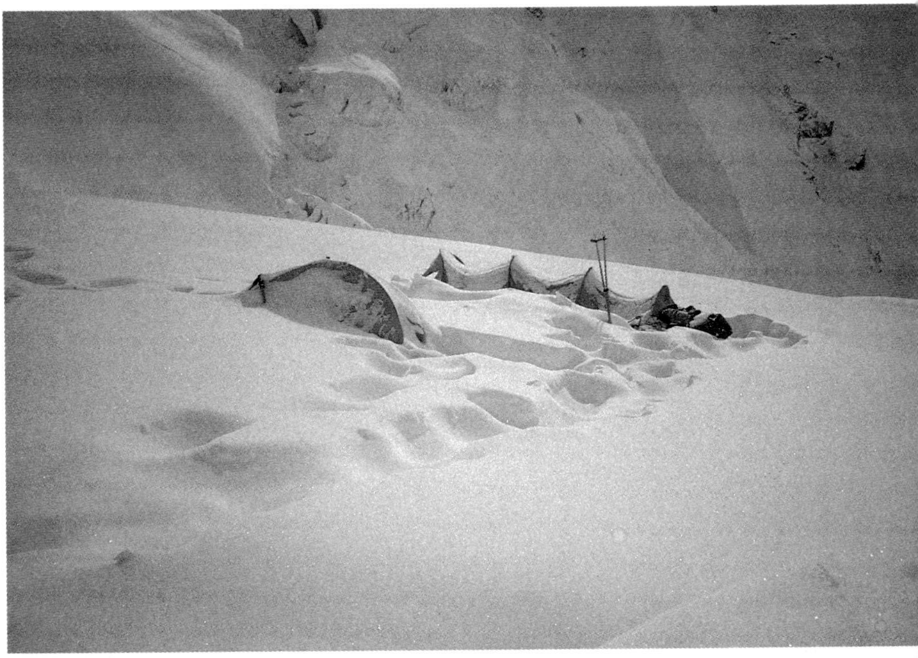

23. *Kangchuntse (Makalu 2), 7640m – Camp 1 after the storm.* (A V Saunders) (p 17)

24. *Kangchenjunga massif showing routes and high altitude camps. Summits (L to R): Yalung Kang, main summit, central summit, S summit.* (p 24)

25. *Manaslu S face.* (Alan Hinkes) (p 242)

26. *Manaslu S face from 5500m – high winds on the summit.* (Alan Hinkes) (p 242)

27. *Expedition Manaslu – avalanche off P29.* (Alan Hinkes) (p 242)

28. *L Mike Banks (aged 66) and R Joss Lynam (aged 65).* (p 46)

29. *Members of the Saga Magazine Himalayan Expedition 1989 to Jaonli (6632m). L to R: Alan Blackshaw, C P Ravichandra, Mike Banks, Don Roberts, Chewang Thundup, Karan, Joss Lynam, Paddy O'Leary.* (p 46)

We returned to Chamonix very pleased with ourselves, spent a day shopping and on 25 July Tom and I walked from Montenvers to the foot of the N face of the Dru, and bivouacked on the rognon with our backs to the huge and frightening cliff. It was my first bivouac, and I will never forget the night we spent huddled together on the cold rock. The sky was clear and star-lit, and the town of Chamonix was a blaze of lights at our feet. Our plan was to leave the sleeping-bags there and climb over to the Charpoua hut where our friends would be waiting for us. At that time the N face of the Dru had a tremendous reputation. It was first climbed in 1935, and by 1949 there had been something like 30 or 35 ascents. Tom and I left the bivouac at 5am the next day, carrying a double nylon rope, a spare rope for hauling up the rucksacks and wearing vibram-soled boots. My ideas had had a good shaking up since 1949. We had some rope slings, some karabiners, a few pitons, a hammer each, one ice axe and one pair of crampons. Luckily the rock was dry and in perfect condition. We hardly noticed the Fissure Lambert, which is regarded as the first major difficulty. I had certainly led part of it before I realized what it was. When we got to the hard bit, the Fissure Allain, there was no argument: we climbed the Fissure Martinetti which is a lot easier, and a much more sensible way. The last 150m were steep and covered in verglas, which made them rather serious. The ascent lasted 8½ hours. Our earlier plan to traverse over the Grand Dru came to nothing. There was a thick mist and the weather looked bad. Instead we descended the Petit Dru by a long series of tedious and difficult abseils. Viney and Saxby were waiting for us in the Charpoua hut and gave us a tremendous welcome.

I was all for doing another climb, but my companions would have none of it. We must return to Chamonix and have a celebration. Viney and Saxby had to return home, leaving Tom and me on our own for the last week. Richard Myer joined us for the Aiguille de Roc-Grépon traverse. This involved a 32m abseil from the summit of the Roc, all of it overhanging and very uncomfortable using the classical trouser-friction technique. The day did not end well. Our return to the tree-line just above Chamonix coincided with pitch darkness and we got hopelessly lost in the woods, tracking to and fro without torches, till we staggered into the town at midnight and had supper in a night-club, to the amazement of the other people who were dancing.

My 1951 season started off with the Mer de Glace face of the Grépon, with Johnnie Sims. This climb had by then become very popular. Westmacott and Rawlinson had done it in 1950, as had Godfrey Francis and McNaught-Davis. 1951 was not a good year, but in 1952 Dan Stewart and I had tremendous plans. We warmed up on the Aiguille Mummery by its SW face, then walked over to the Leschaux hut which was empty apart from ourselves and a rather attractive *gardienne*. '*Que vous êtes beau!*' she cried, seeing Dan coming in through the door. I expect she was lonely, and Dan had a certain rugged Scottish charm. Much might have come of this encounter, had it not been for our plan to leave early next morning to attempt the Hirondelles ridge of the Grandes Jorasses. Unfortunately this failed to come off owing to a silly route-finding error on the Hirondelles col. Two days later we climbed the Innominata ridge of Mont Blanc and were back in Chamonix again after a

17-hour day. After a day of rest we climbed to the Envers des Aiguilles hut, aiming for the E ridge of the Crocodile. We were off before dawn and by about 5am had reached a point high on the glacier where it is quite steep. Dan was leading, and it was here that the accident took place. I saw it happening quite clearly. He was carrying too many coils of rope, and his right cramponned foot caught in one of the coils. He tripped and fell and within a second he was going like a train. There was nothing I could do to stop him. Together we fell down the entire length of the Envers des Aiguilles glacier. The bottom of this glacier is a mass of jumbled seracs and huge crevasses where it topples over and tumbles into the Mer de Glace. Both of us could easily have been killed. What happened was an amazing piece of luck. I shot into one of the larger crevasses, and Dan went over the top of it: the rope held. Dan was completely uninjured, and proceeded to pull me out. This was not easy as I was semi-conscious and had a broken jaw, and a very painful back.

Having pulled me out of the crevasse, Dan frog-marched me to the hut. There was no one else there, it was unguarded, and was still in fact under construction. Dan set off on his own down to Chamonix, and two days later he returned with a rescue party from the *Compagnie des Guides de Chamonix*. I was put in a carrying stretcher, like a parcel, and humped unceremoniously down to the Chamonix hospital. My stay in this establishment was not pleasant. I was X-rayed, and had my temperature taken twice daily *per rectum*. Apart from this, I was neither fed nor attended to. They must have felt that with a broken jaw I could eat nothing. My friends from the Chalet Biolay came to see me every day, and smuggled in tubes of condensed milk (*Lait Mont Blanc*) which I was able to force between my jaws. I think it was Dave Thomas who eventually decided that this could not go on. I was flown back from Geneva by plane, and within three hours of my arrival in London had had my jaw set and wired in the Middlesex Hospital.

For me this episode was a disaster. A successful 1952 season would have strengthened my claims for a place on the Mount Everest expedition of 1953. As it was, I could not possibly be considered, having suffered two falls in quick succession, one on Zero Gully of Ben Nevis with Anthony Rawlinson in 1951, and now this. The fact that Dan's slip was an act of uncharacteristic though inexcusable incompetence cut no ice with the selectors. I was written off as dangerous, and given a place as a reserve.

Our ascent of the N face of the Dru in 1950 had a marked effect on British alpinism, and in the next two or three years climbers from Oxford and Cambridge Universities continued to raise the standard. Cym and Nancy Smith from Cambridge were already doing big things in 1950, but soon after Cym was killed in a motor-cycle accident. By 1952 Oxford and Cambridge were sharing the honours. In 1951 Ian McNaught-Davis appeared on the scene with Godfrey Francis, an Oxford geologist who had defected to Cambridge. Mac was from Manchester, and added his strength to the Cambridge teams. In 1951 he climbed the Ryan route on the Plan with Roger Chorley (Cambridge) and Tony Moulam. This was one of Moulam's rare appearances in the Alps at that time. Dave Fisher and George Band repeated the Roc-Grépon traverse in 1951, but the big season for Cambridge climbers was 1952. Band and Chorley began by hacking out an ice cave on Monte Rosa. This was paid employment from which, in odd moments, they climbed the Cresta di Santa Caterina of the Nordend and did the Liskamm-Castor-Pollux traverse; then, moving over to Chamonix, they climbed the N ridge of the Peigne (with Arthur Dolphin and McNaught-Davis), and the S ridge of the Aiguille Noire de Peuterey (with Francis and Wrangham). Streetly and Band climbed the N ridge of the Dent Blanche, and the Tronchey ridge of the Grandes Jorasses was climbed in 1953 by Viney, Rawlinson, Wrangham, Harris and Jones.

But it would not be true to say that it was all Oxford and Cambridge in those years. Neil Mather climbed the Peuterey ridge with McNaught-Davis in 1952, and the Ryan route with Pigott in 1953. Then, in 1954, the Oxbridge dominance came to an abrupt end, when the Rock and Ice Club appeared in Chamonix for the second time. Joe Brown and Don Whillans climbed the celebrated W face of the Dru in two days in August 1954. This was a third ascent. In the same year they made an important first ascent on the W face of the Blaitière. This contained two pitches of Grade 6, one of which was the famous 'Fissure Brown'. British climbers had at last arrived in the post-war Alps.

My 1953 season was a great success. Once again I went out by train, carrying a good supply of Viking nylon ropes which one could sell or barter in Chamonix. My first companion was Michael Cunnington, also from Balliol College, Oxford. After an easy climb on the Argentière I became progressively more ill with a raging sore throat. The doctor in Chamonix, Dr Bousquet, seemed quite concerned. '*Vous couchez sur la paille?*' he enquired anxiously. We all stayed in the French Alpine Club refuge in those days. It was called the Biolay, was extremely primitive, and had sleeping quarters on straw upstairs and a few tables and a cooking area downstairs, rather too near the villainous hole in the ground which passed as a toilet. On 17 July Michael Cunnington and I walked up to the Requin hut in poor weather, and we remained there for three days during which it got steadily worse. By the 19th there was nobody else left in the hut. At midday the weather cleared miraculously and, in a foot or two of new snow, we plodded up to the bivouac hut on the Col de la Fourche, carrying all that was left of the food – a tin of pemmican and a few biscuits. At the Fourche hut I wedged the petrol stove in a crack between the floor-boards, and propped a billy-can across it, balanced on two stones. The inevitable happened: the stove fell over, and our precious pemmican flowed into a gutter between the floor-boards, where we had to fall upon it with our spoons before it all disappeared. At 1.45am the next morning Michael and I set off for the Old Brenva route on Mont Blanc. Thanks to the recent snowfalls, there was a foot of soft avalanchy snow over ice on the entire upper half of the Old Brenva above the ice arête. It went on endlessly, and I lost all count of time. We reached the summit of Mont Blanc at 5pm and descended in a trance of fatigue, hunger and thirst to the Goûter hut. This hut is well above the snow-line, and all water has to be melted from snow by the guardian, so it was a very thirsty night. The next day at the terminus of the mountain railway called Mont Lachat, not far below the hut, a trainful of French tourists was disembarking. They each had their picnic hampers and looked well fed. We shamelessly begged food from them – peaches, pears and sandwiches – then sat down behind a stone and scoffed the lot.

It did not take very long to recover from all this in Chamonix and next day I was off with Alan Blackshaw to the forester's hut in the woods near Montenvers. We climbed the Pointe Albert by its W face; this was the first *extrêmement difficile* (ED) climbed by a British party in the Western Alps. It was one of the new post-war ED rock-climbs, and had been first climbed in 1945. Ours must have been one of the earlier re-ascents.

On 25 July Alan Blackshaw and I walked up to the Torino hut and heard that Arthur Dolphin had been killed. He was climbing on the Dent du Géant, and had met his death on the easy rocks below the summit-spire. He was one of the best-known English rock-climbers of the day, the author of innumerable first ascents in the Lake District, including the well-known Kipling Grooves on Gimmer. Two days later Alan and I set off to attempt the S ridge of the Aiguille Noire, but Alan fell ill on the lower rocks of the mountain and was forced to turn back. At this point Pat Vaughan arrived in the Noire hut with a very large party, including Gwen and Dennis Greenald, Dick Tomes and Geof Milwood. The S ridge of the Noire had been climbed in 1930 by K Brendel and H Schaller, and was one of the most popular rock-climbs on Mont Blanc. Normally one had to bivouac somewhere on the ascent or descent. Next day Pat and I set off so fast that the others soon dropped behind, and we did not see them again that day. We climbed the whole ridge in 10½ hours and were back in the hut by 10pm. The others got back to the Noire hut two days later, just as a search party was setting out to look for them.

For six days the weather was bad, and Alan had to go home. On 3 August I met Ted Wrangham, a noted Cambridge alpinist, at the Torino hut and we decided to join forces. I was once again living on *Lait Mont Blanc*, this time because an impacted wisdom tooth made it impossible for me to open my mouth. Ted wanted to climb the NW ridge of the Grands Charmoz which had only been climbed once, by Allain and Schatz in 1950. On the Nantillons glacier just before the rocky part of the climb we bumped into Lionel Terray, the famous French guide, who had a client in tow. He told us that the upper part of our ridge was very hard. He was right. At one point one has to pendulum across a blank wall, and this particular section cannot be reversed. Above this lies the crux. Ted, suffering from cramp in his fingers, had to prise them open with his teeth. I won't ever forget the final pitch. There we were, Ted and I, huddled on a tiny ledge, with an immense drop under our feet going down 1000m to the Nantillons glacier, and above us an overhang, a vertical wall, a thin crack and then easier ground to the summit ridge. First I had to stand on Ted's shoulders to surmount the overhang, both of us belayed from one tiny piton. The thin crack was the hard bit, and here I tried to protect myself by placing a piton. To my horror I found that my efforts were demolishing the only remaining handholds. It was now or never. 'Watch it, Ted, I might come off!' I need not have told him. He knew. I gripped a tiny hold with my right hand and climbed it desperately: we were up. It was certainly Grade 6. Ted followed on a tight rope.

Five days later Ted and I tackled the S ridge of the Pointe Gugliermina on the Aiguille Blanche de Peuterey. This has since become very popular with British climbers. Ted and I had driven over to Courmayeur in Ted's Mark 7 Jaguar, and then quite a long way up the Val Veni until a rickety bridge over the

Doire prevented further progress in such a huge car. We walked straight up to the Gamba hut, had tea with the guardian, and then crossed the Frêney glacier to bivouac on a rocky ledge at the bottom of the cliff. Next day we were climbing by 6am. It was one of the most delightful free climbs that either of us had ever done. Two days later in Courmayeur we met Gaston Rébuffat and Paul Habrun, after their successful ascent of the E face of the Grand Capucin. We took them by car up to their camp-site at Purtud, and they there entertained us with vermouth and cigarettes. When I next met Rébuffat at the Alpine Club in London, he had absolutely no recollection of this encounter. By now the Italian towns were filling up for the holidays and Ted was having difficulty finding accommodation. These problems did not concern me very much, as I slept on the back seat of his car in the hotel garage.

By 17 August the weather, which had been bad, improved, and Ted and I climbed the S face of the Géant, a short, hard and mainly overhanging rock-climb. We must have been fairly fit by this time, because two days later we were half-way up the Route Major, on the Brenva face of Mont Blanc. Ted was leading at a blistering pace across the lower slopes below the Sentinelle Rouge, while I was crawling slowly after him, suffering from the trots. Toni Gobbi had advised us to take his direct route up the centre of the upper buttress on the Route Major, which was graded 5. We got up in 12 hours and were back in Chamonix by supper-time. My entire six weeks' holiday, including transport there and back, had cost £42.

In 1954 it was common knowledge that a major expedition was being planned to climb Kangchenjunga in the following year. I began to wonder what qualifications were necessary for such a trip. By this time my alpine record was equal to most, and better than some. However, no letter of invitation ever came. 1956 was the last year of my medical studies, and I simply had to pass the final examinations in December. When I was asked to take part in the triumphant expedition led by John Hartog to the Muztagh tower in 1956, I had to refuse. By the summer of 1956 my finances had reached an all-time low, and I faced the dubious prospect of surviving for six months in London on no money. I was rescued from this predicament by a generous grant of £100 from St Thomas's Hospital.

1955 was to be my last big alpine season, possibly for a number of years. In mid-July I left London with Ted Wrangham in his Jaguar car, and met Tom Bourdillon, who was to be my climbing companion, in Chamonix the next day. The N ridge of the Peigne was to be our training expedition. In those days the Plan des Aiguilles lift had not been completed, but there was a useful workman's lift which most of the climbers knew about. It was a plank suspended from a wire: you got there by 5am, sat on it, and miraculously it set off into space, high above the pine-trees, giving you a spectacular view of the Chamonix valley. The N ridge of the Peigne was a great deal less exciting.

Next morning we sat on the plank at 6am and reversed the procedure. Our next climb really *was* the E ridge of the Crocodile, and this time there were no accidents and no mistakes. We were up and down in a day, slept in the next morning, and then set off late to cross the Torino pass into Italy, in a bad storm. Our intention was to stay at the Albergo della Funivia at the bottom end of the

Torino lift, where we made a dramatic entry, bursting into the dining-room in the middle of a dinner party, our dripping anoraks and voluminous coils of rope making a slow puddle in the middle of the dining-room floor. Next day we set off at 2am for the Gamba hut. There were thick clouds spreading across the sky from the French side, and beyond Purtud it began to rain. When we arrived at the Gamba hut at 7am it did not look as if the W face of the Aiguille Noire de Peuterey was a good idea.

Next morning the guardian pinched my toes and said: '*Une heure, Monsieur, il fait beau.*' I rolled off my bunk, fumbled my way to the door, and saw outside a brilliant starry night. Thanks to an earlier recce, and some handy steps across the Frêney glacier left by a descending party, we were already starting up the W face of the Noire at 6.45am. It was steep at first, and one has to aim for a little ridge which is a feature of the middle section of the face. The ridge is quite easy, and we could move together carrying coils of rope. The end of this section was marked by a snow-filled gully. Tom pulled the ice-axe out of his rucksack and cut steps across it. On the other side of the gully the climbing suddenly became more serious, the rock blacker, steeper and more greasy. It was very cold. I was looking for the Grade 6 crack which was going to take me up to the Ratti bivouac ledge. The crack was wet, and here and there were patches of ice. Then I was struck clean on the forehead by a drop of water. Another followed. The water came from the lip of the great overhang, and fell a clear distance of 60m. Somewhere up there, there was a space where the bivouac ledge must be.

I turned my attention to the crack, which was about 6cm wide, and for 25m I jammed it, laybacked it, and was sometimes forced to bridge across the corner. I emerged on to the bivouac ledge. Quite a few important climbers had spent the night here, and had left their cigarette packets and sardine tins behind as mementos. It was wide and long enough to lie down full-length, but its chief merit was the huge overhang which acted like a roof; one might have been indoors. From the ledge a crack could be seen running up the overhanging wall, and in it were half a dozen pitons. By 5pm we were both up, and we could see the summit quite easily, about 300m away. At 6.45pm, exactly 12 hours from the glacier, we reached the summit of the Aiguille Noire de Peuterey and bivouacked on the E ridge, a few feet below the summit. Next day the washerwomen at Entrèves turned and stared at us walking past. I had a huge tear in my trousers and wondered if anybody would be able to mend them. Ours was the 10th ascent of the Ratti route, which had first been climbed in 1939.

For five days it rained in Chamonix. Then it cleared enough to allow us to make an attempt on the E face of the Grand Capucin. This climb is so steep that it clears rapidly after bad weather. Our sacks contained food for three days, bivouac equipment, 35 pitons and wooden wedges and 110m of rope. It was a hard flog up the glacier in soft new snow, sometimes wading thigh-deep. The bivouac platform which is well placed within 15m of the first Grade 6 pitch was covered with 60cm of soft snow. It was 8.30pm, and it would soon be dark. After a bit of shovelling with piton hammers an area measuring three metres by one emerged with a gravel base, much better than one might have expected. Tom lit the petrol stove, I cut a few lumps of ice from the cornice behind me, tipped our 20 hard-boiled eggs out of the saucepan in which they had travelled protected, and started to make soup. Our bivouac gear was quite primitive. There were two reasons for this: we were too poor to buy any, and if you carry a lot of stuff you will almost certainly have to use it, because it slows you down. We each had a cagoule and an eiderdown jacket, and nothing else. A bad storm would have caused serious problems. At 3am two little lights could be seen crossing the glacier. Competitors! So breakfast was a hurried affair, and we started climbing at 6am. Tom and I pressed on upwards quite slowly, at a rate of about 15m per hour. Each pitch needed 10 or 15 pitons or wedges, and few were *in situ*. By 4pm we had reached the 40m wall which is said to be the crux of the climb. This wall is continuously overhanging and has to be done in two sections, with a stance in the middle, standing most precariously in étriers. It took us four hours to climb the wall, and it was 8pm by the time we reached the second Bonatti bivouac. This was the largest ledge on the climb so far; it was covered in one metre of snow, but a lot of vigorous stamping and sweeping produced a sort of cave, just big enough for two people to sit down but not to stretch out. I smoked a cigarette and waited for dawn, chin on knee.

Breakfast was eggs, soup and super-milk concentrate, pretty nauseating, and it took two hours. It was still too cold to move off, but by 7am I was into the 25m sinuous crack which, in those days, had not a single piton in it. I put in 15, and it took an hour to lead. Just above this Bonatti had spent his third night. He must have been standing on one leg. At 5pm we reached the summit, abseiled down into the gap behind the Capucin, and rejoined our rucksacks by descending a snowy gully. We reached the Requin hut after midnight. This was the fifth ascent of the E face of the Grand Capucin.

By 1955 there were a lot of British climbers in the Alps. The Oxford and Cambridge contingents had been joined by the Scots and other Northerners. In 1955 Tom Patey climbed the N face of the Plan, and Rawlinson and Westmacott climbed the S ridge of the Fou and the Ryan-Lochmatter route on the Plan. The ascent by Blackshaw and Downes of the N face of the Triolet in the same year was one of the first big ice-climbs by a British party. The Couturier couloir of the Verte was climbed by Moseley, Dance, Noyce, Sutton and Brook; this was before the days of the curved pick, when it was still quite an undertaking. The Cassin route on the Piz Badile fell to Blackshaw, Sutton, Downes and Langmuir in 1956.

In 1956 I had my final examinations in medicine and had not intended to go climbing, but Tom persuaded me to come. The journey began and continued badly. Tom had suffered all summer with an acute infection of one finger, which had made his right hand very much weaker than the left. On our way along the shores of the Lake of Geneva he lost his glasses while having a swim. On a Friday evening the party arrived at the village of Baltschied and camped on the extreme edge of a hay-field. Although nothing was said, the villagers did seem to be very unfriendly. Later in the evening the farmer diverted the irrigation stream to flood our camp-site, and he did this quite deliberately. We woke up at 1am in 10cm of water. On Saturday I remained in the valley to see Mary, my future wife, off on her journey to Venice by train. Tom and Dick Viney, with Roger Chorley and John Tyson, walked up the path to the Baltschiedertal hut. I followed the next day, but without a map I got lost and spent a night in a hay-loft. It was 10am on Monday morning when I reached the hut, to find John and Roger alone. Tom and Dick had not returned from their climb. We walked up to the glacier at the foot of the E face of the Jägihorn and found them both there, on the glacier, roped together. They were dead. Their deaths ended the golden age of Oxford mountaineering in the 1950s, and certainly ended my climbing career at that time. I did not climb again for four years.

Tom and Dick were buried in a little cemetery in Visp. I acted as one of the pall-bearers, my eyes blinded with tears. Whenever I can, I visit the grave and read the inscription on it: 'They were most rightly reputed valiant, who, though they perfectly apprehend both what is dangerous and what is easy, are never the more thereby diverted from adventuring.'

The Stunt

ANNE SAUVY

(*Translated by Edward Peck*)

'Must find something to do,' grumbled Meriadoc.

'Yes, but what?' groaned Ethelbert.

'Dunno. You're the clever one. Use your brains. Me, I can't bear to think in this heat.'

It really was very hot. The needle on the barometer had reached the second 'R' in 'Very Dry' and, something that had never happened before, a family of marmots had been seen coming down from the Charlanon screes to cool off in the swimming-pool. Snow and ice were melting so fast that Wilfrid, Meriadoc's great rival, had just succeeded in making the first descent of Mont Blanc by sail-board.

Meriadoc hadn't thought of that one in time. 'You know,' he reminded his usual climbing partner, 'you know that my publisher insists that I get myself mentioned three times in the press this summer before the book comes out.'

'I'm ever so sorry for you! There can't be many lads who have been asked to write their memoirs before they're twenty-one. What about the descent of the couloir of the Tour des Courtes by kayak? There were two dailies who put you on the front page for that.'

'Three,' Meriadoc corrected him. 'But there's one article I didn't care for. The one where it said that we were nothing but a bunch of ascetics who thought only about keeping fit and training for success. I know we do 250 pull-ups on each little finger each morning before even going for a pee. But the pleasures of life, we know about them as well as anyone else. We know what it's like to have a good blow-out on yoghurt!'

'Quite right,' agreed Ethelbert, his eyes suddenly gleaming with greed. 'But never mind what stories they tell. The main thing is that they should talk about you. After all, you have opened up a mass of firsts this summer, both on the cliffs and in the mountains – nothing less than Grades 7(c) and 8. Let's see . . . there was "Nietzsche's Nick", and then "No Edelweiss for Mrs Wilkinson". And "Saussure's Assassination". And don't forget "Another one Edlinger won't get"!'

'Pooh! And the papers didn't even mention them, there are so many new routes being opened up nowadays. What I need, don't you see, is to manage one really big success, pretty quick.'

'Well,' suggested Ethelbert, 'suppose you did something funny . . . eye-catching, of course, but entirely comic. Say a first on the SSE face of the buttress of Gendarme 3876, wearing flippers and a diving-mask. You could call it the

"Saint-Tropez Gendarme". Headline in the press: "So hot in the Alps that climbers think they are on the *Côte d'Azur*." The mask would be a bit of a nuisance, but not too much. And there ought to be enough room under the flippers for the edge of a climbing boot to stick out. I'm sure it's possible. Are you listening?'

'Hm. You don't say. What a lot of eyewash,' protested Meriadoc. 'Know what I think? I think it would look just a bit artificial!'

'Well, then, what about a descent on skis of a completely rocky face? That hasn't been done yet. Say the W face of the Dru! Not joking. Why not? With a film tacked on to it, as well!'

'Bah! You know – skiing, skiing, that's all old hat. You can ski down an overhang, and it wouldn't surprise anyone any more. As for the W face, even on a monoski . . .'

'Oh, you make me tired. I don't know what else to suggest. Perhaps you could beat the endurance record for the Rubik Cube, hanging on an étrier? On the side of the Aiguille du Midi so that the journalists could watch?'

'But I don't know how to do the Rubik Cube.'

'That's just the point! If you did, it would be over too quickly. And with a bit of luck you might get into the *Guinness Book of Records*.'

'No, that wouldn't cut any ice.'

'Well, then there are only the three other possibilities that I've told you about. The Frêney Pillar in 59 minutes . . .'

'So what's new?'

'Something on the N face of the Aiguille du Goûter, where the rock is so rotten that almost all the routes still have to be done.'

'Pah!'

'Or set off an avalanche on the Verte after the first fall of powder and go down on top of it on a surf-board.'

'I've already told you that that gives me the pip.'

'Well, what the hell do you want me to dream up for you? Blast it! How about a sex-change, and do as a ladies' first something you've already done first as a man. That would make a splash! You could call yourself Marinette. No other climber would have managed that one before you! And you'd be likely to keep the exclusive rights for ages.'

'You're pulling my leg,' said Meriadoc in a threatening voice.

'Well, then, go up the Italian side of the Matterhorn with a rising parachute and come down the N face in a barrel.'

'I think that's already been done,' sighed Meriadoc. 'No, you see . . . the public, the newspapermen, they need to be taken by surprise . . . to be *really* surprised! Get it?'

'That's it!' exclaimed Ethelbert suddenly. 'I've got a super idea. The walk round Mont Blanc!'

'What do you mean – walk round Mont Blanc?' Meriadoc asked thoughtfully. 'Surely that isn't done any more? With all the impossible stunts people are racking their brains to invent, are there really any types left who want to just plod around Mont Blanc?'

'I believe so, I'm sure of it!' replied Ethelbert.

'But how should I do it? In less than five hours? Backwards, or hopping on one foot?'

'No, quite the opposite. Make it absolutely simple. Take a week over it. Just the normal way. To prove that you're not only a demi-god, but also human like everyone else.'

'Perfect. Absolutely perfect! Out of this world. It takes someone like you to dream up a ploy like that!'

The undertaking was a tremendous success. Accompanied by a few journalists, Meriadoc touched the heart of the crowds by the human side of his act. All the papers published the photo where, sitting by the edge of a path, his forehead bathed in sweat, he was dressing his blisters. It was the start of his real career.

Tragedy in the Ortler

JOHANNA MERZ

(*Plates* 49–52)

The Königsspitze (3859m), which dominates the Ortles-Cevedale group of mountains, is not the highest peak in the range but it is undoubtedly the most striking. Rising in a great dome of shattered, rust-coloured limestone, topped with a coronet of snow, it looks majestic when seen from a distance and awe-inspiring when you stand directly beneath it. A long and steep ridge of rock and snow divides its southern side from the difficult N face on the Stelvio side of the mountain. The normal route from the south attains this SE ridge by way of a narrow snow gully, prone to rock-fall, leading up to a shoulder, the Passo della Bottiglia (Königsjoch) at 3293m. The section of the route leading from the shoulder to the summit is steep but, given good snow conditions, it is not difficult. When the snow is out of condition, however, it can be very dangerous.

When I arrived in Bormio towards the end of July, my friend and guide, Maurizio, came round to the hotel in the evening with the news that the Gran Zebrù (the Italian name for the Königsspitze) was in perfect condition and that we must certainly attempt it the next day. I had hoped to start with something easier; however, I was very keen to climb this 'king' of mountains, and I readily agreed with his suggestion.

I had first met Maurizio two years before, when I came to Bormio for a skiing holiday and particularly enjoyed the run down from the 3000m Cima Bianca. From that splendid viewpoint I had seen an enticing-looking range of mountains along the NE skyline and had decided, there and then, to return in the summer to investigate. One of the ski instructors introduced me to Maurizio Zappa ('the best guide in Bormio') and we arranged to climb for a few days at the beginning of my Alpine season the following September. When I returned to Bormio in the late summer, I hoped to climb the three highest peaks of the range – the Cevedale (3769m), the Gran Zebrù (3859m) and the Ortles (3905m) – but in the Alps things rarely turn out as planned.

We had walked up to the Rifugio Casati but, on arrival, we heard that someone coming down from the Cevedale, unroped, had fallen into a crevasse. As the smallest guide in the hut, Maurizio volunteered to go down. An hour or two later I watched from the windows as the sad litle rescue party returned with the news that the man had died from a 40m fall – with the rope still coiled round his shoulders. The following morning Maurizio had to help to retrieve the body, but first he arranged for me to join another party to climb the Cevedale. The mountain was in deep mist, so there was little chance of having a look at the other peaks in the range. However, I was assured that the Gran Zebrù was out of condition (too icy). I decided to cut my losses and come back the following year, and I made a date with Maurizio for the end of July 1989 – a whole week, this time – to make sure of really getting to grips with this out-of-the-way and intriguing range.

In the meantime I found out a bit more about the Ortler group and looked through some early accounts in the *Alpine Journal*. In the very first volume, Francis Fox Tuckett gave a detailed description of the range as a whole and, in particular, of his first ascent of the Königsspitze in 1864. In a later volume (1918), Claude Wilson wrote about some superb ridge expeditions:

> [The Ortler] is, *par excellence*, the land of the ridge wanderer. One can walk or climb over summit after summit along every one of the sky-lines of the district . . . in the Ortler *all* the ridges 'go'. And yet the mountain forms are grand, and the outlines often singularly bold, and few can have examined Mr Tuckett's beautifully drawn panoramas in the first volume of the *Journal* without experiencing the desire to ascend those striking peaks.[1]

When July came round I made a new plan. We would start with a three-day traverse of the '13 Cime', which curl round from the Pizzo Tresero, above Santa Caterina, to the Cevedale. But, on the first evening, my plans were already changing and I had agreed to start off with the Gran Zebrù.

Maurizio and his cousin Nino picked me up from the hotel at 5 next morning and we set out on the bone-shaking ride up a track which eventually petered out high on the mountain. This saved us from having to stay overnight at the Rifugio Pizzini. A tongue of glacier rose above a boulder-field towards an unlikely-looking narrow snow gully. Once we were actually on it, the gully turned out to be less steep than it appeared to be from below. The surrounding rocks were described by Tuckett: 'The fact was that a more utterly disintegrated, rotten, and untrustworthy collection of stones professing to be rocks I never saw . . . doubt and distrust were the garment of our minds.'[2] However, apart from odd bits of falling rock no bigger than a golf-ball, the gully presented no difficulty, and we soon attained the Passo della Bottiglia. The SE ridge rises another 500m above this shoulder and, though steep, it was by no means desperate. My main problem was a touch of altitude sickness, on this my first day, combined with a splitting headache. But after eating and resting on the summit I felt a lot better. Tuckett considered the view from the top 'of the grandest description, and . . . must be decidedly the finest in the whole district'.[3]

Several other groups had passed us on the way up and now, one after the other, we all moved off. One of them, a party of four young men, was making heavy weather of the descent; they seemed to be rooted to the spot, unable to proceed. We edged our way past them, and then Maurizio said, 'I really think I should help those people, because I'd rather do so now than have to arrange for a helicopter to take them off later on.' So Nino and I continued down very slowly and carefully, while Maurizio secured the young men over the difficult bit. They were grateful for his help and certainly not too proud to accept it. It's not often, I thought, that a guide is willing to help another party and I admired his initiative. Once down the gully, the young men were able to continue on their own.

As we made our way down the glacier, Maurizio told me about his own and Nino's involvement in the mountain rescue service for the Valtellina. Maurizio is head of the Bormio team and trains the younger guides in advanced mountain rescue techniques. Nino looks after the necessary administration, records, accounting, etc – all on a voluntary basis. In addition, Maurizio spends 24 hours once a fortnight on stand-by duty at Sondrio, with a helicopter pilot and a doctor, ready at a moment's notice to go wherever they are needed. Maurizio and Nino have even designed a special wigwam-shaped structure, made of collapsible steel poles, which can be placed over a crevasse so that the victim can be pulled clear more quickly than by conventional methods. Their system has now been adopted and used successfully all over the Valtellina.

The following evening Maurizio called at the hotel to discuss further plans. I still wanted to do the 13 Cime. 'It's not difficult,' Maurizio said, 'But it's very long and, with the present humid temperatures and thundery weather, I would not recommend it.' For the last day or two the thermometer had not fallen below zero. He suggested, instead, that we should go up the Pizzo Tresero from which, if all went well, we could continue to the Punta San Matteo via a snow and rock traverse, and from there return, in a triangle, to our starting point at the Berni hut. This was, in any case, the first leg of the 13 Cime.

We set out the next morning at 5. The hotel owner's wife, Claudia, again insisted on producing breakfast at that uncivilized hour, which I felt was way beyond the call of duty. As usual, Nino came with us and was useful as a photographer – he kept grabbing my camera, and also took plenty of pictures of his own. (In the end, he made me a present of all the slides he had taken – a typical example of the spontaneous kindness of the Italians.) As we parked the jeep outside the Berni hut I was full of anticipation, having been re-reading Tuckett's account of his first ascent, in 1865, of the two peaks, the Punta San Matteo (3678m) (which he called the Pizzo della Mare) and the Pizzo Tresèro (3594m):

> We started at 1 this morning, and at 7.30 stood on the summit of the Pizzo della Mare, a peak lying behind the Tresèro . . . The

> atmosphere was wonderfully clear, and though the wind was high and extremely cold, we contrived to get sufficient shelter to enable us to spend three hours on the summit in the enjoyment of one of the most wonderful views that I have ever beheld. Not only were the mountains of the Orteler group, the Lombard Alps (Presanella, Adamello, etc.), the whole range of the Dolomites, and the Bavarian and the Engadine peaks perfectly clear, but Monte Rosa, Mt. Blanc (distant 185 miles), and Monte Viso (distant 210 miles) were distinctly visible to the W., while in the E. the eye ranged as far as the Gross Glockner and even beyond . . . Having gazed our fill, we next proceeded to attack the Tresèro, reached its summit without any serious difficulty, spent another delightful hour there, and then dropped straight down upon this place [ie Santa Caterina] at 5 o'clock. Two new peaks, each nearly 12,000 feet in height, accomplished in one day, and under such perfect conditions of weather, are a prize that only rarely falls to the lot of the mountaineer, and you may imagine that we are jubilant in proportion.[4]

We planned to follow Tuckett's route in reverse and, having crossed the bridge 'over the Gavia torrent', we circled around the massif, following a waymarked path which mounted higher and higher towards the beginning of the glacier. As we gained height, the perfect cone of the Tresero gradually revealed itself above us, while, to the west, Tuckett's wonderful panorama started to unfold. First the Disgrazia, with its long and graceful Corda Molla route clearly etched against the skyline; then the Adamello and Presanella and, coming into view higher up, the Bernina.

At the glacier we roped up and, in an hour, reached a col on the SW arête. From this vantage point we looked down on several other parties making their way up the Tresero by way of the glacier on the other side of the ridge. Above our heads, the shattered limestone of the SW ridge reared up towards the summit, like a series of flying buttresses. Our route mounted the very crest and mostly we moved together, but there were several short sections which required a belay. These added interest to the climb and the time flew by; it took us three hours of scrambling to reach the summit.

We were blessed with a marvellously clear day, like the one Tuckett enjoyed on the first ascent. Not only were the peaks which he saw laid out before us (though I was only able to identify a few of them), but I gained a clear view and appreciation of the 13 Cime which I had so nonchalantly believed I could toss off during my first three days in the Alps. A delectable-looking snow ridge led off to the east, broken by the rock pile of the Cima Dosegu, and continued to the elegant San Matteo. As my eye followed the other summits, curving majestically round to the pure snow dome of the Cevedale, I realized that in scale and grandeur this was a much larger undertaking than I had imagined when studying it on the map. Maurizio had been most tactful, and instead of saying bluntly, 'No, of course you can't do the 13 Cime,' he had allowed it gradually to become self-evident that my original scheme was, for the moment, impracticable. He himself had only done the circuit once the previous year, and *that* had been when conditions were perfect and with a very strong party!

By now it was already midday; the weather was humid and the snow soft. It seemed prudent to return straight down the glacier and to forget the two-hour-long traverse to the Punta San Matteo. Maurizio reported our position over the radio and was told, in turn, that elsewhere everything was *a posto*. We would have a carefree afternoon descending the long glacier on the E side of the ridge and eventually joining up with the path on which we had started, near the Berni hut. We could see an enormous black cloud coming in from the north, so we hurried down and were just clear of the glacier when it started to rain, hail and thunder! But this in no way spoiled the splendid mountain day we had enjoyed.

Back at the hotel, Maurizio and Nino were immediately involved in a long, unintelligible conversation in double-quick Italian with Nino's brother, the proprietor of the Hotel Dante, and someone from the guide's bureau. They all rushed off and Claudia, Nino's sister-in-law, told me what had happened. There had been a terrible accident on the Gran Zebrù. On the steep bit, just below the summit, a snow-slide had swept away the guide, Valentino Sosio, and his three clients. One of the clients had survived and was in hospital with serious injuries, from which he subsequently died. After supper, Maurizio and his wife Marisa joined me for coffee. It seemed that the three friends, with their guide, had fallen over 500m down the mountain and a rescue team from Solda had recovered the bodies and flown the survivor to hospital. This was not the first time, Maurizio said, that people had been killed at that particular point; he had often urged that a rope should be fixed over the steepest section (like the one on the Matterhorn), but nothing had been done. I asked the inevitable question: 'Would *you* have taken a party up the Gran Zebrù today in this humid weather?' 'No,' Maurizio replied, 'I wouldn't have wanted to take anyone up there in the present dangerous snow conditions.'

The next morning we went rock-climbing. There are several good crags around Bormio and Maurizio had in mind a nice, easy route for me at about Grade III. It turned out to be VS, but somehow, with much help from above, I managed to struggle up it. Later we talked of what was on both our minds. The Italian newspaper reports had spoken of an avalanche, but now Maurizio had been given an eye-witness account. While descending the steep section below the summit, on the normal route, the first client on Valentino's rope had tripped and fallen forward over his crampons. The second man had little chance of arresting such a fall and was wrenched from his stance, followed by the third man and finally by the guide. There was nothing Valentino could do to hold the fall of the three men, particularly in such soft snow, and they had all disappeared down the steep slopes on the N side of the mountain.

As a climax to our week we had hoped to climb the Ortles, the highest peak in the range. But this plan now had to be abandoned, since Maurizio and Marisa – who had been close friends of Valentino's – were spending the nights at the house of his widow and her two children. However, we could climb another one-day route, and we decided on the Cima Viola in the Val Dosdè.

The following evening, Maurizio and Marisa invited me to their house for coffee. Everything was immaculately clean and tidy, even though Marisa works all day in a dress-shop. You could have eaten a meal off their kitchen floor! Maurizio returned to the subject of the accident, which was still very much on his mind. He was barely on speaking terms (he said) with the other guides, who all persisted in declaring that the accident was simply *la destina* and nobody's fault. None of them was willing to try to establish the true causes of the accident, both direct and indirect. Being so much involved with mountain rescue, Maurizio was particularly sensitive about these issues and he felt resentful that financial considerations were sometimes allowed to override the highest standards of safety. A few years ago four people and a guide, all on one rope, had fallen on the Matteo. Many bones were broken but fortunately, on that occasion, no one was killed. But now he believed that if only certain changes had been made then; if the guides' tests had been tightened up; if climbs had no longer been undertaken in bad weather or adverse snow conditions; if clients had been required to establish that they had the necessary experience for a particular climb; and, above all, if the ratio of clients to guide on the steeper climbs had been fixed at no more than 2:1; then the present accident, he believed, and the death of his close friend, might have been avoided.

I was having plenty of 'rest' days, which I spent going for long walks, and I felt in excellent form when Maurizio and Nino presented themselves at the hotel early on my last morning. Soon we were enjoying a beautiful dawn from the Val Viola, which runs from the Valdidentro, west of Bormio, right up to the Swiss frontier. We parked the jeep near a farm at the foot of the Val Dosdè, which branches off south-westwards and, following the stream, circles round to reveal, after an hour or so, the remote Cima Viola (3374m). The peak is not part of the Ortler range, is little known and we had it all to ourselves. The mountain is well named – it's a shy violet hiding itself away at the top of a remote valley. It is even viola-shaped, with a snow dome flanked on each side by lower rocky outcrops. The Capanna Dosdè, which we reached in two hours, is magnificently sited with views over the western Dolomites. We paused here while Maurizio made a brew, and then we started up the mountain itself.

It was a delightful climb – varied and interesting – a boulder-field, followed by some enjoyable rock scrambling on soft granite, a tramp over a gentle snow-slope and, finally, a long, wide glacier which we took in one continous movement without stopping. In no time we were mounting the summit rocks and, suddenly, there was the cross which marked the topmost point. Maurizio reported our position on the radio. It was still only 11am, but we didn't stay too long on the summit as the weather looked uncertain. This was the first climb any of us had done since the accident and, although nothing was said, all three of us were being exceptionally careful, especially on the descent. Nino led, with Maurizio as anchorman. When we reached the boulders we were able to relax and stop for a second lunch.

On the way back up the long valley we stopped again by the river, where there was a little bridge, and refilled our water bottles. The sun had come out now, and I thought that, in spite of the shadow cast by the accident, what a pleasure it was to be there, pleasantly tired after climbing a delightful and little-known mountain with a romantic and appropriate name. Circumstances had prevented us from achieving the highest peak in the Ortler range; but the Ortles would still be there another year – something exciting to lure me back to this beautiful and challenging range of mountains, and the friendly people of Bormio.

REFERENCES

1 C Wilson, in 'The Ortler in 1911'. *AJ*32, 176, 1918.
2 F F Tuckett, in 'Contributions to the Topography of the Orteler and Lombard Alps'. *AJ*1, 406, 1864.
3 Ibid, 405.
4 F F Tuckett, *A Pioneer in the High Alps*. Arnold, 1920, p237.

Alpine Mattins

EDWARD WILLIAMS

That brilliant light on Altels' lethal slope;
So near, so clear, can that be Venus here?
Over the Gemmi the huge full moon gives hope
To two tiny figures plodding without fear
Slowly, steadily, one with the solitude's silent grandeur
Of silver peaks, sepia shadows, and shining ice;
Forging to a further fastness of inanimate nature
Their peak, on eggshell blue, now etched to entice.

A wondrous speechless mattins to quintessential essence
Of God's so pure and palpably perfect presence.

Weissmies

EDWARD WILLIAMS

Years had passed:
Mirroring the passing time,
The moon was well beyond the full;
And Venus, contrasted with before,
But brightly shining still,
Could barely penetrate the morning mist
As two tiny figures' torches,
Bobbing with many an uphill twist,
Mimicked Nature's greater forces.

The wraith-like silent figures slowly wandered,
Climbing the listening eerie landscape below
To the lighter, stiller, stillness –
Of the snow;
And opposite, the ghost of alpenglow;
Higher yet, until a brilliant carpet spread below,
Radiant, vast,
Setting off the intense azure world
Of the sun – about to come.

Wildspitz 1972

TERRY GIFFORD

Incompetence was rife (Richard Gilbert, 1989)

Everyone and their grandma
Hustled for the highest point
And the queues strung back
Between summits and below
The icy ramp of bucket steps
Stamped up the Mitterkar Joch.

Grandma wore a headscarf
And a woollen skirt. It was
An Austrian family holiday
Hiking hut to hut. For us
It was a helmet job, hard men
In the making, moleskins and smocks.

But two steps down the ramp
A crampon came free. I went
Sledging on my sac, unable to roll over
Amongst glacier cream, sweets, shouts.
Nick thought I was glissading
And leapt off behind me

Whooping past the cursing guides.

Black Rock

GERRIE FELLOWS

I

In my kitchen   musing   one rain-splashed
evening on the old plans of women climbing
I turn my face against your jacket's hollow
nap   asking   How can this have happened

        And there is no answer   No words

but the rooks' rough melody over Applegarth
or against the roof of Black Rock the clatter
of the wind mimicking your restless dreams
the night breathing through your empty bed

II

It seems as if we kept coming back to make
those moves   In drifting heat the mind
floating   only the rope (umbilical cord
of the flung body) moving through the hands
teaching the fingerprints the route's codes
its hesitations   the tug to clip a runner

If I climbed now   your gear clanking
from my harness   would your tall shadow
with its rough grace   reappear

III

I dreamt you were Persephone   given time
in the living world   woke to some kind
of salve   or sweating mistaken   having
cut your skirt to fit my shape   found you
were still alive

After three years   your presence in these
clothes   the shrunken jersey   the jeans
nipped in at the waist   is odourless
no more   than a ghost   You are gone

IV

And yet   in August   putting away the stove
and zipping the tent and last of all lacing
our boots and trudging up to the glacier
through the casually rigorous afternoon
not climbing yet   not expecting stonefall
on the path   I thought   over and over
This is how it was

Helen   memorials are fixed or moving   They
are the lethal spin of a pebble in a gully
or on a route   a rockfall's thunder
and in all these mountains   the mounds
of scree   your true gravestone

Robert Townson – The Great Explorer of the Tatra

JERZY W GAJEWSKI

(*Plates 53, 54*)

Robert Townson played an important part in the exploration of the Tatra mountains which, at the time of his visit in 1793, formed part of the border between Hungary and Poland. I believe that the story of Townson's trip, which included an ascent of Mt Lomnický (2632m), might be of interest to readers of the *Alpine Journal.*

The sources I have used in writing this article are listed in Reference 1; they include Townson's own account of his visit to the Tatra. In the last few years, many articles have been published on the history of mountaineering in the Tatra and most of them have used some basic material derived from these books.

But who was Robert Townson? His name is not to be found in the standard encyclopaedias. However, in *The Concise Dictionary of National Biography, Part I: From the Beginnings to 1900* (Oxford University Press, 1961) there is a short notice about him: 'traveller and mineralogist; M.D. Göttingen, 1795; chief work "The Philosophy of Mineralogy", 1798'. More details are given in the (main) *Dictionary of National Biography*, and by J Szaflarski in his book *The Exploration of the Tatra.*[1]

Townson was probably born in Yorkshire, and studied in Edinburgh under Alexander Monro. He graduated in natural history, so botany, zoology and geology would have been of especial interest to him. After his journey to Hungary in 1793 he studied medical science at Göttingen, where he obtained his doctorate in 1795. His later vicissitudes are not known, but perhaps he was working at a Scottish university.[2]

Townson was not the first explorer of the Tatra. It is likely that shepherds and mountain men, mostly hunters, were in the area long before it was visited by tourists and scientists. The northern, Polish, side was settled much later than the southern, Slovak, side; therefore the first trips into these mountains were undertaken from the south, often from Kežmarok, an important town in the region of Spiš, at the foot of the Tatra. Many of the early visitors to the Tatra lived and worked in Kežmarok.

The earliest information about a tourist trip into these mountains dates from the 16th century: in 1565 a Pole, Beata Łaska (1515–1576), wife of the *starost* (noble civil servant) of the Spiš district, is thought to have visited the Kežmarskej Bielej Vody valley and the Green Lake, situated in the upper part of this valley at a height of 1545m. In 1615 the 'highest peak' was climbed by

David Frölich (1595–1648), a teacher with the honoured title of 'imperial-royal mathematician and practical astronomer of the Hungarian Kingdom'. Historians argue about which peak was his goal: Mt Lomnický (2632m), Mt Slavkovský (2452m) or Mt Kežmarský (2558m), but W H Paryski has no doubt that he attained the last of these.

Another person who lived in Kežmarok was Christian Augustini ab Hortis (1598–1650). He hiked through the Tatra, but no details of his trips are known. As a physician he was interested in collecting resin from the dwarf mountain-pines (*pinus mughus*) and stone-pines (*pinus cembra*) which he used as a medicine.

In 1683 a book was published, entitled *Ungarischer Oder Dacianischer Simplicissimus, Vorstellend Seinen wunderlichen Lebens-Lauff, und sonderliche Begebenheiten gethaner Raisen, Nebenst Wahrhafter Beschreibung dess vormals im Flor gestandenen und offters verunruhigten Urgerlands*. . . . It included a diary of climbing on Mt Kežmarský in 1654. The Simplicissimus of Hungary, whose identity was kept secret, was Daniel Speer (1636–1707) from Silesia, musician and composer.

The next significant explorer of the Tatra was Georg Buchholz Sen (1643–1724) who climbed Mt Slavkovský in 1664. In 1719 he wrote a description of the High Tatra, *Das weit und breit erschollene Ziepser-Schnee-Gebürg*, which was not published until 1899. It concerned the area around Mt Kriváň (2494m), but his opinion that the Tatra could be seen from Łowicz – a town about 80km west of Warsaw – is complete nonsense, of course. Soon afterwards, between 1736 and 1742, Mathias Bel (1684–1749) published in Vienna a description of the Western Tatra in *Notitia Hungariae novea historica-geographica*.

Other important figures in the exploration of the Tatra were Georg Buchholz jr (1688–1737), teacher in Kežmarok, who drafted the first panorama of the Tatra, and his brother Jakob (1696–1754?). Jakob Buchholz sent samples of mountain rocks and minerals to Vienna in 1746; this collection attracted the personal interest of the Emperor of Austria, who set up a scientific commission which visited the Tatra in 1751, with Jakob Buchholz as guide.

At the end of the 18th century and the beginning of the 19th, many well-known scientists and travellers explored the Tatra, among them the Rev Andreas Jonas Czirbesz (1732–1813), Balthasar Hacquet (1739?–1815), the Pole Stanislaw Staszic (1755–1826) who climbed Mt Lomnický in 1802 or 1804, Johann Asbóth (1768–1823), the brothers Genersich, the Rev Thomas Mauksch (1749–1832), known as the leading expert on the Tatra in his time (he accompanied Townson, too) and the Swede Göran Wahlenberg (1780–1851). The visit, between 1766 and 1768, of an unusual character, Friar Cyprian from Červený Kláštor (Red Abbey) in the Pieninys, is also worth mentioning: this legendary constructor of an early type of hang-glider may actually have used it himself to fly over the Tatra.

Two of the above-mentioned men visited the Tatra before Townson's trip. The Rev A J Czirbesz subsequently published two papers including a description of the first documented ascent of Mt Kriváň in 1772 or 1773. B Hacquet, well-known as an explorer of the Eastern Alps, was born in France

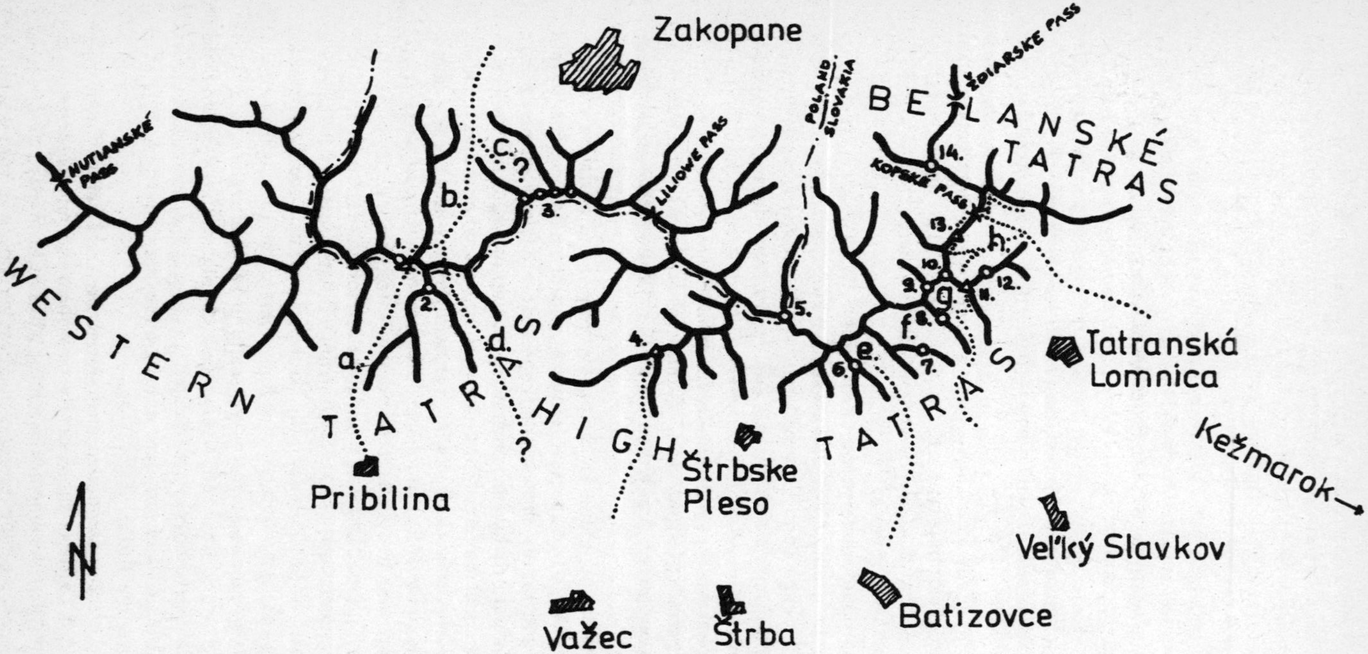

. . . .Townson's routes in the Tatra; △ the peaks attained by him. *Valleys*: a – Račková, b – Kościeliska, c – Miętusia, d – Kamenistá, e – Velická, f – Vel'ka Studená, g – Malá Studená & Five Spiš Lakes, h – Kežmarskej Bielej vody; *peaks*: 1 – Starorobociański, 2 – Bystra, 3 – Red Peaks, 4 – Kriváň, 5 – Rysy, 6 – Gerlachovský, 7 – Slavkovský, 8 – Prostredny hrot, 9 – L'adovy, 10 – Baranie rohy, 11 – Lomnický, 12 – Kežmarský, 13 – Jahňaci, 14 –

and was a physician to the French and Austrian armies. He was also a professor of surgery, anatomy and natural history, and a lecturer at the universities of Ljubljana, Lvov, Cracow and Vienna. He travelled all over the Carpathians and published in Nuremberg his observations entitled *Neueste physikalisch-politische Reisen in den Jahren 1787–1795 durch die dacischen und sarmatischen oder nördlichen Karpathen*. In 1792 he spent some time on the northern side of the Tatra, travelling from Nowy Targ to Witów village and to the Western Tatra, climbing Mt Kriváň twice and visiting the main areas of the Polish Tatra: the Five Polish Lakes valley and the Morskie Oko Lake. In fact, he was better known as an explorer of the Carpathians in general rather than of the Tatra, where his observations were mainly concerned with mining activities.

Robert Townson recorded his trip to the Tatra in a book entitled *Travels to Hungary, with a short account of Vienna in the year 1793*. The book, which was 'illustrated with a map and sixteen other copper-plates', was published in London in 1797; a translation by C Cantwell, *Voyage en Hongrie*, was published in Paris in 1798–99.

Townson's book describes his impressions and experiences in travelling from Italy, where he spent the winter of 1792, to Budapest (May 1793), to the Matra mountains (north-east of the Hungarian capital), Debrecen, Oradea (now a town in Romania), the Tokay Valley (famous for fine wines), Košice in Slovakia and the area of Slovenský kras. Along the Hornád River he came to Levoča, a town not far from the Tatra, where he was arrested as a Jacobin. Some time later, luckily free again, he arrived at the foot of the Tatra. Unfortunately, owing to bad weather, he had to stay in the Spiš villages and in Kežmarok.

The first trip Townson made was to the Green Lake, along the same trail which B Łaska had followed almost 200 years earlier. He arrived there after three hours' walk, saw traces of a bear, and started some botanical experiments which were interrupted by a change in the weather. During his second trip to the Green Lake he saw much more: his book gives descriptions of the Iron Gate (known today as the Rocky Gate) and fascinating views of the limestone rocks of the Belanské Tatra, the range situated to the north-east of the High Tatra. As a naturalist Townson was especially interested in this 'green' area of the Belanské where the flora was so much richer than in the inhospitable granite rocks of the High Tatra. He spent a night camping near the lake, among dwarf mountain-pines; his guides made a fire and told him stories about treasure-seekers and ruby jewels to be found at the top of Jastrabia veža (the Hawk's Crag, 2139m, a peak towering over the lake and known in Townson's time as Ruby Crag).

Next day, he 'ascended by a small cascade into a higher valley, where still more snow was lying'. It was the Vel'ká Zmrzlá valley, known as the Wild Valley in the Polish language. And it really is a wild valley, hanging over the Green Lake. This beautiful cirque is surrounded by the walls of high peaks: Kežmarský, Lomnický, Pyšny, Baranie rohy and Čierny, which descend steeply to Copper Dale, the site of copper mines in the 18th century and earlier. The snow-field in the upper part of the cirque was supposed by some authors to form a small glacier, but this is not true. On 6 August Townson decided to climb Mt Lomnický from Copper Dale on its northern side, in the company of a highlander guide. An approaching storm and a stone avalanche thwarted their plan, but they attained a height of almost 2000m and were the first climbers in the history of Tatra mountaineering to attempt this mountain from the north.

After climbing alone in the Belanské Tatra, where his guide refused to accompany him, Townson was joined by another guide, Hans Gross, and they organized (on 9 August) a trip to Mt Jahňaci (2229m), then known as the Weisseespitze. This peak is easily reached by a marked trail today, one of the few in this part of the Slovak Tatra National Park. They took a similar route through the Červená valley (the second known passage into this valley), over the Kolové pass (2097m) and along the SW ridge of Mt Jahňaci. This ridge is now known as Townson's ridge (Townsonov hrebeň), and thousands of hikers follow in his footsteps every year. The way back led over the Kopské pass (1749m) which divides the High and Belanské Tatra, but the details of their route are not known.

After a short rest in Kežmarok, Townson arranged his next trip on 14 August; he hired a horse and asked two guides to accompany him. By the time they had reached what was probably Hrebienok (today a funicular goes there), Townson had satisfied himself that the horse was useless and sent it back down. Next day the hikers came to the 'koleba' – a hollow under a big rock, situated in the Malá Studená valley. While sheltering there Townson suffered a personal 'tragedy' – his servant broke the bottle of alcohol! – and he met three treasure-seekers who had been digging for 12 years without success.

Townson also visited the upper part of this valley, known as the Valley of the Five Lakes of Spiš, surrounded by Mt Prostredný hrot, L'adový, Baranie rohy, Pyšny and Lomnický. The next morning, because of bad weather, he decided to send his servant down for provisions (brandy and wine being top of the list), while he himself continued to the rocky ridge dividing the Malá Studená and Vel'ká Studená valleys. This ridge is of particular interest for climbers to the top of Prostredný hrot (2440m), but Townson visited only the lower part of the ridge. Did he reach the pass of Sedlo za Oštepmi? He noted only that it was a precipitous ridge.

The top of Mt Lomnický, the goal of Townson's trip, was not attained on this occasion; and the chances are that Jacob Fabri sen (1740–1817) reached the top before Townson. Then, on 16 August, when the weather improved a little, he and two highlander guides started to climb from the south-west. After two hours' walk from the 'koleba' they were on the Lomnické pass (2190m), at the foot of the S ridge of Mt Lomnický. Unfortunately clouds covered the pass, there was no view and both guides wanted to go back; but a drop of vodka changed their minds. The hikers reached the top by a difficult and complicated route: it was probably the trail known later among Polish climbers as 'over Wrótka route', parallel to the S ridge of the mountain.

Townson, equipped as usual with a barometer, decided to determine the height of the peak. His measurement, 2634m above sea-level, was very precise – the accepted height is 2632m. On the way back clouds covered the mountains and the splendid panorama could not be seen. Today this view is admired by passengers on the cable-railway from Tatranská Lomnica.

Our hero finally left Kežmarok on 20 August. He passed through Vel'ký

Slavkov (where he met the Rev T Mauksch); Batizovce, leading to the big Velická valley at the foot of Mt Gerlachovský (the highest peak in the Tatra, though not known as such at that time); and other villages situated along the foot of the Tatra: Štrba, Štrbské Pleso and Važec.

From this last village Townson prepared for his next trip – to the top of Mt Kriváň. At the start he was accompanied by the Rev T Mauksch, the Rev J Ursing, his servant and a guide; but, after a night spent in a miner's hut, the wind was strong and only Townson, the servant and – without enthusiasm – the guide started for the summit. The guide later maintained that he had never been on Mt Kriváň, but that was not true: on the top he looked for coins left there by other travellers whom he had accompanied before Townson. Their route lay on the south side of the mountain, where today there are marked trails, easy and monotonous.

Townson's book also contains recollections of his trip to the Polish side of the range. He crossed the Western Tatra and reached the Kościeliska valley, where he visited a few mines; and probably also the Miętusia valley, since his report on the geology of the Red Peaks which rise above this valley is remarkably complete and accurate. On 6 September, after visits to salt mines in Wieliczka and Bochnia and a visit to Cracow, he started his journey back south. On 10 September he was seen in the village of Pribylina, at the entrance to the Račkova valley in the Western Tatra, and in October he was in Bratislava. By November he was in Vienna and his historic trip was over. I believe that it played a significant part in the story of mountaineering and scientific observation in the Tatra mountains.

The book about this trip was not Townson's only work. He was the author of geological and botanical observations which had never been made before. A short chapter of his book deals with the life of shepherds in the mountain pastures. For many years his measurements of the heights of the peaks caused Mt Lomnický to be accepted as the highest top in the Tatra. We have to admire his persistence in the face of difficulties and hardship, bearing in mind especially that the weather in the summer of 1793 was poor and not favourable for mountaineering.

It is noteworthy that Townson chose for his trips the areas in the Tatra with the most fascinating scenery, in particular rocky cirques surrounded by the inaccessible walls of the highest peaks, which even today are considered difficult ascents for both walkers and climbers.

REFERENCES

1 J Szaflarski, *Poznanie Tatr* (*The Exploration of the Tatra*), published in Poland in 1972; W H Paryski, *Tatry Wysokie* (*The High Tatra*), a climbers' guide, published in 25 volumes in the years 1952–1988; and Z & W H Paryski, *Encyklopedia Tatrzańska* (*The Encyclopaedia of the Tatra Mountains*), published in 1973. See also A Kuś, 'British Alpinists in the Tatra', *AJ79*, 153–161, 1974 (in this article Townson appears as Townshend).

2 J Szaflarski (Reference 1) lists three articles in his references which can be consulted for further information: 'Prvý výstrup na Lomnický štit', *Krasy Slovenska XII*, 1933; H Seidel, 'Robert Townson, ein Tatraforscher des 18. Jahrhunderts', *Globus XCVIII, Nr 21–23*, 1908; H Seidel, 'Der englische Naturforscher R. Townson', *Jahrbuch des Ungarischen Karpathenvereines XXXVIII*, 1908.

Appointment with the Sun

KEV REYNOLDS

(*Plates* 55–57)

June, so far, had been abominable. By the end of the second week we'd already had twice the average rainfall for the whole month. Cold too, and blustery, it was more like March than light bright summer, with trees bowing to the east under a bullying, forceful wind. So when the invitation came to join a group wandering over Corsica, I jumped at it. Shrugging clouds, I had an appointment in the sun.

There are ranges and landscapes that stay close to the mind. Mountains that once were mere names become living realities, characters almost – like members of one's family. Obsessions grow from daydreams; daydreams to ambition; ambition to obsession. It's natural progression, unless kept firmly in check.

But there are others, secondary places of which you are only vaguely aware, that play no part in one's hours of insomnia. These mountains, valleys, massifs are part of Earth's upland fraternity; they people the globe, but are treated so often as no more than bit-players on the scene; members of a crowd. One's obsessions alone take centre stage and top billing.

Yet now and again fate lends a hand and the bit-players are suddenly thrust forward. So it was with Corsica.

'A mountain rising from the sea,' the brochures announced. 'Corsica, the nearest of the faraway isles.'

There were cobbled alleys where of an evening the day's warmth was trapped, and calm set in while swifts raced screeching overhead. Stone stairways and wrought-iron grilles, lilies on the rooftops and distant voices duffed through peeling shutters. An accordion player tilted his chair on two legs against the crumbling façade of a tall pink building, with washing hanging out to dry on one dubious balcony above another. (Don't slam the door or an acre of plaster, two shirts and a dozen socks will come crashing down.)

There were time-scooped bays caressed by a six-inch tide. Gently slapping, yachts sighed against a sun-bleached jetty. Beautiful people drifted to the sand, their teeth dazzled the Mediterranean sunlight, their naked bodies turned to copper and from copper to bronze as June simmered. Inland, on the mountains, snow still hugged dark corries.

Col de Bavella was the nearest thing to the Dolomites I'd seen for years. The Cornes d'Asinao braced against the morning, rising like fence-posts of stone from a strip of pine. From a distance you could almost feel the texture of that lovely, lovely rock. It wasn't dolomitic, though, but granite. And oh, what a thrill to amble on. Not scramble but amble. The only ropes were those fixed in place for aid on a steep pitch with a back-pack. At the base of each pitch, it seemed, berberis thorned the horizontals. In full yellow flower, fragrant as honey, it drew the bees. Hundreds of bees. Nay, thousands. They came out of the valley with thunder in their wings and burst with a fever of industry about us: the loud boom of berberis in June.

In the valleys and on the lower hillsides flowers thrashed one's senses. Drawn by the sun, every head demanded attention: broom and heather, hellebore and asphodel – while saxifrage and thrift painted the rocks to which we were inevitably led. Inspired by the sun, aromatic plants drenched the air with fragrance: peppermint, thyme, juniper, rosemary, honeysuckle. I wandered in a haze of intoxication.

Monte Incudine was the first summit. If you collect such things it will do, yet in truth it was merely the highest rock around, brazen with a large cross and climbed by Freshfield in 1880. But views were all and I peered in glory at that craggy spine, at dark-shadowed peaks far off, at softer hills wearing shawls of cloud-shadows, at blue-distant summits and the ever-present sea moulding in bays against the sky. Wandering north then, to a ridge that was no real ridge but rather akin to a moorland plateau falling in the east, we later skirted westward and dropped to beechwoods and a tent by a stream. It was only a day later that we discovered real crests that went on for ever and grew in quality with each successive summit gained.

GR20 is the way to take across these mountains; the hill-walker's route *par excellence*. Old shepherds' paths, so they say, linked together to form a continuous trail along the island's spine. Yet where were those shepherds whose way we trod? Waymark flashes on boulder and tree did most of the guiding and a Braille of cairns where doubts might otherwise occur. But it was not so much the mountains that confused and conjured doubt, as their slopes. The dreaded maquis. That deadly undergrowth became an overgrowth; it swallowed paths, rocks, boulders, people. Alder scrub and scrub oak with groping tentacles to scrape at legs, arms and rucksacks as a route was fought off the ridge and into a valley that beckoned. We bivvied in meadows by tumbling streams and there doctored our wounds; next day we had to fight our way through again to get on to the spine once more.

Day by day we strode towards the knotty heart of Corsica, checking its pulse as we went. And it took no time at all to become captivated by the scented isle and every single facet of it. The light had something to do with it, of that I'm sure. Out of the Pyrenees I'd never known anything quite so pure. You couldn't describe it. You couldn't feel it, smell it, touch it. But wandering on those ridges the light absorbed mountains and men. Perhaps its intensity belonged to the Mediterranean whose influence was all around. Certainly it was fresh as spring water; edifying, unadulterated. Like the streams that poured through the valleys – jade-green pools trapped among the boulders, cascades of persistent spray that sparkled in the light, then tossed globules and rainbows on to wayside fronds. Valleys were green by these streams, as green as ever you'll find. But the mountains often were white. Not white with snow, but white with the rough light-spinning crystals of stone that made this island in the sun such a raw and magnificent lump of delight.

30. The N face of Kolahoi and the ice fall from near the snout of the Kolahoi glacier. (Dave Comins) (p 50)

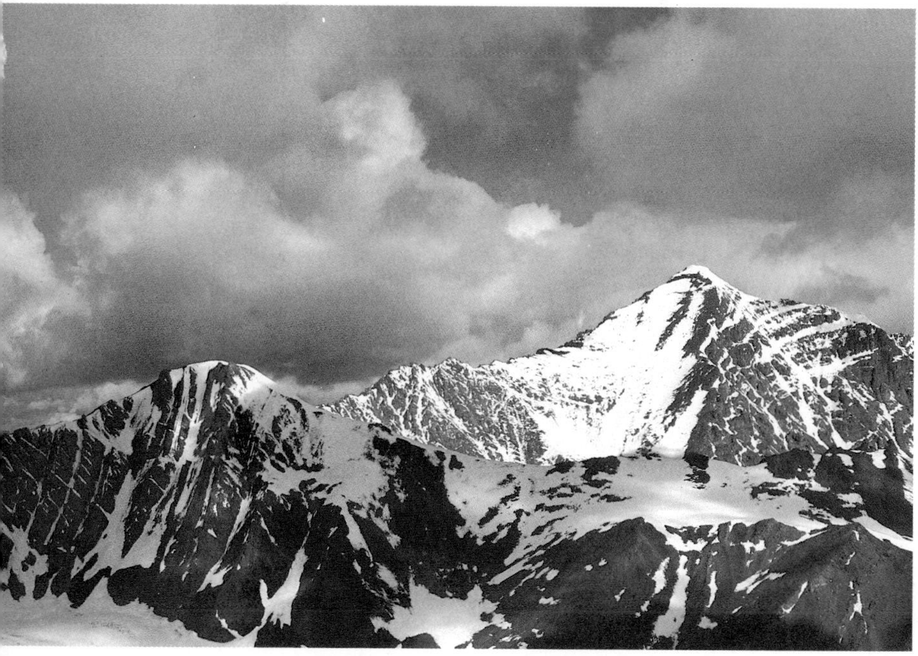

31. The E face of Stok Kangri from the summit of Gulap Kangri. (Dave Comins) (p 50)

32. Elderly Ladakhi lady with prayer wheel.
(Ivar Hellberg) (p 54)

33. Ivar Hellberg on the summit of Saser Ka

ave Orange) (p 54)

34. Dave Orange on the summit of Saser Kangri IV. (Ivar Hellberg) (p 54)

35. Saser Kangri I, 7672m. (Ivar Hellberg) (p 54)

Monte Renoso was a dome of snow rising from the blue of Lac de Bastani, yet its summit was bare. It was bare of snow; a wind-blown pile of rocks on a wind-blown plateau. Huge views spun a panorama flattened by a grey scum of cloud that had no right to be here in the Mediterranean in June. Across that plateau we faced the wind heading north. And then the broad crest made a convex slope and gave a new dimension as pinnacles rose defiantly ahead. Lovely, those pinnacles were. They played at real mountains. One close-shaved pair clutched between them an almost circular boulder high above the cairned route. Teased by a dozen possible routes and another dozen impossible for us to climb, we turned our backs away from them and instead picked a way down to the ever-threatening maquis.

On the far side of Col de Vizzavona, Monte d'Oro wore a cap of cloud, yet, the day we took to the Agnone valley leading to it, summer had returned in full splendour. We wandered through the valley on one of those magical mornings when in the lower woods we trod stepping-stones of light dappling the path. Above the woods there was the maquis zone and, above that, rose sturdy ribs of the mountain itself. Hitting the ridge we looked across a void and gazed into the northern corrie, then scrambled over towers and into hollows of scree, and finally up a series of steep little couloirs to the summit. A most satisfying diversion, that was, but then so was the next day away from the true path when we strayed into the arms of Monte Rotondo.

Rotondo is the second highest peak on the island, although it looks modest enough from most angles and is indeed amenable to parties of limited experience. Gathered round Refuge de Pietra Piana we looked to the tumbling mists that had appeared from nowhere. A wild pig, black and undeterred by massed humanity, came quizzing for food, poked its head inside a rucksack and made off with a plastic mug. Two of us took up the chase and wrestled it back, then set off up into those mists.

Long strips of snow took us into the mountain's rough inner sanctum. There, with barely a blade of vegetation and with black tarns holding no vestige of summer, we prepared to bivvy. Rotondo's ridges curled in an embrace and covered us with their excess vapours. A cold night followed and, while others grumbled, I lay there with a smile of contentment. After all, they were paying for the privilege of an uncomfortable night in a poly bag; I, at least, was at work!

Sunrise drew us out. That daily gift to the earth worked its miracle and we thrashed up the south ridge growing warmer by the minute, and on the crown spread the world in an orange hue. Summit panoramas are not always satisfactory. Rotondo's was. It was an unreal conglomerate of ridge and crag, of tarn and scree, of valley and distant scoop of bay, of shadow and sunbeam and stream and snow-field twisted and patched in a carpet of wonder. Half an hour breathing the warmth of early morning, then down. Down to Restonica's bursting cascades, flowers, trees and streams with pools to entice. Down away from GR20 for a long loop of waywardness.

Corsica won my heart with her wild and empty uplands. I gazed on deserted bergeries, and dreamed. I heard pigs snorting in the tangled maquis and watched buzzards soaring overhead. The shadows of Tavignano's forested gorge were brightened with cyclamen; I bathed in her deep placid pools and inhaled the incense of her aromatic plants. The drug worked. For who can turn away from the Scented Isle and not crave to return? Not I. I'm hooked.

Daydreams then, lead to ambition; ambition to obsession – and the list of mountain landscapes that fill the hours of insomnia has lengthened.

Napoleon's Mountains

R WENDELL JONES

By a mist-girt church under Monte Giove, 600m above the sea, Elba's only emperor met his Polish mistress. He was Napoleon; she, the countess who had already borne his son.

A century and three-quarters later I trudged up the stone steps of the Pilgrims' Way leading to the shrine of Madonna del Monte, and pondered why they should have chosen to renew their liaison in the modest outbuildings of this isolated place. For Napoleon, passion usually took second place to politics. He may still have hoped that the Austrian archduchess who had succeeded Josephine as his empress would be allowed to join him; if so, a little discretion in the conduct of his amours might have been desirable. Did his mistress still see him as the man whose armies had ranged from Moscow to the Tagus? Or was there a more prosaic reason? Was she carrying messages from Europe, just another agent in the great game of deception being played out between Napoleon and the great Powers who had forced his abdication? Whatever the truth, she was dispatched equally secretly in a small boat which was nearly lost in a tempest on the short journey back to the mainland. With that voyage she vanishes from history; her lover's fate is high drama, passing through escape and triumph to ultimate disaster on the field of Waterloo.

The island donated to Napoleon by the Allies after his first abdication is 30km long, with a width varying from four kilometres at its narrow waist to 18 at its eastern end, parallel to the Tuscan coast. 'Half the size of the Isle of Wight and four times as high', said the guidebook. But its shape is very different, with scarce 200m of straight road anywhere. While there is a small airstrip at Marina di Campo in the west, the usual access is by ferry from Piombino, an unattractive port 65km south of Livorno (Leghorn).

Jenny and I had spent the previous week absorbing culture in a very damp Florence, and the prospect of little bays and villages, backed by limestone mountains, was a welcome change after numberless marbled galleries and museums. In these hills precious iron ore has been mined from the time of the Ancient Greeks, fought over by Romans and Spaniards, and exported until 1945. Then the mines were shut down and tourism took over.

We arrived at Portoferraio, the island's capital and only substantial town (about 10,000 people) on a sunny May afternoon. Napoleon, too, came in May, escorted by the British navy. He was a little uncertain of his reception but was welcomed with enthusiasm by the islanders, who were flattered to have gained so famous a man as their ruler. He set about his duties and by nightfall had dictated memoranda giving instructions for the improvement of the island's roads and the installation of a sewerage system.

Almost equal enthusiasm was displayed by the large Elban lady who seized our luggage. Brief identification problems were soon resolved and Brunhild, as we christened our taxi-driver, was soon speeding along the road to Marciana Marina, tyres squealing at every bend.

Marciana Marina is a small fishing port a few miles to the west of Portoferraio, its little harbour dominated by the ancient Pisan tower which stands astride the mole. It has only a shingle beach and perhaps for this reason has escaped the worst evils of tourist development. Our hotel was an attractive two-storey building about half a mile from the shore. After a brief assault on the mosquitoes which had forgathered in our room, I lay back in a deck-chair beside the pool. Beyond the town and overlooking it stood two hill villages backed by slopes of maquis and a promising granite ridge.

After breakfast Jenny departed to paint the harbour and the multi-coloured houses which backed on to it. Eschewing the bus which klaxoned its way up the hairpins about three times a day, I set out on the almost traffic-free old road to Marciana, passing by olive groves and occasional small vineyards. After an hour I reached the main road from Poggio to Marciana, ignoring a further track leading off to the Cabinovia di Monte Capanne which, I knew, was not working.

Marciana itself, a traffic-free walled village, looked down to the Ligurian Sea, as it had looked down for a thousand years. Behind its walls the inhabitants of the coastal villages had fled from many invaders, and in particular from the slave-seeking North African corsairs of Dragut and Barbarossa whose galleys had once terrorized these shores. More recently, the islanders had had the experience of being 'liberated' by the Free French, whose Moroccan and Senegalese troops had interpreted 'free' as 'make free' and had behaved almost as badly as the original pirates. Nowadays Marciana seems sinister, a place of horizontal alleys divided by steep medieval steps.

I passed by the old fort at the apex of the village and found a path which climbed further up the maquis-covered hillside. A little further on it developed a contour-hugging syndrome – 15m up to the next spur, followed by 15m down to the next ravine. Students of forestry roads will be familiar with the process. After a little scrambling I reached a second parallel path and then one which led diagonally upwards. Hitting the ridge between the summits of La Stretta and Monte di Cote, I gained the twin boulder-piled summits of the latter. The granite felt good.

The first section of the main ridge was broad and allegedly crossed by a path; it led on to the Tavola whose rocks were surmounted without much difficulty.

Further on, La Galera (950m), a summit whose wedge-shaped face seems impressive when viewed from Marciana Marina, gave a little more trouble. A good scramble up pleasant rocks on the crest led to the summit. An unroped descent on the opposite side seemed imprudent, and an open corner proved a little more awkward in practice than it appeared from above. One of the less engaging features of the ridge is the intrusion of an extremely sharp species of thorn between the rocks. In arresting a small slip, I put an incautious hand into one of the bushes; much of that evening was spent extracting great black thorns from the hand.

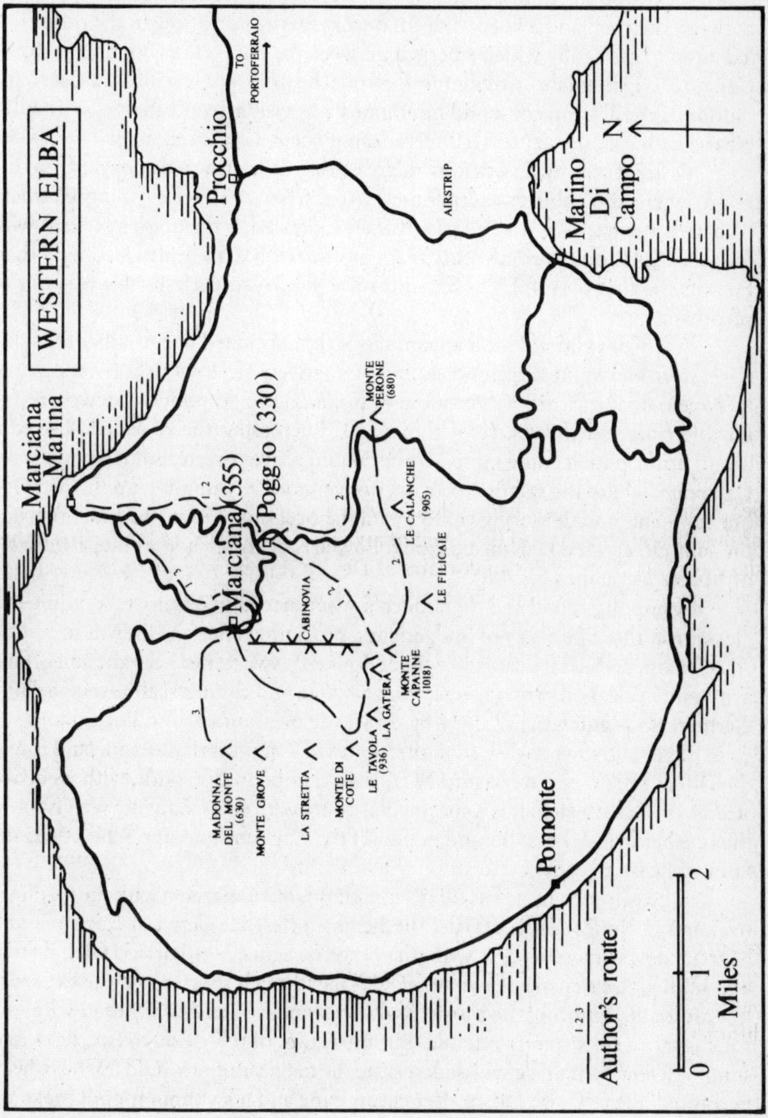
WESTERN ELBA
Marciana Marina
Procchio
TO PORTOFERRAIO
Marciana (355)
Poggio (330)
Marino Di Campo
AIRSTRIP
N
MONTE PERONE (680)
LE CALANCHE (905)
LE FILICAIE
CABINOVIA
MONTE CAPANNE (1018)
LA GATERA
LE TAVOLA (936)
MONTE DI COTE
LA STRETTA
MONTE GROVE
MADONNA DEL MONTE (630)
Pomonte
1 2 3
Author's route
0 1 2
Miles

The ridge-crest leading to the next summit produced a profusion of downward-sloping holds. After a brief foray, discretion found a passage between the rock and a bevy of thorn bushes on the north side of the ridge; this led into an open gully which emerged between the wire fences bounding Monte Capanne's Fylingdales-like summit. While heat-haze concealed Corsica, the outline of the Tuscan coast and mountains was visible over Elba's eastern hills. Nearer at hand, the azure Mediterranean glistened on three sides.

Descent was by an obvious ridge leading down towards Poggio from the point where the cable-car terminated. At this stage I met a young German. 'Where is the bar?' he wanted to know. We glanced at the map, inscribed with the word BAR quite prominently. And our thirsts had to be satisfied with that. He was the first person I had seen for some hours, so perhaps this was not so surprising.

A few days later, I took advantage of the continued fine weather to tackle the eastern end of the ridge. A little unimaginatively I followed the twisting road to Poggio as far as Monte Perone (680m), a good and popular viewpoint for Portoferraio and the centre of the island. Recrossing the road, I followed a broad bridle path leading up to Monte Maolo past a forester's hut and on to Le Calanche, where the granite took over once more. Scrambling up the crest for one moment, and detouring off to avoid the occasional *mauvais pas*, I reached the summit, crossed Le Finicaie, and followed easy rocks up the eastern buttress of Monte Capanne (1018m).

A buzzing sound and the sudden appearance of two tourists standing in a glass jar, rather like a pair of budgerigars, proclaimed that the lift was in action. Alas, again, no bar! It was so hot that I donned a sweater to keep the sun off my arms and neck. Today there were more walkers and climbers, almost invariably German, so I 'guten tag'd' my way down the pleasant path to Poggio.

The following day we took the bus up to Poggio and Marciana and round the cliffs of the western coast to Marina di Campo in the south, with its broad stretch of sandy beach. It is a spectacular route with ever-changing sea vistas on the one hand and the rocks and gullies of the Capanne massif on the other; the faint of heart are advised to sit on the near side.

How should one assess Elba's mountains? Comparison with the Cuillin is overstating things a little. True, the height difference between Capanne and Marciana Marina compares with that between Sgurr Alasdair and Glen Brittle, and both give extensive sea views. The ridge is much shorter and the exposure less although, ignoring the thorns and occasional stretches of barbed wire, the rock is more consistently reliable. But the legion of television masts, discs and sundry defence antennae which desecrate the main summit would not have been permitted above Coire Lagan. Yet cheap wine and a swimming-pool make up for quite a lot.

A low cloud base on the first day prompted a visit to Napoleon's rendezvous. It was a little eerie in the mist and an insect raised a lump an inch high on my leg. Could its ancestor have bitten Napoleon and explained his swift departure?

Moroccan Odyssey

DENNIS GRAY

(*Plates 60–63*)

Guide us on the straight path, the path of those to whom thou hast been gracious; with whom thou art not angry, and who go not astray.

The Koran

Mustapha

I was frightened, not for myself but for my companion Mustapha. We were climbing up smooth waterworn slabs, set high in a gully above the Ourika Valley. Our objective was to reach a small summit, set on a grassy ridge high above us; this, we hoped, would be a good viewpoint from which to see Toubkal (4167m), the highest mountain in the Atlas ranges.

In Marrakech, that most wondrous of Moroccan cities, there is, at the side of the Koutoubia mosque, a Cheshire Home. It is one of many scattered throughout the world, founded by Leonard Cheshire who, having been a British observer in the 'plane which atom-bombed Hiroshima, was so appalled by the suffering caused by that deed that he subsequently devoted his life to helping others. The Cheshire Home in Marrakech, underfunded and terribly overcrowded, looks after boys who have been stricken with polio, many of them Berbers from remote villages. Polio is rife throughout North Africa and only now, with the help of the World Health Organisation and charitable foundations such as Rotary International, is a mass vaccination programme under way. I defy any hardened cragsman to visit the Home in Marrakech and remain unmoved. Children have to sleep three in a bed, two at the top and one at the bottom, but despite all there is cheer and song to be found there.

It was there that I had met Mustapha who was 18 years old and, unlike some of the other boys, he was an Arab. The population of Morocco is made up of Berbers and Arabs, with the former in the majority. Mustapha had been stricken with polio when he was 15 and, as a member of a large family, had been abandoned to his fate, reduced to begging in the streets of Marrakech until he was taken into the Cheshire Home.

He was very intelligent, of medium height with the upper body of an athlete, his skin a deep brown as were his eyes; he had flashing white teeth and black wavy hair. His great ambition, I learned, was to climb to the summits of the Atlas Mountains. This I had found incredible, for when I first met him he was sitting in his ancient wheelchair, which nevertheless he had used to good effect in taking part in the recent Paris marathon.

He badgered me to take him with me into the mountains, and by way of inducement he acted as my guide around Marrakech, taking me into the souks, the Saadian tombs, introducing me to the Gnaoua trance musicians and dealing with the hustlers in the Djemma Square, surely only surpassed in their craft by those found in Tangier. Mustapha was on these occasions swinging along on crutches; he moved so fast that I could not keep up with him, and in the tropical sun he soon had me gasping for a *thé à la menthe*.

Two days later we left by bus, first to the village of Dar Caid Ourika, where it was market day; then we managed a lift with Berber tribesmen to Setti Fatma, high in the Ourika valley, running up into the high peaks of the Atlas, about 70km south-east of Marrakech.

We slogged up the valley in the heat of the day, a superb October afternoon, surrounded by greenery, waterfalls and granite boulders, following a cool clear stream – such a contrast to the dry, arid plains which surround Marrakech.

From afar we had spotted a gully leading out of the valley and up on to the summit ridges; it seemed an easy means of ascent, with its entry about 300m above us. From below it looked wide and easy angled, and as we climbed the first steep slopes I marvelled at Mustapha's dexterity. The slopes were as steep as Cwm Glas, but he kept right on my heels, balancing on his crutches. All had seemed well when we reached the gully, but above us – hidden from below by a jutting spur – was a difficult section: a barrier of rock-slabs right across the whole route. On arriving at its base, in the lead, I had stopped, wondering what to do. Could we avoid the slabs by traversing out of the gully? Or would we have to retreat? We were dressed in track-suits, had trainers on our feet and no climbing equipment and, although the slabs were easy, they were nevertheless technical climbing.

While I was wavering Mustapha took the decision for us: he swung past me and started to work his way up the rock-face. I held my breath and watched, fascinated. His left leg was atrophied and useless; his right could take his weight but could not be moved unaided. Somehow, using his crutches as bridging devices, he climbed; when this ceased to work he used them as hooks; and when this technique began to fail he simply mantled on them. It mattered not that he had never been on a mountain before in his life, he knew intuitively how to climb.

After about 40m he had to stop; the effort had been enormous and he was lathered in sweat. I climbed past him, anxious to see what lay ahead, and I was worried by the fact that the slabs steepened at their top into a head-wall. Only a few metres high, but quite an obstacle, and on reaching it I found it hard to climb, what with the altitude, the heat and my inadequate footgear. It might have been Very Difficult in standard. I tried to imagine what it would be like on crutches and shuddered: a fall would mean serious injury, and we were in a remote mountain area.

I waited at the top of the obstacle as Mustapha climbed bravely up to join me. My heart went out to him and I started to climb down and grabbed hold of him. I was astonished at his reaction, for he spat at me! He cursed me in French: 'Don't touch me. I am free, I am nobody's slave!' Somehow he dragged himself up to join me, the muscles bulging in his forehead. He did allow me to take one of his crutches, and how sorry I felt. I was helpless, and if he fell he would be badly injured because of me. I need not have worried, for the strength of his upper body saw him up, and he managed to crawl on to the ledge at my feet above the difficulties.

We struggled up the rest of the gully together in silence, my mind in a turmoil. I had hurt and offended Mustapha, for clumsily I had not realized how proud he was. But, when we finally reached the elusive summit ridge – which, as on all mountains, kept receding away from us – he swung over and held on to me for a moment, to show his gratitude. The view was magnificent, we could see so many mountains including Toubkal, but I was too choked with emotion to take it in.

'Can we climb Toubkal, *mon père*?' Mustapha pleaded. I was sorry not to be able to grant him his wish, for I was flying back to London the next morning. But here was a true climber and I felt I owed him a promise, one that he could cling to once he was back at the Cheshire Home, often in black depths of despair at his predicament. 'I will come back next year and together we will somehow get to the top of Toubkal, Insh' Allah.' 'Insh' Allah,' Mustapha cried happily.

Six months later, sitting in a café at the Tafraoute Oasis, watching television with several Berber tribesmen (the world is shrinking fast), I was looking at a telecast of the Casablanca marathon which had been run that day. I almost jumped out of my chair when one of the first to cross the finishing line appeared on the screen. It was Mustapha in his battered old wheelchair!

On the Buses

Away from the tourist fleshpots such as Tangier, Agadir and Fez, Moroccans are both friendly and courteous. They can also be very proud, as I found when climbing with Mustapha. Their country is a wonderland, the nearest to Europe that is definitely different! I travelled thousands of miles at Christmas and New Year 1987/88 by bus, and saw many interesting sights. Taroudannt, the magnificent walled city, the Valley of the Dadès with its kasbahs or fortified villages, and the huge Todhra Gorge. This is set to become a major climbing ground; inevitably the French have been here, but so far they have not truly realized its potential. Imagine Gordale Scar, only three miles long and many times the scale in height, a gorge through which you can drive a car because its stream-bed is like a rough road, but which is narrow enough to hit the walls with a stone thrown from either side at its entrance. In several places French climbers have tried to climb the walls on both sides of the gorge, but it appears from the abseil slings in places that they have so far not succeeded. You can see how far they reached by looking at the end of their line of bolts. In the entrance they have completed some short routes and it is sad, very sad, to see these lines of shiny steel bolts all the way up the rock-face. Somehow they have no place for me in Africa, for Africa and Morocco are about adventure.

In the south of the country I did have an adventure. Kif is still grown in huge quantities in Morocco, particularly in the Rif Mountains, and of course it is a part of the populist hippie past of the country, but now dealing in the drug, or possessing it, are illegal. The penalties for a tourist who is caught are severe: a massive fine, a jail sentence, or both. I met a French youth who had been caught and who had spent some time in jail; his stories would have put off any would-be cannabis commodity dealer.

I had been running in the desert outside Tiznit, and as I jogged back through the town two young Berbers joined in and followed me back to my hotel. Moroccans are very keen on sport, particularly soccer and athletics, and you never get jeered at when running as you sometimes do in Britain; there are always shouts of encouragement. Just round the corner from where I was staying was the public *douche*. Contrary to the beliefs of some, Berbers and Arabs – if given the chance – are very keen on bodily cleanliness. The Berbers followed me into the shower and I had to physically stop them from trying to get into the cubicle with me! When I came out they were still waiting and insisted I went with them to their father's hotel, which was the barest and cheapest I have yet seen in North Africa. After many glasses of mint tea I was allowed to depart, but only after promising that I would return later that night for a special dinner that they would prepare for me, for they knew the importance to us Christians, us Nazarenes, of Christmas Eve.

Surprisingly, despite the Spartan nature of the hotel, the meal was delicious. Conspiratorially, my young Berber acquaintances insisted at its end that I accompany them upstairs. There, waiting for us in the corridor, was the most evil-looking fellow I have yet set eyes on, one-eyed, unshaven and wearing a turban and djbella. It transpired that he was a Kif dealer from the north of the country. My young Berbers wanted to give me a Christmas present, and from the man they obtained a carrier-bag full of the stuff and handed it over. I had not understood their whispers in French, Arabic and Berber, but now I felt in great danger. I had been told how the Kif dealers set tourists up: they unload a pile of the stuff on to you, then go off and warn the police who jump you. If you are caught in possession you might be fined a large sum, the drug dealers get a reward and it is rumoured that they get the Kif back to start all over again. '*Je ne fume pas*', I stammered as I returned the gift. The two young Berbers looked amazed, then a hurt expression came into their faces and they tried to make me take it, but I refused again. They then became agitated and annoyed and ran off down the stairs, leaving me blocked in the corridor with old one-eye. In a few minutes they were back, this time clutching a much smaller bag; evidently they thought I had refused the Kif because there was too much for me to smoke all on my own! Travelling alone can be quite a trial, and I now realized that they were genuine and that I was not being set up. Berbers are marvellous friends but terrible enemies; no one has ever 'conquered' them and, when they are annoyed, they can be quite frightening. I accepted their gift with trepidation, thanking them from the bottom of my sinking heart, praying they would not insist that we all start smoking the stuff there and then in the corridor, but even they obviously felt that this was too dangerous for me and let me go back to my hotel where, I assured them, I would get liberally 'stoned' behind locked doors.

I bade them farewell next morning with real sadness. That they do not think or feel as we do might be no bad thing, but in truth they meant me nothing but kindness. I spent the next four days travelling on buses and wondering how I could ditch the Kif. I kept putting off the evil moment, for I was seldom on my own – you rarely are in Morocco – although the only time I spoke English in three weeks was when I met a Scot who had been travelling for six and a half years around the world. On the fourth day, down at Tinerhir on the edge of the desert, in stifling heat, the bus was stopped by a police road-block. This almost caused me a heart attack, especially when they climbed aboard – and of course, as I was the only European on board, they made a beeline for me. I was travelling light with only a sports-bag which I normally took everywhere with me, never letting it out of my sight. But on this occasion, as I boarded the bus in Ouazazate, the driver had insisted that it go up on the roof, the same as every other passenger's luggage. After a spirited argument I had given way, and now, up on the roof and wrapped inside my towel, was the bag of Kif with enough cannabis for hundreds of joints.

'*Passeport*, *bagages*', they demanded. Fortunately, like all good bureaucrats, I had a briefcase with me and thrust this into the gendarme's hands. He searched this again and again, shaking his head. 'Oh, god,' I thought, 'they have had a tip-off.' '*C'est tout?*' he demanded. '*C'est tout!*' I replied, feeling sick, remembering that my French acquaintance had been caught in similar circumstances and had then spent six months in jail, unable on occasion to lie down so crowded was the cell. The policeman smiled at me. '*Bonjour, monsieur*,' and he got off the bus, still shaking his head. I could guess what he was thinking. 'What a strange people the British seem to be, out in the middle of nowhere, with nothing more than a camera and a briefcase . . .'

On arrival at Tinerhir I walked into the backstreets looking for a barber to have a cut-throat shave. I badly needed one and, like so much else, they are very cheap in Morocco. I found a barber, a very kind and friendly man who, when he had finished, refused any payment. I was the first Nazarene he had ever shaved, and he was very happy to do this for nothing. On an impulse I took a quick look outside his shop; nobody seemed to be about or waiting, so I picked up my sports-bag, opened it, fished out the Kif and pushed it into his hands. He looked at it for a moment absolutely astonished, then he smiled and stuck it away out of sight in a drawer. '*L'Hamdullah*, *l'Hamdullah*, *Shokran*.' I grinned and quickly left him, still wide-eyed in amazement. Truly there is adventure to be found aplenty on the buses in Morocco.

The Oasis

I lay on my back watching Ron Fawcett edge his way up the middle of a smooth slab, set on a boulder above the Tafraoute Oasis in Southern Morocco. It was a perfect March day, just like the preceding five days. The temperature I guessed to be around 90°F, and though this was too hot for me to enjoy climbing, Ron with his massive dedication was up there and fighting. I had known him from his boyhood and had followed his progress from the time when he had first emerged as a local star of the Yorkshire outcrops, then on to the national scene and finally to the late 1970s when he had established himself on the world rock-climbing stage; for a while he had then been on a pinnacle ahead of the whole damn pack.

His tall angular frame, without an ounce of surplus fat or any sign of the ageing process, carried him on up the slab and I heard a little squeal of delight: 'cracked it'. I marvelled at his enthusiasm, for he was as keen as ever and had been out climbing almost since our arrival, sunrise to sunset.

My other companion, equally dedicated to his art, was John Beatty. He was here to take pictures, have a well-earned rest and take yet more pictures. For as it grew dark, or as the sun rose, he would be setting forth into the desert. A desert so different from its appearance at Christmas for, after the heaviest spell of rain which anyone could remember, every hour that passed in that hot sun brought it more and more into life, a life of greenery and blossom. Almond trees, orange trees, with flowers like a carpet stretching endlessly into the sand. A land full of milk and honey, with flocks of birds stopping off on their way back to the spring of Europe. It was psychedelic!

A year before I had been reading some of the writings of the American Paul Bowles, who lives in Tangier. He had written: 'The area around the Tafraoute Oasis is like the badlands of Southern Dakota, only writ large, with fingers of granite, and high peaks all around.' It is an old Foreign Legion post in the sub-Sahara, situated on the south side of the Anti-Atlas range. I decided to check it out and, arriving there on Christmas Day, I was unable to believe my eyes, for I had never seen so much granite in one place before. For miles and miles around the Oasis there were boulders and crags, some of which were hundreds of feet high, set on a plateau with a backdrop of the Anti-Atlas mountains rising to almost 3000m, above the Ameln Valley to the north.

On my first day there I had walked out into the desert, a desert not like Hollywood Beau Geste movies with large dunes but flat, sandy and stony. I went first to a rock above the village of Agard Oudad, a large pinnacle hundreds of feet high with real climbing potential, known as the *Chapeau Napoleon*; then, with the help of a Berber tribesman, I had 'found' the painted boulders!

These were right out in the desert: a Belgian artist had recently spent months there, painting the rock-faces in bold, primary colours. At this first visit they were staggering, for the scale is huge. Imagine the cliffs of Poll Dubh painted orange, red or blue, or the Unconquerables at Stanage purple. Some of the painted surfaces are 30m high, while some of the detached boulders are painted all over, without an easy route to their summits. This painter must be some climber, and I wondered if he had received a grant for his work from the Belgian Arts Council? When I asked the Berber who was with me what he thought about it all he simply shrugged his shoulders and murmured, '*Labass*!' ('It's okay').

I returned to the UK uncertain what to say or do about Tafraoute. It is already much visited by tourists, for it is truly a classic oasis site, with palm trees, the lot, but as far as I could ascertain from the local people no one had climbed there before my visit. It is, I suppose, to be compared with Joshua Tree in the USA, but as I was there on my own, climbing solo, only wearing trainers, I found it hard to assess its true worth as a future rock-climbing centre. It is incredibly beautiful: the light is so bright, the views are breathtaking and some of the sunsets made all the others I had seen seem weak in comparison. I had some minor epics out in the desert, bouldering. On one occasion, having set the self-timer on the camera, I jumped on to a face of a large wind-eroded granite boulder and started to climb. It was about six metres high, and just below the top I became stuck. I could not get down, and the top was all rounded. Imagine the surprise when suddenly, over the top of that boulder, appeared a hand as if by magic, for me to grab. It turned out to belong to a Berber out herding goats. He had seen me, but I had not seen him (you never will unless they want you to); he had scaled the easier opposite face of the rock.

Tafraoute is a paradise, especially up in the hills around the oasis. In the latter you can live very cheaply in a simple hotel, and my initial idea was not to tell anyone in the climbing world about the place, but to keep going back there and to enjoy myself in my own way. The locals had never seen anyone climb before, and they thought it crazy. Good things, however, have to be shared with one's friends, and in the end I told John Beatty; he talked to Ron Fawcett, and the next thing I knew Ali Baba (the name by which the former became known in the oasis because of his beard) had the three of us organized to go to Tafraoute in March 1988 via a charter flight to Agadir. This was a cheap and ghastly experience, herded in with all the package-tour victims on their way to the beaches. Tafraoute is easily reached in a full day from Agadir via Tiznit, if you can get the buses and taxis right, and we were to enjoy an idyllic week there.

It was the boulders which captured our party's imagination. There are many square kilometres of them, in all sizes, some as high as Stanage Edge, others only a few metres. The granite is mainly bad, but there is some superb rock as well. Everything we touched was unclimbed, although now there are one or two test-pieces and I vividly recall one near the painted rocks, climbed by Ron: a wall climb where I only succeeded by jumping for the top, and nearly had a fit when, grasping it, I found it as smooth as a parrot's cage! It was about five metres off the ground, with an unusually bad landing; it is frightening climbing with such a giant.

Not just the immediate area but the whole plateau is climbing territory. John Beatty and I one day had a memorable time, traversing across rockfaces high up at the head of a valley, set above a Berber village to the south of Tafraoute, off the Tiznit road. We found incredible wind-eroded formations, one like a huge elephant, trunk and all. Afterwards, comparing notes, we found that, although we had been on separate excursions, we had almost dogged each other's footsteps, yet we had never seen each other. There is nobody about up there but the tribesmen and, as I have already mentioned, they will only let you see them if they wish it.

The weather at Tafraoute can almost be guaranteed, but in the summer months it will be much too hot to climb, the temperature reaching 50°C on some days. The late autumn, the winter and early spring are all superb, although it may rain around November or March. You can live in a rough and ready hotel for about £2 a day, including food, if there are two or three of you sharing costs, and the major expense is getting there. It is possible to get a hire-car in Agadir, and this would enable one to explore much further afield. Out to Ait Baha there are many cliffs that I saw at Christmas 1987, and many of these would be worth investigating. Be warned, though: the local bus has only just been restored, having previously gone off the road, killing everyone. If you go on it, you will soon see how this could happen, for the drops are Himalayan! I will be going back to Tafraoute, for I like it so much there. It is another world, a third world where the locals are most friendly and where climbing is fun. Its greatest appeal for me is that it is all unspoiled – the oasis, the people and the rocks. I hope we in the climbing world can help to keep it that way.

Lengai, Mountain of God

PETER PAYNE

(*Plate* 64)

It is common knowledge that none of the mountains of Britain have a permanent snow cover, and the entire African continent has only a few snow-covered mountains. Where there is such scarcity, lovers of the mountain scene have been known to indulge in make-believe with a substitute for the real thing.

Britain has its 'fake' in the form of the white quartzite screes of Beinn Eighe and in East Africa – although the resemblance is certainly no more than visual – there is the soda-ash cap of Ol Doinyo Lengai. In both cases the effect, like that of snow in summer, is to promote the stature of the mountain, make it more photogenic and enhance its allure through the distinctiveness bestowed on its upper reaches by the unfamiliar cover.

Viewed from the popular Nairobi vantage point of the Ngong Hills, 'Lengai' has other claims to distinction. It is the sole remaining active volcano in this part of the Rift Valley, and its symmetrical form stands in striking contrast to the mass of the Ngorongoro Crater Highlands behind, even from a distance of 170km. It is situated deep in Maasai country, in a remote site at the southern end of the alkaline lake Natron. The Maasai tribe reveres it fittingly as the mountain of God (Ngai). To the outside world its wild individuality makes it an obvious choice as an emblem of the Rift Valley. Its last major eruption was in 1966, when it smothered itself and the surrounding plains in inches of light grey ash. As an active carbonatite volcano it is unique and the relatively low temperature of its lava seems to result in less destruction than might be expected. The surrounding vegetation recovers quite quickly from an eruption, since it is not completely destroyed and re-emerges from its soft ash covering in a comparatively short time. Nevertheless, the lush appearance of Lengai's lower slopes during rainy seasons comes as a surprise, bearing in mind its recent history.

There are many sub-alpine mountains spread across East Africa which provide a great variety of interest to adventurous hikers and back-packers, but invariably involve route-finding through sometimes dense forest. Precipitation rises with altitude and results in rich forest cover on many hills in the region between 1600 and 3200m in height. Where not greatly disturbed, this forest is still the haunt of big game which can provide additional interest and excitement to hill-climbing here, to say nothing of the verdant beauty of the virgin forest itself. Due to its active volcanic nature, the vegetation on Lengai has not developed beyond grass, herbs and low scrub. Although the surrounding plains are at times brought to life by a rich and diverse fauna of migrating game (zebra, wildebeest, oryx etc) and birds, on the treeless, waterless slopes of Lengai you are unlikely to meet more than an occasional small antelope.

To the climber the mountain is enticingly visible from near Nairobi, but detailed maps of the area are virtually unobtainable and access involves crossing some 150km of dirt-track of uncertain quality. A visit has to be planned as an expedition. Not that this is is a major deterrent: at least one Nairobi resident has climbed the volcano 14 times to date (1989). As a sporting objective Lengai's shape and composition put any attempt on its summit in the category of dedicated exploration, with only a superficial resemblance to what is normally called mountaineering. From a base at about 1200m its slopes rise in an unbroken sweep to the summit on the crater rim which, since the last eruption, has stood at 2970m. It thus offers approximately 1800m of 'grind', initially in the inferno of one of the hotter parts of the Rift Valley close to the equator. Without the vegetation cover to give grip the slopes – which carry you, at a moderate but unrelenting and steepening angle, up into cooler, breezier air – would be acutely tiresome and difficult. With care it is possible to steer a viable course between dense, progress-impeding herb and scrub and the edge of one of the colossal erosion gullies that rend the volcano for most of its height. The scale of these gullies is difficult to appreciate from a distance and, once on the mountain and experiencing the extremely friable nature of its very juvenile rock, you find it difficult to believe that such formations, perhaps 60–90m deep, can endure without collapse. But the only slightly firmer chalk of Beachy Head is over 150m high and has offered climbing routes. Ultimately no rock formations are permanent and it is really a matter of the time-scale of their stability that decides our attitude to them.

Eventually the vegetation peters out and on the northern side you are brought out on to the white, soda-ash region which appears to feed, almost glacier-like, the gullies lower down. To the uninitiated this rather peculiar material is intimidating, but it is soft without being grossly unstable and brings you near the crater rim. Although not quite glissadable it allows scree-running in descent and is not as untrustworthy as it looks.

The exciting thing about volcanic cones that provides not a little incentive to endure the toil of their ascent is the prospect of seeing a new and hidden landscape once the crater rim is reached. On an active volcano no one can be quite sure what will be found. On Lengai anticipation is enhanced as you become aware of the build-up of sulphurous fumes as the rim is approached. Then, quite suddenly, the view ahead which had seemed depressingly unchanging for so many laborious hours is transformed. The 35m-deep crater is a grey-white sterile world, devoid of life but with steam vents gasping and sighing like some great aquatic mammal. Apart from the steam vents the crater floor, perhaps 300m across, is the level surface of welled-up lava waiting for the build-up of subterranean pressure to eject it, as it did 22 years ago. There is no fire and not much brimstone, but it is a dramatic and satisfying culmination to the climb. As with other free-standing mountains the views are stupendous, down to another mineral dominated landscape – the flamingo-breeding soda-flats of lake Natron and across, in the distance, to the genuine snow cap of Kilimanjaro.

Background Note

The mountains of East Africa that do not support equatorial snow or unique Afro-alpine vegetation because of their lower altitude – of which Lengai is one particularly striking example – comprise a diverse and fascinating resource which is still very under-explored. Sporadic attention by climbers since the 1960s has produced a few routes of outstanding quality in splendid, remote surroundings and has shown potential for much more. Botanically there is still much to be learnt. Although it is, of course, unlikely that there are any major secrets of natural history still to be uncovered, a large mammal – the Giant Forest Hog – of the Aberdare range in Kenya remained undiscovered until 1904 and the yeti-like phenomenon of the 'Nandi Bear' from the Nandi hills in western Kenya has yet to be explained. The literature, both technical and popular, is comparatively sparse and mostly out of date. Recent publications include a new, extensively revised edition of *The Mountains of Kenya*, and *Snowcaps on the Equator*, a generously illustrated book showing the scenic splendour of the East African hills and mountains.

REFERENCES

C Nyamweru, 'Activity of Ol Doinyo Lengai Volcano, Tanzania, 1983–1987'. *Journal of African Earth Sciences* 7, 603–610, 1988.

A Wielochowski, *East Africa International Mountain Guide*. Reading, 1986.

L Brown, *East African Mountains and Lakes*. Nairobi, 1971.

Time-Life Books, *The Rift Valley*. (An aerial view of the Lengai crater is the cover feature.)

P Clarke, *The Mountains of Kenya*. Mountain Club of Kenya, 1989.

I Allan, G Boy and C Ward, *Snowcaps on the Equator*. Jonathan Cape, 1990.

A Return to East Africa 1989

JOHN A JACKSON

(*Plates* 58, 59)

My first journeys to Mount Kenya and Kilimanjaro were made during the first three months of 1943 while I was stationed at RAF Nakuru in the Kenya Highlands.

Taking part in operational training and 'crewing up' on Mark V Blenheims meant that my journeys were by air and not on foot. None of my fellow aircrews were interested in mountains, and in any case both Kenya and Kilimanjaro were too far away for a weekend furlough. Fortunately, the nearness of the Bell Inn at Naivasha did allow solo ascents of Mount Longonot and the Eburu Escarpment.

My pilot 'Jock' Wicks had some sympathy for my interest in mountains, and on 7 February 1943, following a flight to Lake Rudolph and Southern Abyssinia, we refuelled at RAF Nanyuki. We then flew over Mount Kenya and practised 'low-level' flying over the, then, much more extensive Lewis and Gregory glaciers of Point Lenana. It was frustrating not to be there on the ground, and shortly afterwards I remember the envy (as well as admiration) I felt on learning that, later in the month, three Italian mountaineers (POWs) had escaped from Nanyuki camp and ascended that third-highest point of Mount Kenya. For me, going absent without leave while on active service couldn't be considered! In March 1943 (my flying log-book tells me it was the 18th) we flew to Moshi in Tanganyika and on return flew across the Mawenzi Saddle. There, just above us, as Hemingway wrote: 'As wide as all the world, great, high and unbelievably white in the sun, was the square top of Kilimanjaro.' These exhilarating flights to the mountains of East Africa were a sustaining memory during the following two years of operational flying in Assam and Burma, and I often promised myself that I would return.

Despite a delay of 46 years, it turned out that 1989 was a good year to go back to Kenya and at last, on foot, to cross the Lewis glacier to Point Lenana; then later, in what was now Tanzania, to reach the summit of Kilimanjaro. It was a year of anniversaries.

At Lenana summit my companions remembered the 'no picnic' journey made by the Italians Benuzzi, Barsotti and Balletto. However, they were even more intrigued to learn that exactly 90 years before, in September 1899, Mackinder with the guides Brocherel and Ollier had made the first ascent of Batian, the higher of the two summits of Mount Kenya which could be seen just across the glacier saddle. Later, in the Teleki valley, as we camped among the Giant Senecio and Lobelia, we looked up the Diamond couloir to the Diamond glacier, the numerical connotation of its name a reminder that 60 years before, in 1929, Shipton and Wyn Harris had made the first ascent of the summit of Nelion which we could see beyond the 'Gate of the Mists'.

As anniveraries go, though, it was probably the centenary ascent of Kilimanjaro that provided the main interest. No one in their right senses would ever describe the Marangu route as an exciting mountaineering ascent, though environmentally it is – and was. In Moshi there was much hustle and bustle while television crews led by Wolfgang Benn (a great-grandson of Hans Meyer, the first ascensionist in 1889) prepared to record their ascent to the summit at the beginning of October. With a good deal of alacrity we left Moshi before them, taking the route through the forest, moorland and high desert zones to reach Uhuru Peak (5895m) in the last week of September. The weather was good: warm, clear and dry. A pair of Auger buzzards greeted our arrival at Gillman's Point, and bathed in warming sunshine we looked across a sea of cumulus clouds to the rock serrations of Mawenzi, then photographed the rose-tinted seracs of the eastern ice-field. An hour or so later, at the Uhuru summit, fluted pillars and terraces of ice characterized the arctic terrain, but the diminishing 'Great Northern Glacier' was a reminder that the equatorial sun is rapidly removing the ice-sheet that formerly filled the crater. Surprisingly, even at this centenary period, there was no one else at the summit and lower down, at Gillman's Point, we had met just three other walkers. As with the circuit of Mount Kenya, we had the mountain virtually to ourselves.

It was a joy to return to the mountains of East Africa in 1989, but two pronounced changes were a particular reminder that mankind must strive harder to conserve the environment of planet Earth. First, I noted the appalling reduction in wildlife compared with 46 years ago and, secondly, it was astonishing to see the shrinkage in the size of thc ice-sheet and the glaciers which had taken place on both Mount Kenya and Kilimanjaro in the same length of time. May they all still be there in 2039!

The Birdman of Gars-Bheinn

RICHARD ANDERSON

The Greater Traverse of the Cuillin Ridge in Skye (the Main Ridge plus Clach Glas and Blaven) was first completed by Charleson and Forde in June 1939. 'This *tour de force* is not likely to become everyone's cup of tea' is the rider given in *Classic Rock*.[1] It seemed to make it a perfect target for Chris Stephens and myself, both middle-aged and intent on doing something challenging before descending into a totally sedentary existence.

Murray and Donaldson also made an early successful attempt, armed with their secret weapon 'Mummery's Blood', a repulsive-sounding mixture of rum and Bovril with which they fortified themselves before doing the final Clach Glas-Blaven section. Murray's account[2] makes tremendous reading, and Humble[3] also has a wealth of colourful information about early parties. One notices, when reading these accounts, that – as so often with advances in mountaineering – there was a psychological barrier to be overcome: describing the background to his attempt, Murray writes: 'The first practical difficulty was to convince my own mountaineering friends that the proposition was not an impossibility. And for three years I was unsuccessful.' It seemed right that we should be embarking on the Traverse 50 years after those great pioneers, but whether 4500m of ascent over 20km could be construed as 'an easy day for a lady' was still open to question!

It was clear that this trip would require quite a bit of planning. The end of May and beginning of June, which coincided with my half-term, seemed an obvious time to go, with near maximum daylight and minimal midge factor, but where we should base ourselves for the Traverse was less obvious. The early parties had started from Sligachan or Glen Brittle, but both of these approaches entail long trudges before or after the Traverse. The more we thought about it, the more attractive Camasunary looked as a start/finish point. The approach from there to Gars-bheinn is shorter and more interesting than the mind-numbing trog from Glen Brittle, and it lies literally at the foot of Blaven. There was also the bothy, a rather unknown quantity, but we could always camp if it proved uninhabitable.

At some stage during the preparations I decided to get my attempt sponsored, with money going to the Gurkha Welfare Trust. We would not be out to break any records (even in 1944 Menlove Edwards had done the Greater Traverse, Glen Brittle to Glen Brittle, in 24 hours, with apparently zero reconnaissance and no more food than 'the usual packet of sandwiches supplied to climbers at Glen Brittle House'[3]). The rules we set ourselves were that we would try to make a continuous traverse, with time being no object. We would carry all food, but would pre-position a water dump on the ridge. We planned to start in the evening from Camasunary, bivouac on Gars-bheinn, at the start of the ridge, with the option of a further bivouac should we need it. It was obviously essential to be very fit and we concentrated on building up stamina. I ran in Wytham Woods, the nearest convenient bumps to North Oxford; Chris commuted on his folding Bickerton. We met, when we could, for weekends in that still empty part of Wales, west of Hay, to tramp across miles of bog discovering unknown, enchanting valleys.

Then, on 25 May 1989, we took the familiar road north, marvelling to see the Buchaille, for once clear of cloud, standing guard at the entrance of Glencoe. The weather was still brilliant when we reached the coast and took the old Kylerhea ferry over to Skye, and as we approached the start of our walk-in from the Elgol road our hearts sank at the number of parked cars. Had our careful plans to beat the weekend rush to grab places in the Camasunary bothy been dashed? But they were only day-walkers and we established ourselves, after two carries from the road, without trouble. Camasunary proved to be an excellent choice: the bothy was spacious, in good repair and right by the sea, with plenty of driftwood for a fire and nothing but rabbits and sheep for company.

Low cloud and rain woke us next morning; the weather was changing. We made a late start for the Druim Hain pass into Coruisk and, finding an outcrop at the back of Coire Riabhach, we returned to the rock. It was glorious to be climbing once again on rough gabbro. We returned to Camasunary by the coast, relieved to see that there had been no further attempts to 'smooth' the Bad Step.

We decided that Bealach na Glaic Moire would be as good a place as any to put our water dump, and so trudged round the next day, up Coir' Uisg to the col, the cloud lifting from the top of Bidein as we approached. We cached four litres of water under the S summit and then followed the Main Ridge over Bidein, reminding ourselves of the complexities of the route and trying to commit the easiest line to memory, for it is a confusing place to be in mist. We thought we could get off Bidein on to the Druim nan Ramh ridge, which would make an interesting return to Camasunary. However, there appeared to be no direct way off the centre summit without an abseil, so we moved north along the Main Ridge and dropped off into the top of Harta Corrie, only managing to regain the Druim nan Ramh ridge after an interesting exposed scramble whose outcome remained in doubt until the end.

The weather was still poor on Monday, but we had to look at the unfamiliar Clach Glas-Blaven section. The cloud held off sufficiently, allowing us a great day. The Clach Glas-Blaven Traverse is a superb expedition, never more than Moderate, but what a Moderate! The route continually weaves round difficulties; every moment one expects the way to be barred by some impossible overhang or gendarme, but always it goes, as so often in the Cuillin, by the most improbable line. As we made the long descent from Blaven back to the bothy, we felt we were now in position to have a go, but would the weather be with us?

In the morning there was the familiar cloud, with ominous snow on the tops. We retreated to the Broadford Hotel for coffee and the *Scotsman*'s weather forecast. It was not good: 'Unstable northerly airstream, showers, snow on high ground. . .' Our window was beginning to close and the time had come for decisions: it was either tonight or Wednesday night; Thursday would be too late to allow a second attempt if the weather was bad. We chose Wednesday which would give us maximum rest, and there was a slight suggestion that the weather might marginally improve. So it was off to the fleshpots of Portree.

Wednesday dawned unpromisingly, but the cloud lifted towards midday. We ate, brewed, passed the time with a horde of rock-chipping geologists and generally got ready for our bivouac on Gars–bheinn. Ascending this hill from Coruisk was a little less straightforward than we had imagined, but eventually we gained the summit ridge by a hard-packed snow gully. It had been cold in the gully and it was a relief to emerge into the evening sunlight and look across a golden seascape that might have been Mediterranean if it weren't for the temperature. We found a bivouac-site and settled in: Chris in his custom-built Goretex bag, me in a fly-sheet and ancient Icelandic which had seen some distinguished service. Stars shone intermittently through the cloud. The croak of a solitary raven (no sound of Murray's foxes) and an orange glow far to the south (Oban?) reminded us that we were not alone on the planet. We were finally in position, everything was in place, with months of thinking, planning and training behind us . . . a confused sleep overtook me. Something was falling on my face – I hoped it was rain.

We shook ourselves awake at 3.45am, to a white and frozen dawn. The Icelandic had torn in the night and I emerged in a cloud of feathers. 'The Birdman of Gars-bheinn,' Chris remarked, but it was the only humorous thing about the situation. The scene was appalling: our dreams were buried under two inches of fresh snow, putting paid to any chance of the Traverse. It would take us hours to get to the Thearlaich-Dubh Gap, which would probably be iced up anyway – we were not into the winter game. We descended slowly, picking our way carefully over vile, wet, snow-covered scree towards the coast. We were back in the bothy by 9am, thoroughly soaked and disappointed.

The weather was even worse on Friday, not even good enough for a compensatory climb on Blaven; we slunk back to England completely defeated. I did raise about £1600 for the Gurkha Welfare Trust, many friends being generous enough to overlook the fact that snow had stopped play. Let Louis MacNeice have the last word:

> The glass is falling hour by hour, the glass will fall for ever,
> But if you break the bloody glass you won't hold up the weather.

REFERENCES

1 K Wilson, *Classic Rock*. Granada, 1978.
2 W H Murray, *Mountaineering in Scotland*. Dent, 1947.
3 B H Humble, *The Cuillin of Skye*. Robert Hale, 1952.

Doorpost

SHEILA HARRISON

The epitome of Cornish climbing, exposed throughout

And down drops the monkey on my back
In two shakes he's thrown the weighted net
Arms buckled hard around the head
Toes dug in sharp behind slack knees
Strapped in a rusted spider's web.
Scrawling skin and claws
Grabbing at straws on inch-deep ledges
to reach for a landing that funnels to the sea
Feet slapping down with a flat footfall
A lateral place where tunnel-thinking eases
and jokes and touch and breathing crack the spell.
Let's go, it's ball and socket time:

Foot rocking to a warrior beat
Knees dipping to a chantdown sound
Rock slotting in a folded hand
Head stepping up jugs of air

Till we stop under the sky
On the wheeling stone,
Turning for home, stepping over the threshhold.

Humpty Dumpty sitting in the rocking-chair
Turf and boulders piled against the door
Left ajar to see the threshing floor.
Tiny flywheels spin off nubs of granite
Putting it all together again, forever again.
Under their breath the earth-struck stones roar
Humming the necessity of shadows.

Liverpool Land

TIM KING

Liverpool Land lies north of Scoresby Sound in East Greenland, between latitudes 71°25′N and 71°58′N, and is almost severed from the mainland by the thin north-south fiord known as Hurry Inlet. It has not attracted much attention from climbers mainly because, until Mestersvig closed, the more obvious delights of the Staunings Alps provided an irresistible pull. Now that the Arco Oil seismic survey has opened up Constable Point airfield, Liverpool Land is a few hours' boating away. Although the terrain is rugged, the mountains are much lower than the Staunings and for the most part technically easy. In summer boats can be used to ferry men and stores to any point on the W and S coasts. For a party of mixed experience, as we were in July 1989, with limited time to spend on long approaches, it was an ideal area for a training expedition.

We landed at Constable Point on 17 July. There were eight of us; five Army, one Royal Marine and two civilians. After two days of barging through the pack-ice in Hurry Fiord we pitched our first shore camp at Pytelv. A day's march brought us to the head of Kalkdal. The weather was disappointing. We were obviously too far south and east of the Arctic Riviera to avoid the Gulf Stream influence, and almost half of our month's journeying was to be done in poor weather. In the first week we climbed five of the northernmost peaks, notably Points 1262 and 1180. The latter had received two previous ascents, one by Bertram, Lack and Roberts in 1933 and the other by Edelston, Ralph and Chapman in 1976. Colin Bertram says that they approached from Hurry Inlet. The note left by the 1976 party said, 'NW Fiord to Scoresbysund', presumably involving a traverse of Jameson Land from the South Staunings: a long undertaking.

Our plan to traverse the central (north-south) spine of Liverpool Land from Kalkdal had to be abandoned because of the bad weather and our next peak was climbed from a camp at the head of Sødal. This was Korsbjerg or Pt1400, approached by a long ridge that bordered the true right bank of the Hans glacier. There were no signs of a previous ascent. John Muston's altimeter recorded a height of 1396m. We were unable to judge with certainty whether our peak or one of similar height a mile to the east was *the* Korsbjerg, and so we distinguished between them by using 'west' and 'east' suffixes.

By now we were half-way through the time available to us and moved base to Gubbedal. Here we made ascents of Pt1040 and Pt1362, on either side of the Grete glacier. In the summit cairn on the latter peak were further interesting notes. The first two were placed in the cairn by Kurt Bungi on 20 July 1933. Bungi was a member of the Akademische Alpen Club, Bern, and an assistant of Lauge Koch on his coastal survey of 1933. The other inscription was by Grame Niels -- (Nielsen?) of the Danish Geodetic Institute in August 1969.

To complete our movement southwards we traversed the col between Skåldal and Nissedal and walked out the 24km or so between there and the Scoresbysund settlement. If Ejnar Mikkelsen could see it now! On our return, five of us completed the circumnavigation of Pt1346 via the unnamed glacier at the head of Jaettedal and the col between it and the Grete glacier.

A day later two members climbed Pt1346 from the Skål-Nisse col. It had a cairn but no record. Malcolm Slesser may have climbed it and it was almost certainly a station for the 1969 survey. Our final sortie was to the highest point on Liverpool Land: Pt1430 or Tvillingerne. This looked like being the most interesting climb from a technical point of view, but during our approach up the Grete glacier we were hit by a storm and forced to bivouac in a corrie beneath

Pt1362. The storm continued unabated and we were tent-bound for three days. Eventually the tents started to break up and an uncomfortable retreat had to be made to safer ground. It was now 12 August and time for the return of the expedition to Constable Point.

We had had serious problems with our two boat engines throughout the expedition. During the return trip to Constable Point the reserve engine finally died on us in the middle of Hurry Fiord. A two-mile row up the Thames in a coxed eight is quite pleasant: the same distance in an overloaded Gemini with a 30-knot sidewind over a five-knot tide is not! It took us four hours of hard paddling to reach Jameson Land. We left Constable Point for the UK on 16 August. Considering the very poor weather and the inexperience of five of our members, some of whom had done nothing more serious than a little winter scrambling, we were very happy with our results. We had walked for 360km, climbed 21,500m of vertical interval, learned a great deal and enjoyed the experience – and left ourselves some unfinished business, an ideal excuse for returning as soon as possible.

Members: M T King, A J Muston, D O'Neil, I Kidd, I Smith, D Bore, R Crawley, I Drew.

Maps: Danish Geod Inst 1:250,000 Sheet 70–01 Scoresby Sound.

1933 Report: *Geographical Journal Vol LXXXV No 3*, 234–251, 1935. (This covers the Scott Polar Research Institute Expedition of 1933.)

1989 Report: A full report has been submitted to the Alpine Club.

Excursion to Alaska

The first ascent of the South Face of Mount Hunter

JONATHAN PRESTON

(*Plates* 65–70)

People frequently ask me what my mountaineering ambitions are, and after successful trips to India, East Africa and South America I was finding it increasingly difficult to answer this question. But while attending the 1988 Alpine Club Symposium, which that year concentrated on Alpine and Arctic North America, it became apparent to me that Alaska begged further exploration. The state is enormous, covering 1.5 million square kilometres. It is six times the size of the UK, and with a population of only 400,000 – many of whom live in Anchorage – this is truly one of the greatest pristine wilderness areas on earth.

Fortunately I chanced upon both a climbing partner and a potential objective that weekend. I fell into conversation with Roy Ruddle, a Nottingham-based climber, and we discovered that we both had independently attempted the same W face route on a peak in a remote area of the Cordillera Huayhuash. I felt a kindred spirit and, while poring over black and white photographs of the McKinley range, we alighted on a particularly striking shot of the S side of Mt Foraker. An enormous ridge snaked its way down from the summit in splendid isolation from all other obvious features on the mountain. Our eyes met over the picture and it was love at first sight (for the ridge, not the eyes!).

Though Alaska abounds in mountain ranges, from the coastal Chugach and Wrangell mountains, boasting peaks over 4800m high, to the less elevated but more remote Brooks range in the north, the allure of the McKinley massif is compelling. Mt Foraker, 5300m, is the sixth highest peak in North America and has various pseudonyms. Early Russian explorers called the mountain 'Bolshy Gora'. The Tanaina Indians called it 'Sultana', meaning 'His Wife' (Denali's). Finally, in 1899 Joseph B Foraker's name stuck, despite the fact that he was later driven from public life following a bribery scandal. The mountain was first climbed in 1934 by a party led by T Graham Brown via the W ridge, and 12 routes have been completed on it to date. In 1976 a French team under the leadership of Henri Agresti made a memorable ascent of the SSE ridge. This ridge is 7km long, rises 3200 vertical metres and contains sustained technical difficulties on rock and ice. The team fixed cumulatively a total of 7300m of rope during their six-week ascent of the mountain. We aimed to spend anything up to 10 days climbing the ridge alpine-style and descending the SE ridge (the line of the 1963 second ascent).

In preparation for the trip we had to re-equip in various departments, despite the fact that both of us had climbed at altitude before. We upgraded boots, duvets and tents to withstand severe arctic storm conditions. For this reason, coupled with the fact that airfares to Anchorage are not cheap, an initial expedition to Alaska can be a fairly costly affair. Offset against this, though, are the lack of peak fees, porters' wages and liaison officer's welfare that are incumbent on a Himalayan venture. We aimed to climb during the second half of May and early June when temperatures might be slightly higher than in April and early May, though the weather could be less settled.

Our forward planning worked to perfection. So much so that we enjoyed the somewhat surreal experience of finding ourselves on the morning of 15 May 1989 ambling round Heathrow's Terminal 3, casually trying to check in 130kg worth of crunch-bars, soup-packets, skis, snow stakes etc, while on the morning of the 16th the MSR stove was purring contentedly as we assembled our dome tent and built an igloo in full view of Alaska's 'big three' – McKinley, Foraker and Hunter. 36 hours had elapsed, during which time we had crossed the Atlantic, been met at Anchorage, filled our bellies with caribou stew, bought food at a late-night supermarket, driven the 180km to Talkeetna (a tundra bush-town), registered at the Ranger station, collected white spirit and plastic sleds at the airstrip and jumped aboard a Cessna 185 light aircraft. The company's motto is 'Fly an hour or Walk a week' – we chose the former.

It can be quite an exciting flight to the Kahiltna glacier, even though we chanced upon the first fine day for several weeks, as the pilot sets a beeline course for the only notch in a long ridge on the edge of the range, known as 'One Shot Gap', for obvious reasons. Safely through the gap, we landed on the flat, uncrevassed W fork of the glacier, below the SE ridge of Foraker, and set up Base Camp more or less on the spot, the silence ringing in our ears.

We were at 2000m with the summit of Foraker looming 3300m above (about the same height difference as between Everest Base Camp and the highest point on Earth). The colossal scale was illustrated by the aircraft which had brought us and all our gear in now being reduced to the merest speck as it took an age to fly across the SE face of the mountain. The whole of the W flank of Mt Hunter (4442m), stretching 8km from the N to the S summit, lay across the glacier from us, while the S side of Mt McKinley, with the Cassin ridge showing prominently, stood etched impressively in the bright sunshine. The Rangers had informed us that there was an all-time record number of 367 people ensconced on the W buttress route of McKinley at that time. More than 90 per cent of climbers in the range opt for this route, which means that the rest of the peaks are virtually untouched. We met two people on the glacier and four on Mt Hunter during our five-week stay.

We explored the local area on skis, inspecting the French ridge from close quarters and looking down over the vast Lacuna glacier. We were utterly alone, the very occasional drone of a light aircraft flying into the permanently manned Kahiltna Base Camp on the SE fork of the glacier the only reminder of any other form of life. Though CB radios are widely used by climbing parties, we had concluded that a rescue on the French ridge would not be feasible and so had forgone this potential lifeline.

We aimed to acclimatize before tackling Foraker and though we made one abortive attempt over three days on the W ridge of Mt Hunter (one of the ubiquitous Heinrich Harrer's first ascents and not repeated in a quicker time since), retreating from a severely creaking snow-slope, we still needed to spend time high-up. So we then packed up food and fuel for eight days and set off in 'Tilmanesque' style towards a tributary glacier on the S side of Hunter. Forget envelopes, the plans we had would have fitted on the back of a postage stamp!

We ski'd 10km across the gently undulating Kahiltna glacier, weaving our way through one icefall, to set up the two-man single-skin Goretex tent at 2000m in spectacular surroundings, with 900m of rock and ice walls on one side and the S side of Mt Hunter on the other. We had come here to explore and we both spotted what looked to be a likely line up the impressive S flank of Mt Hunter and decided, somewhat impulsively, to climb it. The line seemed to be the only safe route through a series of hanging glaciers, with access to the summit plateau barred by a large rock buttress. The weather was fine, hot and sunny for the fourth day in succession, and we decided to set off as soon as possible.

The following day, 25 May, we waited for the sun to move off the face and at 9.30pm, shouldering as heavy a pack as I have ever encountered outside an Outward Bound centre, we gained the first 300m on skis. Though conditions were warm at first as we ploughed up through knee- and thigh-deep snow to the crest of a well-defined ridge, the temperature soon plummeted as the sun slid down for its brief disappearance below the horizon. We moved along the ridge and entered a shallow gully that separated a steep broken glacier on one side from a rock buttress on the other. The snow here was of good quality and we moved together up the grade II-ish gully for 450m, pausing for a snowstake belay near the top to overcome a steep, powdery bulge. The snowy crest of another ridge led to a big, glaciated icefield that we traversed first left and then right, before finally taking a rock belay at around 3200m, below an enormous area of rock buttresses that stretched up to the SW ridge. Here we chewed on a frozen crunch-bar and put on an extra layer of clothing, overseen by a pink-red moon which was in oddly close juxtaposition to the brightening north-eastern skyline.

Thirteen pitches of grade III mixed and ice climbing followed. The rough, blocky granite provided good belays throughout except for one taken on ice. Route finding was intricate as we traversed right for four pitches to avoid blank rock. Roy then found a way upwards via a broad couloir, and I led on up an ice gully to disappear through a crumbling cornice that provided a link back to the main rock buttresses. Roy then led the hardest pitch on the route, a precarious mixed affair reminiscent of classic Cairngorm buttress climbing, though carrying a tent stove and several days' food makes teetering and scratching on front points all the more ungainly. After a couple more short rock-steps, pure ice followed for several pitches and, although exhaustion and altitude were beginning to take their toll, I felt on familiar ground as resoundingly good axe and hammer placements followed one after the other. We were leaving the bulk of the rock buttresses behind us now and soon emerged, after a brief disappearance into a snow-covered bergschrund on to a flattish section of the SW ridge, just below the summit plateau that contains both the S and N peaks of Mt Hunter. Coincidentally, Roy had pulled on to the ridge close to a four-man

American team's camp, so I was greeted as I stumbled off the face by a hand proffering hot orange juice, an unexpected pleasure in such a hostile environment.

It was 2pm on 26 May and we had climbed flat out for 17 hours, gaining 1400m from the point at which we had left our skis. The light had been quite bright enough for climbing throughout. It had been cold during the early hours of the morning, especially when windy (alpine winter-type temperatures), but we had only stopped a couple of times to rewarm frozen fingers. The weather had held while we were climbing, but it deteriorated as we started to dig the tent in and soon it began to snow, continuing solidly for 36 hours.

Three of the Americans had just repeated the 1978 route up the SW ridge and had survived a minor avalanche while returning to their camp. For us, continuing on to the top of Mt Hunter's S peak was unfortunately now out of the question, as more than a foot of fresh snow now loaded the slopes above. We sat out the storm until the morning of 28 May when the wind stopped rattling the tent and, though visibility was poor, we decided to descend with the Americans. The descent involved six 50m abseils from ice-screws and snow pickets. With a sense of enthused abandon, the first American disappeared down the ropes into the mist. Unfortunately he happened to be a two-metre giant of a man, whose weight stretched the ropes so much that no one else could reach the next anchor-point without downclimbing. We were operating as two teams of three, and I found myself in the unenviable position of being last man down, which entailed removing the back-up screw at the top and clambering off the ropes at the bottom to front-point down, totally unattached, to the next belay, tugging the ropes through at the same time. With relief we reached a col, from where a 600m curving couloir led back down to the glacier. One short abseil, a lot of front-pointing and eventually a long, long glissade, including an exciting airborne moment clearing the gaping bergschrund, landed us safely back a few hundred feet from our skis. It had taken a full day to descend the SW ridge and we spent the 'night' in happy revelry on the tributary glacier before making tracks back to our Base Camp the following day.

From the next day (30 May) onwards the weather became very unstable and it snowed heavily for eight days, almost continously. We lay in our tent, the Walkman music punctuated by regular rumblings as layers of snow clattered down from Foraker's ridges. We had already witnessed one enormous serac avalanche that scoured the entire tributary valley in which we had camped south of Hunter, and reluctantly we had to concede that, after so much snowfall, Foraker was totally out of condition.

We had one brief foray on McKinley's W buttress, the only route free of avalanche danger at the time, before being whisked back to the comforts of Talkeetna. The Rangers here confirmed that our climb on Hunter was the first time that the S face had been penetrated and we decided to name the route 'Eroica', after much time spent in the company of Beethoven on the glacier. It is an Alaskan grade 4; McKinley's W buttress is 2, the Cassin ridge 5. Overall, the route can be compared with Route Major on Mont Blanc, but it is longer and harder.

Alaska is certainly the most serious climbing environment that I have ever been in, and is definitely not a place for the faint-hearted or unprepared. While passing through 'One Shot Gap' on the flight back from the Kahiltna glacier, I noticed a maxim on the pilot's joystick that read, 'If in doubt, don't'; sound advice generally for any activity in the McKinley Range.

The Roof of Colombia

The first ascent of Simon Bolivar, Sierra Nevada de Santa Marta, Colombia, was made 50 years ago on 2 February 1939

JORGE RUIZ

(*Plates 73, 74*)

The Sierra Nevada de Santa Marta is located in the north-west of Colombia, rising from the sea-level of the Caribbean. It is the highest massif on earth so close to the sea, and includes the mountains Bolivar and Colón, both 5794m high. At Parque Tayrona, north of Santa Marta (an important Colombian port), the Sierra drops sharply into the sea.

The fact that these two mountains share the highest altitude in the country has made the history of their first ascent both exciting and confusing. This article attempts to clarify the fog surrounding the subject and then describes a recent climb of Ojeda (5490m), another of the Sierra's high summits.

Erwin Kraus, a Colombian of German origin – with Enrico Praolini, an Italian, and Gustav Pichler, an Austrian – conquered the summit of Bolivar on 2 February 1939. They named the mountain 'Pico Olaya Herrera', after a liberal president, but a conservative head of the Geographical Office was not willing to include such a name on the official maps.

With Heinz Franke and Alex Stiernon, Kraus left Bogotá with the aim of climbing the highest summit in the Sierra Nevada de Santa Marta. But at Valledupar they met Praolini and Pichler, who had climbed Tayrona the previous year. There were no maps then, and it took them three weeks to reach Base Camp from the sea. The approach walk was hard, and Stiernon and Franke abandoned the group. Kraus, Pichler and Praolini built their Base Camp near the S face of El Guardián and from there attacked Bolivar. Nowadays, Base Camps are usually set up at Naboba Lakes.

On the summit the three men used a hypsometer to determine the altitude, taking into account some additional data such as time of day, latitude and temperature, and the Trautwein Tables. Kraus's original reading was 5520m, but this was later corrected to 5794m by the Office of Longitudes and Frontiers at Bogotá (today *Instituto Geográfico Agustin Codazzi*). Another estimate, 5834m, was given by Dr Enrique Uribe White.[1]

Although the hypsometer was invented by a Colombian scientist, El Sabio Caldas (Francisco José de Caldas, 1768-1816), Kraus's instrument was manufactured in Berlin and weighed 6kg. Even though Kraus never climbed Colón, his estimate of almost identical heights for the two mountains seems to be right. A recent climb by Cristobal von Rotrich and Juan Pablo Ruiz to both summits gave readings, with an altimeter, of 5790m for Bolivar and 5775m for Colón.

36. *Duncan Francis abseiling during the traverse around the rock tower, Shani SE face, 2nd day.* (Peter Leeming) (p 62)

37. Duncan Francis makes a parapente descent to Base Camp. Shani (5800m) in the background. (Peter Leeming) (p 62)

38. Summit buttresses and summit ridge of Shani from Base Camp (Peter Leeming) (p 62)

39. The S face of Tapadan Sar from the gloomy depths of the Moorkhun Gorge. (Lindsay Griffin) (p 69)

40. JurJur Khona Sar from the S face of Tapadan Sar. Above Camp 1. (Lindsay Griffin) (p 69)

41. Barn Bluff from Lake Windermere. (John Harding) (p 77)

42. The Tasmanian Olympus. (John Harding) (p 77)

43. *View NW of Tasmanian Olympus.* (John Harding) (p 77)

44. *Cradle Mountain.* (John Harding) (p 77)

45. *W face of Aiguille Noire de Peuterey 1955. Ratti-Vitali on L. Boccalatte on R.* (T D Bourdillon) (p 85)

·6. *H G Nicol on N ridge of Peigne 1955.* (T D Bourdillon) (p 85)

7. *T D Bourdillon on E face of Capucin 1955.* (H G Nicol) (p 85)

48. *H G Nicol on Aiguille Noire de Peuterey. Starting to lead the Grade VI pitch which leads to the famous bivouac ledge. 1955.* (T D Bourdillon) (p 85)

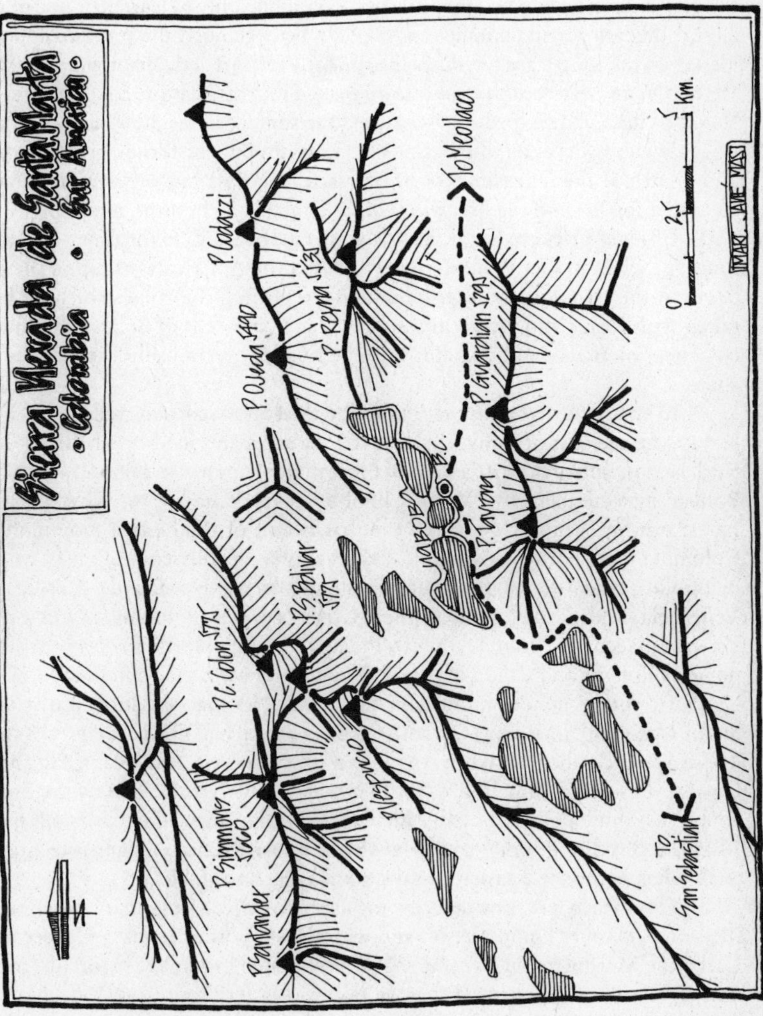
Sierra Nevada de Santa Marta
• Colombia • Sur America •
P. Codazzi
P. Bolivar
P. Santander
To San Sebastian
Km.

When Kraus left Bogotá, he did not know that an expedition to the Sierra Nevada de Santa Marta was being organized in New York; this was the Cabot Expedition of the New York Geographical Society. It is easy to imagine the faces of the North Americans when they reached Colombia, only to learn that one of the Sierra's highest virgin summits had already been climbed the previous month. However, the Americans hired a plane and took the first aerial photographs of the Sierra. On 16 March of the same year, 1939, Praolini – with A Bakewell and W Wood of the Cabot Expedition – reached the summit of neighbouring Colón.

Evelio Echevarría, the Latin-American climbing historian, gives the date and names of the first climbers of Bolivar correctly[2], but other writers have created a fog around the first climb of Colombia's highest mountain.

Ullman[3] gives credit for the first ascent in the Sierra to the Americans and Praolini, when in fact Praolini merely guided the Americans as far as the col between the two equally high mountains, repeating the route which he had taken with Kraus and Pichler during the true first ascent of Bolivar. From the col, the Americans and Praolini ascended Colón, technically a much easier route.

In an article in the *Alpine Journal* by D M Snoswell[4], no credit is given to Kraus's first ascent of Bolivar; nor is this ascent mentioned by M Kurz.[5] The truth is that, unlike the first ascent of other major summits in Latin America (eg Bolivar in Venezuela by Weiss, Chimborazo in Ecuador by Whymper, or Huascarán in Peru by Ms Peck), the first ascent of the highest mountain in Colombia was led by a national of the country. In this context, it is worth mentioning that the highest summit in the Sierra Nevada de Mérida, in Venezuela, is also called Bolivar (see L Griffin's article in the *Alpine Journal*[6]). However, according to the Arhuaco Indians who inhabit the territory, the real name of Bolivar and Colón in the Sierra de Santa Marta is 'Chundua'.

The other major summits in the Sierra Nevada de Santa Marta are: Simons (5660m), La Reina (5535m), Ojeda (5490m) and El Guardián (5285m). These were climbed between 1941 and 1943 by the Americans Elisabeth Cowles, Elisabeth Knowlton, Max Eberli and Paul Petzold, and by the Swiss couple Marmillod. It is possible that El Guardián was climbed in 1898 by Joseph de Brettes, but one wonders why he chose to climb the most technical peak when higher and easier virgin summits were available.

This article will now describe my ascent of Ojeda in January 1988, with the British climber Philip Nelson and with the support of Lindsay Harper and Catherine Marquette. In December 1987 we visited Erwin Kraus for advice on our expedition. He suggested that we take the eastern route via Donachui, an Arhuaco town, reckoning that this was the easiest way into the Naboba Lakes area. A Base Camp at Naboba would be well placed for all the summits of the Sierra Nevada de Santa Marta. We also borrowed from him a map which Kraus himself had helped to prepare, giving detailed information about the glaciers.

We managed to get all the food for our expedition from local supermarkets in Bogotá, except for dried fruit which we obtained from health food-shops. At a hardware shop we bought gas cylinders and long-life batteries. (European climbers should note that head-torches must be equipped with an AA battery adaptor.)

All expeditions to the Sierra Nevada de Santa Marta start from Valledupar, an agricultural town south of the Sierra from which there are at least four different routes to it. The town can be reached by plane from Bogotá in under an hour. Although it is possible to reach Base Camp (Naboba Lakes) from the west (from Santa Marta), there are many reasons against this; guerrilla activity is just one of them.

After driving for a day in a slow Land Rover from Bogotá, we arrived at Bucaramanga to stay the night at the hotel of the local country club. The next day we should have reached Valledupar, but an electrical fault with the car forced us to stay at Caracoli. Travellers from abroad need not go via Bogotá, unless they want to do some rock-climbing at Suesca.[7] Alternatively, one can fly from London to Caracas, change planes for Cartagena or Barranquilla, and from there drive or fly to Valledupar.

There are only two aboriginal tribes left in the Sierra Nevada de Santa Marta, the Arhuaco and the Kogi. Formerly there were also the Wiwa and Canguamo tribes.[8] While the two tribes share much the same environment, the former are more accessible to the white man than the latter and it is nearly always the Arhuacos who act as guides; they use mules rather than the donkeys favoured by the Kogis.

To enter the Sierra one is supposed, in theory, to have a permit from the Indian authority. Unfortunately, we arrived at the weekend and the office in Valledupar was closed. Since we were unwilling to hang around until the office reopened, we took the risk of entering the Sierra without a permit. In fact, possession of a permit is no guarantee that a climbing team will not be turned back when it meets the authorities of the tribes within one of their territories.

Most expeditions enter the Sierra by driving from Valledupar to San Sebastián de Rápagos (1940m), the largest settlement of the Arhuaco Indians.[9] This was Snoswell's route with the Royal Military College of Science.[4] From San Sebastián the approach starts on mules, through a series of valleys and many ups and downs, gaining height and losing it again. However, our own team took Kraus's advice and entered the Sierra via the eastern route: Valledupar-Atanques-Chemesquemena-Donachui; a 'less documented' route, according to Snoswell. A jeep goes as far as Chemesquemena. From here the mules carried our rucksacks – and some presents that we hoped might be acceptable instead of our missing permits. On the first morning we let our guides load the mules, but it soon became obvious that their abilities left much to be desired. Loads were distributed unevenly, and the mules were being injured by the ice-axes. From then on, we supervised the loading ourselves, and we always kept the ice-axes in a separate bag. At the beginning the food, in a heavy 60kg duffle-bag, was easier to manage if loaded on to just one mule. In general, we found that the animals were able to carry two fully-loaded rucksacks and one light one. Mules must be carefully looked after, not only for their own well-being but also for the sake of one's belongings. It would be hard to find anyone who has been to the Sierra Nevada de Santa Marta without 'losing' something. Unfortunately, one hour before reaching Naboba, one of our own mules collapsed while crossing a small river.

The trip was not straightforward. For instance, the Arhuaco Indians normally live on their farms and use their towns only for social gatherings at weekends. We arrived at Donachui on a Sunday, after a six-hour walk, and, being the only aliens in town at the weekend, we were easy prey for the picking. Our first guide had escorted us only as far as Donachui; our next guide did not show up at sunrise next day, as planned. Thus, we had to visit several *fincas* (farms) before acquiring enough mules.

It was strange to walk through crops and see coca leaves being grown. This is legal only for Indians. As with other tribal groups, the government respects the Indians' custom of chewing the coca leaf. In fact, one Arhuaco mentioned to us that he travelled outside his reservation with fewer problems if he brought along his 'poporo' and coca leaves. A poporo is a wooden instrument containing sea-shells. The powder is placed on the tongue with a stick when the Arhuaco is chewing coca leaves. A base is used to neutralize the acidity of the leaves. The mixture adheres to the stick, which is later rubbed against the poporo, making the ring wider and wider.

With our new guides we went through Sogrome, another aboriginal town like Donachui. Both towns have houses built in the rectangular or square shape characteristic of the Arhuacos. The Kogis, on the other hand, build their houses in a circular shape. However, the Kogis have been displaced by the Arhuacos, so that sometimes one finds an Arhuaco living in a circular house that formerly belonged to a Kogi. Probably the easiest way to distinguish an Arhuaco from a Kogi is by the hat worn by the former but not the latter.

During the approach walk, we had to feed the Indian guides and provide them with sleeping-bags and a tent. Fortunately this was no problem for us, but it was something we had to bear in mind when dealing with climbing logistics. The altitude gained in just one day was amazing. While coffee and plantain are grown around Donachui, only potatoes will grow around Meollaca.

On the third day we arrived at Naboba Lakes in the early afternnon. Here we set up our Base Camp at 4600m. Other climbers, whom we met at Naboba, confirmed that 'the living history of Colombian mountaineering' (Kraus) was right. The San Sebastian route is considerably longer and the vegetation is scarce. Our own route, via Chemesquemena-Donachui-Sogrome-Naboba Lakes, was both pleasant and shorter.

After a two-day rest, we made our first attempt on Ojeda. However, poor acclimatization prevented us from going very far. We attempted to reach the glacier via a col which can be identified by a helicopter wreck. This accident occurred some years ago when an American diplomat was being 'rescued', when he was actually safe and back in civilization. We returned to Naboba and the next day climbed Tayrona, a mountain with a small fast-disappearing glacier. Two days later we moved our camp to the border of the lake by La Reina. Just before sunrise, Philip and I left for our final attack on Ojeda; this time it was Philip who felt the altitude and our progress was slow. We followed a series of cairns. A couple of times we roped up, but the unstable rock made protection difficult. The weather was brilliant and the views of La Reina and El Guardián were magnificent. I agree with the many climbers who consider El Guardián the most beautiful mountain in Colombia. It looked like a true alpine peak. Near the summit of Ojeda there was an exposed bit, but the rock at this altitude was granite and gave good protection. From the flattened summit, 10m of rock and ice, there was a superb view of Codazzi.

Going down we sometimes strayed from our route, but every now and then we would recognize a reassuring cairn. The weather, fortunately, remained fine; in bad weather the scramble could be lethal. Because of our slowness earlier in the day, it was dusk when we arrived at our last camp; this prevented us from returning to our original Base Camp at Naboba and meeting our guide the next day. There was no alternative but to spend the night at our Camp 1, and to walk at first light to Base Camp and on to Meollaca in search of the guide and mules. At our Naboba Base Camp we split into pairs: two remained at the camp and two took just a tent (food was already running short) as far as Meollaca in order to get the mules for the return trip. The highest Arhuaco farm in the area is owned by Don Antonio; it is easily recognized by a huge hole in the mountain which lies directly behind his farm. We learned that Don Antonio could supply fresh or dried meat (beef, lamb or pork) and even potatoes. Catherine and I, the pair who had gone down, spent a night at Don Antonio's house and he kindly sent two of his sons, with our tent, back up to Base Camp. They left at 7pm and were back, with Lindsay and Philip, before noon the next day. Our last night was spent at a *finca* somewhere between Sogrome and Donachui. Unfortunately it was not a pleasant one and, as before, we were picked on as aliens. Finally we arrived once again at Chemesquemena, and of course enjoyed the pleasure of a cold beer. For the trip back we chose another route – via Cartagena, a beautiful colonial port on the Caribbean – and from there continued to Medellin, arriving only three days after leaving the Sierra. In spite of being careful with the water (always putting in one of those pills), Philip became very sick after leaving Cartagena. A week later the rest of us suffered the same affliction (Montezuma's revenge?).

If you would like more information about rock and ice climbing in Colombia, the place to go in Bogotá is the *Centro Nacional de Montaña*, located in the north of the city (Transversal 10 No 106–35, tel 214 0884). The centre has a library, an outdoor gymnasium and a café with warm fireplaces.

The author is indebted to Erwin Kraus and Marc Jané for their kind collaboration.

REFERENCES

1 E Kraus, 'Ascenso a la Sierra Nevada de Santa Marta'. *Revista PAN*, June 1939

2 E Echevarría, 'A survey of Andean ascents'. *American Alpine Journal* 13, 155–192, 1962.

3 J R Ullman, *Grandes Conquistas*. Barcelona (Ed Juventud), 1954, p108.

4 D M Snoswell, 'The Sierra Nevada de Santa Marta'. *AJ78*, 78–82, 1973.

5 M Kurz, 'Kolumbien'. *Berge der Welt* 3, 344–350, 1948.

6 L Griffin, 'The Sierra Nevada de Mérida'. *AJ*92, 20–26, 1987.
7 J Ruiz, 'Rock-climbing in Suesca'. *High* 76, 40, 1989.
8 'El Mundo Kogi'. *El Tiempo*, 28 December 1988, p2.
9 H Frank, 'Trekking a la Sierra Nevada de Santa Marta'. *Revista Campo Abierto*, No 3, April-June 1978.

See also:

Le Ande – 67 (concise history of first ascents in the Sierra Nevada de Santa Marta); and

J Ruiz, 'Kraus Pisada Alta'. *El Tiempo*, 13 February 1989.

Una Cameron's Climbs and Expeditions

JANET ADAM SMITH

When Una Cameron was elected President of the Ladies' Alpine Club in its Jubilee year, 1957, it was a recognition of her outstanding record, unmatched by any other member, in the Alps and far beyond them. I could only briefly summarize her climbing career in the obituary in the 1988/89 *Journal*; in this article I hope to give a fuller account. Una herself published little beyond a few articles in the *LAC Journal*, but she left various manuscript books, folders of typescripts and a diary of her trip to East Africa in 1938. I thank her nephew Major John Getley for letting me use this material before it is given to the National Library of Scotland, where it will make an important addition to the mountaineering collection started by the bequests of R W Lloyd and T Graham Brown.

I can find no accounts of Una's early climbs: the classic routes recorded in her application to join the LAC in 1929 (which included Matterhorn by the Zmutt and Italian ridges, Viereselgrat of the Dent Blanche, hard routes on the Cinque Torri and Punta Fiammes); and the Grépon, Grandes Jorasses and Meije in 1930 and 1931. Of the climbs in the Dolomites that year there are some sprightly accounts by Hazel Jackson, an American sculptor whom Una had met at art school in Rome. She gives some characteristic glimpses – Una 'partaking of many grogs' in a hut while waiting for the weather to improve; cursing 'Hell's own highway' as she faced an overhanging red wall; weaving herself a little basket of rope in which to descend a tricky pitch (like those monks of the Meteora who are let down from their monastic perch in a net); picking up a big brown beetle adrift in the snow and laying it on a nice warm stone.

In 1932 Una's own tales begin, with her trip to the Caucasus with the Courmayeur guides Edouard Bareux and Elisée Croux, with whom she had climbed in the Mont Blanc range. Hardly any British climbers had been to the Caucasus since the Russian Revolution: 'To travel independently in Russia requires the purse of a rich man or the qualities of the gipsy and Spartan,' W R Rickmers warned readers of the Lonsdale Library *Mountaineering*. Una was well off, but she also had the qualities of the gipsy and Spartan, and this was just the challenge for her. 'The Caucasus seemed to suggest beautiful horses, a wild handsome people, and mountains never climbed before. There was added interest in the uncertainty connected with such a trip, the maps were secret, and the Intourist bureau had no knowledge of such an expedition.' Not surprisingly, her account dwells more on the hazards of getting to and from the mountains than with the climbs themselves. From Tiflis they went by bus along the Georgian Military Highway to Kasbek, where they collected a hunter Nikolai

... AND SOME
HAPPY CHERUBIMS
UPHELD
THE ROCK - -

to look after the horses. 'He had a hook nose, fierce slanting eyes and wore a fur hat and wrote poetry and best of all had a map. . . . When the horses finally turned up they looked quite presentable, but the minute anything was put on their backs, they sighed heavily and hung their heads.' The caravan lurched its way up roads that were really river-beds to Karkutchia, where the villagers presented them with 15-inch trout and warned them that 'the people beyond were wild and unfriendly, and they have no use for police or roads.' But though the men of Djuita carried swords, they did nothing more threatening than try to do a deal for Una's boots. The climbing began, the weather was mostly awful, and so was the rock.

> The mountains in that district are from 3800 to 4000 metres high, and the rock is very dangerous, a sinister mix of stone books and suitcases that rattle down just as you are about to put a finger on it, and it cuts the boots badly, which is worse. The grass grows up very high and so there is very little feeling of height.
>
> Climbing on loose rock may be dangerous, but it has no comparison with being taken for a doctor as I was, and being asked to prescribe for someone with a high fever, whose heart and breathing have both gone wrong, and who lived too far away for me even to see if I had understood the symptoms correctly. We hoped aspirin was a universal cure.
>
> Most of the nights sleep was impossible, hail rattled on the tent and everything was lit up with white lightning and thunder roared among the hills. The weather was always unexpected, a serene evening meant that the tent would be nearly blown away or punctured by hail in an hour or two, and a wild cloudy morning probably meant that we could climb all day and never have a drop of rain.

However, they did manage to climb five of the Tschauchee towers (all, as far as they could make out, first ascents), but blizzards thwarted their two attempts on Kasbek. The return journey presented a new hazard: no banks at Kasbek meant no money for the bus fare to Tiflis till they had sold their horses. 'We spent four days continually talking and making new acquaintances among the charming, friendly people, until the miraculous day when we managed to sell the horses and buy a ticket and leave for Batum. What an expenditure of time, money and patience for 7 peaks and 6 fine days! but I am going again.'

She never did revisit the Caucasus: the next climbing expedition beyond the Alps was to East Africa in 1938, again with Edouard and Elisée. This time she kept a full diary. They arrived at Mombasa by sea on 15 January, took a train to Nairobi where they hired a lorry, engaged a cook and driver, and set off for Uganda and the Ruwenzori – her aim there, she told the *East African Standard*, being to collect plants and seeds for her own garden from the Mountains of the Moon, as well as to climb them. Auspiciously, when they stopped at a hotel at Mubende, advertisements for Dewar's Whisky were prominently displayed beside royal portraits – Dewar's being the family firm which made such expeditions possible for Una. The five-day trudge up the mountain with porters hired at Bugaye – 'hell-fire hot through elephant grass and banana trees' – wasn't much fun, but there were new flowers to note and porters to doctor. 'Anything with a bandage gives satisfaction, a poisoned hand looked very sinister, but hydrogen peroxide fizzed v. satisfactorily on all wounds.' On 1 February, from a bivouac at 4400m, they started for the Alexandra Peak of Mt Stanley.

> Set off in a mist – full of hope. Slowly, waiting every 100 metres to see if it wd. clear or where we were going, we came to some comic local seracs. V. light and decorative (black ice v. hard) like Christmas tree decorations and candles hanging wrong way up. In the dark we got to some sort of a summit which we thought might be Alexandra, but on trying to reach what might be Margherita we found a tin with Shipton and Tilman's names and a card from the Belgian expedition 1932 proving us to be on Alexandra. Waited ½ hour to try to get a view of Margherita but the mist only lifted a few seconds showing v. complicated ice formations and not far enough to show the connecting col. Came down in a thicker mist than in the morning following tracks gratefully and collected some wood at the regulation camping place to add to the defective Primus's usefulness.

Two days later, after much 'plunging over roots and fallen trees and sinking into green moss which becomes black mud' they crossed the Stuhlmann Pass to bivouac at the Leopard's Lair cave from which they climbed Mt Speke in mist, rain and hail ('we never climb on fine days'). On 8 February the Luigi di Savoia provided more interesting climbing, with a hole in the rock to be negotiated; three days later it was actually clear when they reached the top of Mt Baker by a new route from the Scott Elliott Pass.

> The rocks were comparatively clear of snow and beautifully steep, and in 4½ hours we were on the summit ridge, looking at our first clear view of the range as a whole, able to understand and see at

U.C.

> last how the mountains and valleys fitted into the map. It was the finest climb we did in the chain, and the first time that the mountain was climbed by this route. We followed the ridge across Semper Peak to the summit of Mt Baker, then traversing down reached our old track, where the plants were beaten down and the rocks peeled clear.

Una came out of the Ruwenzori with a gashed and infected leg which was dressed at the Fort Portal hospital; at Tororo she delighted in a hotelier who called his cat Rachel 'because she wept for her children', and warned guests that he charged '2/- extra for those who do not bathe'. She rested her leg with friends near Nairobi before making for Mt Kenya. The approach was from Chogokia to the east of the range; and how pleasantly the three-day walk up to Carr's hut contrasted with the struggle on the Ruwenzori. First, 'the grandest real African wood, enormously high trees and pretty flowers, monkeys and birds'. Further up, 'we never caught our faces on branches. Gosh! what a change!'; and when they got to the heather moors, the dry paths were a joy. And so was the rock on Mt Kenya after the wet snows of the Ruwenzori.

> *March 5*. Set off in a gale for Mt Kenya. This decided me to leave my hat at the foot of the climb and the 2 guides 'le casque touche partout'. It was v. hot until we reached the ridge where a fresh breeze improved matters a lot. The rock was good and the climbing interesting although it made us blow a lot – anything in the way of a chimney made me blow myself purple . . . The summit at 12.00 when we shouted down to our impressed friends but we were practically surrounded in mist. That fool Ghiglione had left an Italian flag and we found a new book for Batian left by the Carr (?) party so we set off down to the col. That made us think – having 2 prs rubber and 1 cloth pr boots, no ice-axe and no crampons! The wickedest ice with a thick layer of snow and sheer on both sides. Very cunningly the two fixed up a rappel and first Elisée went over with success, then self with less, and one wicked swing followed by *à cheval* down the ridge and we were all over and hurrying up good rock to Batian where the mist was thicker. Ate some marvellous tinned strawberries, left the book in tin and came down, crossed the ice col with relief, over Nelion and coming through hail and mist reached glacier in 2 h. Two v. nice Sladens camping here now, doing Kenya tomorrow.

The day after Una had been the first woman up Batian and on the Gate of the Mists (she had been preceded on Nelion earlier that year by Carol Carroll), she watched Geraldine Sladen and her brother repeat her climb, and as they clanked down the last stretch in the dark she went out to meet them with lanterns.

Plodding from hut to hut up Kilimanjaro was boring and induced bad temper. From the Kibo hut 'started off feeling sullen. Suggested after an eternity (5 mins. according to my companions) going back to bed. Slid about in leprous scree, stopping often and feeling short of air and ready to kick the cat'. But once up, there was the 'interesting crater with queer ice-cliffs', though clouds hid everything else. Down at Moshi she met Dr Reusch: 'A King! Quite unbelievable. Small, king climber, hand-kisser and linguist and full of charm . . . One of the most interesting people I have met. Ex-Cossack officer, Georgian, D.D. of Leipzig, climbed Kilimanjaro 32 times.' Then they headed for home – rail to Tanga where Edouard and Elisée had swimming lessons and Una suffered the humiliation of being weighed before the flight to Mombasa and the steamer home.

Henriette d'Angeville, the first lady (though second female) up Mont Blanc in 1838 called herself 'The Fiancée of Mt Blanc'. Una would have scoffed at such romantic notions – but she was indeed passionately devoted to the mountain under which she built the Villa Cameron at La Palud above Courmayeur. From 1933 it was the centre of her climbing: between then and the war, with Edouard and Elisée, she climbed most of the peaks in the massif and traversed Mont Blanc itself again and again by different lines. In 1933, between 10 and 29 July, the party's tally was Aiguille Blanche de Peuterey, Aiguille Rouge de Triolet, Col de Rochefort and Col du Midi on ski, up Mont Blanc from the Col du Géant and down by the Dôme route, again up by the Brenva Ridge and down to Chamonix, three of the four Dames Anglaises. Una has left no description of these, but two of next year's expeditions are fully recorded in a manuscript book: the Innominata and the Brouillard. For the Innominata, their base was the Gamba hut (which in comfort and provisioning easily trumped any hotel in the Caucasus).

> Rising early being such a tedious proceeding we decided to sup late and not go to bed at all . . . Outside it was very black and the going over the scree in the dark was pretty lousy, so we were glad to get on to the glacier and put on our crampons, lightening the sacks and giving me the feeling of my feet being all melted into one with the iron toes, without noticeably adding to their weight.
>
> The glacier was steep and complicated in places, so we decided to wait for the dawn somewhere near the base of the rise to the Col Emile Rey. As usual Edouard was a comfort to others. Elisée and I draped ourselves over him and put a sleeping sack over our knees and went to sleep, while he sat up stiff and cold.

When day dawned they succeeded in finding a way through the maze of crevasses.

> It was an interesting sight, the towering ice teeth and great blue-green caverns. I was in poor training and had plenty of time to take it all in. As we came up the steep slope to the Col Eccles and looked down towards the glacier it was an impressive sight to see the snow loosened by the sun rolling down in avalanches. We cleared away some snow on the rocks and sat in the sun on the Col. We could see for miles all the hills we knew and interested ourselves in three men

on the Aiguille Blanche who were going along well, while we discussed possibilities and plans for the future. [These may have included the Aiguilles du Diable and the then unclimbed E face of the Grandes Jorasses. A postcard from Elisée to Una that September describes his reconnaissance of these two routes; but there is no record of any later attempt by Una's party on them.] It would have been easy to have stayed as long as the sun lasted in that blissful spot, but the climb was just beginning, so I knocked out my pipe, Edouard put a brown cigarette end in his pocket for future use, and Elisée woke up; how easily he sleeps and with what accuracy he finds the only place possible to stretch himself out in full comfort.

Then we started up the rocks. Gosh! and they were steep too, but what lovely rock, not a great many holds but sufficient and good. There was still a lot of snow, more than the guides cared for as they had to clear out most of the holds, I only got the snow down my neck and good clean places to put my hands much better! Later we turned a corner with a steep fall beside it and our rucksacks playfully bumped against the rocks seemingly doing their best to knock us down the hillside and yet the difficulty was not grand enough to warrant us pulling them along on the rope; each was muttering to himself or herself a very degrading family tree for the rucksacks and when that difficulty was over, a sinister hole appeared that had to be got through. Holes are always more accommodating than they seem but I was relieved to find myself through and not needing to be dislodged with masons' tools.

It was such a glorious day that we took it slowly and it seemed that we had the world to ourselves. Plenty of handy drips that we mixed with lemonade powder at every step. It was a luxury trip. After we had crossed the broad wicked couloir that was constantly being swept with avalanches, it seemed to me that the summit could not be far away, but the guides said that that was merely a lovely fancy.

From then on the route was less interesting, and we reached the Brouillard ridge at sunset; it was colder and there was a slight wind blowing. We slugged along the ridge and across the snow, and the wind blew harder, then Harder and HARDER. We stalked along with heads down muttering. I felt that it was handy to be heavy or we might be blown away and still we walked over the snow, and glory, the last pull in a gale is unending seemingly.

At last we could climb no higher. Far below were the lights of Chamonix signalling cheerily but we only blinked through an ice-fringe of eyelashes and passe-montagne and went down as fast as the wind would let us, digging in our crampons and ice-axes and feeling like flags on a house-top. Still the gale blew but we could distinguish the Refuge Vallot and soon we were at the door and inside. No one there, how comfortable the shelter was, and what a

Una Cameron

Miage Glacier from the Gonella hut

> fine lot of blankets. Edouard soon had the Primus going and Ovaltine was made and we ate some of anything handy, foie gras and hard bread lying on a shelf below a heap of blankets while the wind howled outside.

Next day, down by the Dôme and over the Aiguilles Grises to the Gonella hut where 'all tiredness vanished like a hat blown off in the wind and we came in and got our clothes mended and dried and sat round the table in blankets and were social'.

A few days later they went up to the Quintino Sella hut where they found 'two Everesters' also bound for the Brouillard. (*AJ*46, 410, 1934 records an ascent of Mont Blanc by the Brouillard by Messrs Crawford and Brocklebank, members of the 1933 Everest expedition. 'They consider the difficulty to be greater than what is commonly stated.')

> We put our crampons on and cut practically directly across to the base of the couloir Emile Rey by the light of the moon. Neither the rocks nor the ice were in any way difficult and the couloir looked quite as long as the previous instructions had described it to be. We plodded up, very very slowly, and as we reached the top day was dawning and my inside was dead, stomach-ache accompanied by a sullen tiredness. However, we cleared away some snow, ate something and looked at the slabs uncomfortably covered in ice and very unpleasant looking . . . The slabs were very steep and they seemed to me very difficult and I can't believe that at any time I would rush up them with a happy laugh. After that the going was easy but tedious, there was a lot of snow everywhere and quite a strong wind blowing from the ridge. On the Pic Luigi Amadeo we stopped a while and roared down to the hut, but the wind was against us and our voices did not carry any distance.
>
> Realising that there were several rock towers to be climbed or traversed there could not be much lagging. At last we reached the final ridge and it was as cold as the last time and we felt the wind even sooner but we were all in better trim and so did not need to stop though I would have liked to have explained to the company my views on strong winds in the hills but luckily I didn't bother them as I'm sure they thought them as leprous as I did and even worse if I'd compelled them to stop! 'Let us bivouac,' I suggested (having a good sack and being tired of fighting against the wind). 'Ough,' they said, 'the Vallot hut's not far and we'll be better there.' Of course they were right and the minute we could start off downhill I agreed with them, bivouacing on Mt Blanc is a poor game.

This time they had to share the Vallot with three Frenchmen, and next day went down by the Tête Rousse and round by train to Chamonix. 'It had been a good party and we never felt more unsafe on our feet than we did skidding across the parquet-floored dining-room to our table before the bulging eyes of high society!'

1935 was Peuterey year. The plan was to traverse the whole ridge in one expedition: the first bivouac would be near the summit of the Aiguille Noire, the second (provisioned by porters) at the Brèche Noire des Dames Anglaises. In the event bad weather forced them down from the Aiguille Noire to the Brenva glacier – an unplanned first descent, paid for by two extremely uncomfortable bivouacs. Here they are starting from the first, intended, bivouac near the top of the Aiguille Noire.

AIGUILLE NOIRE DE PÉTÉRET AND DAMES ANGLAISES

Woodcut by Una Cameron

It was tiring getting to the top, even after a good night's sleep, bivouacing takes it out of you; pushing knowledgeable faces over the ridge at 20 metres from the summit the guides decided to descend. The Germans they said had kept to the Frêney side, so we chose the Brenva instead. The rappel was fixed, Edouard went down the steep wall, gosh! there was a lot of snow, I followed, the rope would not run, Elisée followed me, and no faster either. Slowly two rappels were run out. We had not been able to get any idea of the amount of snow and it was deep everywhere. Periodically someone said, 'Are you sure you are holding on well?' and Edouard advanced in a wonderful way clearing snow away with his hands and then cutting the ice into holds where it was not possible to reach the rock, while Elisée equally miraculously came down from above, the last man. We were of course wet with the snow so was the rope and coming down, though sure, was many times slower than normal climbing. How about going up again, I suggested, but apparently that was only angels' or birds' work so perforce we had to go down. We tried to pretend we didn't notice the rain developing into snow, but Elisée saw what looked like a fine bivouac at about 2 p.m. and we made for it, glad to be off the steep wall even if the bed-chamber were not true comfort. The best-looking place from above was a chimney for wind and full of snow and no good for anyone, so we roped down a few metres where there was shelter, a sloping roof, room to sit down and protected from the North and West, facing East so we would get the first of any sun. We used the remains of the *Daily Sketch* to sit on, economised with the one day's provisions we had, smoked and sucked prune stones. Edouard lay on a sloping ledge and put on a passe-montagne, thought he was on his bed at home, closed his eyes and went to sleep. I put my feet in my rucksack, gave anyone who wanted them my boots for a pillow, put on all the extra things I had and considered my surroundings and slept fitfully. Elisée suggested a change of position. We shivered quite a lot, after a while having more fat I suggested he slept on the inside, so we changed places. Luckily I did too, only the shoulders of the outer occupant were on solid ground and the feet tied in a rucksack were so very vague in their movements that they hardly counted and the great beam had air all round! It just jutted over the edge. We rested or slept by turns and the lights from the valley shone in an aggravating manner seeming to speak of mattresses and plenty of room to spread oneself. Well, if the weather were to break, we'd be safer where we were than moving towards a real roof and shelter – still, blast!

It was possible to start, we were stiff and had nothing to drink except the whisky which was naturally being kept until it was really needed. We ate a little dried fruit and talked of Canadian breakfasts [they had been skiing in the Rockies that spring]. I was sorry for the men but, for myself, I hardly eat in the hills, it is only cities and doing nothing that make me a food-hog, but I looked round for a handy drip – everything still frozen stiff, though thank goodness for the rather pale yellow sun.

We were still damp, the rope was wet, the fresh snow that had fallen had melted away but far too much still stuck to the rocks. Soon we also were as wet as the snow and rocks, each rappel made our wet trousers wring themselves on to their unfortunate owners. We found drips to drink from, Edouard found a really lovely crystal and all the time we were on the face with offensive stones whizzing past, it was difficult to lie flat without a preliminary glance to see where the whistle was coming from. All the time Edouard and Elisée were the same good company of the Café Gay, even when a great stone landed on Ed's rucksack breaking his pipe and bending his tobacco tin he retained his good humour; during half-an-hour's rain-storm we sheltered pressing out our knees in a shale couloir and began to realise that we would have another night with the full benefit of unadulterated mountain air and not a chance of completing the ridge.

The snow, ice, loose rock and flying stones were all trying and I was glad to be across the steep couloir intact. We made for the old bivouac below the Dames Anglaises, and found a choice of several, we were far lower down and were sure to be warmer, also it was quite safe to go about unroped which made for added comfort and convenience. We were all entirely soaked as compared with the damp of the night before and in various ways tried to make for comfort. As I knew my company I considered my skin, or wet clothes. No one turned a hair when I decided after trial to retain wet trousers, with a drawing book inside for a seat. The floor was nearly flat carefully arranged with stones. I found a foot shelter but it was rather cramped though dry so when I was shifting about rattling stones when another rain-storm came on Edouard said, 'Elisée isn't here, you can have his place now.' Down I flopped full-length pullman comfort after the previous foot-hole. Next thing was down, by then we were sure to be back in Courmayeur that day so we waited to get warmed with the sun.

We had a real drunks' breakfast, whisky and smokes and started off down the snow couloir to the Brenva glacier. We were glad we had not attempted that frightfully twisting, rhymeless and reasonless glacier at night.

What will I eat? What will I drink?? What will I do any minute now??? I thought comfortably to myself because soon anything would be possible. Elisée ahead said, 'Hullo, who's that?' Mario and Messilia appeared panting up the hillside. 'You're all right?' they said, 'my, we're glad, how we called yesterday and today and no answer. We met old father Croux and he said you weren't back so we started right up in case you needed help, but told no one in Courmayeur.'

BIVOUAC—BRÈCHE N. DES DAMES ANGLAISES

> So sound! And as well as the telescope they had fetched at Messilia's house hot coffee and chocolate and bread. In a moment Messilia was off again to get Alexis to bring the car up to Entrèves and if possible as far as the little beer-house, what a thoughtful pair, and just so pleased to see us we felt gratified. We lay up on the spiky grass and looked up at our bivouacs, it had been an interesting experience and for me goes to show how little I really mind sleeping out and that it does no harm beyond stiff joints in old age and you'd probably get that anyhow living in England.
>
> How we'll sleep tonight! we all said, a great meal when we get down, a hot bath, and then arrears of sleep to be made up for. Not a bit of it, we slept our usual and met again next day at eleven for a friendly drink and went round to get my photos developed.
>
> The Peuterey ridge from one end to the other still remains for me, the bits and pieces only whet the appetite.

How that appetite was satisfied a few days later is told by Dora de Beer, who with Mario Rey and Mario Cossa joined Una for the expedition. The quotations are from her account in the *LAC Journal* for 1936.

> I had never climbed in that district, so when she suggested that we do the Peuterey ridge, I thought it was just one of the usual routes . . . Possibly because of this preconception, and also no doubt because of ideal weather, the climb did not strike me as very difficult, though certain parts were too giddy for my liking. It was not till afterwards, when we were down at the Dôme hut, that I learnt we were the first women to go up Mont Blanc by that route.

After a rather nightmarish ascent to the Brèche Nord des Dames Anglaises – 'a nasty place, very steep, with no good holds and rocks on either side that moved at a touch', they bivouacked in the tiny cabin. Progress was slow next morning, for Una 'admitted to feeling like death', so they sat in the sun till she recovered, then continued up, mainly on the Brenva side. It was clear that at this rate they would have to bivouac – the guides contrived a sort of platform 50 metres below the first summit of the Aiguille Blanche . . .

> . . . where we could all six lie in a row with all our toes projecting

> into space. The two Alpine ropes were our mattresses, and as a bivouac had not been contemplated, there were no extra coverings beyond the usual windjackets etc and no means of making a hot drink . . . U.C. appeared a trifle surprised when I spoke of the temperature. Before we met she had been playing about on the Aiguille Noire with three nights out in bad weather. She seemed to regard this bivouac as true comfort.

The long narrow ridge up to the Aiguille Blanche was 'sensational, falling steeply away to the Frêney and Brouillard glaciers' – then an hour of step-cutting down to the Col Peuterey ('a wonderful spot, a little level breathing-space in the middle of tremendous peaks').

> After a short rest we roped up again and attacked the steep snow slope that led up to a band of greenish rock. From now on the snow was good and steps could be kicked, except for one or two icy patches; the rocks were good, in spite of some loose stuff; in fact, everything was good but my breathing. Above the rock came more steep snow and yet more, all the way to the top of Mont Blanc de Courmayeur . . . From below the route looked like a delicate shaded line, curving this way and that as it mounted upward, but when on it, one realised the line was a well-defined ridge. It was not really windy . . . We kept on and on and at last, about 6 p.m., poked our heads through the cornice just below the level top. A cold wind was blowing up stormy-looking clouds, so we pushed on again and down to the Vallot Hut. It was half full, grimy and uncomfortable, with ice on the floor, but I for one slept soundly.

Down next morning to the Dôme hut, a day's rest there, then across the Miage glacier to the Quintino Sella hut, up Mont Blanc again by the Rochers, down again to the Dôme hut. Six full days of Mont Blanc! And three days later Una was off again, to the Red Sentinel.

This route on the Brenva Face, and the Route Major, had been pioneered by T Graham Brown and F S Smythe in 1927 and 1928: Graham Brown lectured on them to the LAC in 1932. Una was the only British climber to repeat the routes before the war. I have found no account of these splendid climbs beyond the laconic entries in a small notebook about Mont Blanc. But among the Graham Brown papers in the National Library of Scotland I came across a letter to him from Una, with slightly more detail.

> *23 Feb 1936*. Thank you very much for your letter and the print, so much improved, of the photograph I took on the Sentinel Route. I have asked various people about times and dates etc as I do not take much notice of them myself, and the Sentinel Route information is as follows.
>
> > *July 31*. Torino Hut to Col de la Fourche 2 h.
> > *Aug. 1*. Left bivouac 3.20 a.m. Reached position of the photograph, i.e. across wide snow couloir after the red

> sentinel on the rock rib about 9 a.m. Summit about 2 p.m. – very strong wind once we reached the snow.

She goes on to give Graham Brown news of other climbs by her own and other parties in the Mont Blanc range in 1935: owning to 'a singularly unimpressive performance' by herself on the Aiguille Blanche where she had felt like death.

Her notes on the Route Major climb on 2/3 August 1938 are slightly fuller than those for the Red Sentinel:

> Left Col de la Fourche fixed bivouac approx 2 a.m. Passed other party at Col Moore. Crossed couloir after sentinel. Much step-cutting. Fine day, rocks dry, snow and ice in crevices and cracks. Two pitches required consideration. Steep throughout. Snow covered the ridge – much step-cutting. Tracks led to ice-filled chimney – impossible without piton. Traversed round at base of rocks, piton in rock face left by others no use to us – hours of step-cutting – began to snow. Decided to bivouac in the shelter of the rocks. Left in the morning when the sun had warmed us along below rocks then straight up to seracs and through them to saddle between summits, hence to Mont Blanc. Smoked in calm and sunshine. Igloo on summit, 2 inmates. Vallot (observatoire and tea) new hut unfinished, approx. midday. Slept. Left about 3 p.m. Glacier du Dôme v. bad, crevasses, miles of detour.

'The most enjoyable climb I have ever done,' she told Graham Brown. Una hoped to complete what he had called the Triptych of the Brenva Face by climbing the Pear route, pioneered by him and his guides in 1933, but the war intervened. Afterwards, she would tell visitors to the Villa Cameron that she was 'getting in training for the Pear' – but that was as far as it went. She did traverse Mont Blanc again in 1947, and also climbed the Tour Ronde, Aiguille de Rochefort, Aiguille Rouge de Triolet, and Monte Rosa (which she had climbed in 1937 from the Italian side by the Marinelli couloir). But climbing friends were now more likely to find her at the Villa Cameron, ready to hear about their doings and suggest expeditions. I remember a most enjoyable day on the Aiguille Joseph Croux above the Gamba hut as one of her recommendations.

There were also two winter ascents of Mont Blanc on ski. 'Feb. 33 as far as the Vallot from the Dôme hut, v. cold, windy,' and 'Feb. 1937. Traverse Dôme hut up to Vallot, down to Chamonix.' Nothing more on these; but she wrote full accounts of ski-tours in the Silvretta group (January 1934), the Monte Rosa massif (April 1934), the Ötztal (over New Year 1935), the Canadian Rockies (March–April 1935) and the Monte Viso region (March 1936). In the Silvretta and Ötztal she took a local guide; the other tours were with Edouard or Elisée or both; Hazel Jackson (and dog) joined them on the Monte Rosa trip. Una kept clear of skiing centres and didn't care for piste skiing; she always hoped to take in a summit or two. In her narratives she does not flatter herself as a skier. 'You would get on better if you did not get so angry when you fell,' Edouard told her in the Rockies. At Ochsenbergscharte in the

Silvretta, 'the others whizzed off down, while I set off in great stem turns, stately and slow, rather like mother on a bicycle', but she does allow that she executed some stylish christianias on the way down from Monte Rosa to the Val d'Ayas, and records one compliment, from a local who came with them to Monte Viso: 'I had no idea that a great fat person like you could go so well.' (She enjoyed mocking her appearance: 'I looked like a rich Eastern potentate with my red flannel waistband round the bulging middle and a shirt on my ski-sticks keeping the sun off.') But she had great strength and endurance and she could travel light: 'A few days skiing soon discovers that a spare ski-tip, an extra pair of socks, tobacco and a book are all that is needed.' One supposes that her companions carried the food.

What comes out of these accounts is her immense enjoyment of so much more than the actual skiing. She relished the conviviality in huts and inns:

> After supper all Compatsch came in. We were an excellent free entertainment and they sat and watched with fascinated interest while we conversed internationally with a dictionary and bits of any language that made our meaning clearer.

In the course of one such polyglot evening a Dutchman congratulated Una: 'You speak English well, where do you come from?' 'I was completely winded and could only reply in a stately manner, "I am Scottish . . ." The Dutchman asked what was exactly the difference between a Scot and an Englishman, and he heard for the first time that Scotland had never been conquered.'

Above all, it was the sheer happiness of being in the mountains. On the Col des Cimes Blanches: 'Gosh! and that was comfort and a foretaste of heaven in this so-called vale of tears, warm flat rocks, the sun shining in the blue sky, and all around the high hills.' At the Quintino Sella hut on Monte Rosa after a stiff climb from Fiéry: 'It was one of the best evenings in the mountains that I have ever enjoyed, glaciers and snow all round, only kindred spirits, "snows and skis and dear gentlemen" [one was Hazel's dog Argos]. A hoot for cities!'

Una was for once skiing alone on an afternoon in February 1933, up the Val Ferret, when she came on the Courmayeur guide Othon Bron, also on his own, who had fallen and broken a leg. He couldn't get himself out of the snow, and a cold night was coming on. Una gave him first aid, ski'd back down the valley to give the alarm, and a rescue party brought Othon down on a stretcher. The local papers made much of '*la famosa signora Una Kamerum, la nota esploratrice del Caucaso*'; and when I first met Othon Bron next year he had much to say of his rescuer. It was only slowly that I realized that this spirited female '*qui porte le pantalon et fume la pipe*' was the Una Cameron I had known slightly at school. My first real meetings with her were after the war when I came over from the Graians with a mixed party of veterans and schoolboys, and Una helped us find cheap quarters at the inn near her villa. In the years since Othon had first spoken of her to me, he and Michael Roberts and I had climbed from Courmayeur, Chamonix and Zermatt, and in the Dauphiné, always – as Una was with Edouard and Elisée – more as friends climbing together than as clients with a guide; then Othon was killed in 1938 when a snow-bridge gave way on the Glacier du Géant; and Michael died in 1948.

Othon's grave was in the cemetery at Courmayeur; Michael's was in London, and I wanted a memorial of him among the mountains. I mentioned this to Una, who at once offered to help. With Edouard Bareux's assistance, she got the necessary permissions from the cemetery and from the Bron family, and dealt with the stone-mason; so now on a small plaque beside Othon's memorial is engraved: 'In memory of Michael Roberts 1902–1948 who climbed these mountains with Ottone Bron.' I owe Una great thanks for this help so readily given, and I hope that in compiling this record of her splendid climbs I have made some kind of repayment.

When Things Went Wrong

ASHLEY GREENWOOD

Characters in order of appearance: Sandy Wedderburn, Tommy Wedderburn, Pat Baird, Donald Ross, Tom Peacocke, Rosemary Greenwood, Paul Roberts, Norman Gubbey, Jen Solt

December 1932. Idwal Slabs, Hope

I was in my early days of climbing. The Slabs were wet and I wore nailed boots. Half-way along the delicate traverse I paused, perplexed by the next move. 'Oh well,' I said to myself, 'you've led it before' (in the summer in rubbers), 'it must be OK.' Forgetting the recessed fingerhold, I launched myself.

A moment later I was sliding upright down the Slabs. 'He will stop in a moment' piped up that part of my mind which immediately detached itself from my body. And I did – fortunately, as Sandy's belay had at that moment slipped off. My foot had slid neatly into the one hold on the pitch that was large enough for it. Shaken, I descended the parallel cracks. 'Try again, or you'll lose your nerve,' said Sandy. And that's what I did.

March 1934. Ben Nevis, NE Buttress, 8pm

It had never occurred to me that there was any climb in the UK that could not be completed in a day. Tommy and I had started from the CIC hut at 9am and here we were at 8pm, torchless, just above the Man-Trap but still 100m below the summit plateau of the Ben, and it was too dark to continue. Cramponless we had worked our way slowly upwards all day, clearing holds on the ice-sheathed buttress with an old-fashioned long ice-axe. The Man-Trap alone had exacted an hour and a half to clear, climb and hoist my diminutive and fortunately lightweight companion.

Now we had to sit it out, inadequately clothed (cotton shirt and golfing jacket), for 11 hours. We dug out seats from the ice, sat down, hitched the rope round a poor belay, and sang and dozed, waking at one moment to find the belay off. We were encouraged by shouts and flashes from the hut, signals from our two friends who had wisely turned back from the adjacent Tower Ridge before it was too late. So, by the time we were exercising our stiff limbs and restoring circulation at 7am the next day, there was Pat abseiling down to us from above to help us to the top. No harm came to us except for fingertips skinned from sticking to ice-axes, but we were wiser climbers when we settled down in the hut to eat and sleep off hunger and exhaustion.

July 1937. Mer de Glace, below the Montenvers Hotel

Bad weather had delayed our start for the Dent du Géant from the Rifugio Torino till noon, and we were a party of five. Nevertheless we were still in good time on the descent of the Géant glacier, when an evil genius tempted us to stop and linger over a late cup of tea at the Requin hut. And so it got dark while we blundered around, looking for the path from the glacier to the Montenvers Hotel, without which we deemed it too risky to scale the worn slabs by the side of the glacier. So after a long and fruitless search we sat down and waited for dawn. Hot Ovomaltine from our pocket stove cheered us, and it was a tolerable and shortish night. As darkness began to fade into dawn we espied the lights of a party descending to the glacier *only about 40 yards away*. We looked at each other sheepishly and walked up the path to Montenvers.

August 1954. High on the Schalligletscher, midnight

Why on earth, I asked myself, did we turn back two-thirds of the way up the Schalligrat at about 2pm on a cloudless day. There was no hope of descending to the Weisshorn hut that afternoon by the normal route via the Schallijoch (there was no fixed bivouac there at that time) – that would have been much too dangerous because of falling stones. The others thought we might find a way down the Schalligletscher. I doubted it and thought it would be better to run the risk of being benighted on the way down the E ridge of the Weisshorn rather than on the Schalligletscher. But it was not mine to reason why; I had not been leading up over the snow-covered rocks. Needless to say, there was no way through the maze of crevasses; so, after hours of searching, we wearily climbed up and traversed to a rib of rock on the side of the glacier and sat shivering there till dawn, when it was safe to descend to the Weisshorn hut by the way we had come up. It was miserable for all, but particularly so for Donald, who had a severe cold. Ever since then, Tom and I have regretted not going on up the Grat.

Christmas Day 1957. Otira Gorge, New Zealand (South Island)

Rosemary and I had failed to get to the top of Mount Rolleston from Arthur's Pass that day. The approach and the ridge were too long, and we had started too late. On the descent it got unnaturally warm. Never before or since have I seen snow begin to roll down in balls on such gentle slopes. But it did not avalanche, and back on Arthur's Pass we ate our Christmas dinner of chicken legs by the roadside. Then after driving our hired car westwards down towards Greymouth, we pitched camp by the wooden bridge over the Otira river. Ignorant in those days of the weather portents in New Zealand, we stayed on the bank opposite to the town of Otira. At dusk it began to rain and, by the time it stopped 12 hours later, 13 inches had fallen. The bridge was gone except for one span, and the road to the pass behind us had been washed away to such an extent that it took 18 months before it could be reopened. It was a frightening time that night, beside the rising river thundering continuously with the big rocks being swept down. I had stuck my ice-axe in the ground and decided that, when the waters reached it, we must strike camp; and they got within inches of it. Three days later I was able to wade the river and make my way to Otira to buy food. The road was submerged by rocks which reached almost to the tops of the telegraph poles. Two days later the bulldozers, which had been building up the river banks to save Otira from further flooding, could afford time to divert the river under the surviving span of the bridge, build a ramp and tow our hired car out. That night we pitched camp on top of a hillock, and once more the rain began to teem down. There was no more climbing that holiday, and broken bridges stopped us even reaching the Fox and Franz Joseph glaciers on the West Coast.

July 1980. Macusani, Cordillera Carabaya, Peru, 11.30pm

It was the worst establishment calling itself a hotel that I had ever known; the loo was beyond description and the bedrooms were like prison cells. But it was nearly midnight, and I was thankful to get into it. We had been climbing for a fortnight in the Cordillera Carabaya. I was tired, and said so, as we crossed a 5150m pass to descend to the lake and road 20km from Macusani where a lorry had deposited us two weeks earlier and was to meet us next morning. On the descent I had lagged behind, had lost sight of the others and had strayed from the right direction. When I enquired at a primitive llama herdsman's hut if other gringos had been seen, I was given the wrong direction. Reaching the Macusani road too low, I had walked back up it for half an hour and met no one (and, had I known it, had reached within a few hundred yards of where the others were camped). I decided that my only sensible course was to walk the 20km to Macusani. By now it was after dark, and more than 12 hours since we had left camp to climb the 600m to the pass. I had had practically nothing to eat all day and had only a couple of sweets in my pocket. The road was long and I was frequently assailed by fierce dogs which I drove off with stones. The lights of Macusani when they appeared seemed never to get nearer, and I began to have hallucinations and see huge rocks far away by the roadside; when reached in a few yards, they turned out to be piffling little stones. On arriving at Macusani I found a shop still open and devoured some rolls before braving three dogs into the courtyard of the mayor's house where I knew that Paul and some of the rest of the party who had descended by another route would be staying. After the third attempt to arouse someone – the dogs by now had become really friendly – and all my knocking had elicited no response, I gave up. My compatriots had in fact been in the mayor's house and had ignored what they imagined to be a burglar, or at least a drunken reveller. So, the unspeakable hotel it was.

Next morning I intended to intercept the lorry before it left to fetch the roadside campers, but it had left early. An hour later it returned with Norman, intent on organizing a large search party. He told me that the campers thought I must have had a heart attack and would not have survived a bitter night on the mountain, such as those we had been having. They had searched for me half the night, and poor Rosemary had resigned herself to widowhood. We were soon reunited.

Crevasse Trouble

May 1949. Gross Venediger

If it hadn't been for defeats two days running, I don't think we would have persisted to the top on the third day. The weather was thick, the visibility minimal on the upper part and the snow abominable. Coming down we were stemming slowly down our up tracks when in I went up to the armpits, skis dangling below, and myself so precariously balanced that I dared not move till Jen arrived and proffered a ski stick, with the aid of which I pulled myself out. We had a rope, but I was carrying it!

July 1969. Presanella

We were unroped on the descent and I was not far behind the other two, when I disappeared into a bergschrund. This time, following their tracks precisely, I had gone right in but landed on a snow bridge 10ft down. Escape was so easy that they had only just noticed my absence when my head reappeared above the surface. They seemed to find it very funny.

9 January 1971. Breithorn

It was glorious weather but a bitter north wind was blowing when we set out on skis for the Breithorn from Trockener Steg. We followed up beside the pylons of a small meat-hook ski-lift, used for summer skiing but out of action in winter. We stopped for a snack in the operator's hut at the top and I took off my skis and descended a few yards to relieve nature. I was standing *between the pylons* where the ski track would have been and had just unzipped my trousers when in I went up to the armpits but was stopped by snow jamming against the sides of the crevasse. Looking down through the hole I could see that the crevasse widened and disappeared into the gloom. I was out in a moment, somewhat shocked.

March 1989. Moel Siabod

We started at 5pm from Capel Curig to traverse the mountain by the circuit, up past the lake, along the ridge and down the grass slopes to Old Capel. I thought we could do it before dark – expected at about 7.30pm. And so we would have – just – if I had remembered to take a torch to supplement the map and compass I had put in my pocket. As it was we had to decide, when it got dark a bit early owing to the clouds, which lot of lights to aim at. There were no stars and it was too dark to read the map or compass. Four hours later, after innumerable falls, wading through streams and sinking over the knees into bogs, we approached the lights of a village and the outline of a castle loomed into sight, confirming our fears, which had gradually been growing, that the lights were those of Dolwyddellan rather than Capel. However, the pub was still open and beer was obtainable – at 11.30pm! A telephone call produced a taxi in half an hour. On our way back to Capel the driver told us that he was frequently doing the same journey with walkers who on misty days had done exactly what we had done. By 1am we got to the Royal Victoria Hotel at Llanberis for the AC meet.

Not Much of a Mountaineer

IVAN WALLER

The crossing to the Isle of Arran in the car ferry had been as dramatic as ever, with the shapely hills rising 874m above the sea, the great stack of Ailsa Craig visible away to the south, Paddy's Milestone they call it, where the gannets nest, and Holy Isle close inshore to Arran itself. Brodick with its white houses grows closer every minute and in no time I am riding my push-bike along the jetty on to the island. It is August, so my bed and breakfast is booked in advance, but the weather forecast is dreadful, rain all night and two lows with closely packed isobars in quick succession in the morning.

I had climbed, some of them several times, all the higher hills on the island except Beinn Tarsuinn and Beinn Nuis: these were the objective of this short visit, particularly Tarsuinn because it is one of the 221 Corbetts listed as 'lesser heights' in *Munro's Tables*. Seven years ago I finished ticking off all 517 Tops as well as the English, Welsh and Irish equivalents, and have now scored over 100 in Corbett's list. It is a good game when you have grown out of serious mountaineering and it has taken me to a lot of lovely places.

Beinn Tarsuinn can be approached in a clockwise circuit over Beinn Nuis, or widdershins over Beinn Chliabhain. These three hills enclose a corrie from the south of which a mountain stream, the Garbh Allt, flows out and swings east across the moor to run steeply down in a series of waterfalls into Glen Rosa where it joins the Rosa Burn to flow into the sea near Brodick. There is tarmac as far as the camp-site up Glen Rosa, and taken in either direction this should be an easy round even in bad weather, but for 82-year-old legs it could be rather more of an undertaking, as I was to find out.

In the morning all the rivers were in spate so I crossed the Garbh Allt by the bridge down in Glen Rosa, but to reach the moor above there are 150m of height to be gained up a steep and vague path which I found quite an effort. The path went on up the moor towards Beinn Chliabhain but I could find no signs of a track towards Beinn Nuis. The rough wet moorland did not appeal to my old legs, and it looked as if the ridge from Nuis to Tarsuinn was getting the full force of the west wind; so, hoping to find more shelter to the east, I stuck to the path towards Chliabhain. The wet and the wind, although not too bad, were not exactly helping things and, when at last I reached the summit of Beinn Chliabhain, I looked at my watch and at the threatening conditions and decided reluctantly that I had had enough. The col leading to Beinn Tarsuinn looked very close and I must indeed have been feeling pretty feeble not to have gone on at least as far as the foot of the 225m pull-up on to Tarsuinn.

Beinn Chliabhain is little more than 675m in height and to north, east and west there are hills up to 200m higher presenting a fine serrated sky-line while, deep below, Glen Rosa runs south towards the sea. Eleven years ago, a friend had taken me up seven of the island's rock-climbs, and five of them could be seen from this grandstand perch. Chliabhain therefore had plenty to offer me and I could not help feeling a sense of relief that I was not going to land myself on the lofty ridge of Tarsuinn when there had been a gale warning for this very area. On the way down I saw a beautiful herd of deer. The weather improved later in the afternoon and it was lovely down in Glen Rosa, but I never did know what it was really like on the higher ridges. I had seen nobody on the hill all day but there were plenty of people in the glen. The bad weather returned that night and I returned home the next day with very mixed feelings.

I was at Lancing College with Gino Watkins who became a well-known arctic explorer and tragically lost his life in the sea off the E coast of Greenland. It was from him that I first heard about rock-climbing after he had been to the Lake District with my housemaster E B Gordon during the school holidays. Gino had also climbed on the Chamonix Aiguilles and had had a terrible fall in the mountains of Austria. All this made a great impression but at this stage it did not occur to me that I might become a mountaineer. We both went up to Trinity College Cambridge, where Gino's interests turned to arctic exploration; this seemed even further from my scene. After about a year I went to visit Lancing and to see E B Gordon who asked me what exercise I was taking. None, I answered, and when I reminded him that I was no use at games, he recalled that I was always climbing trees and suggested that I might take up mountain climbing, recommending a book by G D Abraham, *First Steps to Climbing*. This I bought and with the book in one hand, so to speak, and the rocks in the other, I taught myself to be a climber.

After a preliminary skirmish on the Salisbury Crags and Arthur's Seat just outside Edinburgh, my first real mountain was Schiehallion, which because of its symmetrical shape and comparative isolation had been used for measuring the mass of the earth. So enjoyable was this ascent that I went back two days later, climbed it again, walked down the far end to Loch Rannoch and back to the car over the mountain again. My next venture was with a friend to climb one of the gullies on Ben Nevis; although it was midsummer, we found to our surprise and delight that it was still full of snow and in perfect condition for kicking steps.

Meanwhile I had bought Mummery's book *My Climbs in the Alps and Caucasus* and had become an armchair alpinist, so that, when I got the chance of a skiing holiday at Wengen in the shadow of the Jungfrau, I furtively concealed in my luggage 60m of Beale's Alpine Line, although I had no clear idea how I was going to use it. The journey out on the continental trains and up from Lauterbrunnen on the rack railway to Wengen was a new and magic experience. The masses of snow on the trees, the crystals sparkling in the sunshine, the great cliffs and frozen waterfalls below Mürren across the valley and the snow-covered hills beyond were for me a fairyland, and when we got off the train at Wengen, there was the Jungfrau utterly detached and remote, right up in the sky with its terraces of rock and glacier and the unbelievable blue of the sky beyond. To me this great mountain wall has always remained the most exciting sight in the Alps.

To get the feel of skis I decided on a visit to Grindelwald by way of the snow-covered roads. First I had to get down to Lauterbrunnen, carrying my skis a lot of the way, then down the road to Zweilütschinen where I could slide freely as there were no cars, only horse-drawn sledges and not many of them. The tramp up the valley to Grindelwald was superb, the most memorable feature being the beautiful old timber bridges with steep wooden roofs to keep off the snow, and the mountains at the head getting nearer and nearer. At last I was there and the Wetterhorn came into full view. It was an easy run down back to Zweilütschinen and I took the train back to Wengen. I already felt part of the country.

The next day I took the train to Kleine Scheidegg and climbed to the top of the Lauberhorn. There were no lifts in those days and I really felt as though I was on a mountain, and what a breathtaking view it was. The great north wall of the Oberland was there in all its glory and seen in wonderful perspective from this lofty viewpoint, extending from the Jungfrau past the Mönch and the Eiger all the way to the Wetterhorn. Today, with lifts and hundreds of skiers, it never feels quite the same. Somehow I managed to ski down to Wengen and the following day I fell in with some English skiers who taught me how to do downhill turns. Then came the thaw, the snow avalanched all over the place, the slopes were left bare and all you could do was walk. This I did, following a path rising northward from the village and signposted 'Hunnenfluh'. After a few kilometres I came to a platform with an iron railing at the top of a great cliff, whiskered with fir trees, and opposite the village of Isenfluh across the Lauterbrunnen valley.

My friends Dennis and Ruth, with each of whom I had done one or two climbs in the Lake District, arrived that evening. The thaw had temporarily put an end to skiing, so I suggested that we might spend the next day roping down from the Hunnenfluh platform. It was New Year, a fine clear day and no wind; we made a leisurely start and it did not look far down, but here I was mistaken. All went well at first until we came to a great overhang. Getting down it was all right, but the rope jammed and we could not pull it down. Climbing as high as I could, I cut off as much of the double rope as possible but only managed to save two 10m lengths which we knotted together. By then it was beginning to get dark, the lights of Isenfluh were still far below us and as we went on and on, from tree to tree, the lights gave the illusion of going down with us. By now the full moon was up and we could see reasonably well, but it was well into the early hours before we reached the easy slopes below, which took us down to a path leading round the base of the cliffs and back up to Wengen.

I joined the Cambridge Mountaineering Club and learned a lot about climbing from Jack Longland on the rocks of Derbyshire, North Wales and the Lake District, but I never learned to stand in nailed boots on outward-sloping ledges the way he could. Easter in a tent on top of Ben Nevis with Freddy Chapman – the author of *The Jungle is Neutral* – just after he had returned from Greenland with Gino Watkins, was a great experience, and I shall never forget his joy when we saw a flight of snow buntings, birds which he had last seen in the Arctic. After two nights on the top of Scotland we ski'd down, left our skis and tent at Achintee to be collected later, and walked the same day by Sgurr a

Mhaim and Am Bodach over the Mamores, thence by the Devil's Staircase into Glencoe to bivouac on the moor above Kingshouse for a climb on the Crowberry Ridge the next day. In the morning I was woken by a crunching sound, and when I opened my eyes I saw a stag with huge antlers, chewing away a few centimetres above my head. I quickly closed my eyes again.

My real alpine climbing started when I went out to Kandersteg intending to climb some easy mountains on my own, but on the station when I arrived there were Smythe and Graham Brown whom I had met in Snowdonia, and they invited me to join them. After an ascent of the Altels from a lovely bivouac round a camp-fire to which we returned for another night after the climb, we crossed the Gemmi Pass with its fantastic descent to the south, and went on to Chamonix. From the old Couvercle hut we attempted a new route on the Courtes, but near the top we found a cairn of broken bottles. Finally we did the classic traverse of the Grépon but they both needed aid on three of the pitches, and after some major haulage operations I arrived exhausted and terrified on the summit. In terror I roped off down the Knubel Crack and scrambled via the Brèche Balfour to wait for them down at the CP gap, while they slept for three-quarters of an hour on the top. After I had gone home they went on to do the first ascent of the Route Major on the Brenva face of Mont Blanc.

The following year, 1929, I somehow became a member of a small party planning to make a January ascent of Piz Bernina. I was somewhat overawed to be in such distinguished company, for our leader was Bentley Beetham who had been on the Third Everest Expedition five years before; his friend Tim Thompson was a university rowing coach and the other member of the party, besides myself who had no claim to fame, was Basil Goodfellow whom I had met on the summit of Buachaille Etive Mor and who, 24 years later, played a leading role in launching the successful British Everest expedition of 1953. The weather was clear but very cold and I retreated with Basil from the Labyrinth, an icefall at the head of the Morteratsch glacier, to the Boval hut with a slightly frostbitten finger. The other two spent a miserable night at the Marco e Rosa hut and made a tricky descent in the morning without attempting the summit.

The next year Basil asked me and another friend to join him in the Alps in the summer. We had five most enjoyable climbs, the most impressive being the traverse of the Aletschhorn from the Oberaletsch hut and down the Hasler Rib to Konkordiaplatz. Over the years I managed to climb six 4000m peaks, one of them solo when 71 years old (Gran Paradiso, of course, with 250 other people), but the highest I ever climbed was to the Vallot hut. It was in May 1948 when France was short of everything and we were allowed to take out only £25, but a mutual friend arranged with Gaston Rébuffat that I should take out a supply of nylon climbing rope and several large tins of Cow and Gate for the newly born Rébuffat baby in exchange for an attempt to climb Mont Blanc on skis. On the way to the Grands Mulets hut we came upon the French army doing exercises on the Bossons glacier. We saw a rope of four at a bridge over a crevasse; the leader had crossed and the second was half-way across when he fell in. No1 and No3 held him while No4 had already whipped up his camera and photographed the whole procedure. Next day there was another impressive event beyond the Petit Plateau as we were climbing up towards the Col du Dôme. The whole N

49. *Johanna Merz and Maurizio Zappa, the Gran Zebrù (Königsspitze) behind.* (Nino Zappa) (p 98)

50. The Gran Zebrù (Königsspitze), 3859m, out of condition. (Johanna Merz) (p 98)

51. The Pizzo Tresero-Cima Dosegu-Punta San Matteo traverse; the '13 Cime' behind. (Johanna Merz) (p 98)

52. *The Pizzo Tresero, SW ridge.* (Johanna Merz) (p 98)

53. *The refuge at the Green Lake and view into Vel'ka Zmrzlá Valley. In the background Mt Pysny (2623m), Baranie Pass and Baranie rohy (2526m) and (R) Mt Cierny (2434m).* (J W Gajewski) (p 110)

54. *Mt Bystra (2258m) and Pyszna Pasture in the upper Kościeliska Valley (Western Tatras).* (J W Gajewski) (p 110)

55. *Monte d'Oro (2389m), NW face.* (Kev Reynolds) (p 117)

56. Monte Rotondo (2622m) from the south. (Kev Reynolds) (p 117)

'7. *Cornes d'Asinao, southern Corsica.* (Kev Reynolds) (p 117)

'8. *Looking to the Northern Glacier and Reusch Crater from Uhuru Peak, Kilimanjaro.* (John A Jackson) (p 136)

59. *Mount Kenya – the Diamond Couloir leading to the Diamond Glacier and 'Gate of the Mists' between Batian and Nelion.* (John A Jackson) (p 136)

face below the summit of Mont Blanc seemed to break away and a giant avalanche came down which ran right out across the Grand Plateau and we were enveloped in snow dust. At the Vallot hut Gaston decided that the wind was too strong and that we might be blown off the ridge if we tried to continue to the summit of Mont Blanc, so we skied back down.

In my old age I have had two holidays climbing in the Alps with Charles Warren and Iain Ogilvie. I have been climbing with Charles on and off since the Cambridge days. He was on the last three Everest attempts before the Second World War and was Honorary Keeper of the Club's Pictures, and all three of us are members of the Scottish Mountaineering Club. Iain, although suffering from the after-effects of a stroke and serious heart trouble, recently compleated the Munros. (The spelling is a foible of the SMC, presumably after Isaac Walton's *The Compleat Angler*.) After several nice mountains in Switzerland, we went on to Italy for the wonderfully attractive traverse of the Disgrazia by the NNE ridge, the Corda Molla, and down the broken face on the other side of the mountain to the Ponti hut. The other holiday was in the Dauphiné and the Ecrins – the most southerly of the alpine 4000m peaks – was included.

However, my last long snow climb was in Scotland on Easter Monday 1984 at the end of an SMC meet. Oliver Turnbull and I left the Glen Affric Hotel at Cannich after an early breakfast and drove to Achintee at the start of the Ben Nevis footpath. Walking up by Lochan an t-Suidhe we reached the CIC hut at lunchtime where we had food and a rest, and then set off to climb the Tower Ridge. The Observatory Gully was choked full of old avalanche snow, as indeed it had been on a solo visit 17 years before, but the snow on the ridge was perfect and we did not rope up until shortly before the Little Tower. After a climb of alpine beauty we arrived on the summit plateau at 6pm. We slept that night at Lagangarbh, the SMC hut in Glencoe, after a day in a lifetime with brilliant sunshine, lots of snow and not a breath of wind.

Note

The heading of this article is a parody on the title *Not Much of an Engineer* given to his autobiography by the late Sir Stanley Hooker, in which he described his work on aero-engine superchargers and gas turbines. It is also a paradox in as much as Stanley was brilliantly successful and his achievements have been of benefit worldwide, whereas my title . . .

Waller's Crack

STEPHEN REID

(*Plates* 71, 72)

Every climber knows of Ivan Waller, the man who in 1927 with Stuart Palmer climbed Belle View Bastion to the jazz tune of a gramophone on the terrace above. A remarkable lead for its time, that alone has been enough to ensure him a reverential place in several history books. One would expect such a capable leader to have a string of similar firsts to his name, but this is not the case and, though he has seconded some famous new routes, Ivan himself can recall only two others where he has been at the sharp end; Fallen Block Crack on Clogwyn y Ddysgl and an obscure short route on Harrison's Stickle in Langdale known as Waller's Crack.

I first met Ivan through what Sid Cross disparagingly refers to as the 'Alpayne Club' (obviously to Sid's mind even more toffee-nosed than the 'quate plum-in-the-mouth enough Claymers Club'). Despite his advanced age of 78 years we teamed up on the 1985 AC Grasmere meet where, to Ivan's indubitable delight, we succeeded in overtaking another AC party (mere striplings in their fifties) on Westmorland's Route. I usually meet up with Ivan at these Lakeland do's, if not to climb, at least at the evening dinner where in general I try to steer the conversation round to his fascinating reminiscences of the early days: Mickledore Grooves with Kirkus, or the time he called Smythe 'a silly ***' on the Grépon, and such-like. Sometimes Waller's Crack would be mentioned and Ivan always looked up hopefully at this point and said, 'Have you done it?' And I always, not having quite got my Pikes sorted out from my Stickles and thus not really being a hundred per cent certain as to where Waller's Crack actually was, replied rather guiltily that no I hadn't, not yet.

There is something rather special about these AC meets. I think it is the sense of meeting living history on the hoof, so to speak. Everywhere one looks in the crowded basement room of the suitably lacklustre lakeside hotel, one sees faces straight from the books on one's bookshelf. The lines more deeply etched, the hair now grey or non-existent, the owners apologetic for their physical shortcomings of age, it is true, but the glint in the eye for the lady, the enthusiasm in the far-fetched tale is as strong as ever. Lectures are listened to with rapt attention and speakers shoud be prepared for some searching and well-informed questions.

Typically one such speaker, a fellow whose reputation for being somewhat economical with the truth has preceded him, who had just proudly announced his recent 'second ascent' of a well-known Karakoram pinnacle, was surprised to be informed courteously by a diffident but insistent elderly gentleman that his was actually the third ascent. The French had apparently made the second ascent a few days after the success of the original British team.

The elderly gentleman turned out to have been the leader of that team and at the end of the talk he again stuck in a mischievous oar by innocently enquiring of the speaker how he had managed the awkward rock-step between the first and second summits, the second apparently being slightly higher. The ambivalence of the squirming lecturer's answer would have done credit to a politician coming under heavy fire on Sir Robin Day's 'Question Time', and there was a considerable increase in the banging of walking-sticks and deliberate coughing that forms the normal accompaniment to such lectures. In fact these meets are usually so entertaining that this year I finally persuaded my wife Jill to accompany me.

By some strange quirk the weather turned out to be gorgeous and the dog was panting hard by the time we reached Gimmer. He wasn't the only one. The crag was crowded but we found a couple of free places in the Chimney and started up. On a good weekend in the Lakes, on a popular crag, one is unfortunately generally guaranteed to see some fairly silly climbing techniques on display. The pair who belayed on a single small wire and then chalked their way up the Strenuous Chimney probably won the 'Wally Award' for that day, though the leader who later led the Neat Bit and then belayed 20 feet to the right without putting in any protection for his second definitely came a close runner-up (if you'll excuse the pun). By the time we had reached the top I had a pounding headache which even the clear unwallied air of Pike o' Stickle took some time to dispel.

By now it was tea-time and folk were heading down. Yet the sky was clear blue tinged with gold, whisked egg-white clouds sat like meringue topping along the length of Crinkle Crags, and as the shadows lengthened our dog finally found a muddy hole to wallow in. It seemed a shame to leave such a beautiful scene, especially as the dinner wasn't until eight. Across the plateau a short crack set in a gilded wall glistened in the sun. Surely that was Harrison's Stickle . . . and if so that must be Waller's Crack . . . Just the thing . . . Jilly could hold the ropes, I would climb the route and then abseil down to get the gear. The new guidebook said VS, 12m, and put it almost at the bottom of the graded list, so it shouldn't take that long. It would be pleasant to be able to say to Ivan, 'Oh by the way, I climbed your crack today.' I could hardly wait to see his face.

From the bottom the climb seemed somewhat steeper than it had done from the far side of the Upper Dungeon Ghyll bogs. Off-width and overhanging too, and as I lurched off the ground to what looked like a good rest but wasn't, my heart lurched a little in sympathy. I hurriedly fumbled in a poor runner.

The crack now revealed itself to be far too wide to jam, but too narrow to get more than an arm and a leg into. Moreover, it was too deep to get at some tantalizing holds at the back. A few feet up was a small chockstone which I couldn't quite reach. Eventually I udged up to it but it was deep in the crack and this left me nothing to stand on. I slithered helplessly and in final desperation resorted to my usual ploy when *in extremis* – friend stuffing! Fortunately for Jilly, who was anxiously anticipating holding her first leader fall, the friend found purchase midst the moss and a certain amount of entirely accidental rope tension allowed me to thread the recalcitrant chock. A few feet higher a second slimy stone proved just as elusive. Almost an hour of udging, thrutching and further friend stuffing gained me a yard and a welcome handhold out on the left wall. Unfortunately at this point the crack narrowed slightly and provided no further handholds when facing left. Even the few available footholds were placed in such a position as to require painful contortions of the user. I made a poorly controlled descent back to my non-good rest, breathed deeply, swore even more deeply and tried it facing right.

The problem with this approach was that, although there were now some poor sidepulls, there were no footholds whatsoever. More slithering ensued. I tried it both ways and several times. Despite the coolness of the evening, sweat was pouring from my brow, my eyes were filled with specks of lichen and my clothing was becoming tattered. My fingers were bleeding, my arms ached and my mouth was, as they say down under, as dry as a dead dingo's donger. Worse, I was beginning to feel somewhat silly. But I couldn't not do it, or Ivan would have a field day and several drinks at my expense. Standing on my non-rest, I tried to examine the situation logically with studied calm. As usual, this proved totally hopeless. But years of experience in such situations had not been in vain – with my last protection point almost at waist-level any fool could see that another runner was called for. I udged back to my high point and vaguely waved a bunch of wires at a hidden hairline crack. One of them stuck and provided a modicum of Dutch courage. I recalled other chimneys I had known – Deer Bield Crack for instance – but this seemed far harder. I thought of Winking Crack at Gogarth where the secret had been simply to move further out of the crack than seemed possible without falling off. The pitches seemed similar in difficulty despite the grading difference and I resolved to try the same here. Another udge up, facing left. I reached down and grabbed my left ankle, wrenched it up and placed it on the good handhold – meanwhile jamming my right knee deep in the crack. My hamstrings twanged in protest, but at least now I could try taking my hands off . . . Ooooer! I tried again, this time managing to twist round and grab a small flat hold behind me. At this point my right leg slipped out of the crack and I spun round, dangling from the handhold. I tried to jump my right foot up on to some small dimple, but couldn't get it high enough. After several failures I let go of the hold with my right hand, grabbed the reluctant foot and heaved it on to the hold. A desperate manoeuvre, but it paid off – I was in balance and a few steep bridging moves saw me to the top.

It took two abseils to recover the gear, and what with taking the wrong path on the way down and having to get changed amid the puddles of the Old Dungeon Ghyll car park, we felt lucky to get to the venue with five minutes to spare. The dinner was as entertaining as usual, the average age on our table being, I would think, somewhere around the seventy mark, the food and beer as excruciating as ever, and the projector breaking down half-way through the lecture leaving the speaker to conclude bravely with 'Well, the next slide I would have shown you was . . .' I waited until the liqueur stage before I broached the subject most on my mind. . . .

'Oh, by the way, Ivan, I climbed your crack today.'

'Oh . . .' said Ivan mildly, 'did you enjoy it?'

'Er . . . yes . . . ,' I lied. 'When did you do it?'

'Oh, about 1930, with Jack Longland.'

'Did you lead it?'

'Yes.'

'On sight?'

'Yes.'

'Er . . . did you have any runners?'

'No . . . we didn't in those days, you know.'

'Did you find it difficult?'

'Not really, but I was quite thin then, I almost fitted in the crack. I suppose it was a little strenuous.'

'Oh . . .'

It was not only the cold autumn air which exerted a sobering influence as I left the hotel somewhat later that night.

Griffith Pugh

An 80th Birthday Tribute

MICHAEL WARD

(*Plate 75*)

It is a lucky man who finds himself in the right place at the right time, able to use all his talents to the full in order to make a major contribution. But PR was not the forte of this tall, flame-haired scientist whose work marked the start of modern high-altitude mountaineering. Our Honorary Member Griffith Pugh has never written his autobiography, but his life story is worth recording.

On 30 November 1989 only a handful of senior members of the Alpine Club were present at his 80th birthday party, but it was an occasion which the whole membership should celebrate with pleasure and gratitude.

Griffith Pugh, after reading Law for three years at New College Oxford, changed to medicine and qualified in 1938 from St Thomas's Hospital. During his student period he climbed over a number of seasons in the Mont Blanc range, the Engelberg and other regions and took part in University downhill, slalom and langlauf ski races. After competing in the FIS Downhill Championships at Innsbruck he was selected for the 1936 Winter Olympics in the 18km langlauf, but was unable to take part because of injury.

After one year's house jobs he became Medical Officer of a Territorial Battalion, the Bedfordshire Yeomanry, at the outbreak of war in 1939, and later joined the 26th General Field Hospital at the Radcliffe Infirmary, Oxford. Sent to the Middle East after Dunkirk, Pugh spent periods in Jerusalem doing tropical medicine, and in Athens where he saw many cases of frostbite during the Greek campaign. When the Germans invaded Greece, he was evacuated to Crete and then Cairo. From there he went to Iraq and, being fluent in German, escorted German refugees to the Turkish border. In the summer of 1942 he was in Teheran and Meshed looking after Russian children and Poles evacuated from Russia, and having to deal with a typhus epidemic.

In late 1942 he was summoned from Meshed at the request of the Chief Instructor, W J Riddell, to join the Ski Wing of the Mountain Warfare Training Centre at the Cedars of Lebanon, 2100m. (A D M Cox was the Chief Instructor of the Mountain Wing.) Individuals were sent from various units, some specialist such as the Long Range Desert Group (now the SAS), and others in the Middle East. Of these only 25 per cent were considered suitable for training.

Pugh remained at the Cedars until the summer of 1944 when he spent a short period as MO to the 44th Royal Tank Regiment in Sicily. However, between 1942 and 1944 he had also written a number of papers on personnel selection, fitness tests, load-carrying, nutrition and other relevant topics. The result was that, later in 1944, he was posted together with Cox and Riddell to

Whitehall where they wrote a series of training manuals covering every aspect of snow and mountain warfare.

Discharged from the army in 1945, Pugh went to see Professor John McMichael at the Postgraduate Medical School at Hammersmith, where he was given a job on the strength of his research work on mountain troops and his great and varied experience. This School was the intellectual powerhouse of British medicine and gained a worldwide reputation which it enjoys to this day. McMichael became an FRS for his work on heart catheterization, the forerunner of cardiac surgery.

In early 1950, partly as a result of the Korean War, the Medical Research Council decided to set up a unit to study the effects of extreme environments on man. Pugh was an obvious choice but, as he had never run a department, he was asked to name a suitable individual. He suggested O G Edholm, at that time Professor of Physiology at the University of Western Ontario, Canada, and towards the end of 1950 this unit, called the Division of Human Physiology, was established at the Medical Research Council Laboratories at Holly Hill, Hampstead.

In early 1951 Murray (leader), Bourdillon, Secord, Tissières and myself proposed a reconnaissance of the Nepalese side of Mount Everest. As Tom Bourdillon's father, Dr R B Bourdillon, was a member of the MRC scientific staff, he questioned me (an RAMC officer in London) about the medical problems and passed me on to Pugh. In early 1951 Pugh had pinpointed the major problems relating to cold and altitude, strokes, dehydration, starvation, effects of supplementary oxygen at high altitude and the beneficial effects of sleeping oxygen. During the 1951 Everest reconnaissance, now led by Shipton, Pugh in London considered how to solve these problems and came to the conclusion that, though much could be done in a laboratory, only field work would provide the optimum solutions. He therefore joined the Cho Oyu 1952 expedition on the understanding that all personnel and equipment would be assessed rigorously. In the event, work on the Menlung La only involved Pugh, Secord, Colledge and Bourdillon; and the fact that the other members played little part in this programme was a factor in Shipton's dismissal from the leadership of the 1953 Everest expedition.

In 1952, too, the Swiss made two attempts on Everest, reaching 8500m, and in his historic report on the Cho Oyu expedition Pugh accurately assessed the reasons for their failure. As a result of the work of Pugh, the Bourdillons and others, the 1953 Everest expedition became the first science-led modern high-altitude party.

Thus the template of the expedition had been accurately crafted and its structure and thrust established by the time Hunt was appointed leader in the middle of September 1952.

After the first ascent of Everest in 1953, this successful *modus operandi* enabled mountaineers world-wide to climb all the 10 highest peaks in the world during the following seven years. Later, with the surge in climbing talent, routes of increasing difficulty became viable, and intensive training led to the first ascent of Everest without supplementary oxygen.

In 1957 Pugh was asked to follow up his Himalayan research by carrying out work in Antarctica, and while there he conceived with Hillary the Silver Hut expedition 1960–61, which wintered for four months at 5800m in the Everest region. Whilst Pugh's work in the Lebanon and in the Himalaya so far had been consumer-orientated – that is, directed towards solving practical problems – this was an investigation into fundamental problems of oxygen transport. It has stood the test of time, is often quoted, and was the catalyst for a dynamic genre of research of increasing significance.

In the mid-1960s Pugh was approached by Kurt Hahn to investigate deaths occurring in young people taking part in adventure training in the British hills. With an average mortality of 30 deaths per year, this was a serious problem. In a brilliant series of field and laboratory experiments Pugh showed that the cooling effects of wind, movement and wetting could rapidly lead to exhaustion and hypothermia even in above-freezing temperatures. Some years later he was involved in the evaluation of athletes at altitude for the Mexico Olympics, the start of the burgeoning subject of Sports Medicine.

In his mountain work Pugh's philosophy was that *ideally*, in this type of field research, the investigator should be as competent, if not more so, than those he was working with, and that he should be able to climb, ski, carry loads and endure all the stresses alongside his team. For over a quarter of a century he lived up to this daunting discipline.

What has never been acknowledged is that he was as physically fit and as well qualified for the task in hand as any other member of the 1953 Everest expedition. Before it was fashionable, Pugh believed in training as it is understood today. More than once, in the friendliest possible way, he said on Everest that we were all amateurs. He was right.

Fame has come to many members of the Alpine Club, but few fully appreciate how much they owe to this redoubtable octogenarian – always ahead of rather than behind the times. Professionally Griff took the long view, provided against the worst and put his trust in knowledge. Since 1951 myriad climbers have been his beneficiaries. *Credite posteri!*

Mountain Medicine and Physiology: A Short History

MICHAEL WARD

(*Plates* 76, 77)

The story of man's attempts to climb higher and higher by his own unaided afforts is one of the most colourful and exciting in the history both of mountaineering and of medicine and physiology. The mountaineer at altitude acts as a model for those at sea-level with oxygen lack due to chronic heart and lung disease, and even the hill-walker, exercising for hours on end over consecutive days, may develop pitting oedema of the ankles, which is also found in a number of medical conditions.

At extreme altitude the mountaineer is exposed to some of the harshest conditions on earth, with temperatures of −50°C, winds gusting to 100mph and more, and – with the barometric pressure a third of the sea-level value on the top of Everest (8848m) – it is surprising that he can survive at all. That he is able to do so is due to a remarkable series of adjustments which enable the internal environment in which his cells live to remain constant. Claude Bernard (1813–78), Professor of Physiology in Paris, first drew attention to this stability: and it is fitting that Paul Bert, the founding father of altitude physiology, followed him in this, the most prestigious chair of natural philosophy in France.

Observations on the effects of high altitude date back many centuries. The Silk Road, which joined the civilizations of the Mediterranean with those of China and India, is the world's oldest, longest and most dangerous land trade route, and it is not surprising, therefore, that the first documented account of mountain sickness should come from Chinese sources, between BC37 and 32. This describes travelling south-west from Yarkand (Shache) to Afghanistan, passing the Great and Little Headache mountains, and alludes to vomiting in both man and cattle.[1] There is a later description of mountain sickness in the accounts of the well-known Chinese traveller Fa-Hsien (AD399–414), who travelled in the same area. He describes what may well have been a case of high-altitude pulmonary oedema, while crossing a high pass, for the victim frothed at the mouth and later died.

Considerable altitudes were also reached in Central and South America, for well-built pre-Columban structures have been found near the summit of Llullaillaco (6712m). These were not permanent dwelling places but were probably associated with mountain worship, since an Inca body has been found at a similar altitude. There is as yet no record of an Asian highlander reaching a comparable altitude until the end of the 19th century; the impetus for the exploration of the world's peaks, passes and glaciers had to await European and other western mountaineers rather than the indigenous inhabitants.

The clinical features of mountain sickness were described for the first time (in Spanish) by a Jesuit priest, Father Joseph de Acosta. His account is compelling and graphic, for he describes the 'casting up of meate, *fleugme*, and choller both yellow and greene'.[2] The local South American names for mountain sickness were Puna, Seroche, Mareo and Veta, and the cause was thought to emanate from the metal antimony. In some regions the vapours of rhubarb, primroses and roses were blamed. De Acosta, in an inspired deduction, thought that the symptoms were due to the 'thin air'.

In Europe the idea that air had weight and therefore exerted pressure on the earth's surface had to wait until the Renaissance for its full realization. It was Torricelli, a pupil of Galileo, who realized that the force of a vacuum was due to the weight or pressure of the atmosphere. An experiment, conceived by Pascal, proved that atmospheric pressure was less on the summits of high peaks, and this of course is the central problem of high altitude: for, as the atmospheric pressure is lowered, so is the oxygen pressure, and less oxygen gets driven through the lungs and less arrives at the cells.

In the 17th century, rumours of Nestorian Christian colonies led to Rome sending missionaries to Central Asia and Tibet. Probably the first European to enter Tibet was Father Andrade, a Jesuit priest, who crossed the Himalaya by the Mana Pass (5450m) in 1624. He, however, was more concerned with hypothermia than with hypoxia. Thirty years later, Fathers Gruber and D'Orville crossed the Tibetan plateau from north to south, visited Lhasa and then crossed the Himalaya. They commented, 'Man cannot breathe in the Langur mountains (Himalaya) because the air is so subtile.' There is a later reference in 1739, by Father Belligate, to the 'deleterious exhalations' found in the mountains. This may have been a reference to La-Drak, 'The Poison of the Pass', which was considered by Tibetans to be exhalations of mischievous Gods who caused earthquakes and avalanches, in addition to mountain sickness.

Mountain sickness was called 'Yen Chang' by the inhabitants of the Koko Nor region, and 'Chang Chi' in Szechuan. Both expressions mean a pestilential vapour thought to be given off by the large quantities of rhubarb that grow in the mountains. Another term was 'Tutek', described by Sven Hedin as occurring in gold mines in North Tibet. This appeared to be a long-standing and often fatal condition in which the victim's body swelled up, his lips turned black and mental disorder occurred. It is possible that this was chronic mountain sickness (Monge's Disease) which was first described by the South American physician Carlos Monge in 1925.

The exploration of the Himalaya began in earnest in the early part of the 19th century, and Paul Bert started his study of the effects of barometric pressure at this time. He collected accounts of altitude illness from all over the world and, in addition to his own work in decompression chambers, became interested in the opportunities available from balloon ascents for the study of altitude physiology. The first 350 pages of his classic work *La Pression Barométrique*, published in 1878[3] are the most authoritative early account of the history of the effects of decreased barometric pressure. His work did not go uncriticized, particularly by Angelo Mosso, Professor of Physiology at Turin, another considerable physiologist who was responsible for the construction of the Capanna Regina Margherita on the Punta Gnifetti (4556m) in the Monte Rosa massif. Rebuilt recently, this still serves as a hut and a laboratory, and is the highest hut in the Alps. Professor Mosso's book *Life of Man on the High Alps*[4] includes the first dramatic clinical description of high-altitude oedema and also an autopsy report.

The early volumes of journals published by the Alpine Club, starting with *Peaks, Passes and Glaciers* in 1859 and continuing with the *Alpine Journal*, contain a number of articles on mountain sickness. Spinal anaemia, dry air and fatigue were all implicated, and Longstaff, who made outstanding contributions to mountain exploration in the Nanda Devi region, on Gurla Mandhata, and who discovered the Siachen glacier in the Karakoram, was the first British mountain scientist to write a comprehensive treatise on mountain sickness. This was published in 1906.[5]

The end of the 19th century and the start of the 20th century saw the discovery of an increase in red blood cells at altitude. There were, in addition, three expeditions of outstanding importance. These took place in a period when there was great controversy over how the lungs worked: whether oxygen was secreted by the lungs or whether it diffused from the air through the lung walls into the blood vessels as a result of the force of atmospheric pressure. Ascent to high altitude would help to solve these problems.

Edward Whymper[6] in 1879 organized an expedition to South America, to observe the effects of low barometric pressure and 'to attain the greatest possible height in order to experience it'. He made many cogent observations on mountain sickness (as well as on other fields of science), and was elected a Fellow of the Royal Society of Edinburgh in 1894, despite his lack of formal scientific training.

The second expedition was that of Conway[7] in the Karakòram, and he acknowledged Whymper's work in South America, calling it a model of its kind. His party traversed the Biafo and Baltoro glaciers and he took recordings of his pulse at regular intervals by means of a pulse sphygmograph. In one reading, at 6100m, his heart rate was exactly half that taken at similar altitudes a few hours before and after. This may have been an incident of transient 2:1 heart block and it focused attention on the heart at high altitude.

The third expedition was that of the Duke of the Abruzzi.[8] His party reached 24,600ft (7500m) on Bride's Peak in the Karakoram and suffered little or no discomfort. However, he gives the first description of high-altitude deterioration, recording that 'the atmosphere of this height did work some evil effect revealing itself only gradually after several weeks of life above 17,500ft'. Later he made the categorical statement that 'perfect adaptation to the surroundings is not possible above 17,500ft', which was confirmed on the Silver Hut expedition to the Everest region in 1960–61. The ascent to 24,000ft amazed many physiologists, for it was thought that not enough oxygen could diffuse through the walls of the lungs at the low barometric pressure of high altitude, particularly when exercising, as such large amounts of oxygen are needed by the muscles.

The arguments in favour of diffusion put by Barcroft of Cambridge, and in favour of oxygen secretion by Haldane at Oxford, ranged over many years. In point of fact the early work in favour of diffusion had been carried out by Krogh in Copenhagen at the turn of the century, but had been 'lost' only to be rediscovered in the 1930s. Eventually Barcroft showed conclusively that diffusion occurred. He did this by having the main artery of his arm exposed by dissection and the oxygen pressure in the blood estimated at ever-increasing altitude. This was always lower than the pressure in the lungs, indicating that diffusion not secretion (when the pressure in the arm artery would have been higher than in the lung) had occurred.[9] The estimation of 'blood gases' is now routine in hospital.

In 1921, after years of prevarication, the government of Tibet gave permission for a British party to explore the northern Tibetan approach to Everest, since the more direct Nepalese southern approach was not feasible politically.

The individual who knew most about the geographical and physiological problems of altitude was Alexander Kellas, a lecturer in chemistry at the Middlesex Hospital Medical School. Before he went on the 1921 Everest reconnaissance he wrote a paper entitled 'A consideration of the possibility of ascending Mt Everest'. This was published in a little-known continental journal, following a meeting in Monte Carlo, and was probably never read by scientists or mountaineers in the UK. Luckily copies of his manuscript were deposited in the archives of both the Alpine Club and the Royal Geographical Society. An appraisal of this article can be found in the *Alpine Journal*.[10] Kellas's insight in asking the correct questions is uncanny and, although a number of his calculations were inevitably wrong, the paper was a landmark in high-altitude physiology. Had it been published in the UK, it might, at the very least, have prompted a careful examination of the scientific factors involved in attempts on Mount Everest.

The series of expeditions to Mount Everest between 1921 and 1938 gives a very important insight into the problems of high altitude and cold. The harsh clinical realities of oxygen lack were set out in each of the Everest books, yet there seems to have been a reluctance to accept the facts. Another important factor was the conflicting evidence from the use of supplementary oxygen. It is easy now, with hindsight, to understand these, but at the time it was not at all clear why some appeared to climb as well at great altitude without supplementary oxygen as with it. In practical terms, a height of 28,000ft (8500m) had been reached in 1924 and, since then, no one had gone any higher either with or without supplementary oxygen.

This was the position at the end of the Second World War. On Everest the post-war era started in the autumn of 1950 with the visit of the Houston party to Sola Khumbu, to which Tilman had a late invitation, the first Europeans to visit the Nepalese side of Everest. From the highest point that he reached on the Khumbu glacier, at Kala Pattar (5554m), Tilman took a photograph of Everest but was very pessimistic about the chances of a route. His pessimism was countered by research in the Royal Geographical Society, where good ground and aerial photographs, taken between 1933 and 1947, showed each section of a possible route up which the mountain was first climbed in 1953. Also important was a 1:50,000 'running' map, drawn by H F Milne of the Drawing Office at the Royal Geographical Society between 1933 and 1945, based on Spender's survey work on the north side of Everest in 1935, aerial photographs taken on the 1933 flight over Everest and other sources. On this map each detail of the eventual route – the Lhotse Face, Geneva Spur, South Col and Ridge and South Summit – were meticulously drawn, with spot heights. All this information was obtained before Shipton, the eventual leader of the 1951 Everest reconnaissance, was even aware that any expedition to Everest was planned.[11]

The provenance of the photographs and Milne's map will be discussed in the *Geographical Journal*.[12] In essence, however, the Holy Grail of Himalayan and mountain exploration, a possible new route up Everest from the south, was 'discovered' without setting foot outside London, always accepting that no route on any peak is feasible until one's nose has been rubbed against the rock and ice of which it is comprised.

In early 1951, too, Dr Griffith Pugh of the Medical Research Council started on the practical physiological problem of the ascent of Everest. As well as suffering from severe oxygen lack, it became apparent that mountaineers at great altitude were starved, severely dehydrated and suffering from cold injury, and some had had strokes. It was a daunting clinical picture that could be overcome only by adequate supplementary oxygen and attention to the detail of providing adequate insulation, good stoves and fuel. The problem was soon apparent, but the solution would require scientific work in the field at an altitude of 5200–5500m, as decompression chamber studies would be inadequate.

After the Everest reconnaissance in the autumn of 1951 had confirmed the existence of the route already identified by photographs and map, a training expedition to Cho Oyu in the spring of 1952 was led by Shipton, while the Swiss attempted Everest in both the spring and the autumn. Pugh joined the Cho Oyu party and, with Tom Bourdillon and two others, worked in a tented laboratory on the Menlung La at 5800m about 24km south of Cho Oyu. Pugh's 'Report on the Cho Oyu Expedition' was published by the Medical Research Council within weeks of his return to the UK in the early autumn of 1952: it revolutionized high-altitude climbing. It determined the organization of the 1953 Everest Expedition – started by Shipton and carried on by Hunt when he was made leader in late 1952. The flexibility provided by adequate supplementary and sleeping oxygen (used often for 18 hours out of the 24 above the Western Cwm) allowed mistakes in planning and execution to be overcome, and contributed overwhelmingly to the good general condition of the climbers. It is no coincidence that by 1960 every 8000m peak had been climbed following the precepts of this report. It is now in the archives of the Alpine Club.[13]

Following the first ascent of Everest by Hillary and Tenzing in 1953 using supplementary oxygen, there was still the tantalizing possibility that the mountain might be climbed without, for, after spending 40 days in a decompression chamber during Operation Everest I in 1946, Houston (in Florida) had exercised on a bicycle ergometer without using supplementary oxygen at an altitude higher than the 'summit of Everest'. However, the first ascent of Everest without oxygen had to wait until 1978.

The next landmark in field investigation was the Himalayan Scientific and Mountaineering (Silver Hut) Expedition to the Everest region in 1960–61, which involved the use of polar techniques. The expedition had Pugh as scientific leader, whilst the overall leader was Hillary who returned to New Zealand during the winter months when the scientific work was completed at 5800m. The results obtained during this period have been basic to understanding the chronic oxygen lack at altitude, and this carries over to other fields of medicine. This expedition also highlighted a number of diseases due to altitude, in particular vascular episodes, and high-altitude deterioration associated with cold injury.[14]

In 1960, in the US, Houston wrote a classic paper on high-altitude pulmonary oedema.[15] This condition had been described previously by Ravenhill, a South American mining doctor, in 1913, but the journal in which his article was published was rather obscure and knowledge of the condition was not widely disseminated. Houston's paper was the starting point of many investigations into fluid shifts in the body due to exercise and altitude.

In the UK during this period the increase in outdoor activities, particularly in hill country, had led to a number of unexplained deaths. As had occurred on Everest, Pugh again solved this problem by laboratory and field work. Essentially, the combination of wind, movement and wetting could and did lead to the hill-walker being exhausted and effectively without insulation, and thus inevitably hypothermic.

The next important milestone was the ascent of Everest by Habeler and Messner in 1978[16], without supplementary oxygen. A vitally important factor in explaining this feat, which had seemed impossible to so many mountaineers and respiratory physiologists, was the realization that the barometric pressure, and hence the oxygen pressure, on Everest was higher than had been previously calculated. This is because in the altitude range 6–16km (Everest is 8848m) there is a pronounced bulge in the barometric pressure near the equator in winter and summer. Since the latitude of Everest is 28°N, the pressure at the summit is considerably higher than it would be for a hypothetical peak of the same height near the Poles. The cause of the pressure bulge is a large mass of cold air in the stratosphere above the equator, brought about by a combination of complex radiation and convection phenomena. Also, the barometric pressure is higher in summer than in winter, and the first winter ascent of Everest without supplementary oxygen (by a Sherpa, Ang Rita) took place only in December 1987.

One of the most important scientific expeditions ever mounted was the American Medical Research Expedition to Everest in 1981.[17] It was led by West, a member of the Silver Hut team of 1960–61. For the first time physiological measurements were made at the summit, and a large number of investigations was completed. Perhaps the most controversial and potentially important finding was that of diminished mental function after a long stay at altitude.

Although sophisticated field studies are now possible and have been carried out by workers of many nationalities, there are still some important investigations too dangerous to be carried out in the mountains, such as estimates of the pressure in the chambers of the heart. These can be completed in a decompression chamber, and in 1985, after five years' preparation, Operation Everest II – a study at the US Army Department of Environmental Health at Natick, Mass – was completed by Houston and his colleagues. Volunteers were decompressed over 40 days and nights to the 'summit of Everest', and many of the findings of AMREE 1981 were confirmed and extended.[18]

One of the most obvious and important effects of high altitude is on breathing, and disordered or periodic breathing has been described, both at altitude and in desperately ill patients at sea-level. Tyndall's book *Glaciers of the Alps*, published in 1860[19], contains the first altitude reference, and Tyndall, whilst resting on the summit of Mont Blanc, was observed by his companion not to have breathed at all for a considerable period. Previous to this, in 1781, John Hunter[20], the father of scientific surgery, had written a crisp, accurate and laconic account in his case notes, now kept in the library of the Royal College of Surgeons of England. He writes '. . . but his breathing was very particular: he would cease breathing for twenty to thirty seconds and then begin to breathe softly, which increased until he breathed extremely strongly or rather with violent strength, which gradually died away until we could not observe that he breathed at all.' The first visual record of periodic, or Cheyne-Stokes, breathing was made by Angelo Mosso on a revolving drum at the Capanna Regina Margherita, and this condition is being intensively investigated in terms of control theory.

Another 'abnormality' of breathing, noted at altitude, is that whereas newcomers are breathing deeply and often, even when taking minimal exercise, the high-altitude resident is breathing quite easily. This is because the acclimatized resident has a blunted response to oxygen lack, which at first sight should produce less oxygen for the cells. This apparent contradiction may be associated with changes at cellular level, possibly the most important factor in acclimatization to oxygen lack.

Indeed, Paul Bert himself in 1878 wondered if the high-altitude dweller functioned better than the sea-level visitor. 'Just as the Basque mountaineer furnished with a piece of bread and a few onions makes expeditions which require of the members of the Alpine Club who accompany him the absorption of a pound of meat, so it may be that the dweller in the high places finally lessens the consumption of oxygen in his organism . . .'[21]

Surprisingly, then, the mountaineer, indulging in his arcane pursuit, thought at one time 'to be perfectly useless even to those that did it', now finds himself to be a useful individual, in particular to those who, due to illness, cannot climb at all.

REFERENCES

1 D L Gilbert, 'The first documented report of mountain sickness. The

China or Headache Mountain story'. *Respiration Physiology* 52, 313–326, 1983.

2 J de Acosta, *The Naturall and Morall Historie of the East and West Indies*, English translation by E. G. Edward Blount and William Aspley, London, 1604, p146.

3 P Bert, *Barometric pressure: researches in experimental physiology* (1878), translated by M A and R A Hitchcock. College Book Co, Columbus, Ohio, 1943.

4 A Mosso, *Life of man on the high Alps*. London (T Fisher Unwin), 1898.

5 T G Longstaff, *Mountain sickness and its probable causes*. London (Spottiswoode), 1906.

6 E Whymper, *Travels amongst the Great Andes of the Equator*. London (Murray), 1892.

7 W M Conway, *Climbing and exploration in the Karakoram-Himalayas*. London (T Fisher Unwin), 1894.

8 F de Filippi, *Karakoram and Western Himalaya 1909*. London (Constable), 1912.

9 J S Milledge, 'The great oxygen secretion controversy'. *Lancet* 2, 1408–11, 1985.

10 J B West, 'A M Kellas: Pioneer Himalayan Physiologist and Mountaineer'. *AJ*94, 207–213, 1989/90.

11 W H Murray, 'The Reconnaissance of Mount Everest, 1951'. *AJ*58, 433–452, 1951–52.

12 M P Ward and P Clark, 'The missing map and photographs of the Mt Everest Reconnaissance Expedition 1951'. *Geographical Journal*, in the press.

13 L G C E Pugh, *Report on Cho Oyu Expedition*. London (Medical Research Council), 1952.

14 L G C E Pugh, 'Physiological and medical aspects of the Himalayan Scientific and Mountaineering Expedition 1960–61'. *British Medical Journal* 2, 621–7, 1962.

15 C S Houston, 'Acute pulmonary edema of high altitude'. *New England Journal of Medicine* 263, 478–80, 1960.

16 R Messner, *Everest, expedition to the ultimate*. London (Kaye and Ward), 1979.

17 J B West, *Everest, the testing place*. New York (McGraw-Hill), 1985.

18 C S Houston, J R Sutton, A Cymerman, J T Reeves, 'Operation Everest II: man at extreme altitude'. *Journal of Applied Physiology* 63, 877–82, 1987.

19 J Tyndall, *Glaciers of the Alps*. London (Murray), 1860, p80.

20 M P Ward, 'Periodic respiration'. *Annals of the Royal College of Surgeons of England* 52, 330–4, 1973.

21 M P Ward, J S Milledge, J B West, *High-altitude medicine and physiology*. London (Chapman and Hall), 1989, p202.

A Few Thoughts on the Ethics of Climbing

GEORGE DVORSKY

The problem of ethics in climbing is not a new one, but recently it seems to have been attracting more and more attention. This is probably because the popularity of climbing and its fast development during the past decades have raised some controversial issues. In the Himalaya our sport has developed very quickly from the first pioneering steps of mountain exploration, through the era of the first ascents, to the present highly competitive approach. 20 years ago, a successful climb in the highest mountains on earth commanded our admiration. Today this is not enough, and we find ourselves evaluating what route was chosen, how large the team was, at which time of the year the peak was climbed, etc.

New technology has helped us to produce equipment which enables climbers to scale the most difficult mountain faces in alpine style, in small teams without large numbers of supporting climbers and high-altitude porters. We consider every spur, face or ridge potentially climbable, and it is only the highest mountains in the greater ranges that can today provide us with real challenges.

Alongside these developments there has been a vast increase in the number of climbers coming to the mountains. Superstition and fear of mountains are things of the past and our sport has been popularized through books, magazines and television. The time is also long since gone when most top climbers knew each other and, as a result, we hear about widely differing ideas, motivations and aims. Some clashes are inevitable and lively discussions take place about what is right and what is wrong. These often develop into full-scale debates about the ethics of climbing, about climbers' attitudes to each other and to the natural environment, and about what the unwritten rules governing our behaviour should be.

It is only natural that we all try to promote our own ideas on these matters – and there is nothing wrong with that. The philosopher Immanuel Kant said: 'Nobody can make me happy by forcing his own ideas of happiness upon me. Everyone should be free to find his own way to happiness, unless by so doing he obstructs others on their way.' If our own primary aim in coming to the mountains is to achieve personal satisfaction, or 'happiness', then we should not deny a similar satisfaction to others, even if their ideas and motivation are different. It is surely up to each person to decide whether he is climbing for his own inner contentment, for wider recognition, or for other reasons.

Climbing has one specific advantage over many other sports – it can bring fulfilment at widely different levels of skill. We probably all remember our first alpine route and the satisfaction it brought us; a great contrast to our feelings when we first hold a tennis racket in our hand. In tennis many hours of practice are needed before one gains enjoyment in one's skill, but I believe there is no intrinsic difference between the feelings of a beginner on an easy mountain route and those of a top climber reaching the summit of a Himalayan giant.

However, I am not suggesting that freedom in the mountains should have no limits. I see such limits defined by the last part of the quotation from Kant: '... unless he obstructs the freedom of others ...' That freedom refers not only to freedom of thought and expression but also to that paramount 'freedom' – the safety of others. And this is where I doubt whether we can depend for much longer on ethical, unwritten rules alone. With increasing numbers of people coming to the mountains to climb, it is unrealistic, where lives are at stake, to rely solely on conventional behaviour and goodwill. There should also be well-established and well-known rules.

The much-discussed tragedy on K2 in 1986 demonstrated the need for such rules; they would help to prevent a similar situation occurring again. We can no longer expect that our own team will be the only one on the mountain at any given time, and there will inevitably be more conflicts of interest between different climbing parties in the future. The kind of problems which are likely to arise – language problems, misunderstandings, conflicting arrangements – should not be allowed to endanger human lives. I believe it would be possible to work out a set of clear rules, so that in cases of conflict the answers would be at hand. The climbing community would be able to judge whether someone had broken these rules deliberately, and one would hope that sponsors would react appropriately. Discussion and debate in the outdoor magazines and climbing clubs could lead to the formulation of a set of fair rules binding everyone.

The clubs and periodicals have a similar task in dealing with the threat to the environment inherent in our sport. That is another example where 'the freedom of others' is relevant. If new equipment and technology allows us to climb even the most difficult terrain, it should also help us to remove all signs of our presence in the mountains.

I am eagerly awaiting the time when every expedition report announces that all used and unused equipment has been brought back to civilization and that Base Camp has been left exactly as it was found. Why should the next party have to camp on the smelling tip left by its predecessors, or stumble over the remains of old camps and fixed ropes? I know the descent is sometimes a fight for survival, but that is not always the case. Many parties manage to retrieve their most expensive pieces of equipment while leaving everything else behind. Anyone who has seen pictures of the much frequented Base Camps and of Everest's South Col, or has been to these places, will know what I am talking about.

Would it not be possible for the journals and magazines which publish the climbing reports to ask for details of what condition the route was found in by the expedition, and in what state it was left? That is another sphere where current behaviour is not good enough, and we should not hesitate to criticize those who endanger the very existence of our sport and 'our way to happiness'.

I believe that a positive response from the climbing community on these matters could change established attitudes and lead to some harsher measures when required. We could even exert pressure on countries which are less environmentally conscious than we are to stop issuing climbing permits to those who neglect the environment or break accepted rules of ethical conduct.

Perhaps Mountains should *not* be Climbed?

MIKE BURNS

Why climb mountains? The question is older than mountaineering itself and there are many possible answers to it, all arising from the fact that mountaineering is an addictive pastime which can be enjoyed in many different ways. This article, however, aims to show why mountains should *not* be climbed!

Mountains, especially high mountains, are among the few natural habitats left. They are affected by atmospheric pollution, such as acid rain or radiation, but compared with other environments they remain relatively untouched. Unlike many habitats, neither the living nor the non-living parts of mountains need active protection, except from people like ourselves. At best our presence has only a minimal effect upon the mountain environment, but any effect we do have will be an alteration to one of the few untouched natural habitats left.

Habitat damage may be minimal on a snow-capped peak, but often crampons scrape across rock which may be supporting lichen and moss plants, or heavy boots kick off a snowy foothold, taking with them some soil which is the home of plants and animals. We no longer like to place pitons if we can slot in a nut, but this sensible attitude to conservation may be prompted more by the wish to keep routes looking tidy for our own enjoyment than out of respect for the mountain itself. Mountains have survived intact because they are inaccessible and can only be tackled safely by properly equipped people such as ourselves. Alpine plants already have difficulty in surviving on their steep, unstable and climatically extreme habitats, and our feet are yet another factor which can do them nothing but harm.

The harmful effects of deforestation, which can only be worsened by trekking and mountaineering, are obvious to everyone. But dramatic, wide-scale deforestation for economic gain may, in the long run, be better than the slow erosion of forests, if it leads to more sensible forestry strategies in the future.

Cultural damage, or at least alteration, has been another adverse consequence of mountaineering on distant ranges. We, as mountaineers, have the power to influence endemic populations and their economies, although I suspect that the people of Nepal, for instance, would not complain of cultural change if it benefited their economy.

We consume a great deal of fossil fuel when we travel to distant mountains or even drive to the nearest crag, but perhaps we would use up just as much irreplaceable fuel and generate just as much atmospheric carbon dioxide whatever pastime we chose.

It is ironic that environmental awareness and concern have been unprecedented in the last 20 years, but so too has the rate of destruction. The Alpine Club promotes further damage by encouraging us to climb and by publishing a journal full of excellent articles and photographs which fire our imagination and enthusiasm. Our most knowledgeable and experienced members have probably done the most damage. The person who simply reads or talks about climbing does least disservice to the environment.

What therefore do I think we should do to help protect the mountain environment? Give up mountaineering, I suspect! Personally I cannot resist mountaineering and I'm a knowing sinner. At the same time, I know that there's a price to pay in terms of my over-burdened conscience.

One Hundred Years Ago

(*with extracts from the Alpine Journal*)

C A RUSSELL

(*Plates 78–81*)

> Heavy snowfalls in December had made the conditions rather different from the previous year, and a week's 'Föhn' wind made mountaineering at first impossible. So soft was the snow that it took us 8 hrs to get up the Faulhorn, which we had done the previous year in a little over three. Everything comes, however, to the man who waits – even mountains – and on January 6 our patience was rewarded by a change of weather, the precursor of as brilliant a week, I should think, in point of weather, as was ever seen at Grindelwald in winter.

The splendid weather, described by Theodore Cornish, which was experienced in the Bernese Oberland during the second week of January 1890 was immediately utilized by the climbing parties staying at Grindelwald, and within a few days several climbs of note had been completed. On 7 January C W Mead and G F Woodroffe, with Ulrich Kaufmann and Christian Jossi, made the first winter ascent of the Eiger, reaching the summit by way of the SW flank and W ridge. 'Much step-cutting was required, but otherwise there were no serious difficulties. The weather was so perfect that through the telescope of the "Bear" a guide could be seen on the summit in the act of striking a match in the approved Swiss fashion and handing it to his "Herr", who, after lighting his pipe, let it burn out.' On the same day Cornish, who on arrival at the Bergli hut had been disappointed to find that he could not attempt the Eiger from that direction, succeeded with Hans and Ulrich Almer in reaching the summit of the Jungfrau. On 8 January Cornish and his guides climbed the Gross Fiescherhorn, a feat repeated by the other party two days later.

In February W A B Coolidge and Frederick Gardiner arrived in Grindelwald where they enjoyed three weeks of fine weather. 'Bright sunshine gladdened our eyes every morning and lasted far longer than in January, so that we were not merely able to have our lunch in the open whenever we liked, but to lounge on benches outside the house, in both cases being forced occasionally to seek for shelter in the shade against a sun which was at times overpowering.' Coolidge, who recalled the charm of their arrival by sleigh, 'could not help regretting that this delightful three hours' drive will soon be entirely superseded by an hour's run in the train, as the railway up the valley is to be opened on July 1 next.'

First winter ascents were also completed in other districts. In the Bernina

Alps on 27 February W H Bulpett and J H Wainewright, with the brothers C C and H C Grass, climbed the E peak of Piz Palü in fine but intensely cold weather, with a bitter wind. Two weeks later, on 13 March, the summit of the Presanella in the Adamello group was reached by Orazio de Falkner and Count Armandi Avogli.

The winter sunshine was followed, in all regions of the Alps, by long periods of unsettled weather which, with the exception of one fine spell in July, continued without interruption to the end of the climbing season. Many routes on the higher peaks were out of condition throughout a summer which was notable for several violent storms, and all in all it was not the best of years for climbing. Nevertheless many determined parties were active in all the principal regions and a surprising number of new ascents were completed.

In the Mont Blanc range an early success was achieved by Ludwig Purtscheller who on 17 June made the first ascent, solo, of the distinctive aiguille above the Tour glacier which bears his name. On 23 July C H Pasteur, his two sisters Isabel and Mary Pasteur and Claude Wilson, with Auguste Cupelin made the first ascent and traverse of La Nonne, the lowest of the three peaks on the ridge between the Aiguille Verte and the Aiguille du Moine. A few days later, on 31 July, V Attinger, A Barbey and H Pascal, with Justin and Joseph Bessard reached the summit of the unclimbed Petit Darrey, above the Saleina glacier.

In the Arolla district a notable achievement, on 13 August, was the ascent of the N face of Mont Collon by John Hopkinson, with Jean and Antoine Maître. This climb, which had been planned by Jean Maître and was completed in ideal snow conditions, established the first of the three principal routes on the face. Five days later the same party – with the addition of Hopkinson's son Bertram – traversed to the E peak of the Petit Mont Collon after reaching the slightly lower W peak by way of the unclimbed NW ridge. Above the Arolla valley two routes on the Blanche de Perroc, the N peak of the Dent de Perroc, were climbed for the first time; the NW ridge on 28 July by Walter Leaf, G W Prothero and R L Nettleship, with Clemens Zurbriggen and Aloys Kalbermatten, and the NE ridge on 31 July by A G Topham, with the Maître brothers.

Elsewhere in the Pennine Alps the Leaf party, without Kalbermatten, reached the summit of Mont Pleureur above Mauvoisin by way of the unclimbed SW ridge on 23 July, and the first recorded ascent of the Petit Combin was completed on 25 July by Charles de la Harpe and E W Viollier, with Justin Bessard. To the east two new routes to the highest point of the Portjengrat were established; the E ridge by Moritz von Kuffner, with Alexander Burgener and J P Ruppen on 15 July, and a direct line on the W face by A F de Fonblanque and G F Berney, with Xaver and Moritz Imseng on 11 August.

In the Bernina Alps the outstanding achievements of the season were undoubtedly those of Ludwig Norman-Neruda who with Christian Klucker completed three major new routes in the space of ten days; the first ascent – and descent – of the NW face of Piz Scerscen on 9 July; an ascent of the unclimbed NE face of Piz Roseg on 16 July; and, on 18 July, the first direct ascent of the NE wall of Piz Bernina. The last of these routes was completed in deteriorating weather and after being caught in a severe thunderstorm high on the N ridge of Piz Bernina the party endured six hours of unpleasant descent to the Roseg valley. Addressing the Alpine Club in the following year, Norman-Neruda explained that he had wished to attempt the climb on Piz Scerscen but would not have thought of the other routes

> . . . had not the conditions of snow and ice, which caused 1890 to be called a bad year for climbing, enabled us to do much we should have had to leave undone under more generally favourable circumstances, for in our ascents of the Piz Roseg and the Piz Bernina we had to conquer steep, in many places quite exceptionally steep ice slopes which at other times, in a good mountaineering season, would in all likelihood present insurmountable difficulties. But we found at nearly every point a sufficient coat of snow covering the ice, and steps had scarcely ever to be cut through the snow into the ice, as would infallibly have been the case in a dry summer, and often half a dozen kicks were enough to produce as many steps; consequently the work necessitated by step-cutting was not only of a comparatively little fatiguing nature, but we got through it in time to reach our two goals – the summit and our own comfortable bed – the same day we had started.

All three climbs were remarkable for the period and the ascent of the NE face of Piz Roseg, an impressive ice wall 700m high, was not to be repeated for more than 30 years.

Norman-Neruda and Klucker then moved to the Zermatt district where on 31 July they made a determined attempt to climb the NNE face of the Dent Blanche, reaching 3900m before dangerous snow conditions and icy rocks forced a retreat by way of the ENE ridge. On the following day, after traversing the Wellenkuppe, this formidable party made the first complete ascent of the ENE ridge of the Ober Gabelhorn and on 9 August, with the addition of Joseph Reinstadler, reached the E summit of the Lyskamm by a direct route up the unclimbed NE face.

Four other climbs completed during the season are worthy of note. In the Dauphiné on 24 July Alfred Holmes, with Maximin Gaspard and Basil Andenmatten, made the first ascent of the Pic du Glacier Carré below the Grand Pic of the Meije, and in the Mont Blanc range on 28 July the Pic Sans Nom, on the ridge between the Aiguille Verte and the Aiguille du Dru, was climbed for the first time by the guideless party of Ellis Carr, G H Morse and J H Wicks. In the Dolomites, also on 28 July, Hans Helversen with Sepp Innerkofler succeeded in completing a route up the unclimbed N face of the Kleine Zinne or Cima Piccola di Lavaredo. On 8 August Robert Hans Schmitt and Johann Santner, without guides, made the first ascent of the highest point of the Fünffingerspitze or Punta delle Cinque Dita. In his account of the climb Schmitt, who was regarded by Coolidge as 'a remarkable personality among the most daring climbers of his day', wrote that it was by far the most difficult which he had ever undertaken and issued a challenge to other parties to retrieve his card from the summit.

On Mont Blanc a famous landmark was established when Joseph Vallot, with the assistance of 110 guides, constructed his first observatory on the rocks of the Bosses ridge.

> It consists of two rooms, one for ordinary travellers, the second reserved for the storage of instruments and the use of observers. The traveller's room is warmed by an oil-stove, and well furnished with rugs. The building is a wooden framework with loose stone walls piled round it, and the roof is well furnished with lightening conductors.

In August an early visitor to the new hut was Dr Janssen, the celebrated astronomer and the President of the French Alpine Club

> . . . who, being lame, was dragged to the summit of Mont Blanc on a sledge. M. Janssen's principal scientific object was to determine, by means of spectroscopic observations, the presence or absence of oxygen in the solar atmosphere. Briefly, M. Janssen considers it an established fact, from his observations, that oxygen is absent from the solar atmosphere. Physicists may or may not agree as to the sufficiency of proof, but no doubt the contribution to the settlement of a most important and difficult question – one affecting the very existence of life on our planet – is very valuable.

One of the first climbers to visit the hut was Achille Ratti – the future Pope Pius XI – whose party completed a traverse on Mont Blanc on 1 August.

The storms which occurred during the last two weeks of August were severe, and a violent gale on 19 August forced the Janssen party to remain in the Vallot observatory for three days before the ascent could be continued. A week later a second terrible storm claimed a tragic victim. In an appeal made in the *Daily Graphic* on 20 September, Edward Whymper recalled that

> . . . when telegrams came in, about three weeks ago, stating that Jean-Antoine Carrel had died from fatigue on the south side of the Matterhorn, those who knew the man scarcely credited the report. It was not likely that this tough and hardy mountaineer would die from fatigue anywhere, still less was it probable that he would succumb upon 'his own mountain'. But it is true.

During the night of 25–26 August Carrel, the great guide who with J B Bich had made the first ascent of the Matterhorn from the Italian side, died of exhaustion on the lowest rocks of the mountain after safely bringing his party down through the storm from the hut on the Italian ridge. Generous provision for Carrel's family was made in response to eloquent appeals by Whymper who, in his book *Scrambles Amongst the Alps*, had written that Carrel 'was *the* man, of all those who attempted the ascent of the Matterhorn, who most deserved to be the first upon its summit. He was the first to doubt its inaccessibility, and he was the only man who persisted in believing that its ascent would be accomplished.'

On 14 December the death occurred of Gottlieb Studer who 'in the course of his life made more than 600 ascents over 10,000 feet. These extend over the period from 1825 to 1883. At the age of 68 he ascended Mont Blanc, and at 78 the Matterhorn.' In a tribute to Studer, one of the original members of the Swiss Alpine Club, Coolidge noted that

> . . . by the death of Gottlieb Studer the Alps have lost their most devoted friend, for no one (save Mr. John Ball) has ever known them as thoroughly as he did, or has done as much to make them known to others. He was elected an honorary member of our own Club in July 1859, the first foreigner to receive this honour, to which certainly no one had a better right.

In the Caucasus exploration of the range was continued by several parties and a number of climbs were completed. In August J G Cockin and H W Holder, accompanied by Ulrich Almer, made their second visit to the central chain. Starting from bases in the southern valleys they scaled three unclimbed peaks in the Adai Khokh group including on 26 August Adai Khokh or Uilpata (4638m), the highest summit, by way of the SE ridge. In his account of the climb read before the Alpine Club in the following year, Holder described the approach to the ridge across the large undulating snowfield at the foot of the peak.

> At this time the sky was almost cloudless and the sun shone brilliantly; the snow glittered and sparkled like diamonds. The magnificence of the snowfield, surpassing anything we had previously seen, profoundly impressed us all. Silently we marched, each possessed by his own thoughts and feelings, and gradually the heat, the glare, and the monotony of the march began to tell, and we almost fell asleep as we finished this part of our journey. There was no crevasse to stumble over; nothing to strain our energies; no demand on skill and previous experience: simply a steady tramp through the snow.

The party then attempted to reach the unclimbed W and higher peak of Jangi Tau (5051m) from the south but were forced to retreat late in the day from a point high on the route.

> We worked up rocks till five in the afternoon. We calculated we had still two hours' work before us, as there were steep and difficult rocks to be surmounted ere we reached the final slope of ice or snow. Most reluctantly we concluded that the only prudent course was to abandon the climb. We were soon benighted, spent the greater part of the night in descending by lantern-light, and at very considerable risk, the rocks we had easily climbed by daylight.

A F Mummery, who had made the first ascent of Dykh Tau (5204m) two years earlier, explored a number of valleys to the south of the central chain with his brother-in-law W J Petherick, but no ascents of note were recorded. Other visitors were George Yeld and G P Baker, who while exploring the eastern end of the range in perfect weather climbed Bazar-Juzi (4480m) in Daghestan on 22 August, and Vittorio Sella who with three Italian porters again travelled extensively, making a number of ascents in the central region. Although bad weather interfered with Sella's photographic work on several occasions, he was able to obtain some fine panoramas of the central chain from the south, ten different views of Ushba and many photographs of the southern valleys and villages.

Further afield, P W Thomas explored part of the San Juan range in the Colorado Rockies and on 1 September, with N G Douglass, ascended a peak which he identified as Mount Wilson (4342m). Following a detailed study of Thomas's description, it has since been suggested by local authorities that the summit he reached was, in fact, that of the neighbouring peak now named El Diente (4315m).

In Canada the facilities provided by the Canadian Pacific Railway Company were enabling an increasing number of climbers to investigate the peaks of the Selkirk range. The principal achievement of the season in this region was the first ascent of the imposing mountain originally named Syndicate Peak but renamed Mount Sir Donald after Sir Donald Alexander Smith, later Lord Strathcona and Mount Royal, who five years earlier had performed the 'last spike' ceremony to complete the transcontinental line. Starting from the Glacier House Hotel the Swiss climbers Emil Huber and Carl Sulzer with Harry Cooper, a young man engaged as porter, spent a miserable night in the open after their tent had been 'placed upon the top of a bush in order to secure it against the teeth of the many ravenous rodents which abound in those mountains. Already before, the mosquitoes, which pestered us in the Selkirks, had forced many an uncouth word from our lips, but in such thick swarms as here they had never tortured us.'

On 24 July Huber and Sulzer continued the climb to make the first ascent of Uto Peak (2930m). 'Directly opposite us the shadowed, dark, really magnificent figure of Mt Sir Donald towered into the sky, mounting with a sudden leap 1,000 metres from glaciers and heaps of debris to a lofty peak.' Two days later the whole party reached the summit of Mount Sir Donald (3297m) by way of the SW face and the SE ridge. After a stiff climb up rough rocks with good holds the ridge was followed 'partly along its uppermost edge, partly along the shelving of the west flank. Many a difficulty was overcome, but the peak always approached nearer and nearer. We were sure of it by this time, and a little after 10 o'clock a loud "Hurrah S.A.C.!" burst forth into the blue sky.'

The tent had been provided by H W Topham, who had returned to Glacier House with his two porters after making the first ascents of Mount Donkin (2955m) and Mount Fox (3224m), the peaks named by the Rev W S Green in memory of W F Donkin and Harry Fox whose expedition to the Caucasus two years earlier had ended in tragedy. Other peaks in the Selkirk range climbed for the first time were Mount Selwyn (3357m) by Topham and H E Forster; Mount Sugar Loaf (3271m) on 14 August and Mount Purity (3187m) on 29 August by Topham, Forster and Huber; and Swiss Peak (3205m), also on 29 August, by Sulzer and a porter. All the peaks were difficult of approach and on one occasion a pack-horse 'which growled like a bear' had to be left behind 'for it was impossible to get him through the tangled forest'.

Topham later recalled that 'we had great difficulty in forcing our way through the dense undergrowth, which renders walking below timber-line almost impossible. There is one golden rule to be observed in the Selkirks: "Keep above timber-line."'

Interest in the Canadian mountains following the completion of the railway was increased by the publication during the year of Green's book, *Among the Selkirk Glaciers*, in which he gave vivid descriptions of his own experiences in the range.

A number of expeditions of interest was undertaken in other distant regions. In East Africa on 17 February a party including F J Jackson and Ernest Gedge reached the crater rim of Mount Elgon (4321m) on the Kenya-Uganda border, and in the Southern Alps in December G E Mannering and Marmaduke Dixon reached a point only 40m below the summit of Mount Cook (3764m).

At the end of June Francis Younghusband left Simla on another of his adventurous journeys, having been commissioned to investigate the Pamir region. After crossing the Karakoram and staying at Yarkand Younghusband and his companion George Macartney, afterwards British Consul-General at Kashgar, spent the month of October exploring a large area of the Pamirs, crossing several high passes and camping beside the Great Karakul lake before descending to their winter quarters at Kashgar. 'This is a fine lake more than a dozen miles in length, and the day on which we reached it it presented a magnificent spectacle. A terrific wind was blowing, lashing the water into waves till the whole was a mass of foam. Heavy snow-clouds were scudding across the scene, and through them, beyond the tossing lake, could be seen dark rocky masses; and high above all this turmoil below, appeared the majestic Peak Kaufmann[1], twenty-three thousand feet in height.'

At home two first ascents by ladies are worthy of note. In the Lake District on 31 March Miss D J Koecher, her brother O J Koecher, H B Dixon and A M Marshall made the fifth ascent of the Napes Needle. On the Isle of Skye at Whitsuntide Charles Pilkington and his wife Mabel traversed the Inaccessible Pinnacle, the highest point of Sgurr Dearg, as members of a party led by C T Dent. Interest in rock-climbing, which had been growing for some years, was increased considerably by the publication in the *Pall Mall Budget* on 5 June of an illustrated article on the Needle, giving details of how it might be climbed.

During the year W M Conway published the *Climbers' Guide to the Central Pennine Alps*, the first of a series of Alpine guide-books developed from his *Zermatt Pocket-Book* which had appeared nine years earlier. The guide, produced in collaboration with Coolidge, was soon in demand and was reviewed in the *Alpine Journal*:

> The present instalment covers the ground from the Great St. Bernard to the Theodul, Mr. Conway having (as he with perhaps somewhat brutal frankness admits) divided the book at the latter point in order to make it necessary for climbers settled at Zermatt to buy both volumes. The method is much the same as that of the original 'Pocket Book', except that more attention is paid to bibliography, wherein we may doubtless see the hand of Mr.

> Conway's collaborator; the arrangement is somewhat altered. Formerly it was by districts; now it is rather by ridges. In its present form, in short, the book treats rather of the ways in which to reach given points, than of the point to be reached from a given place; and so far may be regarded as illustrating the author's sentiments in regard to 'centres'.

On 4 March, in a paper entitled 'The Dom from the Domjoch' read before the Alpine Club, Conway had initiated one of the great debates of the time in climbing circles by attacking 'centrism' – the practice of climbing habitually in the immediate neighbourhood of a chosen centre. After continuing to attack the practice throughout the year, Conway set out his views in a further paper 'The Exploration of the Alps' read before the Club on 15 December, part of which appeared later in the *Alpine Journal* under the title 'Centrists and Excentrists':

> Broadly speaking, I assert that the man who wanders amongst the Alps (or any other large range or set of ranges) is more easily able to keep his eye alert and his mind fresh for the appreciation of the various forms and kinds of beauty which mountain regions offer, than can a man who makes excursions around a centre. Few parts of the world are richer in beauty than a great mountain area, crowned with snow, draped in ice, buttressed by splintered rock, founded on the broad bosom of the earth, and framed in the emerald glories of verdant meadows and mysterious forests. Great is the educational value of mountains to the aesthetic sense; but he that would experience it must open his mind to all the pleasures of the hills. The man who knows only one kind of mountain, only the surroundings of a few centres, does not know even the Alps.
>
> I conclude, therefore, that, except for the gymnast and the man who climbs merely for the sake of enjoying dangerous adventure (and who therefore cares only for the most difficult rocks, which nature kindly arranges in the immediate neighbourhood of a few centres), the excentrist's method of visiting mountain ranges is the best. The Alpine wanderer is more likely to profit by his expedition than the centrist, and I maintain that, in the present condition of affairs, wandering deserves to be practised and encouraged by members of the Alpine Club.

It is fitting that the conclusion to this account should be provided by Conway, the true excentrist and one of the great explorers of his day:

> Members of the Alpine Club are now to be found in almost every great mountain region in the world. They have recently not only flocked to the Caucasus, but they have penetrated into its remoter districts. Daghestan has now been photographed. The Selkirks, in North America, have been further explored. Renewed attention has been paid to the great mountains of Mexico. Moreover, this extension of the mountaineering range is not the result of a

spasmodic and exceptional effort; it is a normal and continuous growth, and may be regarded as merely the promise of greater developments to come.

REFERENCE

1 Now Pik Lenin (7134m).

Correspondence

Bisney Cottage
Shamley Green
Guildford
Surrey GU5 OTB

The Editor
Alpine Journal

15 June 1989

DO MOUNTAINEERS LIVE LONGER?

Sir,

Casual conversations reveal a common belief that 'mountaineers live longer'. A glance through *AJ* obituaries reinforces this belief, and it stimulated W W Naismith to make a brief study (*AJ*34, 266–7, 1921). Of the 16 whose age at death was recorded, the average age on joining the Alpine Club was 37. The Institute of Actuaries was quoted as giving 29.6 years as the expectation of life of a 37-year-old healthy man. Naismith calculated that the 16 lives had had an average increment of about 3½ years beyond this expectation.

In the mid-1970s I made a more detailed study than Naismith's, because my impression was that the average prolongation of life might be significantly more. The correct way to design such a study is a prospective one, that is, to start now with a large population of mountaineers and a matched population of non-mountaineers, then wait until all members of both populations are dead before analysing the data relating to each person's life, cause of death, and age at death: hardly a practicable proposition. I therefore settled for a pseudo-prospective study by using the whole membership of the Club as listed in the 1930 list, and following each, from the Club's records, through the next 45 years.

So far as I could ascertain, virtually the whole membership then belonged to, or in a few years entered, the Registrar-General's Occupational Classes I or II. The Registrar-General's Occupational Mortality Tables in his decennial supplement of 1930–32 recorded life expectancy for men in these two categories to be very close, so, for purposes of comparison, they were averaged. This reference standard was based on data derived from the England and Wales census of 1930, and this had to be taken into account in making a comparison. I assumed that figures in these Classes for Scotland would be similar and that any small difference would be negligible, bearing in mind the small proportion of AC members living in Scotland. I decided, however, to reject from the 'population' of mountaineers those who had spent most of their Club membership life abroad. I also excluded those killed in the Second World War, as the compilers of the reference tables could not have taken into account this future hazard when calculating life expectancy. Naturally I had to exclude those whose records were incomplete, which included those who resigned (most resignations were during the first years of the Great Depression and during the War). The *only two* killed on a mountain were included. All this reduced the 'population' to 334 men ranging in age from 30 to 80+, those aged 20 to 29 being only three and hence too small a cohort to subject to statistical analysis.

The results are shown in the table:

Age (yrs) at 1930	*Average deviation from life expectancy (yrs)*	*Number in this age range*	*P*
30–39	−4.4	17	NS
40–49	+2.7	56	0.05
50–59	+2.7	109	0.005
60–69	+3.9	103	≪0.001
70–79	−5.5	38	NS
80+	−0.68	11	NS

(P is the probability that the result is an example of random fluctuation, e.g., in the 50–59 age group, if 1000 similar studies were made such fluctuations would be expected to give this degree of average increase in life span in five of them, i.e. the increase is highly likely to be a real one. NS means 'not significant' and no conclusion can be drawn. The number of individuals in these age ranges was small and there was a remarkable spread of years greater, and less, than their life expectancy.)

These results confirm the general belief, but the average life increment is remarkably similar to Naismith's findings. This is not the place to analyse the results of the many published studies relating life style to longevity. During the last two decades this has been a popular topic for research and the literature is correspondingly vast. From this one factor stands pre-eminent: family history. If a person comes of a stock notable for delayed ageing and long life, then, apart from infection and accident, that person will probably follow the family pattern. Such predisposition can, of course, be overridden by unhealthy habits, particularly dietary ones. Another factor common to many studies is the favourable effect of exercise and particularly of such exercise as produces in the individual 'endurance fitness'. This is exactly the type of fitness a mountaineer has to maintain if mountaineering is to be enjoyed.

So it is almost self-evident that, on average, a life-long mountaineer can expect a longer life than the average citizen, and a study to establish this with the rigour of experimental design which would satisfy a professional epidemiologist would be a waste of time. We must not forget that the ability to be an active mountaineer for most of one's life is likely to be one of the consequences of

)0. *Mustapha climbing in the Gully, in the Ourika Valley.* (Dennis Gray) (p 125)

)1. *Painted Rocks, Tafraoute, Morocco.* (John Beatty) (p 125)

62. *Ron Fawcett climbing at Tafraoute, Morocco.* (John Beatty) (p 125)

63. *Dennis Gray setting out to rescue Ihad, Tafraoute, Morocco.* (Dennis Gray) (p 125)

64. Ol Doinyo Lengai from the Engare Sero River. (Peter Payne) (p 133)

65. Jonathan Preston on Mt Hunter W ridge, day 1. (Roy Ruddle) (p 145)

56. *Mt Hunter W ridge. Camp at 9000ft, day 2.* (Roy Ruddle) (p 145)

57. *Mt Hunter South peak, from Base Camp. The sunlit ridge (R) is the SW ridge – our descent route.* (Roy Ruddle) (p 145)

68. *Crux buttress section of 'Eroica', Mt Hunter, seen from the glacier.* (Roy Ruddle) (p 145)

69. *Jonathan Preston on the S face of Mt Hunter.* (Roy Ruddle) (p 145)

70. *Jonathan Preston resting below the crux of the buttress. Mt Hunter S face.* (Roy Ruddle) (p 145)

71. *Ivan Waller in Dovedale on the day he climbed Westmorland's Route, 1985.* (Stephen Reid) (p 184)

72. *Stephen Reid, exhausted, at the top of Waller's Crack.* (Jill Reid) (p 184)

factors which also predispose to a longer than average life. The second is not necessarily a result of the first. 'Correlation is not causation.'

Yours faithfully,
Edward Williams

Easter Torrans
Tomintoul
Ballindalloch AB3 9HJ
Scotland

The Editor
Alpine Journal

27 November 1989

GEORGE TRAILL (1792–1847)

Sir,

While recently visiting St Magnus Cathedral in Kirkwall, I came across a marble monument prominently placed in the S transept near the entrance to the choir, to the memory of

George William Traill,
born 1792, Bengal Civil Service, died 1847,
for many years District Commissioner, Kumaon,
where his memory is of a wise and benevolent ruler.

Bells began to ring in my memory. This must be the eponymous discoverer of Traill's Pass, one of the very earliest mountaineers, as opposed to explorers or surveyors, in the Himalaya. Back home, from a rapid reference to Kenneth Mason's *Abode of Snow* and Tom Longstaff's *This My Voyage*, I elicited the following facts. During his period of service as District Commissioner in Kumaon which ended in 1835, Traill made his way from Gwaldam up the Pindari valley to cross this 5400m pass slung between Nanda Devi East, to the NW, and Nanda Kot, to the E. He then descended the Lwanl glacier and the Lawan Gad (below the pleasant camp-site of Narspan Patti, later used by Longstaff), to emerge in the Gori valley at Martoli, some 16km below Milam. This was in 1830, and it was a remarkable achievement to have crossed a pass which is still held difficult under certain conditions today.

Reports have it that the Schlagintweits crossed this pass in the 1850s, but the next recorded passage was not until 1926, this time from N to S, by Hugh Ruttledge, another District Commissioner in Kumaon (and later leader of the 1933 Everest Expedition), together with General R C Wilson, on their way back from a lengthy exploration of the Kailas area of Tibet.

Meanwhile, in 1905, Longstaff had been active in the area, reaching the rim of the Nanda Devi basin from the E, and climbing high on the NE ridge of Nanda Kot, but not actually touching Traill's Pass. A Japanese party completed Longstaff's route on Nanda Kot in 1936, returning over Traill's Pass to the Pindari valley; they were guided by Dewan Singh of Martoli, who had been over it with Ruttledge 10 years earlier.

Traill's Pass was evidently not only an interesting short cut for District Commissioners setting out from their headquarters in Almora to visit the upper Goriganga (and on to Tibet), but also a key factor in attempts to enter the Nanda Devi Sanctuary over the rim, before the classic way was forced up the Rishiganga gorge, first by Longstaff *en route* to Trisul, and then by Shipton and Tilman on their reconnaissance of Nanda Devi in 1934.

I found Traill's Orcadian ancestry less easy to trace. His ancestors came north with the Stewart Earls in the 16th century and were allotted the island of Rousay as their territory. The 18th-century Traill laird was one of the few Jacobite lairds on Orkney, who all sought refuge after the 1745 Rising in the 'Gentlemen's Cave' on the neighbouring island of Westray. The male line of Traills petered out in the mid-19th century, and a General Burroughs who had also served in India and made money there married the last Traill heiress. (I cannot ascertain whether this was George Traill's sister, daughter or niece.) George Traill himself was probably born in the modest house at Westness, which General Traill Burroughs, as he now called himself, abandoned to engage the well-known Victorian architect David Bryce to build the ungainly pile of Trumland House. Burroughs earned a reputation as an exploiter of his island, reducing crofters to labourers and in other ways incurring the censure of Orcadians, using methods of which the 'benevolent despot of Kumaon' would certainly not have approved.

Yours faithfully,
Edward Peck

Buck Croft
Felsted
Dunmow
Essex

The Editor
Alpine Journal

29 December 1989

EVEREST: THE NE RIDGE

Sir,

And so the pinnacles on the NE ridge of Mount Everest have been crossed; but the entire ridge has not yet been climbed.

I wonder how many people know that in the thirties, on Everest, we used affectionately to refer to this ridge as 'Finch's Folly', because legend had it that in 1922 George Finch, that great mountaineer, had suggested that it might be the best way to the summit. Certainly not the easiest, as we now know. But what about *the best*?

Just as the W ridge, in those days, was known as 'Hazard's Folly', for the same reason; nowadays it has fallen to the onslaught of modern mountaineering.

But now, as an old mountaineer, somehow or other I wish that Nature would occasionally triumph over Man. I don't like to think that there is nothing left for us to look for round the next corner: 'For lust of knowing what should not be known.'

I don't really want our great Past-President's ridge on Everest to be climbed.

Yours faithfully,
Charles Warren

AREA NOTES

COMPILED BY A V SAUNDERS

South America 1989

EVELIO ECHEVARRÍA

A distressingly long period of dry weather established itself over most of the world's equatorial regions and areas adjacent to them, reaching as far as 30° latitude north and south. This 1989 drought was ascribed to what the Americans have termed the 'green-house effect', the warming in weather patterns due to the accumulation of automobile and industrial fumes. Several Andean countries were hit hard. Entire valleys were left without water, since their streams simply dried up. Small glaciers and minor névé-fields that still characterized some peaks and high valleys disappeared altogether. Cerro Tolosa (5370m), that landmark of the Mendoza valley in central Argentina, so well known to climbers, seems to have shed about one-half of the glacier that covered the western side. It is not known exactly what impact this long drought has had, or will have, over glaciers and snowfields around the world. The 1989 skiing season (June–September) did not begin in Chile until mid-August and in Argentina until the end of that month.

Otherwise, the general picture of Andean mountaineering has remained much the same as described in Area Notes in the last few years. One great addition has been female mountaineering, which from the viewpoint of high mountain climbing is receiving an increase comparable only with what is practised in some Eastern European countries. Chilean and Argentinian women have been leaders, but representative women from all the other five Andean countries have been constantly participating in prolonged expeditions, as well as in advanced technical climbing. On the political side, peasant and guerrilla attacks have remained at fairly much the same level as in the last few years, although such activity moves from one area to another. The Arequipa region in southern Peru, particularly the long and wide Colca valley, has now been declared unsafe, while the Ayacucho district is now 'safe'. Similarly, Bolivia, a country hitherto wholly safe, is now being infiltrated by Peruvian fighters who are also training their Bolivian counterparts. The area around and south of Illimani was in 1989 less safe than in the last few years. To face this problem, the author recommends the only two solutions that are viable at present: foreigners are advised to travel in rather large groups and to hire a local climber or guide, not a simple camp guard. Local guides are usually experts in local conditions, will do their best to obtain reduced costs and estimates and will solve the language problem. Furthermore, they are generally expert climbers, some having earned their diplomas as guides in the Alps or in Spain.

The activities listed below belong to the calendar year 1989, unless otherwise stated. The bulk of this information came from the Editor of the *American Alpine Journal*, Prof H Adams Carter, from friends in Argentina (Marcelo Scanu, Claudio Bravo, Luis A Parra), Ecuador (Freddy Landázuri), and at times some reports were collected by the author himself when travelling in South America.

Ecuador

Two new routes on well-known mountains were reported by Freddy Landázuri, editor of Quito's *Campo Abierto*. On Cotopaxi (5897m) climbers have always taken a detour from north to west to avoid the 'Yanasacha', a wall of volcanic rock that bars the way on the normal route. On 1 August, Ecuadorians Eduardo Agama, Danilo Mayorga, Jorge Peñafiel and Emilio Salgado went up the north route, climbing over the Yanasacha along the way. Because of the instability of the rock, this north side direct route was not recommended. Tungurahua (5005m) had its SW flank and S ridge climbed for the first time by Paolo Catalán and Alfredo Mensi (26 February). This mountain is usually ascended by the N side, where the Refugio Nicolás Martínez is situated.

Peru

In spite of many reports declaring the Cordillera Blanca district a target for violence on the part of peasants and guerrillas, the magnificent peaks of at least the northern half of the range continued to receive enthusiastic visitors. New routes, if not new peaks, were the main events. Two Peruvian climbers, members of the young Club de Montañeros Américo Tordoya, were apparently the first to scale the very steep SW face of Tocllaraju (6032m), the beautiful ice peak that is one of the main goals for visitors to the Ishinca valley. The route was climbed by Mario Masuelos and Gonzalo Menacho on 21 July. Other new routes opened in the Cordillera Blanca included one on the SW face of Huantsán (or Huanchán), 6395m, by four Frenchmen who, however, could not finish the last 50m on account of the unstable ice (23 July); another was done by four Spaniards, among many existing variants on the dreaded S face of Ocshapalca (5881m), east of the Grassi route; and still another new route was by three Italians on the SE face of Vallunaraju Sur (5640m).

A Scottish party that had set its aims in the Cordillera Huayhuash travelled to the Cordillera Vilcanota in southern Peru instead, so as to avoid attacks by political groups. It claimed the first ascent of three peaks over 5200m situated west of Ausancati, but these may already have been ascended by Basques in 1977. Another group of five from Sheffield, led by Simon Cooke, achieved the first ascent of Colquecruz V (which this expedition reported as

5965m high); it was climbed at the second attempt, by its N face (29 July). The same party made a new route on Colquecruz VI (5970m) by its NW face (25 July). (*Editor's Note.* Simon Cooke was climbing with his right wrist in plaster, having broken the wrist while soloing in the UK two weeks before departure for Peru. He reports that the wrist 'didn't prove to be too much of a hindrance, but did require some modifications, with a hacksaw to fit through my duvet jacket arm and into a Dachstein glove'.)

Bolivia

Since the Cordillera Apolobamba appears isolated enough from the mainstreams of human activity, rightly or wrongly it has been declared by mountaineers themselves to be safe for visitors. The 1988 Smith expedition of the Yorkshire Ramblers' Club was no doubt the cause of two parties from Great Britain coming to the same area in 1989. A three-man group from Bath University climbed the N ridge of Nevado Cololo (5915m). In the Area Notes of last year this route was mistakenly reported as having been ascended by the Smith party, which had in fact used the W ridge. Other ascents by the Bath group were Nevado Nubi (5710m) and Palomani Grande (5768m), the latter almost certainly by a new route, the SW ridge. The second expedition was launched by the Loughborough Students' Mountaineering Club and did the following ascents: Iscacuchu (5650m), second ascent; Huerancollac (5836m), traversed; Cololo (5915m), W ridge; Mita (5500m) and unnamed peaks 5375, 5370 and 5305m.

In the Cordillera Real, Bolivia's greatest range, a North American expedition from Seattle, led by John Hessburg, placed its Base Camp in the neighbourhood of the great peaks of Chearoco and Chachacomani and climbed the latter (6094m) by a new route. The Seattle group tackled 'the crazily cracked north-eastern icefall, about two miles of weaving crevasse work, then traversed up the east ridge' over to the N face and on to the summit. The same party made the second ascent of 'Dome 2', which on this occasion was renamed Nevado Dómine (5708m). Also in the same Cordillera two European groups climbed the W face of Nevado Huayna Potosí (6088m). Austrians Erich Gatt and Martin Wolff did a somewhat zig-zagging variant up the face and had to bivouac close to the summit at −25°C. The same face was visited a month later by Frenchmen Patrice Gabarrou and Yves Astier who scaled it directly; surprisingly, Astier reported warm temperatures and unstable weather. In south-central Bolivia, immediately south of Illimani (which marks the southernmost end of the Cordillera Real), is the Cordillera de Quimsa Cruz. Evelio Echevarría accomplished on foot, alone, the circumnavigation of the range, entering along the way several unvisited valleys and realizing the first ascents of Curicampana del Sur (5200m), Anco Collo (5460m) and the second of Ñuñu Collo (5215m). Weather was stable but cold; on the Amazonian side of the range mists entered the higher valleys in the afternoon (June).

Argentina

The main South American events for the calendar year 1989 took place in the Argentinian Andes and were the work of local mountaineers. Starting with the district of Ojos del Salado, we have the meritorious results of the expedition sent by the Club Andino Tucumán to the area located south of the highest volcano in the world. Leader of the six-man party was veteran Dr Orlando Bravo (65). On the summit of Cerro Chango (4650m) two of the members found scattered wood, probably left in pre-Columbian times by Calchaquí Indians. Luis Salinas and Claudio Bravo attempted Nevado del Cazadero (6660m), but were chased down by deep snow. The same pair, however, made on 12 January the first ascent of Cerro 6050m, situated in the Arenal valley. They named it Cerro Gendarme Argentino; two other members of the expedition repeated the ascent the following day. The leader and Jorge Madozzo made the second ascent of the imposing Volcán del Viento (6200m), climbed by Poles in 1937. Salinas and Claudio Bravo made another ascent, the second of Cerro Nacimiento II (6460m), also climbed previously by Poles, while Antonio Fons and Madozzo were at the same time reaching the summit of Nacimiento V (6320m), hitherto unclimbed.

Farther south, the exceedingly young climbers of the Club Andino Mercedario have been exploring the area inland from their city of San Juan. Taking advantage of the newly opened international road over the Agua Negra pass to Chile, these youths, led by Marcelo Scanu, made several forays during 1989 that resulted in the first ascent of Nevado de Pismanta (5400m) and the twin summits of Nevado de Bauchaceta (5036 and 5100m). An attempt on Negro Aspero (5500m) failed in a blizzard. The San Juan mountaineers are almost unique in South America in that they manage to climb high mountains in any season.

Luis Alberto Parra, the well-known Mendoza guide, summarized the 1988–89 Aconcagua mountaineering season as follows: heaviest activity concentrates on the mountain between early December and end of January; although Aconcagua is visited and climbed all year round, activity outside those six or so weeks greatly decreases; there were 52 expeditions or parties from the United States, 33 Argentinian, 21 German, 20 Spanish, 16 French, 11 Japanese, and the rest distributed among several countries from Latin America and Europe. The 'speed record' by the normal route (base to summit) established in six hours and 15 minutes by the German Michel Dacher was reduced by two minutes in January 1989 by the American Marty Schmidt. Two other noteworthy ascents in Mendoza province were also on very high peaks: Tupungato (6550m), by its SE gully and SE ridge, in only six days from the city of Mendoza and back, by the Argentinian guide Gabriel Cabrera and the Spaniard Mariano Muñoz (28 January); and Cerro de la Plata, the 5860m-high giant that overlooks the pampas, first winter ascent of the steep E face of the N peak, by José Arboleda and Eduardo Ferllén (12 September).

An unknown number of lesser Mendoza peaks, ranging between 4000 and 5400m, remain unclimbed. They have been left alone for a variety of reasons: lack of notoriety or importance, problematic access (mostly swollen rivers in the climbing seasons), rather modest height by Argentinian standards and, above all, poor quality of rock. Even in the Aconcagua Provincial Park such peaks can be found. In February last year an Italian party from Venice ascended an unnamed peak in southern Mendoza and named it Cerro Piré (height and location so far unknown). Evelio Echevarría, travelling alone into unvisited valleys situated north and south of Las Cuevas, on the international road to Chile, climbed in January the peaks he named Peñascoso (4180m), Peñas Amarillas (4400m) and Morro Overo (4437m). The local rock was confirmed as extremely unstable.

The 'Andes Australes', as Chileans and Argentinians call their Andes that fall within Patagonia and Tierra del Fuego, registered an activity that more than ever concentrated only on a good rock-climbing area – the Chaltén district. The following remarkable climbs were noted for the climbing season of December 1988–March 1989:

Attempt on Cerro Pollone (2396m), W buttress, to 100m below summit;
El Mocho (1980m), new route on left side of E buttress;
Torre Innominata (2501m), first ascent of N spur;
Aguja Poincenot (3036m) a variant of normal route; and
Aguja Guillaumet (2539m), SE face; all by Michel Piola and Daniel Anker (Switzerland).

Aguja de la Silla (2978m), E spur, and
Aguja Bífida (2450m), N face, both by Horacio Bresba (Argentina) and Peter Lüthi (Switzerland).

Torre Innominata (2501m), normal route, third ascent (?), by Carlos Domínguez (Argentina) and Peter Lüthi (Switzerland).

H Adams Carter also received from the Argentinian Alberto Tarditti lists of other ascents that are mostly repetitions of normal routes: three climbs of Cerro Torre (Americans, Spaniards and Poles), and numerous ascents of Fitzroy by Italians, Argentinians, Basques and Swiss. All the Patagonian activity reviewed above took place on the Argentinian side of Patagonia.

Józef Nyka adds:

Patagonia: Aguja de l'S

A four-member party from Bulgaria led by Alexandr Ruevski intended to climb Fitzroy but had to cancel this plan because of bad weather. Two members of the team took advantage of a calmer day to make a (probably) new route on the SE/E face of the Aguja de l'S in the St Exupéry ridge. In four hours of climbing up to UIAA IV+ to V− in difficulty they reached the top. The whole enterprise took them 14 hours (up and down). The climbers were Miroslav Sevilevski and Valentin Trenev.

The E face of the Aguja de l'S was climbed in 1987 by the Austrians Hans Bärnthaler and Ewald Lidl (400m, UIAA VI). They gave no further details of their route, which seems to be different from that of the Bulgarian ascent.

David Hillebrandt adds:

First Ascent of Roncagli (2300m) (Cordillera Darwin, Tierra del Fuego, Chile)

David Hillebrandt, Julian Mathias and John Mothersele made the first ascent of this magnificent peak by its NW ridge to the N summit in a 20-hour push from an advanced glacial camp. It gave about 1200m of sustained mixed climbing at about TD. The top was reached on 14 January 1990. This was the fifth British expedition to visit the area and attempt the peak. The line climbed had originally been attempted in 1988 by Iain Peters and David Hillebrandt, after they spotted it as a possible route on this complex peak during their ascent of Pico Ohi.

The expedition was in the area for just under a month. It also made a first ascent of Pico Payes de Galles to the east of the Stoppani glacier.

Morocco 1989

HAMISH M BROWN

(Plates 82–84)

The mountains of Morocco are steadily growing in popularity with British climbers, walkers and ski-mountaineers. This is due both to the quality of the mountains themselves being better known, and to a combination of easy travel, cheapness and freedom from bureaucracy.

Half a dozen UK tour operators offer trekking holidays which cover not only the over-popular Toubkal area, but also the Central (M'Goun) Massif, the Jbel Saghro, the Anti-Atlas, Siroua and the Tichka Plateau above Taroudant. Most are sensitively run and as an introduction to an area can be useful. 'Knowing the ropes' is not easy in Morocco, and time-conscious visitors don't want to waste days over organization. The trekking offered there is as good as anywhere in the world, especially in the spring when the vivid colours and snowy mountains make life among the Berber hillmen a memorable experience.

The Moroccans themselves are now becoming well-organized (the Alps must have been like this 80 years ago), and several professional guides can set up everything required for trekking and climbing almost anywhere: booking hotels, laying on transport, providing mules, food, etc. (Some addresses are given below.) This can save a great deal of time, effort and hassle and in the end is little more expensive than doing one's own thing throughout.

The availability of mules facilitates ski-mountaineering, a side of the game neglected by the British and rather slavishly followed by continentals *en masse* only in the Toubkal area. A traverse of the Central Atlas, the big hills beyond Toubkal, peaks west of the Nfis like Erdouz and round the Tichka Plateau all offer good ski-mountaineering. A few days warm-up at the small resort of Oukaïmeden is recommended. The Middle Atlas (cedar forest country) offers good *langlauf* touring but the snowcover is unpredictable.

Jbel Toubkal (4167m), being the highest peak in all North Africa, is the great lure and the Marrakech-Asni-Imlil-Neltner-Toubkal trail is a busy one and provides the worst of hassles. This notoriety is superficial, however, and if one stays at Imlil rather than just bombing Toubkal then the charms soon come through. The other huts at Tachddirt and Lepiney offer far finer rock-climbing or winter climbing, yet are largely unvisited by British climbers. Rock-climbing on untouched faces is there for the picking in every area and, given the sunny climate even in winter, deserves far more attention. I'd be happy to advise on areas to visit.

Trekking below the snowline in spring in the Toubkal area is rewarding. In the last few years I have worked out a whole pattern of such walks using huts, bivouacs and local houses, and usually ending at one of the gourmet hotels on the Tizi n' Test road!

For some years we have used a house above Imlil as base. This gives greater freedom and the owner, Aït Idir Mohammed (address below), can organize mules etc., circumventing the Imlil hassle. *Ribat Tours* office at Imlil can also provide information.

The authorities have stopped the ready availability of maps on 'security' grounds. As they want to attract tourists, this seems a short-sighted restriction and one of considerable inconvenience to climbers and trekkers. To help a bit, I have prepared illustrated notes to climbing Toubkal and on the area's trekking (see below).

Mountaineers will find spring, March to May, the most rewarding period. Alpine gear is needed then. June to September can be very hot below the mountains but is the popular trekking period for the tour operators, as the high passes (*tizis*) are all open. (Burnt-up and snowless, with vast screes, the hills are, however, far less attractive.) From October to January the weather is very unstable, in February it begins to improve, and this is a good time for the Saghro or Anti-Atlas. West of the Tizi n' Tichka pass Atlantic weather applies and the hills are lived in year-round; east of the pass the weather is 'Tibetan' and transhumance occurs. Winters can produce fierce winds and cold.

The Toubkal Massif is well-enough described in Collomb (qv) and the non-Neltner-based areas are especially recommended. Those wanting things organized a bit could contact Asquarray Lahcen BP 5 or Aït Idir Mohammed, BP 26, Asni (par Marrakech). The guardians at Tachddirt or Lepiney can also help with mules etc from those villages; the latter lives at Tizi Oussem and has rooms for hire.

Local Guides: Asquarray Lahcen (and the *Ribat* Tourist Office at Imlil) or Aït Idir Mohammed (see above), and there are a dozen more listed on the notice board at Imlil. One can simply arrive and fix things on the spot. These guides also lead trips to the other ranges listed, and vice versa.

Central Atlas, culminating in Irghil M'Goun, the only 4000m summit outwith the Toubkal region, is frequently visited by British parties. March to April is best for skiing, May is good, June bearable, then it is arid and hot. Trekking parties operate into June and also in September–October. Easiest access points are the Bou Goumez valley, Demnate, Telo et-Anemiter. Traversing N to S to the Ourzazate-Errachida road is recommended. Winter can produce severe storms.

Local Guides: Mohammed Achari, Douar Iskatafen, Aït Bouguemez, Bureau Tabant (par Azilal).

Jbel Sarhro is never wet and in summer is desert, hot and best avoided. February to April and October to December are the best months. Nights can be frosty, even if days are hot. Dramatic rock towers and memorable trekking have seen this called 'the Hoggar of Morocco'. There are no reports of British climbs and only a few French ascents. Iknioun and east from Agdz are the easy approaches.

Siroua A remote, solitary extinct volcano south of the Toubkal Massif which is seldom climbed by British parties. It has a unique atmosphere and deserves a visit. There are water problems in summer. It is usually reached from Taliouine or Aoulouz, and Lac d'Ifni and Toubkal can also be reached from these bases. The best times are February to May and September to November. It is desert hot in summer.

Local Guide: Jahid Ahmed, Auberge Souktana, Taliouine.

West of Nfis Some big peaks, snowy till late (ski options) with deep valleys, ragged crests and offering largely untouched rock-climbing. Entry from Tizi n' Test road: Ijoukak, Mzouzite or the pass itself. The area is seldom visited (even by Imlil guides) and demanding. Best information in Peyron. Avoid October to February.

Tichka Plateau A strange 'lost world' place with superb trekking and plenty of untouched climbing. Hot approaches in summer but modified at height. Best avoid July, August, October to January. Approaches from Imi n' Tanoute or Timesgadiouine on Agadir-Marrakech road (N) or via Taroudant (S).

Local Guide: Tali abdel Aziz, BP 132, Taroudant (or via the souvenir shop in NE corner of Place Assarag).

Anti Atlas The centre is Tafraoute. An area of fantastic granite formations and big rock peaks above the Ameln valley. There is wide scope for all interests. A few trekking companies alone operate regularly.

Middle Atlas An area of rolling cedar forests and extinct volcanoes, this is primarily an area for *langlauf* ski touring. Snow-cover is unpredictable. Two small ski resorts at Mischliffen and Bou Iblane. Spring trekking would be rewarding. It is little visited by foreigners. East again are ranges with no English references – but see Peyron.

Addresses of Tour Companies Trekking in Morocco

Pioneer Expeditions, 105 Hanover Street, Edinburgh EH2 1DJ.

Waymark Holidays, 295 Lillie Road, London SW6 7LL. (Treks include the area above Taroudant.)

Explore Worldwide, 7 High Street, Aldershot, Hants GU11 1BH.

Exodus Expeditions, All Saints Passage, 100 Wandsworth High Street, London SW18 4LE.

Sherpa Expeditions, 131A Heston Road, Hounslow, Middx.

Guerba Expeditions, 101 Eden Vale Road, Westbury, Wilts BA13 3YB.

Ribat Tours, 3 Ave Moulay Youssef, Esc B No 15, Rabat, Morocco. (Or BP 24, Imlil, Asni, par Marrakech.)

Marrakech to Imlil

Marrakech offers accommodation from the 5-star de luxe *Mamounia* to local hotels in the alleys off the Jemaa el Fna, youth hostel and camp-site. The *Hotel Ali*, Rue Mouley Ismael is much used by walkers and climbers, and the

Moroccan guides. Reliable hot water, good Moroccan food, usefully situated just off the Fna, facing the Place de Foucauld with town buses (No 1 to Gueliz – new town) and *petits/grands taxis* handy. *Hotel de Foucauld*, Rue El Mouahidine is just across the square and the *Tazi*, Rue Bab Agnaou round the corner.

Ten minutes walk from the *Ali* takes one to the Bab er Rob (gateway), outside which buses and communal taxis go to Asni, as and when they are full. A 'place' cost 10dh in 1989, you may be asked for more as a try-on. Taxis are faster and less hassle. A shuttle service (taxi, minibus, *camionette* or truck) operates from Asni to Imlil (10dh). Saturday is very busy due to the local *souk* (well worth a visit), other days you may have to wait an hour. *Grands taxis* can also be hired from the Fna but are much more expensive.

PERSONAL NOTE

I have spent several months at a time, most years since the early sixties, in Morocco; my enthusiasm grows, if anything, year by year. I have put together notes on Toubkal and the spring trekking almost in self-defence as I receive so many requests for information. These, and the Morocco chapter in *The Great Walking Adventure*, should help with the most popular area; the notes above hint at other areas. If further information is wanted I would be happy to help. Sometimes I have maps or publications available. More rarely I may be free to organize or lead small parties to specific areas or for specific interests: skiing, climbing, trekking, bird-watching, botanizing, etc. I also have an extensive Moroccan library and archive collection, a vast library of pictures, and can make study facilities available. Contact H M Brown/Atlas Information, 21 Carlin Craig, Kinghorn, Fife KY3 9RX, Scotland (Tel 0592–890422). The only comparable collection is held by the Alpine Club Library. Please enclose a SAE whenever writing to either.

BIBLIOGRAPHY

The following are useful sources, mainly on the mountains and related subjects, with some background titles as well. Many are out of print or in journals/magazines, so a visit to a specialist library may be needed (see above).

T J Abercrombie, 'Morocco'. *National Geographic*, June 1971.
'Atlas 1969'. *AJ75*, 148–149, 1970. (Aioui etc.)
'The Mountains of Morocco'. *Appalacia*, December 1974, pp 46–65.
N Barbour, *Morocco*. Thames and Hudson, 1965. (Standard work still.)
H Brown, *The Great Walking Adventure*. Oxford Illustrated Press, 1986. (Chapter specifically written with a first visit to Morocco in view, including Toubkal.)

Travels. Scotsman Publications, 1986. (A piece describing a trek down the Agoundis valley in the Toubkal Massif.)

'M'Goun Revisited'. *Scottish Mountaineering Club Journal 33*, 434–441, 1987. (Central Atlas with an ascent of Irghil M'Goun.)

'The Ridge of Dreams', *AJ92*, 150–155, 1987. (Multiday, high-level traverse from near Toubkal along the Iferouane and Taska n' Zat ridges to near the Tizi n' Tichka.)

AJ71, 43–50 and 275–280, 1966. (Rock climbing in the Toubkal area – possibly the only such descriptions in English.)

Treks and Climbs in the Toubkal Area. Pettycur Publishing. (Available from Atlas Information, address above.)

'About Irghil M'Goun and the Bou Goumez'. *AJ84*, 3–10, 1979.

'A Hard Day's Night'. *Scottish Mountaineering Club Journal 28*, 305–308, 1967. (Winter ascent on Aksoual.)

B Clarke, *Berber Village*. Longmans, 1959. (Students studying village life.)

P Cliff, *Ski Mountaineering*. Unwin Hyman, 1987. (Has chapter on *The Moroccan Haute Route*. No glaciers but demanding terrain for the experienced ski-mountaineer. Huts and bivouacs. February to May.)

T v Clarmann, *Der Hohe Atlas*. Wandern, Klettern und Skibergsteigen in Marokko. Munich, 1984. (Useful sketch-maps of Toubkal area.)

R G Collomb, *Atlas Mountains Morocco*, revised edition. West Col, 1987. (Standard guide.)

C Cominelli, *Ski dans le Haut Atlas de Marrakech*. 1984. (Useful sketch maps of Toubkal area.)

B Domenech, *Le Maroc. Les Plus Belles Courses et Randonnées*. Denoél, 1989. (A Rébuffat-style, comprehensively illustrated, coverage which makes it essential for any area, especially outwith the Toubkal massif. Stocked in the UK by Cordee.)

D Dourron, 'Jbel Sarhro'. *La Montagne*, No 1–1989.

J Dresch and J de Lépiney, *Le Massif du Toubkal*. 1938. (Thorough pre-war guide, only in libraries.)

M Ellingham and S McVeigh, *The Rough Guide to Morocco*. Harrap Columbus, 1988. (By far the best practical guide. It is kept updated. Good historical survey, bibliography.)

A Fougerolles, *Le Haut Atlas Central: Guide Alpin*. 1981. (Many maps and pictures make this useful.)

E Gellner, *Saints of the Atlas*. Weidenfeld and Nicholson, 1969.

R Gilbert, *Young Explorers*. York, 1979. (School summer visit.)

R B Cumminghame Graham, *Magreb-el-Acksa*. 1898. (Recently reprinted.)

D Gray, 'Moroccan Odyssey'. *AJ95*, 125–132, 1990/91 (this volume).

W Harris, *Morocco that Was*. Eland Books. (*Times* correspondent early this century. Writes entertainingly.)

J D Hooker and J Ball, *Journal of a Tour in Morocco and the Great Atlas*. Macmillan, 1878. (Botanists' trip but made some early explorations and ascents; interesting reading still.)

S Kay, *Morocco*. Namara Publications, 1980. (Glossy pictures *and* informative text.)

C Kininmonth, *Traveller's Guide to Morocco*. Cape, 1986. (Excellent on history.)

La Montagne: Has many references. The following are the more important and useful: December 1968, February 1971, No 2–1973, No 1–1977, No 2–1981, No 4–1985, No 4–1986, No 1–1989.

O Logan, *Al Maghrib, Photographs of Morocco*. Polygon, 1989.

R Mailly, *Villes et Montagnes Marocaines*. 1964.

G Maxwell, *Lords of the Atlas*. Longmans, 1966. (A Century paperback of this classic work is available.)

B Meakin, *The Land of the Moors*. 1901. (Reprinted Darf Publishing, 1986.)

D Mill, 'The Crossing of Ighil M'Goun'. *Scottish Mountaineering Club Journal* 30, 130–135, 1973.

W Noyce, 'Climbing Solo in the High Atlas'. *AJ*67, 65–72, 1962. (Romps which few will equal, even today.)

A Paccard, *Traditional Islamic Craft in Moroccan Architecture*. Editions Atelier, France, 2 vols. (Huge tomes, magnificently comprehensive.)

R Parker, *A Practical Guide to Islamic Monuments in Morocco*. Baraka Press, USA, 1981. (Good survey of all sites.)

M Peyron, *La Grande Traversée de l'Atlas Marocain*. Rabat, 1984. (Revised 1988.) *Great Atlas Traverse Morocco, Vol 1*. Moussa Gorges to Ayt Bon Wgemmaz. West Col, 1989. (Indispensable volumes. The English one is based on the French but is a new work; vol 2 will cover eastwards to Midelt, the Middle Atlas and Jbel Sarhro.)

D Porch, *The Conquest of Morocco*. Cape, 1986. (Turn-of-the-century take-over bids.)

K Reynolds, 'The High Atlas'. *Off Belay* 39, 21–23, June 1978. 'On Trek in the Atlas'. *Great Outdoors*, February 1987. 'A Pilgrim in the Atlas'. *AJ*93, 155–160, 1988/89.

K Smith, *The Atlas Mountains, A Walker's Guide*. Cicerone Press, 1989. (Mainly concerned with the Toubkal area and circuits in the M'Goun and Jbel Sarhro mountains.)

Teuler and Chraibi, *Ait Imi, Morocco of the Heights*. 1986. (Beautiful picture-book on the Bou Goumez.)

T Weir, 'Spring Climbs in the High Atlas'. *Scottish Mountaineering Club Journal* 26, 138–147, 1957.

Yorkshire Schools Exploring Society, *High Atlas*. 1980. (Wide-ranging report, on trips based below Toubkal.)

East Africa 1989

ANDREW WIELOCHOWSKI

New Routes

Recently the numbers of mountaineers visiting East Africa has grown considerably. Many repeat the old classic routes on the main summits, but ever more are searching out more adventurous itineraries, exploring less well-known summits and venturing into more remote areas to sample the mixed delights of 'bush-climbing'.

On Mount Kenya a new line, Diamond Natasha, has been climbed on the Diamond Buttress. This beautiful rock wall has already provided some of the most magnificent, hard rock climbs in East Africa, and this route has been reported to provide more excellent pitches on perfect rock. The route starts up easy rocks at the right side of the buttress, crosses Southern Slabs, then tackles a line of cracks and corners forming a characteristic letter 'Z' between the Diamond Buttress Original Route and Southern Slabs. These provide several pitches of grade V–VI climbing. A bivouac was taken before tackling the upper section of the buttress; two pitches beyond this the Southern Slabs route was rejoined. The ascent was made in late February 1989 by two Polish climbers, Krzysztof Gwozdz and Zbyszek Wach.

The best time for climbing on the Diamond Buttress (maximum hours of direct sunlight) is in mid to late December. At this time it is also often possible to catch the Diamond Couloir in condition. In January 1990, an unusually late period of very bad weather over New Year allowed the Diamond Couloir to remain in good condition well into the month.

A few new routes have been pioneered on the minor peaks, amongst them a fine corner system on the nose of the Krapf Rognon.

There has been little recorded activity on Kilimanjaro. The glaciers continue to recede, but so far no good rock has appeared as a result! The Breach Wall Icicle, climbed by Messner, is still there. The Heim glacier, however, has suffered from recession; the lower sections are rubble-strewn and breaking up, but with a good snow-cover it could still be an excellent lower-grade snow and ice climb. Under good snow conditions an adventurous walking route up to the crater is by the Oehler ridge and Pengalski glacier; be careful to traverse right immediately after the Ravenstein to avoid ice cliffs.

Only one new climb has been recorded in the Ruwenzori. This is a suspected first ascent of the remote peak Rugendwara, 4300m, by N Woodward, M Wynne-Jones, A Rathmell and S Crofts. The major achievements of this ascent were the ability to find the mountain in the first place, and then to find a way up through the deep, vertiginous vegetation, slimy slabs and eternal mists.

The great cliffs of Poi in Northern Kenya have been revisited but not reclimbed. Attempts at new routes have so far been repulsed, and the East Face route has also repulsed several parties attempting a second ascent. A few bolts have made the lower half of this route safer, and the short aid pitch has all the aid in place now. A few bolts would make the upper half of the route much more pleasant (no bolts were placed on the first ascent).

Bush-climbing cliffs ideally involve no climbing up bushes. Bad route choice can, however, result in this activity living up to its name. Not just bushes, but cacti, thorns and vines adorn certain cliffs which, together with the armies of ants, swarms of bees, snakes, scorpions, vultures and eagles defend fine lines from would-be first ascensionists. The name really comes from the location of the cliffs in bush country such as the Tsavo Game Park, where the bushes are obstacles mainly on the way up to the cliffs. After a particularly dry spell, walking in bush country is considerably easier along the many game trails which have been pushed through the bush – elephant are particularly good path-makers.

Kitchwa Tembo in Tsavo National Park has been visited several times and has had its reputation established as one of Kenya's best bush-climbing areas, with several excellent hard rock-climbs in magnificent settings on cliffs up to 300m high.

Nearer to Nairobi the outcrops at Lukenya have been revisited by axe-men and landscape gardeners. As a result some magnificent outcrop routes have been discovered in the modern style – top-rope inspections with bolts placed where considered essential. Slightly further from Nairobi the cliffs at Hell's Gate are now in a National Park with good camp-sites providing easy access to the climbs.

General

The rate of deterioration of the Tanzanian economy appears to be slowing, and some services are actually improving. Devaluation of the shilling has not made entry to Kilimanjaro any cheaper, as all park entry charges have to be paid at the Marangu Gate in foreign exchange.

On 1 January 1990 some of the park charges went up almost 300 per cent. Each day's camping anywhere on Kilimanjaro now costs $55 per person. Huts on all routes other than the Marangu tourist route are charged at this camping rate. Marangu route charges are $30 a day; these include hut charges. No adequate explanation for this strange charge system has been provided. During the peak New Year period overbookings were commonplace at Marangu route huts, visitors having to share beds or find floor or table spaces to sleep on. Others had to sleep out in leaky tents.

On Mount Kenya the growing popularity of the Chogoria route, combined with rains, has caused the track through the forest to vary from being a sea of mud, negiotiable only by amphibious land-rovers, to forming a scar of ridges and ruts requiring careful balancing acts from vehicles with low clearance. Rumour has it that the track is to have some hardcore put on it. The Naro Moru route provides a more reliable access route for vehicles. Park fees are due to go up, but inclusive of camping or hut fees they should not exceed $10 per day.

The political and economic situation in Uganda is improving rapidly, and the Ruwenzori are gradually regaining their former popularity. A daily bus from Kampala to Kasese provides a reliable service. John Matte has stepped down, and porter and guide services are now provided by an efficient organization called 'Ruwenzori Mountain Services' based in Ibanda which he helped to set up. Various charges have been introduced, some to assist the local communities and some to help improve services in the mountains. Aid money has provided a new bridge across the Mubuku near the Nyabitaba hut. A more controversial project is the construction of a raised causeway of planks across the Bigo Bog (as yet 90 per cent incomplete, according to latest reports). Also there are plans for new huts and camp-sites. Porters are still paid low wages, but they must be provided with a variety of 'perks': food, clothing, blankets, pots and pans, cigarettes etc. As porters work on a rota basis, they might only go up with a group once a year, and these perks form an important supplement to their very meagre yearly incomes. The service they provide is excellent, but they will require double pay for rainy days or for travelling in snow. Be prepared to pay about 80,000 Ugandan shillings per person for all entry fees, porter and guide wages and perks. This is about $150, but it will vary depending on the exchange rates obtained. The huts on the Zaire approach have been refurbished. A standard trip costs about $40 in park entry fees, and a few extra dollars are needed for porter wages. Glacial recession on the western glaciers of Mount Stanley has been very marked.

Maps and Guidebooks

Recent additions include:

Map of the Ruwenzori (1989): three maps on one side (1:20,000, 1:50,000 and 1:400,000) provide detailed information on the central areas of the Ruwenzori, together with details of roads around the mountains. Guide printed on reverse side.

Map of Mount Elgon (1989): Similar design to Ruwenzori map and guide.

Map of Kilimanjaro (1989): The Ordnance Survey World Series. Updated version of the old 1:100,000 map. Information and peak area enlargement on reverse side.

Map of Kilimanjaro (1990): 1:75,000 map of mountain and access routes. On reverse: sketches, general information and enlarged maps of Kibo and Mawenzi.

The above maps are available through West Col Productions, Goring, Reading RG8 9AA.

The Mountains of Kenya (1989): A recently revised, comprehensive guide to all important mountains in Kenya. Only walking routes are described on Mount Kenya. Edited by Paul Clarke and published by the Mountain Club of Kenya. Available only in Nairobi.

Books

Mount Kenya (John Reader 1989): A 'coffee-table' book, well-illustrated, with general information and a description of personal experiences on his visit to the mountain. A follow-up to *Kilimanjaro*.

Africa's Mountains of the Moon (Guy Yeoman 1989): Few people know the Ruwenzori as well as Guy. This book is an account of his extensive travels, with excellent illustrations and beautiful botanical sketches. (The book is reviewed on p272 of this volume.)

I would be grateful if any comments, information about recent developments or changes in East Africa could be sent to me to help update guidebook information: A Wielochowski, 32 Seamill Park Crescent, Worthing BN11 2PN (Tel 0903 37565).

Canadian Arctic and Alaska 1989

TED WHALLEY

Auyuittuq National Park Reserve had only three climbing parties in 1989. Earl Redfern and a companion tried to climb Mounts Thor and Odin but failed because of bad weather. Julie Munsell and Stephen Roberts flew to Broughton Island,[1] crossed to Maktak Fiord by snowmobile and ascended Maktak glacier, crossed the Penny Icecap and descended to the head of South Pangnirtung Fiord. Christopher Holloway, Pia Cole, Josée Auclair, Richard Weber and three dogs crossed the Penny Icecap from Okoa Bay to Pangnirtung Fiord in about 13 days in 1988.[2] Dave MacAdam made his twentieth consecutive summer trip to Baffin Island and continued his lone journeys, visiting Tasialuit valley, which is between and parallel to North Pangnirtung and Kangert Fiords. He climbed one peak of about 1325m, which had been already climbed by a British expedition in about 1978, and several smaller peaks.

G van B Cochrane[3] of the Explorers' Club returned to the Virginia glacier on the E coast of Baffin Island, near Cape Dyer, which he and his companions had surveyed in 1967 to 1977. During the 10 years of the first survey there were only early signs of recession, but marked recessions of many glaciers were reported from their 1989 survey. They deduce from this, somewhat trivially, that the recessions are caused by environmental changes. Four first ascents were made.

The 1988 report from Kluane National Park was too late in arriving, and so is reported this year. There were 60 people in the St Elias Mountains and they spent a total of 1329 nights there. Bob and John Jonas, Jeff Desbecker and Jim McLatchy ski'd in 45 days from the Bagley glacier in Alaska through the Seward glacier and out by the Kaskawulsh glacier in Kluane National Park Reserve. They used specially designed parachutes to help them across the icefields. Paul Hemstride, Chris Jones, Rhonda Markell and Roderick Leighton climbed some mountains near Pinnacle Peak and had eight days of good weather.

Several attempts were made on the E ridge of Mount Logan. A group of 10 from the Canadian Forces failed because of bad weather and avalanches. John Cathro and three others tried the E ridge. One member joined Max Lautenbacher and climbed the E peak. The party ski'd out by the Kaskawulsh glacier. Four members of a Mount Logan expedition were unsuccessful on Alaska King Peak, but four members reached the summit of Mount Logan. Grant McCormack and five others tried the E ridge of Mount Logan but failed because of snow and avalanches.

The W ridge of Mount McArthur was climbed for the first time by Chic Scott, Tim Friesen and Ken Wallator in association with a group calling themselves the PGOC East Ridge Logan. In Denali National Park, the coldest recorded temperature during the winter of 1988–89 was −60°C at 5200m. David Auble and Charlie Townsend made the first ascent of the E face of Mount

Russell on about 18 May 1989. The first winter solo ascent of the W rib of Mount McKinley was made by Dave Staeheli on 12 March 1989. On 13 May 1989, the first parapente descent from the N peak to the 5000m camp on the W buttress was made by Bertrand Doligez and Serge Tuaz.

James Quirk and David Nettle made the first complete ascent of the W face of Mount Huntington about 24 May 1989, and made the second ascent of the German route on the Moose's Tooth. Tod Bibler and Doug Levin made the first ascent of Peak 2300m in the Ruth Gorge, by the W face to the SW ridge. Seth Shaw and Conrad Anker made the first ascent of the W-ridge variation of Mount Hunter. The second ascent of the Infinite Spur on Mount Foraker was made by Jim Nelson and Mark Bebie on 24 June 1989.

Accidents in North American Mountaineering is edited and published by the American Alpine Club and the Alpine Club of Canada. It reports mountaineering accidents in North America, and the 1989 edition reports one accident in Nain, Labrador, one on Mount Marcus Baker in Alaska, eight on Mount McKinley and one on Mount Blackburn. It is well worthwhile owning copies for the lessons we can learn. They can be obtained from The American Alpine Club, 113 East 90th St, New York, NY10128–1589, USA, or The Alpine Club of Canada, PO Box 126, Banff, Alberta, TOL OCO, Canada.

REFERENCES

1 J Munsell and S Roberts. *Can Alp J* 72, 64, 1989.
2 R Weber. *Canadian Geographic*, Feb/March 1990.
3 G van B Cochrane. *The Explorers' Newsletter* 21, Nos 3 and 4, 4, 1989.

Józef Nyka adds:

Japanese Mount McKinley Tragedy

Three well-known Japanese mountaineers, Noboru Yamada, Teruo Saegusa and Kozo Komatsu, were killed attempting a winter ascent of North America's highest mountain. They were seen for the last time on 22 February 1989 at 5200m. On 13 March their bodies were found lying beneath the traverse to Denali Pass by an aeroplane searching for them.

This is a heavy blow for Japanese mountaineering because all three were among the country's leading 'himalayists'. Yamada (39) in 1988 became 'number one' among Japanese Himalayan climbers. Between 1978 and 1988 he collected ascents of nine 8000m peaks, three of them carried out in December, and he climbed Everest three times (in 1983, 1985 and 1988). In 1981 he made the first ascent of Langtang Ri (7205m) and in 1984 the first ascent of Mamostong Kangri (7516m). A series of four eight-thousanders, including Everest, completed within 11 months gave him world-wide publicity. His climbing partner Teruo Saegusa (31) ascended four eight-thousanders, conquering Everest twice. In December 1987, accompanied by Yamada and two other companions, he climbed the British route on Annapurna S face; all four members of this team have now died in three separate accidents. The third victim of Mount McKinley, Kozo Komatsu (35), ascended in 1975 the dangerous Dhaulagiri IV (7661m), and in 1979 he was a member of the party which completed the striking traverse of Dhaulagiri II (7751m), III (7715m) and V (7618m).

During last year a new record-breaking idea had captured the imagination of Yamada. He decided to climb the highest summits of all continents – in winter! He had already ascended wintry Aconcagua, Kilimanjaro and Mont Blanc. After McKinley Elbrus was to follow. It should be recalled that Naomi Uemura, another great Japanese mountaineer and adventurer, disappeared in February 1984 during a winter ascent of Mount McKinley, the first ever solo.

Karakoram 1989

PAUL NUNN

Although 46 parties booked with the intention of climbing in Pakistan, only 44 arrived, according to the Ministry records. It proved a harsh summer for weather, with relatively short periods of fine weather and much that was poor. This was a problem on the high peaks, and probably contributed significantly to the low summit bag everywhere. Of 'official' expeditions only 10 reached their summits. These figures do not include Pakistan military expeditions, nor the 'trekking' permit activities on mountains under the 6000m level. The former are relatively few, but activity on small peaks seems still to be on the increase.

K2 and Broad Peak were unclimbed in 1989 despite both strong parties and more conventional attempts on the standard routes. On K2, Loretan, Troillet and Kurtyka hoped to attempt the W face, but were beset with the two other parties by bad weather. An Austrian climber, Hans Barnthaler, died in a 200m fall while attempting the E face, and a large (Basque) Spanish party failed on the Abruzzi. On Broad Peak all five parties reported very adverse conditions; several were led by very experienced climbers.

In these circumstances the successes on the Gasherbrums were all the more creditable. Three expeditions climbed Gasherbrum 2. Rhona Lampard and Wanda Rutkiewicz reached the top on 12 July, with Wanda filming for a German TV station. This was a considerable achievement for the British womens' party, who did not use high-altitude porters on the mountain as has been common on many ascents. Other climbs of the peaks were completed by Swiss and Spanish parties, the latter suffering the loss of Antonio Jaurequi who fell in descent from the summit on 13 July. South Koreans, a Madrid party and Americans led by Mike Covington all failed. Undoubtedly, conditions here were also dangerous. The British women had one camp destroyed by avalanche, and on Gasherbrum 1 an Austrian party was also avalanched. This party included Willi Bauer, a survivor of the K2 storm of 1986. One member had to be helicoptered out from Base Camp, and they were fortunate to avoid worse consequences. Makato Hara's Japanese Scientific Expedition succeeded on Gasherbrum 1 on 12 July, but Sherpa Tsindi died in a fall during the descent.

On the Trango Tower Wolfgang Güllich returned and did a new route, and a Spanish party of four, led by Miguel Gallego, did a route left of the original British route and close to the unfinished British (Dai Lampard) route of 1984. On Uli Biaho Nick Cradock's New Zealand party was successful, and in the Baltoro Cathedrals Jim Beyer (USA) claimed a solo ascent of Thunmo (5866m). From a camp on the Dunge glacier he started with three difficult aid pitches, taking three days. These were fixed, but the face above was climbed alpine-style; he took nine days to climb 600m of 'big-wall' rock and 1000m of mixed ground, in all graded VII 5.10d A4. This sounds like the most extraordinary feat of the season.

On the Biafo glacier there was little success on the 7000m peaks. A Spanish attempt on Latok 1 and the British on the N face of Baintha Brakk (The Ogre) failed. A report on the latter by Andy Perkins appears at the end of this article. On the West Biafo Wall, Jerry Gore and a companion made the first breach on these large granite walls. They made substantial progress up the central pillar with 'Patience', a rock route with some fine climbing. Much of this was subsequently repeated by Cave and Flewett who confirmed its quality. In the Choktoi Spanish climbers Jon Lazkano and Javi Mugarra climbed the prominent rock-tower (6100m) right of Baintha Brakk in July. The 800m route was fixed to three-quarters height, with a final 22-hour push to the top, and sections of French 6a and A3.

Not far away, in the Hoh valley, French climbers B Domenech, Y Duverney and J Dolby Monet tried the E face of the Sosbun Tower. A first attempt (10–11 July) involved great technical difficulties and was fixed. After much bad weather they climbed 700m of the 1100m face (French 6b A4), but were eventually defeated by more bad weather. A more traditional expedition was successful near the head of Snow Lake. In July a British Metropolitan Police expedition made the first ascent of Lupke Lawa Brakk (Snow Lake Peak, 6590m), via the W ridge. Paul Vardon, Steven Sands, Philip Salt, Peter Stapely, Arthur Collins and Lew Hardy reached the top on 29 July, and got down as weather deteriorated after seven days on the mountain (Alpine D). In the same region an unnamed peak of 6000m was climbed by Tony Walkenden, John Wakefield and Mark Deith (29 July).

British small groups were also active in the Barpu and Hispar glacier areas. In August and September Sean Smith, Simon Yates and Simon Richardson made the first ascent of a 5500m peak at the W end of the Bal Chhish range from the S edge of the Hispar. Yates and Mike Searle climbed another unnamed peak of 5700m on the Hispar-Chomolungma watershed between 14 and 17 September, and Smith and Richardson failed on a difficult peak near Pumari Chhish. On the Barpu, a party from the Wolverhampton MC was active (see Dave Wilkinson's note at the end of this article).

In the Batura, Steve Hart and Kay Bruger (UK) climbed the N face of Shelin Maiden Peak (5973m, 800m AD). On Shispare (7819m) the Japanese Ryukoku University expedition led by Masato Okamoto went very high, but failed because of deep snow near the summit. On Spantik a West German expedition led by Arnold Hasenkopf was successful, but another DAV expedition failed. Diran was climbed by a Hirosaki University expedition, but two members of a South Korean expedition, Sang Woen-Ha and Su Fee-Le, died in an avalanche on 20 June.

A Spanish attempt on Rakaposhi and a French on Minapin peak failed, as did several on Nanga Parbat. There the Pakistan army had a resounding success. Led by Major Sher Khan, they did the Kinshofer route on the Diamir flank, with the leader, Atta, Mohammedullah and Rajab reaching the summit on 13 July. Ekkert Gundelach of West Germany was the only other climber to do so. Kwang Ho-Kim of South Korea died when a fixed rope snapped on the Kinshofer.

In the area south of Masherbrum, Ginette Harrison's group failed on

Masherbrum. There was as usual much action on lower peaks in the Hushe. George Szuca and George Armstrong (UK) climbed five unclimbed peaks: Pata Kha (c6000m) S face, Dru Peak (c6000m) twice, by couloirs on the S and N faces, Tower Peak (5800m) by the N face, Pointed Peak (5400m) NW couloir, and Parantha Peak (5300m) from the route up Pointed Peak. Dave Scott Maxwell and John Ashdown climbed the W face/SW ridge of Raven's Pyramid. This involved 41 pitches up to 5c on excellent granite and about 1000m of climbing, with retreat by abseil back down the route (23–25 August 1989). These are some of the Hushe climbs, but it is known that a large number of climbers were active there and more notable climbs are likely.

In the east of the Karakoram there were some notable events. These are reported in 'India 1989' (pp248–254 of this volume).

Among the tally of 'under 6000m' was the ascent of Shifkitin Sar (c5800m). An Irish expedition examined the Malanguti glacier near Shimshal in 1986, and tried this peak. In September 1989 four Dutch climbers visited the area. From a low base (3300m) they set up two further camps at 4200m and 4600m along the glacier. After a bivouac in a snow hole at 5200m on 16 September, Robert Eckhardt, Rob Lith and Tanja Merkelbach reached the summit. The route ascended snow and ice on the NW of the peak, to the W ridge, without great difficulty. Noes Lautier was the fourth member of the party.

Meanwhile a Japanese expedition explored the vast faces east of Broad Peak, approaching from Xinjiang. For those with the time and money (for it is very expensive), the scope there is enormous. On Nanga Parbat a winter attempt by South Koreans on the Rupal appears to have failed.

Andy Perkins adds:

Baintha Brakk (The Ogre, 7285m)

A British team comprising Andy Cave, Phil Butler, Andy Perkins, Steve Hartland, Chris Flewitt, Tim Jordan, Paul Nunn and Dave Green explored the possibility of climbing the remote N face of this mountain in July and August 1989. After a porter strike on the Biafo glacier (future teams in the area should note that Base Camp is 10 stages from the roadhead and opposite the Sokha La), and attacks at night by a Himalayan brown bear, Advanced Base was established under the N face at the E end of the Sim Gang glacier. All load-carrying was done by ski over the 10 miles between Base Camp and Advanced Base.

On the first attempt on the face, Cave, Flewitt and Perkins were hit by serac fall in the couloir leading to the col on the ridge bounding the left side of the face. Flewitt sustained minor injuries and the three retreated. Soon after, Perkins and Butler had another attempt and reached the col without incident at 5800m. Above this, the ridge (which had appeared to be feasible) turned out to be heavily corniced and heaving with seracs. Poor snow conditions and the impossibility of retreat in bad weather forced abandonment of the attempt.

The prominent central pillars on the face remain a superb but desperate objective. An approach up the lower snow-slopes is raked by avalanche daily and the pillars themselves rise from 6000m to the summit with no respite from steep technical climbing.

Dave Wilkinson adds:

In mid-August, a party from the Wolverhampton MC visited the Barpu glacier, W Karakoram. *Members*: Ralph Atkinson, Ged Campion, Mick Curtin, John Keska, Stewart Muir, Dave Wilkinson.

The approach from Hunza used the jeep road to Hoppar, where local porters were hired for the three-day walk-in to a Base Camp at Girgindil. These porters seemed more co-operative than men from this province of Nagar have proved to be in the past. The weather was variable, but good enough for the three small peaks climbed:

1) 'Girgindil Peak' (5296m), the obvious easy snow-plod above Base Camp. Frequent previous ascents. This party used four separate routes for ascent/descent (NW ridge, NE ridge, two routes on N face), all of them easy (alpine F/PD).

2) 'Girgindil Pyramid'. The obvious symmetrical mountain to the left of Girgindil Peak, as seen from Girgindil. In reality, it is formed by a ridge running SW from the Chukutans group. Not marked on the Polish map. Estimated height 5800m. No record of previous ascent. Climbed and descended by W ridge. Awkward access to the small glacier to its north, then easy snow to the ridge. The ridge (seen in profile from the Barpu walk-in) was easy at first, then some awkward climbing on loose schist to turn the steep section on the right, followed by precarious snow crests. Grade alpine D/TD.

3) 'Yengutz I'. The highest of the Yengutz group, to north of Spantik. No height given on Polish map. Estimated height 5999m! No record of previous ascent. Climbed via Yengutz col, W ridge and SW face, all snow/ice with a detour right to turn the rock-band on the face. Grade alpine AD/D.

Nepal 1989

A V SAUNDERS

(Plates 25–27)

These notes have been arranged in (more or less) height order. The intention has been to report developments and first ascents completed during the year, rather than to list repeat ascents of existing routes.

1989 was not a good year. There were few new routes, and several fatalities. On Everest (8848m), reports of overcrowding have become commonplace; this year they have been linked to outbreaks of viral flu. As if this were not enough, there are now perennial arguments about the fixing of the route through the Khumbu icefall. Apparently the earlier expeditions who set up a route often demand payment from the following expeditions who use the route.

During the spring season, the Polish expedition organized by Eugeniusz Chrobak followed a variation on the W ridge route, avoiding the normal Lho La approach. Following a line with minimum avalanche danger, the team climbed Khumbutse (6640m) before descending to the Rongbuk glacier, where they established Camp 1 at 5850m. The line continued left of previous ascents to gain the W shoulder. Five more camps were established on the ridge and in the Hornbein Couloir. On 24 May Chrobak and Andrzej Marciniak reached the summit. Over the next two days they descended, stripping the camps with the help of two other team members. They reached Camp 1 in deteriorating weather to join another team arriving from base. The next day all the climbers set out for base, up the 600m fixed ropes over Khumbutse. At 1pm the six climbers were struck by an avalanche which broke the ropes. Miroslav Dasal, Miroslav Gardzielewski and Waklaw Otreba did not survive the avalanche. Zygmunt Heinrich died shortly after, and Chrobak expired during the night. Marciniak crawled alone down to Camp 1. He was badly injured and snowblind, but he found a radio and maintained contact with Janusz Majer in Base Camp. Majer radioed Artur Hajzer in Kathmandu, on his way home from Lhotse S face. The Russian embassy in Kathmandu made the necessary diplomatic arrangements with the Chinese (the borders were still closed after Tiananmen Square), and at midnight on the 29th an international team of climbers crossed the frontier. On June 1, Hajzer, Sherpa Zangbu, Sherpa Shiwa, Rob Hall (NZ) and Gary Ball (NZ) reached Marciniak, now without food and little hope of survival. In the autumn a special funeral expedition reached the Lho La (6026m) but found no trace of the five victims. A funeral mass was said and a symbolic burial service performed. Two commemorative tablets were fixed, on the Rongbuk glacier moraine and at Everest Base Camp.

A 30-member Soviet team, supported by 17 Sherpas and led by Eduard Myslovski, accomplished a clean sweep on **Kangchenjunga** (8586m). They completed the first full traverse of all four major summits, in both directions,

and added new routes to the Main Peak and the difficult (IV–V) South Peak. A number of the ascents, though none of the traverses, was done without oxygen, and all summits were reached with the aid of fixed rope. Six camps were placed above the Great Shelf, and three more at or near the summit ridge. The main summit was climbed on 9 April. The other ascents and the establishment of the high camps continued until all was set for the traverse. Starting early on 30 April, a five-member team led by Sergei Bershov traversed the four tops from Yalung Kang (8505m), reaching the S peak at 2.45pm on May Day. They met the second team traversing in the opposite direction on the saddle between the S and central summits. The Soviets made a total of 85 individual ascents in this, their second Himalayan outing. For a fuller account of this expedition, see p24 of this volume.

During the 1989/90 season, a Korean team made the first winter ascent of Yalung Kang via the SE face. Jin Kyo-Sup, Ang Dawa Sherpa and Tshering Tshemba Lama made radio contact from the summit but failed to return, and are presumed to have fallen down the N face.

On **Lhotse** (8516m) the year began with Messner's international team attempt on the S face. They followed a variation to the right of the Polish route, thought to be safer, but failed around 7200m. In the autumn Jerzy Kukuczka and Ryszard Pawlowski followed the Wielicki-Hajzer route to bivouac on 23 October, in fine weather, at 8300m. The next morning Kukuczka fell from the top of the first pitch of the day. His body was recovered at 5400m two days later, and he was buried there in a crevasse. Pawlowski had no rope, the 6mm line had broken just above the belay at what is thought to have been the only runner, and he was unable to reach the tent at Camp 6 that night. Without a head-torch he did not know that he was only metres from the camp. Pawlowski completed the difficult descent without injury. During the following winter both Marc Batard and Christophe Profit failed to solo the S face.

There were two remarkable solo ascents this year, by Tomo Cesen and Pierre Beghin. Beghin's effort was the result of a French expedition to the S face of **Makalu** (8463m). Beghin, Michel Cadot (physician) and rock-star Alain Ghersain fixed the route to 7000m, with Camp 1 at 5800m and Camp 2 at 6600m. The route varied from the 1974 Yugoslav line above about 6000m, taking a direct open couloir to join the top of the icefields below the first band of cliffs. Beghin left the top of the fixed ropes alone, and rejoined the Yugoslav line at about 7200m. After some extremely hard climbing and two bivouacs he reached the summit at 2.45pm on 6 October. There were very high winds and he spent little time on the summit, descending the normal route to 7800m, where he was swept on by a windslab avalanche. He lost an axe, but landed safely 200 metres lower at the Catalan-Spanish Camp 3 where he spent the night. The next day Beghin missed the fixed ropes to the Catalan-Spanish Camp 2 and descended the couloir below the Makalu La, where he again fell victim to a windslab avalanche. This time he went 400 metres, lost his other axe, goggles, hat, camera, radio and the remaining contents of his pockets. He reached Camp (6000m) that afternoon, and his Base Camp the next day. Beghin is a scientist specializing in avalanches.

On 12 May, Alan Hinkes became the first Briton to climb **Manaslu** (8163m), following the W ridge, as part of the commercial *L'Esprit d'Equipe* expedition.

From **Cho Oyu** (8201m) there are bizarre reports that a Frenchman and a Belgian were attacked with fists and sticks by six Sherpas and three Koreans, while sharing (?) the same route. The Frenchman received a head wound and had a rope tied round his neck. According to the report, the Europeans later escaped under cover of dark. Meanwhile Cho Oyu is becoming increasingly popular. On 19 September two Catalan women, Monica Verge and Magda Nos, reached the summit with Sherpa Ang Phuri; they are the first Spanish or Catalan women to climb an 8000m peak.

Tomo Cesen's solo effort took place during the spring on **Jannu** (7710m). On 28 April he completed a 23-hour first ascent of the impressive N face. His route was 2700m long, and of increasing difficulty. The final 500m were compared by Cesen to the overhanging N face of the Cima Ovest. It would be hard to be oversuperlative about this climb.

A British expedition completed a new route on the W face of Makalu II or **Kangchuntse** (7640m) to reach the subsidiary S summit (7600m) on 26 September. (See 'Chaos', pp17–23 of this volume.) A team under the leadership of Franc Pusnic (Yugoslavia) is reported to have completed the first ascent of the

1600m N face of **Gangapurna** (7455m) on 20 September. The climb was a three-day push by a single pair. During the winter season Michel Thodoroff led an expedition which made a new route on **Kanjeralwa** (6612m), while first winter ascents were made of **Langtang Ri** (7205m) and **Langshisa Ri** (6427m). David Etherington (UK) and Jörg Schneider (DDR) completed the ascent of the E ridge of Taweche (6501m).

An international team led by Steve Bell (UK), Russell Brice (NZ) and Paul Bayne (Australia) made the first ascent of the SW ridge of **Himalchuli West** (7540m). Three camps were set up and 3500m of rope was fixed on the ridge which involved rock of grade IV and a vertical ice-step.

On **Nuptse** (7855m) there were two notable efforts. A German team climbed the NW ridge as far as the NW summit (7742m) on 2 November; and an Italian-Canadian team climbed the SE pillar to 6900m, following the Lowe-Twight route past the 1986 high point.

The **Thyangboche Monastery**, the spiritual home of the Sherpa people, was totally destroyed by fire on 12 January. Sir Edmund Hillary has launched a restoration fund: 'The Monastery is a World Heritage site, and it must be rebuilt. We hope that all Himalayan mountaineers will help to rebuild it.' Donations, please, to: Thyangboche Restoration Fund, PO Box 10–274, Christchurch, NZ.

I thank Józef Nyka and Liz Hawley for supplying information.

The Everest Map

Map by the National Geographic Society. Supplement to the National Geographic, *Vol 174, No 5 – High Himalaya, p652A (November 1988)*

MICHAEL WARD

In 1980 Bradford Washburn, who had just retired as Director of the Boston Museum of Science, wished to increase the accuracy of maps of the Everest region and finally obtained permission from the Chinese and Nepalese governments to overfly Everest at 13,000m. The aerial photographs on which the new maps are based were obtained in two overflights carried out in December 1984. The main purpose was to produce maps at 1:10,000 with 20m contours so that geologists and glaciologists would have a large-scale and detailed base from which to plot their field work, and the present 1:50,000 map with 40m contours is a development. In addition there is a sheet at 1:5000, 'Everest over 7000m', while one at 1:2500 of the N face is in preparation. The depiction of ground features, in the unsurpassed style of the *Landeskarte der Schweiz*, is masterly, attractive and accurate, and the whole is the result of extensive international co-operation between the Boston Museum of Science and the National Geographic Society who provided finance, West German photography from the US space shuttle Columbia in December 1983, the Swiss Federal Office of Topography in Berne and, of course, the Chinese and Nepalese governments.

Although it is now clear from Kempson's chapter on the local name of Everest in Ruttledge's book *Everest: The Unfinished Adventure* (1937) that the Tibetans had called the mountain Chomolungma from about AD 750–800 onwards, this was not known to the Survey of India. In 1856, at the suggestion of Waugh, the Surveyor General of India, the name Mount Everest was given to Peak XV, the world's highest, because there seemed to be no single well-defined name or native appellation for the mountain. (See *Proc RGS1*, 345, 1855–57.) Sir George Everest, Waugh's immediate predecessor, had been Superintendent of the Great Trigonometrical Survey.

Modern exploration and mapping of the Everest region began with the Survey of India and in particular the Pandit Hari Ram ('No9' or MH), who circumnavigated the mountain between 1868 and 1888. His observations are included in the Survey of India's maps of Nepal, where work was continued up to glacier level by native surveyors but not by Europeans, who were forbidden to enter the country.

The first detailed map of the N side of the mountain was made by Wheeler on the 1921 Reconnaissance, with additions in 1922, and by the Indian surveyor Hari Singh Thapa in 1924. The next advance was the 1:20,000 photogrammetric survey of the N face by Spender in 1935. Details of the southern, Nepalese, side remained scanty and inaccurate until a remarkably accurate 'running' map with an extremely limited circulation was drawn by

73. Erwin Kraus on the summit of Bolivar, 2 February 1939. Looking W can be seen Santander and Simmons Peaks. (Erwin Kraus) (p 150)

74. *NW face of Pico Guardián, 5295m. If not the highest summit in the Sierra Nevada de Santa Marta, certainly the most technical one.* (Jorge Ruiz) (p 150)

75. *Griffith Pugh – Everest 1953.* (Alpine Club Library Collection) (p 188)

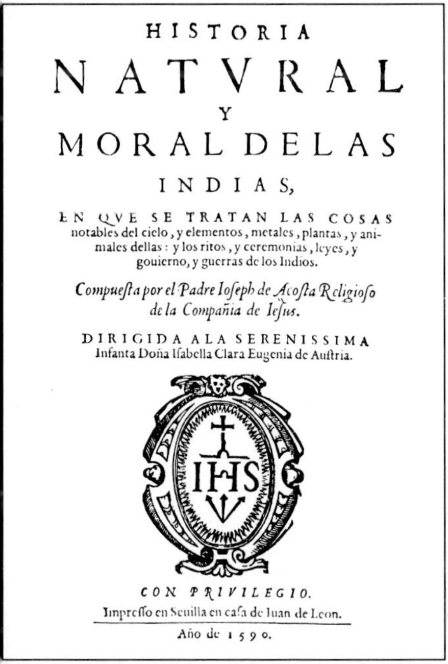
HISTORIA
NATVRAL
Y
MORAL DELAS
INDIAS,
EN QVE SE TRATAN LAS COSAS notables del cielo, y elementos, metales, plantas, y animales dellas: y los ritos, y ceremonias, leyes, y gouierno, y guerras de los Indios.

Compuesta por el Padre Ioseph de Acosta Religioso de la Compañia de Iesus.

DIRIGIDA ALA SERENISSIMA Infanta Doña Isabella Clara Eugenia de Austria.

CON PRIVILEGIO.
Impresso en Seuilla en casa de Iuan de Leon.
Año de 1590.

76. *The title page of Joseph de Acosta's* Historia Natural y Moral de las Indias, *1590.* (From Bodleian Library, Oxford, by permission) (p 191)

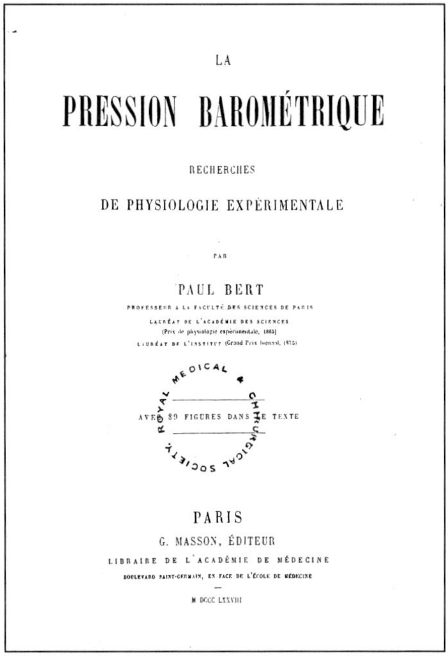
LA
PRESSION BAROMÉTRIQUE
RECHERCHES
DE PHYSIOLOGIE EXPÉRIMENTALE
PAR
PAUL BERT
PROFESSEUR A LA FACULTÉ DES SCIENCES DE PARIS
LAURÉAT DE L'ACADÉMIE DES SCIENCES
(Prix de physiologie expérimentale, 1865)
LAURÉAT DE L'INSTITUT (Grand Prix Lacaze, 1875)

AVEC 89 FIGURES DANS LE TEXTE
PARIS
G. MASSON, ÉDITEUR
LIBRAIRE DE L'ACADÉMIE DE MÉDECINE
BOULEVARD SAINT-GERMAIN, EN FACE DE L'ÉCOLE DE MÉDECINE
M DCCC LXXVIII

77. *The title page of Paul Bert's* La Pression Barométrique, *1878.* (From Library of the Royal Society of Medicine, London, by permission) (p 191)

78. *Fünffingerspitze.* (C Douglas Milner) (p 204)

79. *Uto Peak and Mount Sir Donald.* (Edward C Porter, Alpine Club Library Collection) (p 204)

80. *Piz Roseg, NE face.* (N A Tombazi, Alpine Club Library Collection) (p 204)

81. Obergabelhorn, with (L) ENE ridge. (Frank Solari) (p 204)

Milne of the Drawing Office of the Royal Geographical Society. Compiled between 1933 and 1947 from photographs taken on the 1933 'Flight over Everest' and possibly unofficial flights over Everest in 1945 and 1947, this was available to us on the 1951 Reconnaissance from Nepal, but was never mentioned in any books about this expedition.

These and other maps drawn by French and Austrian mapmakers (most noteworthy among them Erwin Schneider's 1:25,000 map of the southern approaches) were incorporated into the 1961 1:100,000 map by Holland of the Royal Geographical Society. This was revised and extended, with Chinese contributions, in 1975 and could fairly be said to be the first comprehensive map of the Everest region.

The present (1988) 1:50,000 map uses Pin-Yin names in China (Tibet); this has meant a change from Changtse or North Peak to Bei Peak, and the North Col is now the Bei ao, but names on the border are familiar. The map is a major contribution which will give pleasure to those who look at it, and instruction to those who use it.

India 1989

HARISH KAPADIA

(*Plates 85, 86*)

The climbing scene in the Indian Himalaya was active, as always. The East Karakoram area received three expeditions during the year; they differed in style and went to different regions within the area.

The only joint expedition with foreigners was an Indo-British team led by Sonam Palzor. Rimo II (7373m) and Rimo IV (7169m) were climbed on 12 July in separate attempts. They reached the North Terong glacier with 38 porters, intending to climb Rimo III (7233m). The team consisted of Stephen Sustad (USA), Nick Kekus and Doug Scott (UK), Robert Schauer (Austria), Rob and Laurie Wood (Canada) and Sharavati Prabhu (India). Amongst the Indian climbers were Tsewang Smanla, Kanhaiya Lal, Mohan Singh and Sonam Palzor as the leader. Robert Schauer returned early while Rob Wood left on 2 July because of health problems. An altercation developed with student-porters taken from Leh. Deciding to attempt Rimo II first, both teams took different routes to meet higher up. The British team ascended Rimo II via the W buttress to the N ridge. The Indian climbers changed plans and crossed the col between Rimo II and III to climb Rimo IV by W-SW snow-slopes. Rimo II was a first ascent by Nick Kekus and Stephen Sustad, while Rimo IV was a second ascent by T Smanla, Kanhaiya Lal and Mohan Sing. Rimo IV was first climbed in 1984 by a team of Indian Army sappers, approaching from the east. No attempt was made on Rimo III as the leader called off the expedition suddenly after these ascents. There are disquieting reports of poor relations, differences and troubles between the two sides on this expedition. (See also the contributions by Nick Kekus and Doug Scott on pp11–16 and 251–254 of this volume.)

Mamostong Kangri (7516m) was climbed by a huge Indian Army sappers' expedition led by Major M P Yadav. They had ample time and resources, and achieved the third ascent of this peak of 'Thousand Devils'. Their route – the same as that of the first ascent in 1984 by an Indo-Japanese expedition – was via the Mamostong glacier, across the Mamostong col (5885m) to the east, to the Thangman glacier, and through an ice-fall to gain the E ridge of the peak. Six climbers including the leader reached the summit on 10 August 1989. The second summit-team led by Major M C Chhibber narrowly failed to reach the summit on the 11th. The team also climbed Pk6235m and Pk6190m in the Thangman glacier region, to the south-east of Mamostong Kangri. (The second ascent of Mamostong Kangri was made in 1988 by an army team led by Major A M Sethi. They approached from the Thangman glacier direct.)

The third team to the area was a small private group from Bombay led by Harish Kapadia. They visited areas east of the Saser La where few expeditions have been allowed. After many difficulties of terrain and transportation they entered the Aq Tash glacier and recced Aq Tash peak (7016m). This is one of the last three unclimbed 7000ers in the area. They climbed two smaller peaks here. Three members of the team operated in the Chong Kumdan glacier region further north. They recced the unknown Chong Kumdan I peak (7071m) and recorded the historic 'Glacier Dam' at the entrance. This is the famous dam site from where the Shyok floods originated. The last flood was in 1928. The party climbed three peaks here and brought back knowledge and photographs of this unknown area.

It may be noted that all the three teams (including the army team) had access problems. The local commander was not 'mountaineer-friendly' and, despite all the clearance from Delhi, delay was inevitable. Riots at Leh, lack of porters and mules in Nubra and poor weather troubled all. All future expeditions to this area should take the above hindrances into account. It also appears that Westerners do not seem to enjoy the best of relations with Indian Army leaders and teams with which they necessarily have to join.

In Kashmir, Nun Kun continued to attract climbers and commercial expeditions. But the best climbing was in Kishtwar. Hagshu (6330m) was the finest first ascent; this peak had defied many attempts. A British team comprising Robin Beadle, Tim Whitaker, Max Holliday, Phil Booth and Ken Hopper made the first ascent of Hagshu Peak. Holliday, Booth and Hopper reached the summit on 16 September 1989, after a three-day ascent of the E face. Beadle had returned to Base Camp with Whitaker who had contracted pulmonary oedema after the pair had reached c6000m on the NE ridge-E face. Whitaker made a fast recovery once off the mountain, but was unable to make another attempt. Both routes were approached in two days from a Base Camp on the north (Zanskar) side of the mountain. The climbing was relatively easy, but serious, and the ascent was made in alpine style. Earlier, John Barry had been defeated on the N face at 5790m because of bad weather.

Brammah I (6416m) was unsuccessfully attempted by an Indian team. Base Camp was established at Mirchin (Sattarchin) on the Nanth nala. The NE face was followed and the summit attempt was made on 13 September. The climb along the final ridge was stopped at 5790m due to lack of time and resources. No porters or Sherpas were employed above Base Camp. An Australian team also attempted the peak but the route is not known.

A four-member British team led by Michael Spencer climbed in the Haramukh group. All four climbed Haramukh IV (4800m) via the SW ridge on 7 August. Haramukh I (5143m) was climbed on 11 August via the E face and the NE ridge.

Further to the east, Himachal Pradesh had many expeditions. Japanese teams were active on KR3 (6151m), CB13 (6264m), Phabrang (6172m) and others. All the peaks were climbed, sometimes by two routes. One of the finest ascents was achieved on Indrasan (6221m) by a team of eight French and two Indian climbers (21 June). This was a two-day climb from base via the NE ridge.

In Lahul a three-member Indian team from Bombay climbed Menthosa (6443m). This peak above the Miyar nala was climbed from a Base Camp at 4400m and three more camps were established up to 5750m. No porters were employed above Base Camp. Finally, in a 10-hour push, Ajay Tasker (leader), Vinay Hegde and V Shankar reached the summit on 21 August. This was a fine achievement by the team via the route of the first ascent.

Small Indian teams were active in Spiti. Kanamo (5974m) above Kibar village was climbed by an Indian team from Bombay on 7 and 9 August. The route followed the NW approaches and only one camp was established above Base Camp. The peak is on the way to the Parang La and was first climbed by Indians in 1964. It was known as 'Kanikma'.

The first ascent of a remote peak, Gyagar (6400m) in the Lingti valley was made on 1 July. (See the map in *AJ93*, 250, 1988/89.) From Lingti village the team (leader Dhiren Pania) reached the Chaksachan La on 25 June after a gruelling nine-day route over difficult terrain, with yaks. Advanced Base Camp (4570m) and Camp 1 (5180m) were established on the S ridge by which the peak was climbed. The peak is situated near the junction of the Tibet, Ladakh and Spiti borders. Amongst other activities, Manirang (6593m) was attempted by an Indian team, whilst the Border Security Force climbed Shigri Parbat (6526m).

Garhwal and Kumaon were centres of activity for many teams and there were some brilliant attempts. The Para Regiment failed on Mukut Parbat (7240m). This peak, first climbed in 1951 by a New Zealand team, was tried out for the first time. An Indo-Polish expedition was organized to attempt Nanda Devi East (7434m), to celebrate the first ascent of the peak by the Poles in 1939; but the expedition failed to reach the summit. Panwali Dwar (6663m) was attempted by an Indo-American team and Australians by the SE ridge. This peak, first climbed by the Japanese after repeated attempts, has not been climbed since. Yogeshwar (6678m) was attempted by Indians; this high peak in the open area remains an attractive objective, having repulsed two expeditions. However, the most spirited failure was on Jaonli (6632m). A 'Senior Citizens' team consisting of Joss Lynam (65), Mike Banks (66), Patrick O'Leary (54) and Alan Blackshaw (55) intended to climb this peak from the east. However, poor snow and bad weather foiled them. Ultimately Joss Lynam and C P Ravichandra climbed Pk5450m on 10 June at 10.30am. But it is their spirit that matters. (See the article by Mike Banks on pp46–49 of this volume.)

A notable success was the first ascent of peak 6450m, near Shivling, by a Spanish team via the SE face on 18 May. X Gonsalves and J Sorious reached the summit. The team named the peak 'Parvati Parbat'; however, this is a misnomer for this hitherto unnamed peak, as there is a more famous peak of the same name in Kulu. The difficult SW buttress of Bhagirathi III (6454m) was climbed by South Koreans, whilst a Spanish team climbed Shivling (6543m). Nanda Ghunti (6390m) was climbed by the British, and Nanda Kot (6861m) by the Indians. An Indian team from Calcutta climbed the difficult W face of Chaudhara (6510m) near the Kalabaland glacier in Kumaon. They established four camps above the base, and on 8 June three climbers reached the summit. This was the second ascent; the peak was first climbed by a team from Bombay in 1973. An Italian team climbed the W ridge of Kharcha Kund (6612m). Three members reached the summit on 15 August, and two other members summited on the 17th. Some high peaks such as Satopanth (7075m), Kamet (7756m), Gangotri I (6672m) and Sri Kailash (6932m) were climbed, as in every year. Towards the far east Gorichen (6858m) and Pauhunri (7125m) were scheduled for attempts by the armed forces; details are awaited at the time of writing.

The Indian Mountaineering Foundation elected Capt Mohan S Kohli as its new President. Capt Kohli is a well-known mountaineer and has been associated with the mountaineering fraternity the world over. A new set-up is expected at the IMF soon. H C Sarin, who was President for the past 23 years, has been made President-Emeritus for his services to the IMF. A new book, *Mountaineering in India*, by Capt M S Kohli traces the history of the sport in India from the earliest days. It covers all major climbs up to 1987.

The year ended on a sad note with the passing of two Himalayan Club veterans. R E Hawkins, past Vice-President and Hon Asst Editor, died at the age of 82. He had served the Club from 1944 and represented a long British association with the Club in India. Soli Mehta, who also died in November, was Editor of the *Himalayan Journal* for almost 18 years. He had a passionate love for mountain literature and worked for it tirelessly. His remarkable output of publications puts him in the ranks of the senior editors of the mountaineering world. (See the obituary on pp312–314 of this volume.) Both men will be sorely missed.

Józef Nyka adds:

On 30 September 1989 the Yugoslavs Franc Knez and Andreja Hrastnik climbed the (previously attempted) SW face of Bhagirathi II (6512m) in the Garhwal Himalaya, establishing a rock route of 20 pitches graded UIAA V, with four pitches VII to VII+ and two pitches VIII to VIII+. The lower half of the route had been partially fixed with rope the day before the climb. Although the ascent will be disputed because it was made only to the edge of the snow, probably one day's walk from the summit, it was a great event in the history of big-wall free climbing, in which Knez seems to be the world's leading figure.

Doug Scott adds:

The Indo-British Expedition to the Rimo Group: A Commentary

Joint expeditions to India are not always as enjoyable as may appear from reading subsequent reports. Only later, through personal contact with some of the participants, do the problems that beset the undertaking come to light. Clearly there are difficulties for all participants in these joint enterprises, although in 1974 on Changabang and again in 1981 in Gangotri our expeditions under the overall leadership of Col Balwant Sandhu were very enjoyable occasions without controversy. No doubt other mountaineers – particularly Indo-Japanese – have had similar good experiences of joint expeditions.

Our recent Indo-British expedition (with Canadian, US and Austrian participation) to Rimo III in the E Karakoram was beset with problems from the start to its untimely end. The expedition took place in the war zone, where army requirements naturally had priority and where the local Nubra porters are notoriously 'difficult', ie do not take to outsiders who demand that they become beasts of burden. Expeditions here will always prove more complex than in the Garhwal, for example.

Individual relations, man to man, were generally good on our expedition and the financial arrangements were satisfactorily concluded. Difficulties arose through lack of communication and the problem of facing up honestly and realistically to the difference of experience – and therefore mountaineering expectations – of the Indian and the foreigner.

I propose to make what follows as constructive as possible. Suggestions offered here for consideration by the Indian Mountaineering Foundation and others are highlighted as objectively as possible by situations which arose on our expedition and after consultation with the other foreign members and the IMF.

We are very grateful for all the help we received in India; especially to Mr Sarin, the President of the IMF who, despite being unwell, did all that was possible to speed up our permit. Thanks are due to Narinda Kumar, Hukam Singh and Heera Lohia for valuable advice, and Harsh Vardhan of World Expeditions for acting as the expedition agent in Delhi. We also express our gratitude for all the support given by many individuals in the UK and Canada.

Avoid long delays. Most foreigners will have fixed holidays with air tickets booked and jobs and families awaiting their return. Any delays will mean not only less time available for acclimatization and climbing, but also less chance of climbing in good weather. With a delay of three weeks such as we experienced in Leh, team members are bound to become impatient and less tolerant of each other, of the Indian contingent and Indian officials.

The IMF should check with government and with the army that foreign climbers are really wanted in restricted areas. The $2000 royalty payment is taken under false pretences if foreigners are kept waiting because of intransigent politicians and army commanders. One of our members, Robert Schauer, had to return home to Austria before even reaching the road-head.

If government and army do approve of foreign climbers visiting restricted zones, then the following points would help matters:

Alternative peaks should be available if military activity puts the main objectives out of bounds. In a large and bureaucratic country like India, a change of peak inevitably means weeks of delay unless permission can be arranged at the time of the original permit. If onward transport into restricted zones has to be with army convoy, then the army commanders should give this some priority. As far as we could see, at the moment vehicles are made available at the discretion of the local commanders as a favour to the Indian leader. Where porters are difficult to hire because of army presence, the army should offer the expedition the opportunity of paying for helicopter drops of equipment.

Foreigners would do well to allow at least three weeks to cope with unexpected delays.

The individual teams must be compatible. The foreign team and the Indian team must both want to be there. The foreign contingent usually consists of friends who are from the same club or who have climbed together before. The

Indian team might not be so cohesive, and might consist of individuals invited from all over India or individual army personnel invited or co-opted from various army units. Where joint expeditions are concerned, the Indian group should all have climbed with each other, previously and compatibly. They should be in sympathy with their leaders.

The expedition must achieve compatibility between the Indian group and the foreigners. Feelings of inferiority and worries about subsequent 'loss of face' can best be avoided by facing up to each member's previous experience and present expertise in the mountains. It is important that all members know in detail what mountains each has climbed, the technical severity of the routes taken, and also in what style they were climbed. For example, there is a vast difference between a siege ascent of an easy-angled snow peak and, say, the technically difficult E pillar of Shivling climbed in alpine style.

It should be recognized that the Indian members from army units operating in the Himalaya will generally be much stronger and better acclimatized than the foreigners. The co-leaders should be briefed by the IMF and made aware (if this is the case) that the foreigners, on their part, have greater technical climbing experience – most of them will have served their apprenticeship in the Alps when they were teenagers. The Indians should be tolerant of the grumpy Westerners, unable to carry the same loads and move as fast as the stronger Indians, and the foreigners should reciprocate with a conscious effort at co-operation by passing their technical expertise on to the Indian group. Our leader, Sonam Palzor, subsequently recognized our expertise by inviting members of the team back to India to instruct Indo-Tibet Border Police aspirant climbers. Explanations as to precisely how this can be achieved on the mountain should be worked out by the whole group. It is essential that the Indian overall leader is in on the discussions. In our case the Indian leader was often in the rear, pushing up supplies as quickly as possible. With very few porters at his disposal he had to maximize on every carry, and at the critical time he was unable to steer his men into a joint ascent of the safe – but technically more difficult – W rib of Rimo II.

Agreement on what routes are climbed and in what style they are climbed. The broad aims of the expedition can be discussed in Delhi, but the specifics can only be decided in sight of the mountain. If members wish to achieve the limit of their potential, and that potential varies, then there will be problems unless more than one route can be climbed. One solution is for all members to join together for an acclimatization climb (or climbs) and, if possible, to climb the main peak together, using whatever style the least experienced members wish to adopt. This would allow all members to achieve the summit – often felt to be very important on first ascents. Those then wishing to climb a route of greater technicality and in alpine style (ie without fixed ropes, fixed camps, porter support) should have permission to seek out and climb it. The other members should be allowed to climb elsewhere. The Indian overall leader must know and remember the aspirations of the foreign contingent; he should realize the extent of their financial and domestic commitment and of the great effort over a long period of time which goes into their getting to the climb.

Continuous support from non-climbers attached to the expedition is essential until the end. The liaison officer, the doctor, radio operators etc should be briefed that it is hard enough climbing in the Himalaya away from home for such long periods, and the climbers need all the encouragement they can get to continue with the climb. The non-climbers should not put undue pressure on the leader or the team to give up because they themselves are bored or homesick.

Recognition that army mountaineers may have a different attitude to expeditions and mountaineering. Co-opted military personnel usually have no particular time limit. They are also paid while they are on the expedition, so that it becomes part of their job. They may not have the same urgency to reach the mountain, and fail to understand the impatience of the foreigners whose situation is the opposite. Some of our members resented the resigned manner of the Indian team towards the constant delay in Leh. This was most probably simply a difference of attitude; the one Eastern acceptance of fate, the other Western impatience.

The soldier is most probably at risk throughout the year, carrying out his military duties. On the mountain he may wish to avoid any more undue risk and go for the easiest and safest route to the summit. The foreigner will live most of his life in relative comfort and safety. He will, just for a few days, look forward to the exhilaration of risk-taking.

Obviously, military personnel must have intense pride in their country if they are to defend it. Foreign civilians may not understand this, and may be taken aback by the soldier's strong reactions should any derogatory statements be made about his nation. Obviously the foreigner should at all times respect this, not lose his cool in bad manners, and put himself in the other's position.

In conclusion, it is worth repeating Sonam's last words: 'We will never know why things turned out as they have – maybe it is for the best.'

Appendix: The Dolomites – how and why to devastate them?

(Editor's note: as the journal went to press, this statement was received from the Veneto section of the World Wildlife Fund (address: Via Riale 12, 36100 Vicenza, Italy). It is important enough to be included here.)

Cortina d'Ampezzo – Passo Falzarego – Lagazuoi – S Cassiano – Cherz – Settsass – Val Parola – Col Gallina – Cortina, Andraz – Nuvolau; Arabba – Passo Padon – Malga Ciapela – Forca Rossa – Val Franzedas – Passo S Pellegrino – Falcade; Alleghe – S Fosca – Zoldo Alto; S Vito di Cadore – Forcella Puina – Forcella Staulanza – Forcella d'Alleghe; Auronzo – Forcella Maraja – Col de Varda – Misurina; Monte Longara – Monte Fior – Monte Miela.

They are not the most famous Dolomite mountain places, but they are the areas that the Veneto Region (Venice) wants to disembowel by creating new ski-roundabouts. If the 'snow-plan' (*Piano Neve*) is unfortunately approved by the Region, then the natural richness and beauty of the Dolomites will be definitely jeopardized while we are still commemorating the second centenary of the discovery of their name, 'Dolomites'.

But this is not all, of course: dozens of new ski-slopes, ski-lifts, roads (even at the highest levels) and parking-lots will be planned. These and other 'necessary' structures (such as electric cables, phone-lines, new clearings and open spaces in wood and high mountain, building-yards, forest-roads) will involve much greater and graver consequences in the natural environment of the Dolomites: there will be hydrogeologic ruins due to the decrease of vegetal covering (cutting trees, shrubs, digging away the grass), with consequent increase of water surface-flow, impermeability of vast surfaces due to parking, roads etc, with alteration of hydrologic and, as a consequence, ecological processes.

Moreover, many hundreds of thousands of trees (mostly in tall-tree woods) will be knocked down; rock-crests and passes will be levelled; high-level environments jeopardized. These last are, perhaps, the most vulnerable: at first glance they don't look very important, but they include many species very precious and sensitive to anthropic pressure; just consider the typical alpine fauna and the very particular vegetal species that could be lost. These environments are a heritage of genetic richness and biological diversity, whose conservation must be one of the first aims of any long-term use-planning of natural resources.

Most of these 'exploitation' projects include areas designated by the Region as 'regional natural parks', 'highest landscape protection areas', or even areas declared of national interest by the Environment Minister: a famous case (much publicized by the Italian mass-media) is that of Monte Pelmo which has been put under protection by the Minister. The Veneto Region and the other administrations favouring the cementation of the Pelmo have appealed against the Environment Minister's decree.

With regard to the other Dolomite areas named above as part of the Region Project, the situation is very similar to that of Monte Pelmo. In other areas (Alto Comelico, Val Fiorentina, Ampezzo, Cadore, Agordino, Marmolada, Sella, Zoldano, Alpago, Sette Comuni, Fiorentini, Lessinia, M Baldo) 'completions' have been planned, but again the final results would only be many new roads, ski-lifts, ski-slopes, digs, cutting of trees (even in re-afforestations). The kind of tourism that is proposed in these plans is incompatible with the peculiar characteristics of the Dolomites. Moreover, alternatives do exist, in the form of the nature-friendly tourism and the well-balanced and respectful forms of cross-country skiing and mountaineering that the environmental groups have been proposing for this region for many years.

We remember that, at the International Conference for the Protection of the Alps (Berchtesgaden, 9–11 October 1989), the Environment Ministers of the Governments of West Germany, France, Italy, Yugoslavia, Liechtenstein, Austria, Switzerland and the Member for Environmental Protection of the European Commission agreed to limit or to stop the kind of active tourism particularly dangerous to the environment and, on the contrary, to encourage the kind causing less damage to the natural vital basis (point 55 of the resolution).

The South Tyrol has already decreed a moratorium on constructing new ski-installations until 1992. It will never be too late for the Veneto Region to learn from others how to deal with the conservation of its natural resources.

Mount Everest Foundation Notes 1988–89

EDWARD PECK

The following notes summarize reports from expeditions which have received the approval of the Mount Everest Foundation, and this is in most cases accompanied by a grant. MEF approval is generally an important first step to seeking assistance, financial or otherwise, from firms or other organizations. It should be noted that the MEF only 'sponsors' expeditions in exceptional circumstances, e.g. the 1981 Mount Kongur Expedition.

Copies of the full reports of these expeditions are lodged, when available, with the Alpine Club Library and the Archives Section of the Royal Geographical Society, and may be consulted in these places. Some expeditions will already have been described in the *Alpine Journal* and other mountaineering periodicals.

The expeditions summarized in the following notes took place between May 1988 and October 1989 (with one belated exception). These notes are based on reports received up to 1 December 1989.

America, North and South, including Arctic

88/1 *Joint Services Expedition to Borup Fjord, Ellesmere Island* (May–August 1988)

This large mixed Services party aimed to carry out a wide-ranging biological survey of the Borup Fjord area. Groups investigated the arctic char, snow buntings, waders, entomology, vascular flora and did some geological and archaeological research, as well as climbing in the Blue and Krieger Mountains, in particular Mts Leith and Schuchert.

88/29 *Imperial College Expedition to Mount St Elias* (June–July 1988)

Continuous snowfall and avalanche conditions forced this four-man party to retreat on both the SW buttress and the NW spur of Mt St Elias (Alaska), likewise on the N ridge of Mt Newton.

89/3 *South-East Greenland Expedition* (July–September 1989)

From Base Camp on Tasermiut Fjord, this six-member party made the first British ascent of P2511m, but failed in their objective of climbing the two other highest peaks of SE Greenland, owing to the evacuation of one member suffering from appendicitis. Some medical research was carried out into loss of body fluids in Arctic conditions.

89/9 *Milne Island (SE Greenland)* (August 1989)

This eight-member party explored the Korridoren glacier from its E snout up to the 800m contour and climbed seven unclimbed summits including P1867m.

89/10 *British Rye Expedition to Peru* (June 1989)

From camp at Laguna Jatun Pucacocha, all five members of this party climbed the NE ridge of Nevado Tacusiri, and also Ausengate (6372m). Various groups climbed the S faces of Points Linda, Karen and Nina (all 5300–5400m), also the N ridge of Central Sorimani Peak, and the S side of Tacirani.

89/20 *British Mount Foraker Expedition* (May–June 1989)

Abandoning their objective of a first British ascent of the SSE ('French') ridge of Mt Foraker, this two-man team made a successful first ascent of the S face of Mt Hunter to its junction with the SW ridge which, owing to storm, was descended without continuing to the summit.

89/46 *Sheffield Peruvian Expedition* (July–August 1989)

All five members succeeded in the first ascent of Colque Cruz V (5965m) in the Cordillera Vilcanota. Two also made a new direct route on the N face of Colque Cruz VI.

89/48 *Loughborough Students Andes Expedition* (August 1989)

This eight-member party made an extensive exploration of the little-visited Pupuya range in the Cordillera Apolobamba, making ascents of some 18 summits over 5000m. Four members also made the first British ascent (traverse W–N) of Huelanlloc (5805m). They are preparing a sketch map of the area.

89/57 *Patacancha (Peru) Expedition* (April–September 1989)

Teams from this nine-member expedition continued research projects begun in 1987 into the environmental (soil and flora) and settlement patterns, the ethnography, the agro-economic systems and trade routes in and out of the Patacancha valley, with a view to formulating a sustainable development programme. Lake core samples were taken from dry lake-beds at Qewnayoc and Marcacocha. Pre-Hispanic settlements at Tawasaywa and Juchuy Poques were investigated, as well as the main expedition's research into the trade-route to Occobamba. After one early setback they took precautions to avoid areas dominated by the Shining Path guerillas, and used their previous local contacts to good effect for the excavation programme.

Central Asia (China and USSR)

88/18 *Shiwakte Scottish Mountaineering Club Centenary Expedition* (July–August 1988)

The Shiwakte peaks (first sighted by Aurel Stein in 1913 and reconnoitred from a distance by Skrine in 1922–24) lie E of Mt Kongur. This six-member party was obliged by Chinese bureaucracy to approach the E side of the range from the Karakul Lakes and over the Karatash Pass, instead of the more direct approach used by some on the return. One team succeeded in the first ascent of Shiwakte II (6150m) from the S. Others made separate attempts on Shiwakte IIIA and Shiwakte I from the col between the two, and reconnoitred more of this attractive range from the outlying peaks of Aghalistan III and IV.

88/25 *Lancashire Polytechnic Tien Shan Caving Expedition* (July–September 1988)

This reconnaissance expedition was disappointed to find no obvious evidence of karst limestone caves in the Chinese Tien Shan, though there are plenty in the Russian Tien Shan. They investigated the limestone geology of the area and negotiated for a later Sino-British karst cave expedition to the E Kun Lun, described as an 'Alpine Guilin'. (See also 87/4 and 88/12, *AJ94*, 274, 1989/90.)

88/26 *London Mountaineering Club Expedition to Altai* (July–August 1988)

This two-man team failed in their objective of traversing the three peaks of Heroic Korea, Sapoznikov and Sukhov, but instead climbed the N face of Ak Ayuk (3650m) and also, by the normal route, E Bielukha (4506m), the highest peak in the range.

Himalaya

88/19 *British Joint Services Everest W Ridge Expedition* (April–May 1988)

This very large party of 36 officers and men approached Everest by the Rongbuk glacier, intending to climb the mountain by the W ridge. They made three bids for the summit, one group of two reaching c8600m, the other climbers, 25 in all, turning back at c7800m after the crux of the Hornbein Couloir.

88/24 *International Gangotri Expedition* (August–October 1988)

Half of the 17 climbers (Australian, US, South African and four British) succeeded in climbing Kedarnath Dome (6831m), but bad weather caused them to abandon attempts on the S pillar of Shivling.

88/39 *Anglo-Indian Jitchu Drake (6790m)* (May 1988)

Two British men and one Indian woman followed a variation of the 1984 Japanese route up the SE ridge to the S summit of Jitchu Drake (NW Bhutan) and continued to make the first ascent of the N peak.

88/40 *British Makalu Expedition* (August–September 1988)

After discarding their main objective of the W face of Makalu, and also their secondary objective of the Baxter-Jones Couloir, the climbing members of this large party reached the Makalu La at 7000m. Two members attempted the NW ridge reaching 8000m, when an avalanche carried away one man who suffered non-fatal head injuries.

88/50 *British Shivling Expedition* (September–October 1988)

This five-member team's attempt on the NW ridge of Shivling from the Meru glacier was abandoned at 5600m, after two members suffered acute mountain sickness symptoms.

89/1 *Jaonli (Garhwal) Expedition* (June 1989)

This British–Irish–Indian party explored the relatively unvisited Khatling Cirque, were turned back at 5850m on the unclimbed S ridge of Jaonli, but made the first ascent of P5450m (by E face and SE ridge) which they named Saga Parbat.

89/12 *British Kedar Dome Expedition* (August–September 1989)

After the establishment of camps at 5000m for both E and N faces of Kedar Dome (6831m) both attempts were abandoned, the E face 'steepening and becoming blank in sections', the N face as a result of poor snow conditions and broken ankle by leader.

89/22 *East Face Kedarnath Dome Expedition* (August 1989)

This three-man team altered their objective from a pillar in the middle of the unclimbed E face of the Dome to the Polish route leading to the left ridge of the E face. This was abandoned after severe storm about 350m and two days up.

89/30A *Annapurna III Expedition* (September–October 1989)

Owing to prolonged difficulties – delay in arrival of kit, under-equipped porters, difficult approach march and illness including death of Sherpa cook – this strong five-man team only reached 6100m on the E ridge of Annapurna III.

89/40 *British Baruntse Expedition* (April–May 1989)

This six-member party took the long approach route from Dharan up the Barun valley past Makalu Base Camp to attempt the SE ridge of Baruntse (7104m) from the lower Barun glacier. Some members had acclimatization problems, but two reached 6880m on the ridge before snow conditions forced retreat.

89/53 *Polish International Everest W Ridge Spring Expedition* (May–June 1989)

The British member of this disastrous Polish expedition reports that five of the six members who reached the summit of Everest by the W ridge and the Hornbein Couloir were killed by a massive avalanche on the W shoulder. He adds that they made the long but safer approach to the Lo La by traversing Khumbutse instead of the direct line from the Khumbu glacier.

89/55 *London Nilkantha Expedition* (September–October 1989)

This eight-member party approached Nilkantha from the S by the Panapatia-Bamak valley to attempt the unclimbed SE ridge but turned back at 5400m owing to snow conditions. They also reached 5500m on Parvati Parbat and explored the upper reaches of the Panapatia-Bamak valley.

Karakoram

87/34 *Karakoram Traverse* (July 1987)

To mark the 50th anniversary of Shipton's *Blank on the Map* and to continue his interrupted exploration of 1939, this strong three-man team succeeded in their aim of going up the Biafo glacier to Snow Lake, and pushing on over the Kurdopin pass, where Shipton turned back, to descend the Kurdopin glacier to Shimshal. *En route* they made the first ascent of the Solu Tower near the Hispar pass.

88/21 *Charakusa Spires (Hushe Valley)* (August 1988)

This six-member group succeeded in four first ascents: TDK Spire, Mt Beatrice, Mt Poro and Nasa, all between 5350m and 5850m. Detailed climbing directions have been provided for all four.

88/31 *British Malubiting Expedition* (August 1988)

This four-man team was frustrated by bad weather in their attempt on Malubiting (7432m) from its hitherto unclimbed S side. Their approach via Dassu and the Baskal glacier was chosen for its proximity to Gilgit (rather than the long way round via Skardu).

89/14 *New Zealand Uli Biaho Spire* (May–June 1989)

The six-member New Zealand party climbed the magnificent granite tower Uli Biaho (S of the Trango glacier), despite difficult snow conditions, by a route differing slightly from previous Italian and American ascents.

89/15 *British Women's Gasherbrum II Expedition* (July–August 1989)

Two members of this seven-women team reached the summit of Gasherbrum II (8034m) by the SW ridge on 12 July. Others reached c7500m.

89/18 *British Shani Expedition* (August 1989)

Abandoning their original objective of a NE–W traverse, this party made a second ascent of Shani (5800m) from the Naltar valley. (See also 88/46, *AJ*94, 278, 1989/90.)

89/19 *Hushe Valley Expedition* (June–July 1989)

This determined two-man team, despite bad weather, climbed Parantha Peak (5300m), the Dru (6000m) twice (once by the W, once by the S couloir), the N face of Tower Peak (5800m) and the S face of Paisa Peak, all in the Chogolisa glacier area.

89/23 *Indo-British Rimo Group Expedition* (June–July 1989)

Two teams (one mixed, the other Indian) obtained permission to climb the Rimo group in the Upper Siachen glacier 'war zone'. Two members (one British, one American) succeeded in the first ascent of Rimo II, but, instead of a joint attempt on Rimo III, the Indian team diverged to make the second ascent of Rimo IV.

89/27 *British Hushe Valley Expedition* (July–August 1989)

This four-man team climbed Rona Peak (5800m), Fiona Peak (5900m), Ibex Hill (5200m) and Patika Peak (6000m) on the N side of the Charakusa glacier, but failed on two attempts on Ripple Ridge.

89/29 *Snow Lake Expedition* (July–August 1989)

This seven-member party attempted seven peaks from a Base Camp at Shigambarisch in the Snow Lake area at the head of the Hispar glacier. All were abandoned owing to bad snow conditions, though one minor summit was reached and one ascent stopped just below an unstable summit block.

89/49 *Anglo-Irish Shimshal Expedition* (June 1989)

In face of snow conditions this two-man party substituted for their objective of a first ascent of Shiftikin Śar the first ascent of a lower peak (P5200m) to the N. They did not carry out their other objective of exploring the area to the W of the Malangutti glacier.

89/52 *British Masherbrum Expedition* (June–September 1989)

This 12-member party aimed to make the first ascent of Masherbrum by the E ridge and also to climb Masherbrum East (7821m) and to paraglide from the summit. Their highest camp was established on the snow-dome at about 6500m, close to the base of Masherbrum East and just below the SE ridge of Masherbrum. Several attempts on the S face of Masherbrum East were forced back at 6700m by heavy snowfalls. Paragliding was only possible at lower levels.

Book Reviews 1989

COMPILED BY GEOFFREY TEMPLEMAN

Chris Bonington – Mountaineer
Chris Bonington
Diadem Books, 1989, pp192, £17.95

Mountaineer is not really another book by Chris Bonington. It is Chris Bonington redesigned into a sumptuous Christmas package by his long-time editor at Hodder & Stoughton, Margaret Body, and Hodder's new pictorial collaborator, Ken Wilson of Diadem. For once, as Wilson shouts triumphantly in his introductory note, text is subordinated to pictures; and he has done Bonington proud, with a massive selection of colour photos, many of them not previously published, crisply printed in good deep colour saturation on a large-format double-page layout.

The whole Bonington career, spanning over 30 years, is on display, and the sheer variety and excitement of that career are summed up in the opening shots. For the dust-jacket we have a stunning view past a silhouetted figure on the Ogre, out over the Sim Gang glacier and Snow Lake, to the endless array of Hispar peaks beyond. On the back-cover a series of action portraits shows Bonington at different stages of his career. Inside the covers, the frontispiece is another glorious view from the Ogre. Then, as a backdrop for acknowledgements, comes a double spread of the NE ridge of Everest with the bleak vastness of Tibet beyond. Turn over to the contents page and you find what might be a classic Alpine ridge but is in fact the more esoteric Mt Cook massif in New Zealand. Opposite Wilson's introduction there is a dynamic shot of Haston on a steel-cold winter's day on the Grandes Jorasses; then we are off on the first chapter, 'Foundation', introduced by the soft grey light of a summer's day on the N face of Scafell, with just enough contrast to bring out all the architectural detail.

But what of the words? Each of the eight chapters opens with a general essay, followed by more detailed accounts of specific climbs, adventures and expeditions. The scope of Bonington's career – from self-conscious novice in North Wales to pushy alpinist, determined photo-journalist, big-expedition impresario and ultimately fulfilled Old Man of the Mountains, with all the world's ranges at his fingertips – is intrinsically fascinating, but to my mind this particular summing-up is not nearly as compelling as earlier books like *I Chose to Climb*. This is almost inevitable in a pictorial 'coffee-table' book and I suspect that most readers, like me, will tend to skip the text and concentrate on the picture captions, for this is where the real meat of the information lies. Take as an example the opening of Chapter 7, 'Snatched Opportunities'. There is a magnificent full-page picture of the E face of the Moose's Tooth in Alaska, supported by an extended caption packed with succinct historical and topographical information; the general blurb, by comparison, is slightly bland.

Mountaineer makes no claim to be a literary masterpiece, but it is a visual triumph. All but 80 of the several hundred photos are by Bonington himself and, although he is not quite in the same class as, say, Galen Rowell, he is highly competent. His spell as a professional photo-journalist, covered in one of the book's chapters, clearly taught him the discipline to record everything. On the Ogre he shows just how hard that final summit tower was and, broken ribs notwithstanding, he gets the vital shot of Scott abseiling on his knees through the storm, which is worth 100 beautiful views. Alone on Mt Vinson he managed to get the necessary documentary coverage, and his shots of the summit ridge of Everest are among the finest published.

The sheer bulk of good photographs is a tribute to the success of Bonington's career; but a picture album on this scale requires skilful selection, editing and designing. Few people could have made such a good job of it as Ken Wilson, who uses the double-page layout to build up a picture story, working on the principle that big mountain views merit large reproduction while people and incidents can be fitted into smaller spaces. Thus the terrifying grandeur of the Nuptse-Lhotse wall gets a double-page spread, and a previously unpublished shot of the Dru W face – a unique view in a special light capturing fully the architecture of the face – makes a breathtaking full-page introduction to the Alpine chapter. When Bonington's pictures don't come up to scratch or fresh variety is called for, Wilson uses other people's efforts – for instance Nick Estcourt's unusual shot of the Frêney Pillars.

Wilson knows how to present mountains and climbs at their best; but he has not, thank God, confined us to an endless procession of beautiful mountains. He has often been accused of lacking a sense of humour, but there is nothing humourless about this book for, giving the mountains life and meaning, there are people – people like Tom Patey using his North Wall hammer to test the helmet on the head of a young Sandhurst-fresh Bonington, and Joe Brown grinning in his own ridiculous-looking home-made helmet. There is the classic picture of Jim Fotheringham perched high on Menlungtse with the *Financial Times*, there is Blashford-Snell, pith-helmeted, leading the invasion of the Blue Nile, and a priceless shot of Whillans, *en route* for Patagonia, winning the ship's fancy-dress competition in flamboyant drag.

The humour is sometimes tinged with nostalgia for an earlier, more innocent era. I can't help envying Bonington and Whillans their sparse equipment and comfortably weathered jumpers and breeches on the Central Tower of Paine when I compare them with the grotesque 'designer' gear of today but, as well as nostalgia, there is real sadness for lost friends, particularly Nick Estcourt, whose death in the K2 avalanche is graphically chronicled, and Ian Clough, who died on Annapurna. The photograph of his funeral, with all those blank, shocked faces gathered around the roughly-dug grave, is a stark reminder of the risks of Himalayan climbing. Some people might call it voyeuristic, but I think it was brave of Bonington to include it in a book which really does try to cover the total experience of mountaineering.

My only criticism of Wilson's design is that just occasionally, faced with such a wealth of good material, he clutters the page with too many pictures. He is also, perhaps, over-fond of the inset box. For instance, one magnificent double-page spread of Everest's NE ridge, with the dynamic sweep of the N ridge, North Col and Changtse in the background, is spoilt by an unnecessary inset climbing detail. However, these are minor personal niggles, for Hodder & Stoughton's first venture into the pictorial big-format market is overall an outstanding success. I suspect that the *enfant terrible* from Diadem used a lot of bullying and cajoling to bring about that success, but in the end it is Bonington himself, with a little help from his friends, who provided the raw material. There can be few people in the world who could produce such a wealth and variety of mountaineering photographs. My own favourite section of the book is the description of the Ogre ascent, which epitomizes all that is best in Himalayan climbing, plus the uninvited drama of the accident and the epic descent. But all the chapters are good and I felt at the end that, if I had experienced just a quarter of those climbs and adventures, I would feel very happy.

Stephen Venables

Everest Kangshung Face
Stephen Venables
Hodder & Stoughton, 1989, pp236, £14.95

Today Everest has almost as many routes up it as an Alpine peak, has its own guidebook with grades and marked topos and is attempted by around 20 expeditions a year, almost all of them by the classic, existing routes. This made the achievement of Robert Anderson's small expediton to the Kangshung face all the greater and the more interesting. Tucked away on the E side of Everest, away from the glare of the traverse by the South Col and N ridge routes, televised live by a huge Chinese-Nepalese-Japanese expedition, in effect they had the mountain to themselves with all the challenge, fascination, at times fun, at times terror of making a technically difficult new route up the huge and complex face leading to the South Col. It was a classic, small adventurous expedition in the very best sense.

Everest, Kangshung Face is a well-written story of an exceptional mountaineering achievement and yet, in reading it, I was confronted by the problem that faces all expedition books and one which I have grappled with all too often – the unchanging pattern that expeditions follow: the initial concept or invitation, the preparations and approach, the build-up to the climb and then the climb itself. It's difficult to escape this structure; depart from the chronological story and everything tends to become confusing. The variables, of course, are the people concerned, and the strength of their characterization and interaction is what holds the attention.

Venables' portrayal of his fellow climbers is both affectionate and frank. On a surface level he captures the minor but very important irritations of expedition life, his anger at Ed Webster's constant halts to take pictures and the different styles and backgrounds of the climbers, but he doesn't get into their personalities or feelings. At the end of the book there is a slightly cardboard-cut-out quality to Ed Webster, Robert Anderson and Paul Teare, which is frustrating since they are obviously strong, colourful characters. I longed to know more of just how Paul Teare and the others felt when he was forced to descend from the South Col with suspected altitude sickness before their bid for the summit, more of the feelings of Anderson and Webster on that desperate descent.

It is perhaps that splendid British reticence and self-containment which might have limited his portrayal of the other team members, that helped Stephen rise to the extremes of crisis on his descent from the summit of Everest, firstly to join the others on the South Col and then in reversing their route back to Advanced Base. His description, both factual and on the level of personal feeling, is very revealing. His warmth for his fellow team-members and his honesty about the essential sense of self-preservation that must take over in an extreme crisis, when the human body has been stretched so far that it can only care for itself, come through strongly. There is also that quality which the lay person must find very difficult to understand – of slow-motion lassitude and lack of sense of crisis at altitude in what was obviously an extremely dangerous situation. In the heat of the sun, inside a warm sleeping-bag, it is all too easy to be seduced into prevarication, to snatch that extra minute of rest which so easily slips into hours and perhaps eternity.

The book is superbly illustrated and the pictures, particularly of the lower part of the Kangshung face, capture just how challenging and difficult their route was, all the more remarkable that it was put up by this tiny four-man team. It was, however, probably the necessity of working away at the lower slopes for so long which gave them the high level of acclimatization that enabled Venables to reach the summit, and Anderson and Webster to get so close.

The background history of the mountain is skilfully interwoven into the thread of the story and the appendix, on climbing at extreme altitude without supplementary oxygen, is a gift to any researcher. Apart from the frustrating niggle of wanting to see that little bit more into the minds of the four climbers, this is an excellent account of an outstanding mountain achievement, reminding us yet again how thin is the dividing line between staying alive – in this case at a price of lost toes and fingers – and disaster when going for the world's highest mountains.

Chris Bonington

Climbers

M John Harrison

Gollancz, 1989, pp222, £12.95

I didn't like the look of this book when I first opened it at random during the prize-presentation ceremony (Boardman-Tasker Award 1989). I imagine that was the first, and last, reaction of many of the hostile reviewers. One climber wrote in a national newspaper that *Climbers* is not about climbing. Well, the book does break a mould. And it is precisely because it is only 10 per cent about climbing that it is such a good book. This is the first book which really shows *why* people climb, and to do that it has to devote 90 per cent to their backgrounds.

The writing is very good throughout. Urban and natural landscapes merge into one another, as is typical of North England. In a 12-month span (with many flashbacks) we are taken through the lives (and one death) of half a dozen young male misfits in Thatcher's Britain, whose work ranges from porn-shops to steeplejacking. This is not a world of the Alpine Club: there are no Alps, only quarries filled with rubbish and climbing-walls filled with clouds of chalk. The great, filthy British Public is everywhere, as a Greek chorus exuding unlikely bits of dialogue. The relation of the climbers to ordinary life is well-pictured in the funeral scene, where Sankey's ghastly sister and brother-in-law show absolutely no understanding of Sankey's drives, thinking him an idiot when he is merely a misfit.

The book is rather slow at the start, and suffers at times from overwriting (too many similes and adjectives), but soon the story and style become clearer. Harrison is obviously a writer who uses a notebook rather than a word-processor: there are none of those awkward breaks of flow which come from word-processing, and the text is packed with detailed notes on urban and rural living, and vibrates with pop-video humour, convincing rock-sequences and well-researched medical details. The episode of the escaped children who live inside the carcasses of dead sheep rivals Salman Rushdie's prison-hospital scene as a satire of our society. I put down the book knowing more about what makes rock-jocks tick. I found no misprints, and only one factual error: *Samson* was not written *by* Menlove Edwards but *about* him.

Of course, this is a modern novel by a seasoned author, and some readers will have a little difficulty with its method. The 'plot' is understated, even non-existent. It's not clear, for instance, who is sleeping with whose wife – until you have read the whole book. But there are plenty of shining facets to sustain any reader who may feel deprived of narrative: the recurring dream-weather-mirror images, and the focus on fingers and hands, the touching behaviour of Mick who, though 'he always kept his pans filthy', does the laundry and tidies away the pornographic mags when his friend is killed. There is Normal (Norman to his wife) and his 'rock-garden'. There is gentle satire of us VS oldsters who, concedes the central character, are the backbone of the sport. There is delicious interplay of sunlight and shadow, both of rock-climbs and in the bedroom. There is Mike's wife Pauline with her face like a 'becalmed sail', whom he stands up at a rendezvous in King's Cross after separation. And, overall, there are the moors and dales of a far-away country called the North of England.

Ronnie Wathen

Scotland's Winter Mountains
Martin Moran
David and Charles, 1988, pp311, £14.95

A Century of Scottish Mountaineering
Ed W D Brooker
Scottish Mountaineering Trust, 1988, ppxii + 372, £15.95

Scotland has a marvellous wealth of mountaineering adventure available, varying from uncharted summer rock-climbs in remote glens to the thoroughly alpine challenges of the winter season. These two books are a celebration of Scottish mountaineering. *Scotland's Winter Mountains*, by Martin Moran, is an enthusiast's guide to the present and future winter scene; *A Century of Scottish Mountaineering*, edited by Bill Brooker (an anthology of articles taken from the *SMC Journal*), is a homage to the past. Both books are well worth buying; I had purchased both before being asked to review them!

Martin Moran – well known for traversing all the Munro summits during a winter season, while also being an experienced alpinist and Himalayan climber – is now a guide living in Torridon. He is clearly devoted to Scottish winter climbing in all its aspects. This enthusiasm comes over very strongly, perhaps too strongly at times as some of the points are made rather repetitively. The book is essentially a conglomerate of an instruction book, a guidebook, a history, a contemporary commentary and a handbook of Scottish mountain weather. The weather sections are particularly good and, as in all the chapters, are illustrated by short essays describing the reality behind the theory. I liked this personal touch, especially as I share his awe of, and strange attraction to, the worst that a full-blown storm can throw at you. The instructional sections on winter walking, climbing and navigation are admirably clear and full of useful tips. My only complaints are about the dual use of imperial and metric units, which sometimes makes the text unreadable, and his complete underestimation of the usefulness of an altimeter. Properly used – by being re-set at points of known altitude during the day – an altimeter provides the easiest way to navigate in foul conditions and is far more dependable than the suggestion of counting steps. More specialist sections on modern mixed climbing, ski-mountaineering, langlauf skiing and meteorology are contributed by expert guest authors, and the whole is rounded off with appendices on history and much other useful information. This superbly illustrated book is for the committed winter mountaineer, the novice and all those simply interested in modern Scottish winter climbing.

A Century of Scottish Mountaineering is a collection of articles taken from the *SMC Journal* since its foundation 100 years ago. They illustrate all the varied aspects of the Scottish scene from the earliest days of the SMC up to recent times. The emphasis is on the earlier years, which perhaps reflects the current reluctance of the SMC to embrace modern trends, or possibly indicates that the dedication required to aspire to contemporary standards diminishes skill with the pen. With sections devoted to winter climbing, rock-climbing, hill-walking and skiing, as well as obituaries, accident reports, accounts from foreigners and of foreign parts, and contemplative and fictional pieces, the book has something for everyone. I particularly liked the early photographs and articles; the energy and enthusiasm of the pioneers are obvious. This anthology ably illustrates (apart from the frequently poor typesetting) a past of which the SMC is justifiably proud.

If there is one criticism of this anthology, it is of the title. The SMC has never had a monopoly of climbing and exploratory activity in Scotland and thus the true history can never be culled only from the pages of its journal. Unless the SMC can attract into membership a higher proportion of the current activists, the next anthology may be more a history of the SMC than of mountaineering in Scotland.

Roger Everett

Over the Rim of the World. Freya Stark, Selected Letters
Ed Caroline Moorehead
John Murray/Michael Russell, 1988, pp404, £19.95

The letters selected by Caroline Moorehead from the eight volumes edited by her mother and herself cover Dame Freya Stark's life from 1914 to 1980 and range from New York to India. Most reflect her as explorer, and Arab protagonist, in the Arab and Persian lands – over the rim of the Mediterranean world. As befits an Honorary Member of our Club, a number of them disclose glimpses of her intense love of mountain country. The high air acted like champagne over her frail and often suffering body. Her doctor described her constitution as 'an insult to the medical profession'!

Her guided ascent, in July 1924, of the Macugnaga face of Monte Rosa by the 'Cannellone' (Marinelli Couloir) route was the second ascent by a woman of this long and dangerous, though not particularly difficult, route (12 hours from the Marinelli hut, overnight at Capanna Margherita, 12 hours down by the Loccie glacier). The enthusiasm, recorded at the time in her letter to Robert Stark, is reflected 40 years later in her contribution to the *Ladies' Alpine Club Journal* of 1964.

Freya Stark's letters from Persia include her exploration of the Valleys of the Assassins in 1931, which involved some rock-work, and a vivid description of camp at 5200m near Takht-i-Suleiman. Though she did not reach the summit, she corrected much of the topography of the area.

In 1956 she was following in the footsteps of Alexander the Great, wading round the foot of Mount Climax (between Antalya and Phaselis in SW Turkey) and wandering through the mountains of Lycia. She did not scruple to describe the Bithynian Olympus as the 'dullest mountain I have ever seen', but she must be excused since presumably she did not see the eastern precipices.

A brief visit to Simla in 1943 gave her a first glimpse of the Himalaya, and elicited a statement of her mountain faith: 'No human work ever moves me one fraction so deeply as the sight of nature, but especially of mountains.' She was not to revisit the Himalaya until November 1970 when Jimmy Roberts arranged for her, then aged 77, to ride, much of it up those 2000 steps, 'to the crossing of the Himalayan divide between Annapurna and Daulagiri' (sic) – presumably Ghorapani – where she wrote, 'Nothing that I can ever tell you will describe the awe and majesty of this approach, the last terrestrial footsteps to infinity.' And at the age of 83 this intrepid old lady was rafting down the Euphrates in Turkey.

One cannot but admire Dame Freya's indomitable spirit and her capacity for making friends which carried her through bouts of ill-health in lonely places; and one could wish for more glimpses of her mountain experience.

Edward Peck

Africa's Mountains of the Moon
Guy Yeoman
Elm Tree Books, 1989, pp176, £25

Any new book on the marvellous mountain ranges of Africa's Western Rift Valley is welcome. A volume so beautifully illustrated is doubly so, even at the price which has risen by £5 between printing and publication.

A couple of chapters are devoted to the Virunga Volcanoes, but the bulk is given over to the author's accounts of his several visits to the Ruwenzori in the past decade. The impression given is of a rather high suffering-to-success ratio, even allowing for the capacity of the Ruwenzori (and Uganda) to impose the former on visitors.

The central theme, however, is ecological rather than alpine. Yeoman has a mission – to obtain the protection of full National Park and World Heritage Site status for the region's exuberant vegetation, and to promote the interests of the Konjo people who are the greatest threat to it.

To advance the former he organized an expedition around the talents of the botanical artist Christabel King. A dozen or so of her superb illustrations grace the book, and the full collection must make an eloquent plea for the preservation of this unique flora.

Yeoman's text does not approach this high standard. It reads easily, but has too much sugar and not enough spice for my taste. I found the use of conversation as a device to introduce aspects of the area's history irritating, especially in the introduction where a conversation of 45 years ago is presented as verbatim. He should also be careful to get his history correct. On p77, his account confuses the two Poles who in 1939 made the first ascent of the E ridge of Margherita with the three Poles who in 1943 discovered and named the Irene Lakes after the wives of two of them and made the first ascent of the Margherita glacier.

Yeoman has a quixotic tendency to invest the ordinary with an heroic character. When, for example, he sends a messenger down the Mobuku valley to Ibanda, he hails him on his return as a young Philippides. The round trip took about 12 hours. The guidebook gives a time for 'a lightly laden, fit walker' of eleven and a half hours! A good effort by the lad covering in one day what would normally take two, but hardly of epic quality.

There is the same impression of rather tenuous contact with reality in the final chapter. His analysis of the problem is sound if commonplace. There is a population crisis in Africa which will, unchecked, continue to devastate the inhabitable areas of the continent. Overseas aid has increased rather than reduced the problem. His solution is pure Alice in Wonderland – a sort of sexual set-aside scheme backed by an un-family allowance financed by the diversion of funds from existing aid schemes. There could be some difficulty in persuading the aid-giving governments and agencies to divert funds from Save the Children to Prevent the Children! That, however, will be nothing compared with the difficulties faced in getting it accepted and operating honestly in Africa, where birth control is already regularly denounced and widely believed to be a colonialist, racist plot.

Even if the scheme were in being and effective, demographic momentum will still destroy the Ruwenzori montane forests. As Yeoman's map on p31 shows, much has already gone, destroyed by shifting cultivation on the Uganda side. From the evidence of the map, the strict regime of the National Park in Zaire would seem to be giving some protection. It is here that aid money could be used most effectively. The best that can be hoped for on the Ugandan section of the range is the preservation of the vegetation of the higher zones. Even the low pressure of the present tourist traffic is depleting fuel supplies. It would be an elegant irony, however, if some measure of conservation were to result from the discouragingly high prices charged by Ruwenzori Mountaineering Services – set up on the advice of Guy Yeoman.

It might be possible to finance and administer the protection of a limited area. A single valley, not linked to the present tour circuit, could be established as a human-free sanctuary. The remote Lamya valley would be ideal. All the vegetation zones are represented; Yeoman's account of his descent suggests that there is little if any settlement in the valley itself as yet. It is adjacent to the Zaire Park, so there would be the benefit of adequate space for the wider-ranging animals. It is achievable.

John Temple

Fragile Edge

Maria Coffey

Chatto & Windus, 1989, pp183, £12.95

Fragile Edge tells the story of Maria Coffey's love affair with Joe Tasker until he died on Everest with Pete Boardman. After the death of the two climbers, Maria and Hilary Boardman make a pilgrimage to Everest Base Camp to mourn and bury their dead loved ones.

The task of burying the dead was in some ways more clear-cut for Hilary Boardman, in the sense that her life with Pete had had the joy of togetherness and mutual respect. Unhappily for Maria, and perhaps unhappily also for the first half of the book, her relationship with Joe had not had a chance to become established before he died. Maria writes somewhat awkwardly about how she comes to realize that she has, in fact, fallen in love with Joe. This makes her feel uncomfortable because she feels herself losing control – a classic response to love and the reason that Joe, like others before him, had not wanted to 'commit' himself. What follows is a touching if wearisome account of the stereotypical situation where she sits at home waiting for him to come back from his all-consuming adventure; what she risks is the memory of his loss; what he risks, but will never know about, is being whisked away in a puff of snow. In her case this was to happen before the romance had had a chance to blossom.

Stories of unrequited love, or love lost, are less satisfying to read because they speak of impasse or distress. For this reason it is, ironically (and respecting the tragedy of Joe and Pete's death), liberating to reach the stage in the book when Hilary and Maria themselves go climbing. One can't help feeling that Maria should have adopted the classic male response to raised emotional levels and displaced them by taking to the hills earlier. Her account of climbing in the Alps with Hilary, as training prior to making the pilgrimage to Everest to pay homage to two great and loved climbers, was the most exhilarating part of the book.

The most moving and courageous part of the story of lost love was the account of the journey to Everest Base Camp. It is well recognized that a necessary part of the grieving process is to be able, if possible, to see the body but, failing that, to know as much as possible about the circumstances surrounding the death. For those who wait on Himalayan climbers, the arena of death is an unknown, unless the non-climbers themselves go there and try to make sense for themselves of what the magic entails. For Maria, this was to enter a terrain which had been placed beyond her reach by Joe's possessiveness and exclusivity. His tendency to mystify the climbing game made it all the harder for her to get to grips with the reality of the situation. Hence she is left doubting her right to be trespassing on his 'sacred' ground.

Hilary and Maria tackle the horrendous task of having to come to terms with the death of their lovers head-on. At Hilary's suggestion they make the same journey to Everest as Joe and Pete had done before them. They climb as far as Camp 3, from where they continue to gaze up at the Pinnacles where Joe and Pete were last seen, trying to accept what had happened and begin the process of letting go.

The moment of peace comes with acceptance. 'Sitting by the cairn I realized that I would indeed have to turn calmly away the next morning. Joe was gone, he was no longer moving about the earth . . . I had come to be close, to make my peace with Everest and with him, and now I had to leave accepting all.'

Most obituaries dwell on the glorious moments of the lives of our heroes. Most men of action rest on uneasy ground when it comes to looking at their relationships with women. A lot of relationships founder on the fields of adventure. For this reason, reading about them brings more bathos than catharsis. But the vicissitudes of love form the sub-plot to the dramas of the adventurers and need to be told, if only to comfort all the future grass-widows of the climbing sisterhood.

Margaret Urmston and Sheila Harrison

At the Sharp End
Paul Nunn
Unwin Hyman, 1988, ppvi + 202, £14.95

Paul Nunn is a most diffident rock-writer, with minimum emotion or claptrap. This book is a true record of what it has felt like to have been alive in the link-age between the founding of the Alpine Climbing Group in the postwar period and the more recent split of the mountain world into chalkies and snowsloggers.

The cover-pic portrays an elderly man in red-yellow kids' rompers gingerly eyeing an old-fashioned slab: that is to say, the slab is off-the-vertical, diffident, like the man (Paul Nunn). This is not a book of self-congratulation.

The book's weakness is that it is really only a reprint of articles and reviews. It thus lacks continuity, though he has tried to group subjects chrono/geographically. But the result (no rethinks) means authenticity and honesty.

In a *High* article, November 1987, he recalls the K2 deaths and the ugly literary aftermath:

> It is not a pretty literature, and forced me into innovations in method. Each new book was read usually within twenty-four hours of receipt. Post-midnight hours allowed the agonies of the carnage to be tolerated, lubricated by whisky, calibrated in quantities which were intended to anaesthetize. This usually worked – next morning the book was finished, its content assimilated. Feelings took longer, but could at least begin with a new day.

It's a peculiar thing, often noted in recent years, that mountaineering has produced a vast literature out of all apparent proportion to its importance. I have an explanation: the mountains are our country, our home, but we can never possess them. We come down, sit in clubs and stake out our claims in the Kingdom of the Mind. As Nunn says: 'So much time and energy has been expended in such curious ways. Though most things prove senseless at root, a residue of curiosity remains.'

To satisfy our curiosity, Nunn leads us through the years. Yet some things are missing: there is no real account of Don Whillans (Nunn's obituary of Whillans at the time was merely a list of his climbs, and has not been reproduced here), and for a good quote from Joe Brown I had to turn to Peter Gillman's book *In Balance* (Hodder & Stoughton 1989): 'It's not the actual technique – that's easy to keep hold of, though I do get the odd bloody creaking joint. The hard thing is to keep the enthusiasm to drive with. If you get pressure on you it does affect you. But it's not quite as simple as that – you can just go off for no apparent reason at all.'

Yet Nunn's book will be a truer quarry for historians, and there is also some fine avuncular wisdom, as when he castigates 'the use of people's confidences to stab them in the back, and the use of humour without the sympathetic symbiosis, which differentiates it from verbal bullying'.

It remains to be mentioned that the author is an economic historian by trade, and perhaps this explains the book's unusual objectivity.

Ronnie Wathen

High Altitude Medicine and Physiology

Michael Ward, James Milledge and John West

Chapman and Hall, London, 1989, pp515, £50.

Two millennia ago Chinese traders described the Great Headache Mountains as a formidable obstacle on their route to Europe – arguably the earliest reference to mountain sickness. In high central Asia, Mirza Muhammad Haider lost men and animals to altitude in 1550, and a few decades later Father Jose d'Acosta graphically described his sickness while crossing an Andean pass. But only in the last century – and mostly in the last 30 years – has altitude medicine become a popular and sophisticated discipline to which this book is a major contribution.

The authors 'have been there and done that': all are experienced climbers and scholarly leaders in research. The book is well organized into 31 chapters, the first three of which describe the history, geography and demography of mountainous regions and the physics of the atmosphere. Then follow 16 excellent chapters describing the oxygen transport system from ambient air to lung, to blood, to cell and finally to the mitochondria, with frequent reference to the aberrations caused by oxygen lack. Four excellent chapters deal with the varieties of altitude illness, fleshing out the framework established earlier in the book.

The authors' experience in the real world is evident when they examine disorders due to cold and heat and discuss nutrition, sleep and other problems of the mountain setting. The first chapter deals with the history of man's experience with altitude, and each subsequent section adds important, often amusing accounts of how we have learned what we know today. The whole gamut of human response to lack of oxygen is covered and the synergism of cold and hypoxia is recognized. Unfortunately, injuries due to cold are separated from an excellent discussion of thermal balance and there is little mention of problems due to heat.

An important chapter contrasts man at altitude with man short of oxygen due to illness at sea-level, a fascinating subject suggested by Sir Joseph Barcroft more than 50 years ago which still cries out for more study. A brief chapter outlines problems which should keep one from going to altitude.

The authors also describe what is not known; they recognize issues that are controversial, and though they draw most heavily from their own experience their biases intrude only seldom. Here and there disputed data are advanced as fact, and it is particularly interesting to see how scientists from different countries disagree, mostly in terminology but now and then in fundamentals.

Each chapter is extensively referenced, and the bibliograpy is generally excellent and up-to-date. Unfortunately the index is totally inadequate.

Despite some minor flaws, this is the definitive and highly readable text about a subject of growing interest and importance.

Charles Houston

Soldiers and Sherpas. A Taste for Adventure

Brummie Stokes

Michael Joseph, 1988, pp250, £14.95

This book is mainly about soldiers, marginally about Sherpas, and packed with adventure from beginning to end. It is roughly divided into two halves, the first part dealing with Brummie's boyhood and service in the Greenjackets and SAS, and the second with mountaineering, albeit still mostly in his capacity as a soldier.

We start with Brummie's boyhood and youth as a member of a large and loving family living in humble circumstances in the suburbs of Birmingham. During this period, often as a member of a gang of toughies, Brummie performs many daredevil feats in response to challenges by his companions, is in trouble more than once with the police, and when in a serious fix attempts to commit suicide. He always wants to climb and, inspired by Hillary and Tenzing, soon teaches himself rock-climbing on local rocks. He always has Everest in view as his ultimate goal, and he always wants to be a soldier and to join the SAS but, finding that three years' army service is a prerequisite, he enlists in the Greenjackets at the age of 17½, to qualify for eligibility.

Discovering that all his applications for the SAS are being destroyed at source instead of being forwarded, he deserts from Northern Ireland, is caught, escapes and presents himself at the SAS selection headquarters in Hereford. The SAS are sufficiently discerning to let him go ahead in spite of the Greenjackets' efforts to get him back for punishment. After a setback due to a tiff with a sergeant he is accepted in the SAS, and continues his apprenticeship as a climber in North Wales and the Alps. Then follows service in Borneo, Malaya, Hong Kong and Guyana and finally in Dhofar where, because (as he says) of the incompetence of a young officer, he becomes exposed to the fire of the enemy, gets hit in the leg and suffers the removal of a kneecap and other damage. Enough to end the climbing career of a normal person, you would think – but not so for Brummie. Soon he is in Nepal, a member of an Army Mountaineering Association attempt on Nuptse. Selected with his pal Bronco Lane and two other climbers to attack the summit after the first summit party have fallen to their deaths, he is trapped in his tent at the top camp for two days and buried under snow. After digging their way out Brummie and Bronco descend safely, but the other pair also fall to their deaths.

A few years later, as members of a joint British Army and Royal Nepalese Army expedition, Brummie and Bronco climb Everest, but are benighted at 8500m on the descent and Brummie loses all his toes from frostbite. Curtains to climbing for Brummie?

But no – after painstakingly and painfully rehabilitating himself and participating (still in the SAS) in the Falklands War, this amazing man is back on Everest as leader of a party to climb the N face, having first climbed Mount McKinley, as much to test himself as the rest of the party. An avalanche at their Advanced Base Camp carried them half a mile down the mountain; one of the climbers is killed and three others injured and Brummie has his neck broken (a hairline fracture). Undeterred even by this, he is back on Everest in 1986 to lead a strong team of (mostly) civilians in an attempt on the NE ridge, defeated by high winds. Returning in 1988 with a similarly constituted party, he suffers a series of cerebral oedemas and has to be evacuated to Kathmandu. (The party goes on to surmount all the difficulties of the NE ridge, but is deprived of the summit by the weather.)

And there we leave this indomitable man. The book is written in a down-to-earth straightforward style and the writer emerges as a tough and rough-cut person, full of initiative and obviously a great organizer and leader. There is a touch of self-pride and superiority, wholly justified, and a strong contempt for sham and inefficiency. All in all, this enthralling and unusual book should not be missed.

Ashley Greenwood

Mein Weg in den Himalaya. Biographie eines Bergsteigers
Karl Herrligkoffer
Pietsch Verlag, Stuttgart, 1989, pp280, npq.

This autobiography by a well-known controversial name in German mountaineering is extensive. Born in 1916 of a family of modest means in Bavaria, he lost both parents at an early age and was brought up by his aunt. At the age of 18 he learnt of the death of his half-brother Willy Merkl, while leading an expedition on Nanga Parbat. This affected him deeply and is the key to his many Himalayan expeditions, which he regarded in the nature of a pilgrimage. He was, incidentally, upset by Eric Roberts' book *Welzenbach's Climbs* (1980), which he felt cast unwarranted aspersions on Willy Merkl's leadership.

He had many years of medical experience, including research in high-altitude medicine, which was to serve him in good stead. His philosophy on mountaineering, described at some length, sets out the importance of extended physical and mental effort to offset the problems of everyday life. *Ich klettere, also lebe ich.*

His series of Himalayan expeditions was beset by financial problems from the start in the 1950s. The Bavarian government and the German Alpine Club were not forthcoming with financial support, and in 1954 he complained of a press campaign against him as not being fit to be a leader. Nevertheless, his Willy Merkl Memorial Expedition to Nanga Parbat did succeed in 1953, with Hermann Buhl soloing to the top. Over the following 30 years he was in some 20 Himalayan expeditions with varying success, the highlights being Nanga Parbat Rupal face in 1970, Everest in 1972, Kangchenjunga in 1980, and K2 in 1986 in his 70th year.

The book has good photographs. The expeditions are not strictly chronological and tend to be somewhat blow-by-blow accounts. The most remarkable thing of all, however, is that there is no mention of the acrimonious dispute in the climbing press which followed the successful ascent of the Rupal face of Nanga Parbat by the brothers Reinhold and Günther Messner on his expedition in 1970 – no mention of the 'misunderstanding' as to whether Reinhold should make the final bid for the summit 'against Herrligkoffer's instructions'. The account only relates to discovery of the Messner brothers after their descent.

Peter Ledeboer

82. *The classic view to Jbel Toubkal (4167m), the highest peak in North Africa, from above Imlil, Morocco.* (Hamish Brown) (p 225)

83. *'The Camel', in the harsh landscape of the Jbel Sarho, Morocco.* (Hamish Brown) (p 225)

84. The Cascade d'Ouzzoud in the Central Atlas. (Hamish Brown) (p 225)

85. *Aq Tash (7016m), on the Aq Tash glacier, east of the Saser La, East Karakoram.* (Arun Samant) (p 248)

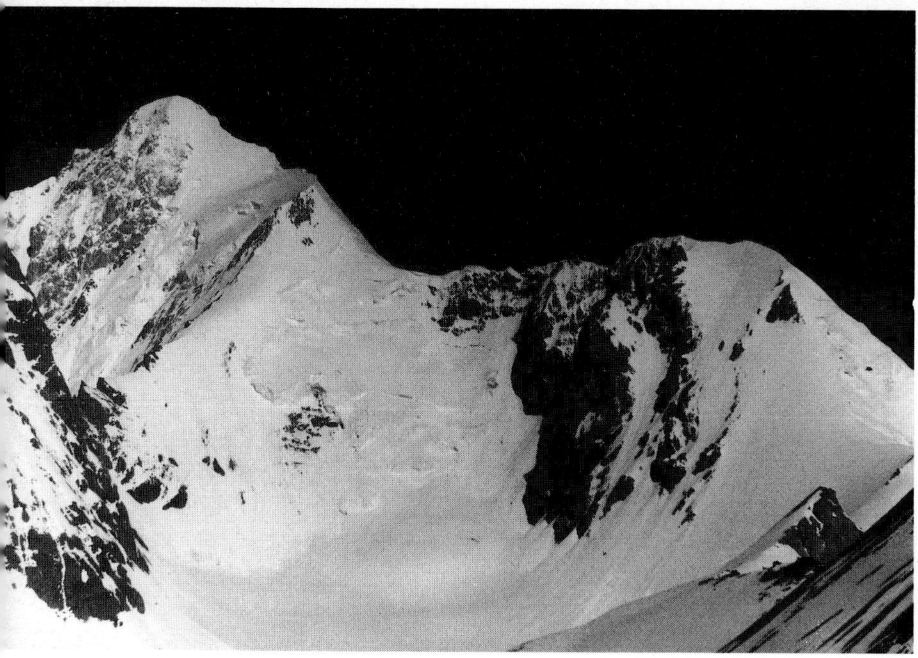

86. *Chong Kumdan I (7071m), SE face, in the East Karakoram.* (Harish Kapadia) (p 248)

87. John Howard (1917–1988) (p 295)

88. Guido Monzino (1928–1988) (p 295)

89. Marco Pallis (1894–1988) (by courtesy of Richard Nicholson) (p 295)

90. Erwin Schneider (1906–1987) during the 1955 International Himalayan Expedition. (Norman G Dyhrenfurth) (p 295)

The Alps

Albrecht von Haller (trans. Stanley Mason)
Walter Amstutz de Clivo Press, 1987, pp84, limited edition

This slim but elegantly produced quarto volume, in its soft covers and protective slip case, comes to us from our revered Honorary Member and Swiss publisher Walter Amstutz, and what a nice addition to the Alpine Club Library it is.

The main purpose of the book is the publication of a modern English translation of Albrecht von Haller's famous poem on 'The Alps'. The translation is printed alongside Haller's German text, and is preceded by an interesting note on the difficulties of the translation by Stanley Mason, the translator.

But not the least interesting contribution to this book is Professor Karl S Guthke's introductory biographical essay on Haller, who was a very remarkable man in his day. A poet in early life, he became famous through his poem *Die Alpen*. But later on he became renowned as a physician, anatomist, botanist and general scientist. It has been claimed that he was perhaps one of the last men of 'universal learning'. He visited England in 1727, where he eventually became so esteemed that both George II and George III tried to persuade him to come and live there.

Haller's poem *Die Alpen* was epoch-making because he was the first Swiss poet to praise the beauties of his native country and to forget about just 'beauty, horror and immensity'. Some years later an English lady, the beautiful Duchess of Devonshire, did the same thing in a rather more lyrical but much less famous poem, 'The Passage of St Gothard'. At this point, I have to confess that I am not qualified to appreciate *Die Alpen* in German. But Mason's translation, which is the main purpose of this publication, is what I am reviewing and I must say that I read it with considerable pleasure. Haller conjures up some beautiful pastoral images of life in the Alps, but rather spoils this by some boring moralizing about the wickedness of city as opposed to pastoral life. He would have us hark back to the golden age, as Rousseau was to do later. I have to admit that in spite of fine passages in the translation of this poem I am unable to become enthusiastic about it; it appears to me to be somewhat pedestrian. Somehow or other, like much of Pope, it seems to miss out a good deal on the true poetic spark of a Milton, or a Wordsworth, in spite of a superficial resemblance, perhaps, to 'The Prelude'.

Maybe it would not be out of place to compare Haller's poem with the work of one of those many highly competent topographical watercolour artists of the eighteenth century, admirable in their way but lacking the inspiration of a J R Cozens, whom Constable apostrophized as 'all poetry'.

Not the least interesting part of this beautifully produced book is its illustrations, mostly from copper-plate engravings of pictures by Gaspar Wolf, the frontispiece being a particularly impressive painting. But, above all, it is a book to be read for the sake of its introduction to us of a very great man in his day.

Charles Warren

I A Richards: His Life and Work

John Paul Russo

Routledge, 1989, ppxx + 843, £40.00

I A Richards the mountaineer is splendidly delineated in his wife Dorothy Pilley's *Climbing Days*. There we see him pioneering climbs in North Wales during and after the First World War (how pleased he was in his eighties when, most unusually, one of his climbs was *up*graded in the latest guidebook), and climbing in the Alps with his wife and Joseph Georges, with first ascents of the N ridges of the Grivola and Dent Blanche. Alpine Club members who heard, or read, Ivor Richards' talk in 1975 on 'Mountains and Mountaineering as Symbols' could be in no doubt as to the part mountains and climbing had played in his life.

So it is rather a disappointment to find that, of the 800 pages of John Paul Russo's *I. A. Richards: His Life and Work*, only 18 cover the climbing (in a chapter called 'Mysterious Mountains' which suggests they are more of a mystery to the biographer than to his subject). But early on in the book there is an intriguing revelation. Richards, having failed to find a teaching job in philosophy in Cambridge in 1919, decided to put in time as a professional climbing guide in the Highlands. Among the friends he asked to help him with introductions was Mansfield Forbes – who promptly recruited him into the English faculty.

Those concerned with Richards' academic and intellectual pursuits will find these fully described and discussed: the critical works which deeply affected university teaching of English, the long campaign for Basic English. Richards' career in Cambridge, China, Harvard, return to Cambridge, and the final heroic trip to China when he was 86, on which he was taken mortally ill, is thoroughly covered, though his wife plays a much smaller part in this account than she did in Ivor's life. Whether on the mountains or in either of the Cambridges, their friends remember them as always together, a remarkable pair.

Janet Adam Smith

K2 Il Nodo Infinito. Sogno e Destino

Kurt Diemberger

dall'Oglio Milan, 1988, pp268, Lire 50,000

This splendid (and expensive) example of book production includes 130 photographs, many of great beauty, mostly taken by the author and Julie Tullis, his assistant and companion. The text is an Italian translation from the German edition (*K2 – Traum und Schicksal*; Bruckmann, München, 1989. An English version will be available from Grafton Books this year). The *Nodo* (knot) in the title, a Buddhist symbol, is applied by the author to the interests and endeavours he shared with Julie. The first third of the book amplifies Kurt's autobiographical article in *AJ89*, 16–20, 1984, and the final two-thirds is a full account of the 1986 tragedies on K2 which were also the subject of notes by Diemberger in *AJ* (Vols 92 and 93). Tables at the end of the book show that of the 66 climbers who have reached the summit, 27 did so in 1986; and of the 26 lives lost on the mountain so far, 13 (including Julie's) were in that year. The special merit of the book is in its detail – in parts it is almost a step-by-step account of Kurt and Julie's climb, with all its nightmare disasters, and the result is a harrowing and unforgettable experience for the reader.

Robin Robinson

Under Storen
A portrait of Utladalen and Vettisfossen
Jan Schwarzott
Sogn og Fjordanes Forlag, 1989

Utladalen, of which this handsome book of photographs is a portrait, is a deep valley about 40km long which stretches from Årdal at the head of Sognefjord into the heart of Jotunheimen. The text, which covers both the topography of the area and its history, is in Nynorsk (New Norwegian) which is rather difficult to understand even for those who can speak Norwegian, but there are both English and German translations at the end of the book.

The area, in which there are more than 50 peaks of over 2000m, is dominated by Storen, as Store Skagastölstind is known locally. Owing to difficulties of access the area was virtually unknown even to Norwegians until the latter half of the last century; it was not until the arrival on the scene of William Cecil Slingsby that it was thoroughly explored and opened up to mountaineers. Storen was first climbed by Slingsby in 1876.

The photographs are impressive if somewhat sombre. It would have been helpful, particularly to English and German readers, if they had carried individual captions.

V S Risoe

Thin Air. Encounters in the Himalayas
Greg Child
Patrick Stephens, 1988, pp192, £12.95

Straightforward 'expedition books' tend to be rather boring, even if well written, if only for the fact that one has read so many over the years. This is why so many authors turn to the 'warts and all' style, hoping that the foibles and idiosyncrasies of their companions will create interest. Greg Child has taken a different tack. He waited until he had three expeditions under his belt before starting his book: Shivling 1981; Lobsang Spire and Broad Peak in 1983; and Gasherbrum IV in 1986. The variety makes for interest, particularly as the style of writing is excellent, but it is the encounters of the title that really make the book. These are treated with humour and insight and are beautifully done. Fresh anecdotes of Whillans, for instance, are always welcome and there are plenty here. In a different vein, the death of Peter Thexton is very moving. Add to this a selection of photos of peaks in or close to the areas described, each marked with various routes of ascent, and you have an enjoyable and useful addition to expedition literature.

Geof Templeman

Western Baltoro Mustagh. Vols 1, 2, 3 & 4
Northern Baltoro Mustagh. Vol 1
Jan Kielkowski
Przewodnik Alpenistyczny, Düsseldorf, 1988/1989, approx pp50, pb, in Polish

These are further volumes in the series of guides (published in Polish) to selected areas in the Himalaya and Karakoram. They feature excellent drawings of the peaks with route diagrams – which make the descriptive text less essential for non-Polish speakers – and maps and climbing histories. The main groups featured are the Uli Biaho, Trango, Baltoro Cathedral, Lobsang Spires and Muztagh Tower in the first volumes, and K2 in the last.

Lakeland Panorama
W A Poucher
Constable, 1989, pp204, £15.95

The late Walter Poucher's son has assembled a further collection of photographs not used in the two previous colour books on the Lakes, although many look very familiar and are probably variations of some already published. All one can say is that it is the mixture as before.

Lottie Dod, Champion of Champions. The Story of an Athlete
Jeffrey Pearson
Countyvise, 1988, pp96, pb, £2.95

Lottie Dod was Wimbledon champion, British Ladies' Golf champion, and represented Britain in archery at the 1908 Olympics. She indulged in other sports as well, but this book is chiefly of interest to AC members because of the descriptions of climbs she did in Switzerland and Norway in 1896 and 1897, the latter with Elizabeth Main (Le Blond) and Joseph Imboden, which included the first ladies' ascent of the Vengetind.

Southwards to Geneva. 200 Years of English Travellers
Mavis Coulson
Alan Sutton, 1988, ppxvi + 156

Between the 1650s and the 1850s, the number of English tourists travelling to Geneva gradually increased, as might be expected. This book selects a few of the more remarkable such as Evelyn, Maria Edgworth, Byron and Shelley, Francis

Danby and some of the early climbers on Mont Blanc, and puts them into the perspective of the Geneva of the time.

Classic Walks in the Lake District
Walt Unsworth
Oxford Illustrated Press, 1988, pp160, £14.95

Another in the *Classic Walks* series, this is a useful volume to join the mass of other guides to walking in the Lakes. Reasonable descriptions and photographs of 40 walks of all lengths and standard, slightly spoilt by the niggling fact that the numbers of the walks do not correspond with the numbers on the maps.

Wainwright on the Lakeland Mountain Passes
A Wainwright
Michael Joseph, 1989, pp224, £14.95

This is the mixture as before, descriptions by Wainwright and photos by Derry Brabbs, but this time it is of 49 Lakeland passes, alphabetically from Black Sail to Wrynose.

Alpinism
Ed Chic Scott, Vol 1, 1988

A new journal, edited in Calgary by Chic Scott, which covers not only Canadian but also international mountaineering. Among the contributors are Greg Child, Jim Bridwell and Voytek Kurtyka, so a good standard of writing on interesting climbs is assured.

Beyond Everest. Quest for the Seven Summits
Patrick Morrow
Camden House/Cordee, 1986, pp176, pb, £10.95

It is now rather late for a review of this book, but it deserves a note. Two years ago we had the Bass/Wells book on climbing the seven highest summits on the continents, in which they mentioned their 'competitor'. Now we have that competitor's own story, slightly different in fact as it substitutes Carstensz for Kosciusko, but vastly different in approach. It is actually Morrow's autobiography and contains far, far more than just the seven summits. In fact, the breadth of his climbing and exploration is immense, and expeditions which would provide other authors with a complete book are here given a few paragraphs sandwiched in between other exploits. In addition to now being involved in the travel business, Morrow is a professional photographer and the numerous examples of his work here are excellently reproduced. The style of writing is good, and it is a book which can be confidently recommended to anyone interested in mountaineering and mountain travel. In addition, there is the bonus of yet another voice added to the tale of the 1982 Canadian Everest expedition!

Montagne Paradis ou le rêve romantique
Samivel
Arthaud, 1988, pp208, F 395

There are none of Samivel's own enchanting pictures in this collection, but he provides an introduction to a selection of alpine prints and pictures, each of which is in colour and accompanied by a relevant contemporary quotation.

Which is the Highest Mountain in the World?
Report of the expedition Ev-K2-CNR to Mt Everest and K2 1987
Prof Ardito Desio, 1988, pp36

When an astronomer from the University of Washington announced in 1987 a revised height for K2 which made it higher than Everest, Prof Desio felt that an expedition should be mounted to take measurements of both mountains under controlled conditions. This gives the findings of that expedition – 8872m for Everest and 8616m for K2. These figures show how accurate the original *Survey of India* heights were – 8848m and 8611m respectively – and how inaccurate was the American figure of 8859m for K2. The report makes fascinating reading, but clearly shows the problems involved in accurate measurement of high mountains.

Classic Rock Climbs in the Lake District
Bill Birkett
Oxford Illustrated Press, 1989, pp142, £14.95

There is already a stream of *Classic Walks* . . . and *Classic Climbs* . . . This volume, apparently the first in a series to cover the five main climbing areas of Britain, is well produced, written and illustrated. Each crag chosen has a brief overall description, then one or two of the classic routes are described and illustrated in detail, often with historical quotations from accounts of the first ascents. If this standard is maintained, it will be a good series.

The Book of the Climbing Year
Ed Cameron McNeish
Patrick Stephens, 1988, pp152, £14.95

12 different months, 12 different climbers each writing of their own experiences

and thoughts in that particular month could be a recipe for nothing more than a collection of magazine articles. However, we have here some of the best writers on the British climbing scene today, and this makes for an interesting compilation.

Classic Walks in Scotland
Cameron McNeish and Roger Smith
Oxford Illustrated Press, 1988, pp144, £14.95

One is getting a little overwhelmed by *Classic Walks* and similar titles with which the public is being bombarded these days. What can one say? Adequate photos and descriptions, minimal maps, and that's about it.

On Foot in North Wales and the Peak
Patrick Monkhouse
Diadem Books, 1988, pp256, £11.95

Two hill-walking classics of the Thirties have here been combined in one volume with numerous new photographs and an excellent introduction by Jim Perrin. Outdoor types of 'a certain age' will have been brought up on these glorious little books and their republication is greatly welcomed.

In the Throne Room of the Mountain Gods
Galen Rowell
Sierra Club Books, 1986, pp xviii + 334, pb, $17.95

A new edition of the 1977 book with a short 'Afterword' summarizing subsequent events in the K2 area, and containing all the original text and black-and-white photos, but with much fresh material and a new selection of colour plates.

Trekking. Great Walks of the World
John Cleare
Unwin Hyman, 1988, pp216, £14.95

This is definitely one of the better compilations of 'world walks'. The areas covered are the Himalaya/Karakoram – Annapurna circuit, K2 and Hidden Peak, and the source of the Ganges; Africa – the High Atlas and the Ruwenzori; the Americas – Vancouver Island, the Wind River Range, the Darien Gap, the Royal Road of the Incas and the Towers of Paine; Europe – the Pyrenean High Route and the Pindos traverse; and New Zealand's Southern Alps. Each section has a description of the trek, excellent photos (as you would expect) and a two-page fact sheet which, in addition, gives brief details of other treks in the area.

Cleare writes three of the sections himself, the others being handled by experts in the particular region.

Mountain Man. The Story of Belmore Browne
Robert H Bates
Amwell Press, 1988, pp xx + 426, $47.50

Robert Bates has produced a magnificent monograph on Belmore Browne which, originally published in a limited edition, is now publicly available. The section of most interest to mountaineers is that on the controversy over Dr Cook's claim to have reached the summit of Mt McKinley in 1906, and of the 1910 expedition in which Browne climbed the mountain and unmasked Cook. Several photos of these expeditions are included, plus details of Browne's life. The major part of the book, however, comprises Browne's own articles, some previously unpublished, on hunting, wildlife and exploration in Alaska and the Yukon, and a portfolio of colour reproductions of 33 of Browne's accomplished oil-paintings.

On the Pennine Way. Poems
Peter Sansom
Littlewood Press, 1988, pp48, £3.00

This slim little book of verse is a poet's reflections on walking half the Pennine Way, from Standedge up to Middleton-inTeesdale. 28 poems are included, so they are not of great length, yet each one captures perfectly the essence of that particular part of the walk and of the people met on the way, varying from elation at walking the moors in fine weather to the depression of camping in bad weather. Drawings by Anna Karvot enhance a nicely produced little volume which repays dipping into again and again.

The Trekking Peaks of Nepal
Bill O'Connor
Crowood Press, 1989, pp224, £14.95

This book is a comprehensive guide to the 18 Nepalese peaks which can, at the present time, be climbed with only a standard trekking permit. In addition, the approach routes to the mountains are covered, together with suggestions for additional treks in each area and good general advice on organizing an expedition, whether for climbing or trekking. While one or two of the peaks are comparatively easy, the term 'trekking peak' also covers some of the more fascinating and difficult mountains in Nepal, and the author points out the many opportunities for new routes that still exist. Well written and illustrated, this book is essential reading for anyone intending to venture among these peaks.

The Peak. A Park for all Seasons
Brian Redhead
Constable/Peak Park Planning Board, 1989, pp184, £15.95

Principally a book of excellent photographs of the Peak Park, Brian Redhead – President of the Council for National Parks – has written an introduction which sums up the Park to perfection. Living a matter of yards outside the boundary, he is well acquainted with both the joys and the problems of the area, the joys being beautifully portrayed in the photographs of the Park in the four seasons.

The Thunder Dragon Kingdom. A Mountaineering Expedition to Bhutan
Steven K Berry
Crowood Press, 1988, pp x + 166, £12.95

This is the story of the expedition to climb Kankar Pünzum, the highest mountain in Bhutan, in 1986, led by Steven Berry. Anything about Bhutan is bound to be of interest, it being a land which still exudes unknown mystery and Berry, who knows it well, gives a delightful picture of the country they passed through. The climb, the third attempt on the peak and ultimately unsuccessful, was a difficult one – almost as hard as the trek to reach the peak! Finally, though, bureaucratic troubles caught up with them even in Bhutan, and the evacuation brought its own problems.

Snowdonia to the Gower. A Coast to Coast Walk across Highest Wales
John Gillham
Diadem, 1988, pp111, £14.95

The idea of a north-to-south footpath down the centre of Wales is not new, and has indeed been resisted on occasion. This book does not describe an 'official' walk, however, but suggests an informal itinerary, with alternative high-level options on a number of sections, diverging to a great extent from the originally proposed Cambrian Way. The walk is split into 11 day-sections and each section is quite a demanding walk, especially if the rougher alternatives are chosen; so it is not a book for the casual 'short-walker', although everyone can enjoy the superb colour photos which are excellently reproduced.

Trekking in Nepal, West Tibet and Bhutan
Hugh Swift
Hodder & Stoughton, 1989, pp xx + 360, pb, £9.95

This most recent trekker's guide deals with Nepal and general aspects of trekking in a thorough and workmanlike way, but additionally has (necessarily briefer) details on Western Tibet and Bhutan.

The Crag Guide to England and Wales
David Jones
Crowood Press, 1989, pp224, pb, £9.95

A useful gazetteer to all the crags in England and Wales, with a paragraph on each crag, notes as to its possibilities, directions on how to reach it and an area map showing all crags in the locality. There are some good photographs. This is really an updated version of Ted Pyatt's *Where to Climb in the British Isles* and, to some extent, of Walt Unsworth's *The English Outcrops*, but neither is mentioned nor acknowledged.

Avonside Explored
Edward H Peck
Privately published, 2nd Edition, 1989, pp64, £3.30

Our member Sir Edward Peck, who is Secretary of the Avonside Conservation Group, has produced this useful guide to Tomintoul and Glenlivet, which traces the Banffshire Avon from its source in Loch Avon under Ben Macdhui to where it joins the Spey. After describing the lower more populated parts of Strathavon, it gives a series of walks and drives centred on Tomintoul, with notes on history, geology and flora and fauna. Although the author encourages people to visit lesser-known places, he is not over-enthusiastic in directing the hordes to the real wilderness areas, as becomes the secretary of a conservation group! Copies can be obtained from the author at Easter Torrans, Tomintoul, Ballindalloch, Banffshire AB3 9HJ.

Flowers of the Himalaya, a supplement
Adam Stainton
OUP Delhi, 1988, pp xii + 86 + 128pp plates, £25.00

This book is a supplement to the late Oleg Polunin's and the author's monumental *Flowers of the Himalaya*, published in 1984. It includes some 350 species not originally included, plus colour plates of these species and those not so illustrated in the original work. Both books are therefore needed, and together they form an unrivalled and indispensable guide.

Anything is Possible
Leo Dickinson
Jonathan Cape, 1989, pp224, £14.95

Many of the photographs in this book, particularly those relating to sky-diving, certainly show that 'anything is possible'. As a follow-up to Dickinson's *Filming the Impossible* it covers still more of the author's adventures, ballooning, sky-diving, cave-diving and filming in the mountains, all accompanied by superb photos. The author does seem to have something of a fixation on falling, whether controlled as in his incredible sky-diving exploits, or uncontrolled as in the deaths of John Harlin and Toni Kurz on the Eiger, where Dickinson went to incredible lengths to film reconstructions of the events. Apart from a short chapter on Don Whillans, the mountaineering content of the book is about the Eigerwand – Harlin's and Kurz's deaths and the first ascent.

Frank Kingdon-Ward. The Last of the Great Plant Hunters
Charles Lyte
John Murray, 1989, pp xvi + 218, £16.95

Frank Kingdon-Ward's plant-hunting expeditions, mostly to China, Tibet, Burma and Assam, occupied most years from 1909 up to 1957, and a number of his numerous books on his exploits have become classics of their type. These books are quoted from extensively in Charles Lyte's fascinating life of Kingdon-Ward, a man for whom exploration and plant-collecting went hand in hand. Some of his descriptions reveal a life of hardship and frugality which rivals Tilman's, and at times he must have been a difficult person to get on with, but it is to him that gardeners owe so many of the rhododendrons, lilies, poppies and other glorious Himalayan plants which are comparatively common in our gardens today.

Alpine Climbing
John Barry
Crowood Press, 1988, pp208, £14.95

Mountaineering instruction books are normally rather 'pedestrian' by the nature of the subject and, provided you have correct information and clear illustrations, you can't ask for more than that. Here, however, you have a bonus in the form of typical Barry asides and reminiscences. An excellent introduction for anyone going on to 'bigger things'.

Great VS Climbs in the Lake District
Tim Noble
David & Charles, 1989, pp160, £16.00

Another compilation of Lake District climbs, described in the blurb as 'The first comprehensive climbing tour of the Lake District'. While some may carp at this statement, it is quite a useful book with some good illustrations, describing 28 VS climbs district by district. Each section is preceded by a walk-in description and then a personal account of the climb in question. As a personal quibble, citing the names of the climbers in each photo does seem an unnecessarily egotistic exercise, particularly as so many are of the author!

On The Big Hill. A Non-climber's Everest
Mark Anderson
Faber & Faber, 1988, pp xii + 174, £12.95

This book has been 'panned' by most reviewers in the mountaineering press and, indeed, compared with something like James Morris's *Coronation Everest*, it does come off very much second-best. Having said that, however, taken as a media man's view of what was to him a completely alien exercise, it shows a most interesting view from the other side. You will have a job to follow the course of the expedition from this book and the personnel becomes hopelessly mixed up in the narrative, but the differences between the film-making team and the climbers are well brought out, as is the hardship of camp life to one unaccustomed to it. An interesting read, therefore, but one that – like the TV film series – does not achieve anything like full marks. For Faber to put a 'Major TV Series' sticker on the cover seems to be pushing it a bit!

Thomas Cook International Top 50 Ski Resorts
Arnold Wilson
Webb & Bower/Michael Joseph, 1989, pp200, £15.95

The author, skiing correspondent of the *Financial Times*, has made a personal choice of 50 resorts which he considers give the best skiing, particularly on virgin powder. The countries covered are Austria, France, Italy, Switzerland, USA, Canada, Argentina and Japan. Each resort has two or three colour photos, a personal assessment and a basic fact sheet.

The Islands of Scotland including Skye
D J Fabian, G E Little, D N Williams
Scottish Mountaineering Trust, 1989, pp x + 406, £18.95

For the past 70 years the SMC has been issuing district guidebooks and, after the first few, the traditional red covers have been instantly recognizable everywhere. Tradition has been broken in this, the first of a new series, as it has a bright blue cover, but there is no fear that any of the previous high standards have been changed. Skye has now been included with all the other islands, and the other change is that many colour photos are now included. This is no doubt reflected in the high price but, as with many recent SMT publications, the result is a book that is excellent both to look at and to use.

Footloose in the Himalaya
Mike Harding
Michael Joseph, 1989, pp xiv + 242, £16.95

Mike Harding leaves his beloved Dales to head for the Himalaya in his latest book. He describes three treks: the first in India with his wife Pat, from Darsha over the Shingo La to Padum and Leh; the second from Pokhara around the foothills of the Annapurna range; and the third on the Everest trail to the top of Kala Pattar. As might be expected the writing is witty and humorous but, what may not be expected by those who have not seen his book *Walking the Dales*, the photographs – and there are many of them – are also excellent.

Canyon Country Climbs
Katy Cassidy and Earl Wiggins
Pruett, Colorado, 1989, pp xvi + 102, $34.95

This large-format book, mainly of superb colour photos but with a reasonable amount of text, covers climbing in the canyon country of south-eastern Utah. In particular it includes Castle Valley, Fisher Towers, Arches National Park, Colorado River Valley, Canyonlands National Park and Indian Creek, with descriptions of first ascents by Layton Kor and other notable desert explorers, including the authors.

The Way Through the Glens
Hamish MacInnes
Constable, 1989, pp216, £15.95

A picture book of 'a pictorial tour of the Highlands', containing not only the expected mountain views but also the usual tourist shots of the Forth Bridge, Iona, Glamis Castle and many others.

Everest. South-West Face
L H Zamistnin
1984, pp224, pb, in Russian.

This account of the 1982 Russian expedition to the SW face of Everest was presented to the Club by Vladimir Balyberdin, one of those who reached the summit. It contains several colour and black-and-white photos, some of which are by Balyberdin.

Mountains. A Natural History and Hiking Guide
Margaret Fuller
John Wiley, 1989, pp256, pb, £8.85

This is an American book, mainly about mountain geology, flora and fauna, and chiefly relating to mountains of the Americas. There is a gazetteer of world mountains at the end, but some of the entries, particularly that on the mountains of Great Britain, show a rather perfunctory knowledge.

Skye. Walking, Scrambling and Exploring
Ralph Storer
David & Charles, 1989, pp224, £12.95

There are many guides to Skye, but this book is rather refreshing in that it covers the entire island, giving equal status to all parts. While many of the best routes in the Cuillin are described, so are beautiful walks and scrambles in Minginish, Sleat, Trotternish and the other areas of the island, with some of the best photographs of coastal scenery seen for some time. Another plus for the visitor from the south is that every Gaelic name has its phonetic pronunciation.

Off the Beaten Track. Women Adventurers and Mountaineers in Western Canada
Cyndi Smith
Coyote Books, Jasper, 1989, pp290, pb

The author is a park warden at Jasper for the Canadian Parks Service and has a great interest in the history of exploration in Western Canada. In this book she describes 14 women explorers, mountaineers and guides who were active in the region from 1885 until the Second World War.

The Crystal Horizon
Reinhold Messner
Crowood Press, 1989, pp324, £16.95

This is the first English edition of *Der Gläserne Horizont*, originally published in 1982, and here translated by Jill Neate and Audrey Salkeld. It tells the story of Messner's solo ascent of Everest in 1980, from Tibet and without oxygen. As usual in a Messner book, there are excellent historical chapters on previous ascents from the north, and the book as a whole is excellently produced. The colour photos are few, being limited to a small selection of the author's own at the rear of the book, and some of John Noel's 'semi-colour' ones at the front. There are many other photos in the text, but all are black-and-white and many quite small, some being hardly worth reproducing. The story of Messner's ascent is well known, but this reviewer at least finds the author's style hard to take in large doses, even though the translation is well done.

Alpine Dictionary
Rudolf Weiss (B M Byrne)
Rother, München (Cordee), 1989, pp452, £12.95

This is a useful dictionary of mountaineering terms in German, English, French and Italian, each language having a separate section with the corresponding terms in the other three languages.

Lightweight Expeditions
Rob Collister
Crowood Press, 1989, pp144, £12.95

There have been quite a few books recently on how to run lightweight expeditions, but this one must rank among the very best. The author has spent the last 20 years travelling and climbing in many parts of the world, and his experience shows in this work. All expected aspects are thoroughly covered, with especially detailed notes on one of the most hazardous operations – river crossing, all spiced with personal comments. A valuable book for what the author describes as 'experienced mountaineers who have climbed on both rock and ice in Britain or the United States and have had at least two seasons of alpine climbing'.

The following guides and other books have also been received:

Safety on Mountains. An Approach to Mountain Adventure for Beginners. John Barry and Tim Jepson. BMC, 1988, pp38, £1.50

Rock Climbing Techniques. Steve Ashton. Crowood Press, 1989, pp128, pb, £6.95

Climbing Days. Dorothy Pilley. Hogarth Press, 1989, pp x + 356, pb, £6.95

Modern Rock and Ice Climbing. Bill Birkett. A&C Black, 1988, pp192, £12.50

Guide to Manuscripts. The Fonds and Collections of the Archives, Whyte Museum of the Canadian Rockies. Banff, Alberta, 1989, pp xvi + 170, npq

Wild Country Camping. Kevin Walker. Constable, 1989, pp180, £8.95

Chamonix Mont Blanc. A Walking Guide. Martin Collins. Cicerone Press, 1988, pp192, £8.25

The Jura. (Two parts.) Walking the Jura High Route. Kev Reynolds. Winter Ski Traverses. R Brian Evans. Cicerone Press, 1989, pp192, £6.50

The Valais, Switzerland. A Walking Guide. Kev Reynolds. Cicerone Press, 1989, pp192, £8.25

Crete Off the Beaten Track. A Guide to Country Walks and Mountain Hikes. Bruce and Naomi Caughey. Cicerone Press, 1989, pp144, £6.95

Escalades dans le Massif des Calanques – Devenson, Castelvieil, Gard. Anne-Françoise Raybaud and Alexis Lucchesi. Édisud, 1989, pp166

Randonnées Pédestres dans le Haut-Var Central et Oriental. Josianne Alor and Alexis Lucchesi. Édisud, 1989, pp176

Appennino Centrale. Vol 1, 2nd Edition. Carlo Landi Vittorj. CAI/TCI, 1989, pp452, L50,000

Walks and Climbs in the Picos de Europa. Robin Walker. Cicerone Press, 1989, pp215, £10.95

Escalades et Randonnées en Corse. Massif de Bavella. Alexis Lucchesi, Jean-Paul Quilici, Bernard Vaucher. Édisud, 1989, pp204, FF85.00

Randonnées Pédestres dans les Calanques. Les Isles, Canaille-Soubeyrane, Saint-Cyr – Carpiagne. Alexis Lucchesi and Josianne Alor. Édisud, 1989, pp160

Massif des Calanques. Nouvelles Escalades á la Bougie. Alexis Lucchesi and Bernard Vaucher. Édisud, 1989, pp12

Góra Zborów. Część Wschodnia. Jan & Małgorzata Kiełkowscy. Przewodnik Wspinaczkowy, Düsseldorf, 1987, pp61

Tung Lung Island Climbing Guide (Hong Kong). Chung Kin Man. Nd, pp12

Rock Climbs in the West Midlands. Doug Kerr. Cicerone Press, 1988, pp116

Mid-Wales. John Sumner. Climbers' Club, 1988, pp232, £9.95

Moorland Gritstone. Chew Valley. Ed Geoff Milburn, BMC, 1988, pp304, £9.50

Staffordshire Gritstone. Ed Geoff Milburn, Comp Gary Gibson. BMC, 1989, pp312, £9.95

Stanage. Ed Geoff Milburn/Graham Hoey. BMC, 1989, pp414, £10.95

Clogwyn Du'r Arddu. Paul Williams. Climbers' Club, 1989, pp166, £8.95

Moorland Challenge. Tony Wimbush. Ernest Press, 1987, pp96, £4.65

Arran, Arrochar and The Southern Highlands. K V Crocket and A Walker. SMC, 1989, pp360

100 Classic Climbs. Lake District. Stephen Reid and Steve Ashton. Crowood Press, 1989, pp240, £9.95

The Pennine Mountains. A Walker's Guide to the Cheviot Hills, the Northern Moors, the Howgill Fells, the Yorkshire Dales and the High Peak. Terry Marsh. Hodder & Stoughton, 1989, pp256, £7.95

North Devon and Cornwall. Iain Peters. Climbers' Club, 1988, pp326, £9.95

New Climbs 1988. Gary Gibson. BMC, 1989, pp252, £5.50

Rock Climbs, Lancashire and The North West. Phil Kelly and Dave Cronshaw. Cicerone Press, 1989, pp394, £12.95

Torridon, A Walker's Guide. Peter Barton. Cicerone Press, 1989, pp168, £5.95

Langdale. D Armstrong, P Rigby and J White. FRCC, 1989, pp264

Hill Walking in Snowdonia. Steve Ashton. Cicerone Press, 1988, pp120, £4.50

Southern Sandstone. Dave Turner. Climbers' Club, 1989, pp208, £8.95

Blue Ice and Black Gold. A Climbers' Guide to the Frozen Waterfalls of Valdez, Alaska. Andrew Embick, 1989, pp130

In Memoriam

COMPILED BY GEOFFREY TEMPLEMAN

(*Plates* 87–90)

The Alpine Club Obituary	*Year of Election*
Aritsune 'Yuko' Maki	1926 (Hon 1970)
J Monroe Thorington	1927 (Hon 1946)
John Armstrong Fergusson Watson	1954
Eleanor Baillie	LAC 1952
Andrew Paul Diamond	1989
Eric Bentley Beauman	1920
Peter Cresswell	ACG 1976
Marjorie B Heys-Jones	LAC 1935
Julian Vincent Anthoine	1969
Soli S Mehta	1974
Julian David Layton	1933
Alison M Barton	LAC 1956
Sir John Hamilton Wedgwood	1939

I am pleased to be able to start this year with tributes to five of our members who appeared in last year's Alpine Club Obituary, and to end with two for well-known climbers who were members for only a short time.

Erwin Schneider 1906–1987

An unusual life, unconventionally led, has ended. It was marked by outstanding achievements in the mountains of his home and of the world. We should remember it; it should be an example to fill the young with enthusiasm.

Erwin Schneider was born on 13 April 1906 in Joachimstal in Bohemia; he attended the modern secondary school in Salzburg, passed the school-leaving examination in 1924 and then began to study mining at the Technische Hochschule in Berlin. He graduated in 1934 as a qualified engineer.

While still at school he had carried out (from Salzburg) sensational climbs on the Untersberg, on the Bischofsmütze and in the Tennengebirge. He called them 'sins of his youth', but very likely these early exploits were already marked by the characteristics which enabled him to grow famous and old as a mountaineer: he was quick, incredibly tough and strong in performance, he was good in assessing risks, using his head and his intuition, and he had the necessary pocketful of luck.

While still a student, Schneider participated in three big expeditions: in 1928, 22 years old, to the Pamir, where he climbed eight peaks of over 6000m, finishing with the first ascent, together with E Allwein and K Wien, of Pik Lenin (7135m); in 1930, under G Dyhrenfurth, to Kangchenjunga, when he made the first ascent of four 7000ers and, with Jongsong Peak (7449m), the ascent of the highest peak climbed at that date; and, in 1932, in the Cordillera Blanca, he made the first ascents of seven peaks, including Huascaran (6768m), the highest mountain of Peru. In 1934, on Nanga Parbat, he was extremely fit and performed outstandingly with Peter Aschenbrenner, but the summit was denied him. After his return from this tragic expedition (three climbers and six porters lost their lives), he was treated with great injustice. He never recovered from this treatment, but maintained an iron silence. In all these expeditions he was present first of all as a climber, but in addition as assistant surveyor to help with the survey activities. In 1936, in the Cordillera Huayhuash (Peru), in addition to five first ascents, he carried out for the first time independent survey measurements and their evaluation.

In 1939, when Schneider was 33, he made a winter ascent of the Biancograt and suffered such severe frost damage to both feet (already damaged by frost on Pik Lenin) that all the toes and the bones of the middle foot had to be amputated. The doctors prophesied he would be limping on crutches for the rest of his life. Schneider answered with a 'tired smile' and embarked upon his great period as daring skier and mountain surveyor.

During the Second World War, and the years immediately following it, he created the basis for the Alpenverein-Maps of the Ötztal Alps and the Arlberg region; and the photography of the Everest region in 1955 was his greatest achievement up to that time; the Everest map has become world-famous. Only he himself exceeded this achievement through his work as Director of the Survey Team of the German Research Enterprise Nepal-Himalaya (1959–1974), when about 11,000km^2 of mainly severe high-mountain country in E Nepal was photographed and measured out for maps. The same period also saw his photographic and evaluation work for the three Alpenverein-Maps of the Wetterstein mountains, for the map of Mt Kenya (1963) and of Huascaran in the Cordillera Blanca (1964). His last project was put into practice in 1983 on the Lewis Glacier (Mt Kenya); this gave him the greatest pleasure on the occasion of his 77th birthday.

Erwin Schneider was a great all-round mountaineer, always according to the motto: 'the longer, the steeper, the better', which led to his exceptional achievements as a mountain surveyor. His maps formed the principal basis for the work of aeroplanes and satellites in the field today, not only for mountaineers but also for earth scientists of all kinds. This was his central aim: to contribute – through the combination of sports and survey activity – to the exploration of mountains, of the 'uneven territory'. That is what he lived for. He was unstintingly generous in handing on the benefit of his experience and, without reservation, he passed on his store of pictures and maps to anyone interested. He always generously supported the young, and often took them along to the greater ranges at his own cost. This sparked off the careers of many young mountaineers and explorers. With his style of life it was not always easy to live with him; he could be demanding, and it required skill and stubbornness to oppose his ideas and his iron will.

He refused all honours and invitations to make public appearances; but he appears to have accepted (as a recognition of his achievements) the designation *excellenti in litteris* granted by Innsbruck University (1959), and the title of professor (1975) bestowed by the Federal President on the basis of a unanimous proposal from the Faculty of Philosophy. He retained his style of life to the end and in December 1986 had his 'last fling', making extensive surveying trips in Nepal. Although he was not supposed to go above 3000m, on this occasion he flew with an Indian pilot, in an open plane without oxygen mask, up to over 7000m towards Kangchengjunga. After 56 years he was delighted and moved to be able to see once more the camp-sites, routes and summits which had been the scene of his first arrival in Nepal in 1930: the country which had become his second home. On his return he immediately made plans for a new flight to the Cordillera Blanca; but this was not to happen.

Erwin Schneider was granted a life that was fulfilled, enviably without routine and active to the end, a life which allowed him to pursue his interests and desires single-minded. His wife Adelheid made this possible. He died in Lech on 18 August 1987, in his 82nd year. 'Forget me' was one of his favourite leave-takings. Sorry, Erwin – that's not possible. 'End of the message' – that's better.

Dr Gernot Patzelt

(Translation of a biographical notice kindly communicated by Norman Dyhrenfurth.)

Guido Monzino 1928–1988

Guido Monzino was born in Milan on 2 March 1928. At a very early age he joined the firm *La Standa Grandi Magazzini* which his father had established throughout Italy. After a hard apprenticeship, which started at the bottom of the ladder, by 1953 he found himself in charge of the business. His rise demonstrated early and exceptional organizing ability coupled with outstanding drive.

At that stage of his life – 1955 – his passion for mountaineering began. His bold, restless spirit displayed itself in ever-changing enterprises: alpine raids, expeditions to Africa, Patagonia, the Karakoram and the Arctic. The means employed varied, but his expeditions always included numerous alpine guides from the Aosta valley.

Early on, Guido Monzino had become aware of the intellectual and physical potential of this new generation of alpinists, distinguished by their passion for mountaineering – a potential which only required a co-ordinator in order to be realized, allowing these men to put themselves to the test in major new undertakings.

Under Monzino's influence the expeditions had an exploratory and scientific character, besides having formative and cultural value for the guides and the various companions whom he selected on different occasions.

A modern explorer whose qualities rested on his overpowering enthusiasm and his capacity for meticulous organization, he had a personal authority which allowed him to obtain optimum results from all who were pledged to his enterprises.

He had the strongest human interest in the people of the countries he visited, and thus his work was one of loyalty, education and proselytism which left a lasting mark.

Monzino had the character of a man of the Italian Renaissance, partaking of the austerity, pragmatism and daring of the great British navigators and explorers. Without any doubt he was one of the elect amongst explorers.

His successes at the North Pole in 1971 and on Everest in 1973, after 10 Arctic expeditions and nine to the Italian Alps, Africa, South America and the Himalaya, bear ample witness to his worldwide designs and his determination in carrying them out. In some cases his exploits were set within the cultural frame, in others the scientific, but always within the human context. Personal honours he spurned, carrying ahead that tradition of courage, professionalism and dedication characteristic of the mountain men chosen by him so as to set an example to all.

In Italy, as sometimes happens, Guido Monzino's achievements received little recognition. Indeed, there was criticism of the large scale of the means employed on the Italian Everest expedition, the critics overlooking the spirit which infused Monzino's ventures.

There is a secure place in the history of exploration and mountaineering for this man, who generously gave all he had – his inspiration, skill and personal qualities – for a goal which served both to raise the human spirit and to offer eternal challenge to nature.

Laurent Ferretti

(Translation of a biographical notice kindly communicated by Efisio Noussan.)

Guido Monzino's Expeditions

Gradatim conscenditur ad alta (Monzino's motto)

1. West Africa (1955)
2. Grandes Murailles (1956)
3. Cerro Paine and Torri del Paine (1957–58)
4. Kanjut Sar (1959)
5. Kilimanjaro (1959–60)
6. West Greenland (66°) (1960)
7. Mount Kenya (1960–61)
8. West Greenland (74°) (1961)
9. Ruwenzori (1961–62)
10. West Greenland (72°, with sledges) (1962)
11. West Greenland (70°) (1962)
12. Staunings Alps (East Greenland) (two expeditions, 1963 and 1964)
13. Tibesti (1963–64)
14. Hoggar (1964–65)
15. West Greenland (nautical) (two expeditions, 1968 and 1970)
16. Jacobshavn-Kanak (with sledges) (1969)

17. Kanak-Cape Columbia (with sledges) (1970)
18. Cape Columbia–North Pole (with sledges) (1971)
19. Everest (1973)

John William Howard 1917–1988

John Howard's climbing career spanned over half a century, from the first entry in his 'Record of Ascents and Passes Crossed' – 'walked up Slieve Donard (Mourne Mountains), August 1929' – to the last record of a walking holiday in the Engadine in June 1986. There were interruptions in the war years but even then, when he was able to get a couple of weeks' leave in 1940, he used it to climb Kilimanjaro, and in 1943 he made two short trips to Mt Kenya.

His abiding love for mountains and mountaineering developed in the university long summer vacations which he spent with a Swiss family in the Val d'Hérens. Officially he was improving his French, but he managed to kill two birds with one stone by learning mountaincraft with the local guides as well. He recorded Alpine seasons in 1935, 1936, 1937 and 1938, and lists the Dent Blanche, Zinalrothorn and Matterhorn among his peaks and passes.

When Howard left Cambridge his degree and personality met the high standards set by the British Colonial Service, and 1939 found him in Kenya as an administrative cadet. This apprenticeship in the art of government was cut short by call-up to the army and posting to the 5th Battalion The King's African Rifles, with whom he served as Intelligence Officer; in Abyssinia against the Italians, where he distinguished himself at the crossing of the Awash River Gorge, and in Madagascar against the Vichy French.

In 1944 the Colonial Government claimed his services once again, and he resumed his career in the Kenya administration. By then too, he had accumulated sufficient expeditions to be elected to the Alpine Club.

1945 saw his third visit to Mt Kenya (*AJ55*, 284–287, 1945–46). In the following year he made his fourth visit there, this time in the company of Arthur Firmin, when this formidable partnership made the first ascent of the S face and SW ridge of Batian. Also in 1946, he was able to return to the Swiss Alps, his first love, where he added the Mittaghorn, the Südlenzspitze-Dom, the Evêque and the Dent de Zaillon to his list. During the same leave from Kenya he renewed his acquaintance with the Lake District.

In 1947, 1948 and 1949 Howard made more ascents on Mt Kenya, including the second ascent of the W ridge of Batian and the SE face of Nelion. In those days a visit to these peaks had almost the glamour of exploration, and few of the present well-trodden routes had been done. He was one of the élite few who helped to change all that. Drawing on his European experience, he took the full gamut of alpinism to colonial Africa. His climbs on Mt Kenya, many with his friend Arthur Firmin, are recorded in *AJ60*, 270–275, 1955. He would be the first to agree that the achievements of some of the 'hard men' of recent years are in a different league from his pioneering climbs. Nonetheless, today's climbers on Mt Kenya are climbing on foundations he helped to lay.

A keen member of the Mountain Club of Kenya, Howard gave unstinting help and encouragement to many. In 1959, with Fullerton, he took Kisoi

Munyao up Shipton's route to become the first African to reach the summit of Mt Kenya.

Then, of course, there was Himal Chuli. The 1955 Kenya Expedition to this 7864m peak grew out of the long and fruitful partnership between Howard and Firmin, who both dreamed of achieving something bigger and higher than anything in Africa or Europe. They were the inspiration and joint leaders of the enterprise.

There were many occasions when Howard's administrative training stood the party in good stead – in encounters with the local administration *en route* to the mountain, but most importantly when the expedition ran into the snowline well below the normal summer level, and many miles from the intended Base Camp. The 70 porters, most of them clad only in thin cotton clothing and without shoes, said they weren't employed to carry over snow – and they certainly weren't equipped to sleep on it. Howard, wearing his 'Bombay bowler' and looking the part, held a good old-fashioned *baraza*, as practised by all proper District Commissioners in Colonial Africa in those days, and remained calm and dignified. After patient negotiations, lasting nearly all day, the porters agreed that several of them would do a carry over the snow the next day, drop their loads and return to sleep – not enough to save the situation, but much better than nothing.

The story of the rest of the expedition, and the tragic death of Arthur Firmin after breaking a leg on easy boulder scree just above Base Camp, has been told by Howard in this journal (*AJ60 et seq*). Firmin's death within a few hours' carry of the 'Shining Hospital' in Pokhara, after the epic struggle to get him off the mounain, was an immensely traumatic experience for Howard which left a lasting effect.

All this took place as Howard was steadily climbing the ladder in the Colonial Service; in 1950 he was selected to run a three-year course in colonial administration at Cambridge University. He spent some time as a District Commissioner, did a spell with the African Land Development Board, and became acting Provincial Commissioner before returning to Britain in 1962.

The following year saw him back in Kenya undertaking a special assignment on boundary demarcation at the time of independence. This was followed by an assignment with the Overseas Development Administration in West Africa. Later he was recalled from retirement to join the cadre of distinguished colonial officials who went to the newly independent Zimbabwe to observe the first general election.

In 1965 he was elected a member of the committee of the Alpine Club, and he continued to make regular trips to the Alps, Wales, Scotland and the Lakes – sometimes just with his family, sometimes with fellow members of the Alpine Club and the Mountain Club of Kenya on their end-of-the-year meet. He was always ready for a walk on the North and South Downs, and he continued with excursions of this kind right up to his death.

All who were privileged to know Howard say that they remember him as much for his outstanding personal qualities as for his climbing capabilities. His life was governed throughout by the strength of his Christian principles which even seemed to manifest themselves at his funeral, described by some who were there as being infused with a happy and quiet confidence. On rock he also had the power to inspire total confidence in those climbing with him: one knew for sure that everything was firmly under control.

John Howard died at the age of 71 after a fall, in no way a climbing accident, while camping in the south of France. He leaves his wife Elizabeth, a member of a well-known Kenya farming family, a son Jonathon who is a regular Army officer and two daughters – one of whom, Sarah, he imbued with his own love of mountains and mountaineering.

John Hull, John Blacker, Charles Richards,
Bob Caukwell, David Wilson
and Sarah Howard

Alexander Harrison 1890–1988

Alexander (Sandy) Harrison, who died in December 1988 in his 99th year, was a remarkable man who – despite being handicapped by blindness in his later years – continued to take a keen interest in current affairs and, particularly, in mountaineering.

Sandy was a grandson of Sir George Harrison, a former Provost of Edinburgh who is remembered for his energy and wide and varied interests, many of which Sandy himself developed in turn. His keen intellect showed at school (Merchiston); afterwards he studied to become a chartered accountant, winning the gold medal of the Scottish Institute for the best candidate.

His career was interrupted by the First World War, in which he was commissioned first in the Royal Scots and then in the Machine Gun Corps (The Suicide Corps); he was one of very few officers in the latter to survive the war. Although listed to travel on the troop train involved in the Gretna disaster, a fortunate last-minute change of plan prevented him from boarding the train.

In professional life Sandy set and maintained a high standard of excellence. His merit and sound judgement were reflected in his appointments which included the Chairmanship of the Standard Life Assurance, of the Edinburgh Investment Trust, of Cowans of Penicuik and of the Edinburgh Savings Bank, and Vice-Chairmanship of the British Linen Bank.

A distinguished mountaineer and a proficient skier, Sandy was elected to the Scottish Mountaineering Club in 1918 and the Alpine Club in 1939. In the 1920s his skill and experience were recognized by an invitation to join one of the expeditions to Mount Everest, which very reluctantly he had to decline due to other commitments. He was one of the first British mountaineers to climb guideless in the Alps, where his companions included Frank Smythe. In 1938 R L G Irving published an anthology which included an article by Smythe graphically portraying how Sandy's endurance and skill enabled the party to descend safely from high on the Schreckhorn in a prolonged storm.

In 1926 Sandy's love of the countryside led him, along with a like-minded group of friends, to found the Association for the Preservation of Rural Scotland. He also played a dominant role in the formation of the National Trust for Scotland in 1931, and he served on various committees of the Trust for many years. As might be expected, he played a very important part in the acquisition of the Trust's mountain properties.

Although latterly handicapped by blindness, Sandy continued to enjoy country walking – with a friend's hand under his elbow when the ground became rough. Always friendly, Sandy is missed not only by his wife Jean and close family, but also by a wide circle of friends.

Bill Wallace

Kenneth Neville Irvine 1906–1988

Kenneth Irvine, who died at Henley-on-Thames on 16 November 1988 aged 82, was the middle of five brothers all at Shrewsbury, most of them notable oarsmen. The one just above him in age was Sandy who, after proving himself a pillar of Shrewsbury and Oxford crews, lost his life on Everest in 1924. Kenneth himself was no mean oarsman at Magdalen in the 1920s. I have happy memories of him at school and at the Oxford of those days. I am sad that I saw less of him in later days, when my spare time went to the world of cricket and his to rowing, but no one could fail to hear of the legendary hospitality which he and his wife Phyl extended to young oarsmen at their home in Henley, particularly to young Salopians.

For many years Kenneth was a popular and trusted doctor at Henley. He had won a Travelling Fellowship to New York after Oxford and became a specialist in tuberculosis vaccine, on which he wrote a number of papers and for which he was awarded an OBE. In the Second World War he served as a Major in the RAMC in Iraq and Belgium.

Kenneth was elected a member of the AC in 1929. His record of climbs when applying for membership shows that he did many of the standard climbs in the Mont Blanc range in the mid-1920s, mostly in guideless parties led by Herbert Carr, but occasionally with such well-known guides as Joseph Knubel and Armand Charlet. In 1929 he was filming with George Finch in the Bernina.

I have one vivid memory of Kenneth in later years. Like myself, he could come only seldom to events at the Club, but we met on that memorable evening when we welcomed back the conquerors of Everest in summer 1953. He and I were standing in a corner, talking of old times, when an official of the Club brought Tenzing and Hillary to introduce to Kenneth. At this stage I modestly bowed out, and have always regretted since that I did not stay on, as a silent fourth, to listen to what must have been an historic conversation – the two men who got to the top talking with the younger brother of the man who may possibly have done so.

Rupert Martin

Aritsune 'Yuko' Maki 1894–1989

Yuko Maki was the first Japanese to climb extensively overseas, and the first to introduce Alpine climbing techniques to Japan. Born in 1894 in Sendai, northern Japan, he climbed Japan's highest peak, Mt Fuji (3720m), at the age of 10. In his early teens he climbed many of the major peaks in Japan, from Goat's

Foot Peak in Hokkaido to the world's largest volcano, Mt Aso, on the southern island of Kyushu. In 1915 he established a mountaineering club at his school, the prestigious Keio University in Tokyo. This was to become one of the 'Big Three' university climbing clubs in Japan, together with those at Kyoto University and at Waseda. After graduating from Keio in 1919 and brief graduate studies in the US and the UK, Maki moved to Switzerland and spent the following two years climbing in the Alps, culminating in the first ascent of the Mittellegi ridge of the Eiger. It was during this apprenticeship in the Alps that Maki, 'that small, short, friendly man from the distant country', became a popular figure amongst the European climbing fraternity.

In 1922 Maki returned to Japan and made the climb for which he became famous in his home country, the first winter ascent of Yarigadake (3180m), the second highest peak in the Northern Alps, the most technically challenging range in Japan. The following January he and two friends attempted Tateyama, the most northerly 3000m peak in Japan, but both friends were injured, one fatally, in the winter ascent. Then, in 1925, Maki led the first Japanese expedition overseas, achieving the first ascent of Mt Alberta (3619m) in the Canadian Rockies.

At this point Maki began entertaining the notion of organizing the first Japanese expedition to the Himalaya and, in order to train and test equipment, he made a number of extreme winter ascents, including Fuji in 1932 and, in 1935, Paektu-san (2744m), the highest peak on the Korean peninsula which sits on what is now the border between North Korea and Chinese Manchuria, overlooking the Siberian plain.

In 1936 a group from Rikyo University technically won the race to the Himalaya by successfully climbing Nanda Kot (6860m). In 1937 war broke out between China and Japan, and Japanese participation in international climbing was suspended until the end of the Second World War. Maki was then placed at the forefront of Japan's post-war alpine re-emergence, as Chairman of the Japanese Mountaineering Association in 1944–45 (and again, from 1951 to 1955). Nepal opened its borders and a new race was on, to climb the giants. The French went for Annapurna, the Swiss and British for Everest, and the Japanese for Manaslu. The first two Japanese expeditions to Manaslu, in 1953 and 1955, both ended in failure but in 1956 Yuko Maki, at the age of 62, led the third Japanese expedition to the world's seventh highest peak. This time they were successful. On 9 May Manaslu became the eighth 8000m peak to be conquered and the Japanese had climbed their first 8000er. For Maki this was the crowning achievement in a lifetime of alpine pioneering. In 1965 he was awarded the Emperor's Prize for Cultural Achievement.

Michael Jardine

John Armstrong Fergusson Watson 1904–1989

John Watson died in 1989 at the age of 84. He had been a member of the Alpine Club for nearly 35 years, but his climbing started in the 1920s when he first began walking and scrambling in the British hills. He was a long-standing member of the Climbers' Club, the Wayfarers and the Rucksack Club.

Throughout the period after the Second World War he was engaged in manufacturing industry in the Midlands, finally running his own company. This facilitated his access to the hills of North Wales and the Lake District, where he was a frequent weekend visitor throughout the 1940s, 1950s and 1960s. During this time he was a dedicated supporter of the Climbers' Club and served almost continuously from 1945 onwards either on the northern subcommitee, the main committee, or as hut custodian.

His first Alpine season was in 1947, when I climbed with him for a fortnight of perfect weather. He climbed the Besso, the Tête Blanche, the Zinalrothorn and the Grand Cornier, as well as the Col Durand and the Pointe de Zinal. Most of his subsequent Alpine climbing was in the Valais. In later years his active climbing was severely curtailed by hip trouble, but he continued to walk in the hills, and he was a regular attender at Alpine Club meetings until well past his 80th birthday.

John was proposed for election to the Alpine Club by Dick Viney, who wrote:

> He is a man of considerable strength of character, of great independence of mind and very strong loyalties. But in spite of being an individualist to the very core of his nature, he devoted great time and trouble to those institutions of which he is a member.

John Watson was a good companion in the hills – a strong, steady and reliable climber who made no claims to be a virtuoso. My most vivid memory of him is of his descent through the night from a point just below the summit of the Täschhorn where, having more or less completed the ascent of the Teufelsgrat, he was struck by falling rocks and suffered a broken shoulder-blade and a dislocated shoulder. His gallant descent is described in *AJ*57, 172–180, 1949–50.

J H Emlyn Jones

Eleanor Baillie d 1989

Eleanor Baillie joined the Ladies' Alpine Club in 1952. She climbed, as most of us did, in the Alps, but it was in more distant lands and in a spirit of exploration that most of her climbing was done, sometimes with other LAC members, sometimes alone. She always showed a tremendous interest not only in the country but also in the people she met, and in their lives and work.

In 1953 she went to Iceland, her 'chief desire being to see the greatest glacier in Europe – the Vatnajökul'. She stayed with Icelandic families, in the towns and on the farms, and so entered into the ordinary life of the Icelandic people and realized the importance to them of their fishing. She travelled widely and, as she says, the natural wonders of Iceland and their variety left her amazed. She climbed Esja, 'the thousand-coloured mountain', and the Hengill mountain and the Tindafjalla.

In 1955 Eleanor, in company with Dorothy Lee and Dorothy Arning, went to Morocco and climbed in the Atlas Mountains. Enquiries made beforehand from the vice-consul in Casablanca gave warning of unrest, but they met with no trouble and received much kindness from both Arabs and French. They climbed Toubkal and Tizi n'Ouagane. Eleanor says of their leader, Aomai, 'he was a born mountaineer, but not a guide.' He climbed the peaks and waited for his clients on the summits.

In 1958 Eleanor again visited Norway and climbed in the Lofoten Islands. The next year she went alone to Crete, climbing, walking and exploring. She had introductions from the Greek Embassy in London and great help locally from the army and the Chief of Police. She says: 'For the mountain lover and the mountaineer, there is the joy of mountains from end to end of the island.' She climbed Mt Ida and also in the Lasithi Mountains and the White Mountains.

In 1960 Eleanor, with Joyce Dunsheath, planned to take a party to the Pamir. This expedition did not materialize quite as planned, through cost and injuries, but the result was that two peaks were climbed – Demavend in Iran and Mir Samir in Afghanistan.

Professionally, Eleanor was a musician, both a teacher and a performer. She was a Fellow of Trinity College and a Licentiate of the Royal Academy of Music.

Mary Starkey

Eric Bentley Beauman 1891–1989

Eric Bentley Beauman was born on 7 February 1891. A six-year-old Victorian at the time of the Queen's Diamond Jubilee in 1897, he was to live on as a man of the twentieth century for over 80 years, playing an essential if modest role in the period spanning two world wars. He chose the path of support and informed, intelligent comment, with consideration and understanding for others. I had the privilege of knowing him when he was 59 and a retired RAF Wing Commander, and I was a young member of the newly-formed RAF Mountaineering Association.

A treasured family photograph of a very youthful Bentley has a note dated 5 March 1978, written in his own hand: 'Self in 25 HP Deperdussin Monoplane in which I took Royal Aero Club Flying Certificate June 1913.' This early involvement with aviation was preceded by a period at Geneva University where he went to learn French after being introduced to the hills as a schoolboy at Malvern College. He came back to England as an alpine mountaineer and skier, with an interest which remained with him throughout his life.

Soon after returning from Switzerland he learned to fly at Hendon, flew in several air displays, then went to France to train under Blériot. His Royal Aero Club Certificate was No 510.

Called up on 3 August 1914 into the Royal Naval Air Service, he reported at Eastchurch and Hendon before being told at the Air Division of the Admiralty that he was now the 'sole air defence of London'. He had neither observer nor armaments and, as he wrote later, 'fortunately no Zeppelin came over the city while I was defending it in this way.' He then served in anti-submarine patrols at home and in the Aegean as well as commanding seaplane stations at Dundee and Newhaven. In 1917 he was mentioned in dispatches.

In 1918 Bentley transferred to the Royal Air Force as a founder member. Two years later he joined the Alpine Club. His application, dated 3 February 1920, proposed by Dennis Murray and seconded by J C Muir, was made as a Flight Lieutenant Regular G D Royal Air Force Officer and Flying Instructor from No 10 Group, Warmash, Hants.

In 1922 he was selected for the first RAF Staff College course held at Bracknell under the direction of Brooke Popham, thereafter a lifelong friend. Here Bentley's literary talent soon emerged; he wrote a play in which several future high-flyers in the RAF took part and Portal was cast as Cromwell. Among other young mountaineers on that first course were R Cochrane and P Drummond.

1926 saw Bentley serving as private secretary to Lord Trenchard, Chief of the Air Staff, and from 1932 to 1933 he was an Instructor at the RAF Staff College. Later on there were other sympathetic people, such as Leo Amery, in high places when extended periods of leave were needed for an RAF officer to take part in the Kamet and Canadian Coast Range expeditions of 1931 and 1934.

Bentley's application for Alpine Club membership, still to be found in the Club records, is an interesting record of the climbs he made between 1909 and 1919, with the omission of the war period 1914–1918. They include in 1910 the third traverse of the entire arête of the Dents Blanches de Champéry, and in 1914 a winter first ascent of the Gross Spannort with the guide Josef Kuster, together with a guideless ascent of the Weisshorn with K de Walteville SAC, his Geneva University climbing companion. Captain Crowe, J W Wyatt AC, G F Whidborne, A J Warner, R B Robertson and T Barstow are also listed as climbing companions.

In Bentley's 1951 *Field* article, 'First Time Up', readers learned that his Lake District climbs before the First World War started like this: 'In the spring of 1914 Dennis Murray and I, after taking flying certificates were waiting to be called up for training in the military and naval wings of the Royal Flying Corps. We had both done a certain amount of climbing in the Alps, and Murray, who also knew some of the Lakeland climbs, was anxious to try out the "very severes"; we had never climbed together before but we were both enthusiastic mountaineers.' Running into difficulties in Oppenheimer's Chimney they found, out to the right, a blind corner which had most satisfactory unseen holds behind it. Later they simply stated: 'The variation of the climb that day saved us from a night near the top of Pillar Mountain and an ignominious rescue next day. It must be unusual for a new route to be made unintentionally.' It often happens that firsts are made out of sheer necessity and the heat of the moment; so was born the 'Alternative finish – D G Murray and E B Beauman' as listed in the contemporary climbing periodicals. The article concludes: 'The excitements of that day were by no means over, for on our way home we were privileged to watch at close quarters one of the most notable feats of British mountaineering – the first ascent of the Central Buttress of Scafell by that brilliant pair S W Herford and G S Sansom.' This is typical of Bentley Beauman's view of his own achievements.

The 25,447ft Kamet in 1931 must have been Bentley's most exciting and at the same time most disappointing experience. The group led by F S Smythe also included E St J Birnie, E E Shipton, C R Greene and R L Holdsworth. Kamet was the first 25,000ft peak to be climbed, and as late as 1942 only Nanda Devi and Kamet had been claimed; Everest, Kangchenjunga, K2 and Nanga Parbat remained inviolate despite the endeavours of British, American, German, Austrian and French mountaineers. Many of the peaks up to 20,000ft had been climbed 50 years earlier, so the success on Kamet on the India-Tibet border in 1931 was a triumph indeed.

Frank Smythe in his account (*Kamet Conquered*, p34) simply describes Wing Commander Beauman of the RAF as 'a mountaineer of many years' standing. He has a large number of first-class Alpine climbs and ski expeditions to his credit.' On page 213 Smythe refers to Bentley's disappointment: '. . . Beauman decided [at Camp 5, 23,500ft] that he would not accompany the second [summit] party. Unselfishly, therefore, he decided not to imperil the safety or success of his companions by risking exhaustion or collapse. It was a wise decision, and one made in accordance with the best traditions of mountaineering.' It should be mentioned that Greene had administered ammonium chloride to himself and Beauman to counteract the lack of oxygen at high altitude; clearly it did not work for Bentley. Years later, in November 1956, Bentley – when noting that the ski record of 23,500ft on Kamet was still held by the Ski Club of Great Britain – typically omitted the small detail that the skier was himself.

During the Kamet march-out to Badrinath he and Greene came across footprints which their porter identified as those of the yeti. In July 1937 Guy Dollman of the British Museum of Natural History wrote in a letter to *The Times*: 'Wing Commander E B Beauman once again revives the rumours of the existence of the "Abominable Snowman of the Himalayas".' Bentley's own scrapbook continues until 1955 with letters on the subject from F S Smythe, H W Tilman, E E Shipton and many others, together with those from the Natural History Museum. I suspect that he had an open mind but enjoyed the whole idea of such a creature; his short article dated 22 September 1955, entitled 'On the trail of the Snowman', written while reviewing Ralph Izzard's book *Abominable Snowman Expedition of 1950*, concludes with the statement of fact: 'So this remarkable mystery still remains to be solved.' Today in 1990 the mystery persists, and I hope for Bentley's sake that this is how it will remain.

Regret that Bentley was not included in the 1933 Everest expedition, two years after Kamet, has recently been expressed by Sir Jack Longland: 'Bentley was a very competent, reliable and safe climber. I still believe we ought to have had him with us on Everest in 1933, but the rules on upper age limits then were pretty strict even if mistakenly so. Apart from the Leader and the Transport Officer, we were all in our twenties or early thirties, and Bentley Beauman would have been 42. All the same I am sure he would have improved our efficiency and enlivened our evenings together.'

As an expert skier Bentley was a natural choice for Sir Norman Watson's pioneer crossing of the Coast Range in British Columbia in 1934. His account was read before the Alpine Club on 30 October 1934 and reported in *AJ47*,

75–86, 1935; he also lectured to the Royal Geographical Society. The crossing was completed by way of the Homathko Valley and river, Lake Twist, Scimitar valley, Scimitar canyon, the 2600m Col Fury Gap and the Franklin glacier down to Knight Inlet, where a Norwegian with his boat waited five days for their safe arrival. To recall a snippet from the second day in the Homathko valley: 'It was necessary for three men with woodman's axes and shovels to go ahead to hack and dig a way for the pony train to cross and recross the river. The trees were the real enemy, old trees, young trees, rotten and burnt trees, Douglas Firs, Jack Pines, Spruce, Poplar and Birch; they formed a tangled mass barring our path forward.' Five days of blizzard with two feet of fresh snow in Scimitar canyon prevented the ponies from making further progress, and the stores had to be manhandled up to Fury Gap and the Col. It appeared that Watson had sought the advice of very few people who knew anything about the district. Those he did ask had not approached it in the winter or spring, and they advised that the attempt should be abandoned. The success of the attempt says much of the team of E J King, Clifford White (Canadian), Camille Couttet (Chamonix guide), Beauman and Pete McCormick, trapper and Yukon 'old-timer', and his 21 mountain ponies pack-train with 150lb loads per pony. Bentley's chapter on the expedition in *Living Dangerously* ends: 'As the little motor boat chugged its way placidly down the great Inlet we turned to take one last farewell of our Valley of Adventure. While we gazed the giant trees guarding its entrance seemed to press more closely together, and once again Mystery Mountain was left in peace to brood over its wild ice kingdom, inhabited only by the wolves and bears.' Today Mystery Mountain is known as Mount Waddington.

Wing Commander E B Beauman was President of the Alpine Ski Club from 1932 to 1935, and an honorary member from 1978. He was made a Vice-President of the newly-formed RAF Mountaineering Association in 1951, having been a stalwart supporter during its formation period in 1947; he could well have been its first Chairman. From 1952 to 1954 he was Chairman of the Touring and Mountaineering Committee of the Ski Club of Great Britain, and from 1947 to 1958 Honorary Librarian of the Alpine Club.

In 1938 Bentley resigned from the RAF to take a permanent post at the Air Ministry, and in June 1940 he married the Public Relations Flight Officer in the WAAF Directorate. In the Second World War, as Taste and Suitability Censor for the RAF, he soon extended his vetting responsibilities by encouraging pilots, at first on a question-and-answer basis, to broadcast after air battles over this country and abroad. He was permitted still to wear uniform and, when he was RAF Liaison Officer with the BBC, a statement that 'here is the Wing Commander as usual' introduced several of the early talks. In 1941 these were published as *Winged Words*, a Book Society choice, with similar acclaim in the USA during 1943 as *We Speak from the Air*. He subsequently wrote for many national newspapers and other publications including *The National Review* and *The Boys' Country Book*, and he was involved in the Kamet film.

From 1952 to 1957 Bentley was Librarian at the Royal United Services Institution. He was on his way to an RUSI window overlooking Whitehall on Coronation Day in 1953 when he heard of the conquest of Everest. His final job, lasting over 20 years, was as Mountaineering Correspondent for *The Field*.

Books then arrived for review, while summer holidays abroad included the Whymper Centenary celebrations at Zermatt and other memory-stirring events.

In December 1951, writing in *The Field* about the eighth expedition to Everest, the first since the Second World War, he had pointed out several interesting features:

a. The approach to the peak was entirely different from that through Tibet.
b. Its lateness, i.e. after the monsoon and not before it, would serve to find out whether autumn conditions were more favourable than the spring.
c. The aim was to force a way into the Western Cwm.

He emphasized that this reconnaissance was led by the experienced and competent Himalayan explorer Eric Shipton, and no better leader could have been found. It was Shipton's judgement and conviction – that a practical route existed from the Western Cwm up to the South Col and thence to the summit itself – that paved the way for success in 1953. But in 1951 Bentley asked the following questions:

a. Should the climbers use oxygen and would the weight outweigh any gains?
b. How big should the party be?

He said that Shipton and Tilman favoured a handier and mobile party of about six climbers with a consequent reduction of stores; comments and observations from a very well-informed, competent and experienced mountaineer which did not fall on deaf ears, although different views prevailed in the end.

One further quote, from his writing of July 1951, concerns the Italian proposal for a Matterhorn railway. In 1907 popular outcry had culminated in a petition from far and wide against the earlier Swiss proposal for a funicular up the mountain, rising 2400m in three stages starting from Zermatt. The Swiss Federal Government withdrew its sanction and the Matterhorn was reprieved from such vandalism. The 1951 proposal was for the cable railway for skiers, which runs from the village of Breuil to the Furggrat, to be extended to the Italian summit. Between 1920 and 1931 Bentley had climbed the Matterhorn on five occasions, each time by a different route, and he made the following plea: 'Let us hope that the noble sentiments expressed during the previous threat of 1907 will again prevail. The high summits of the Alps are the property of the whole people and a symbol of liberty. They are not for sale.'

Without Map or Compass, written in 1957, describes a skiing trip on the Pischahorn with his companion A P Ledger, a member of the RAF Staff College course at Bracknell and later Air Vice-Marshal Ledger of the RAF Mountaineering Association. Bentley tells of a run from the Weissfluhjoch down the Dorftäli valley on a direct run to Davos, in a blizzard, finishing up near Langwies on the way to Arosa. He recalls his shame at '. . . finding ourselves in entirely the wrong valley and horror in crossing the avalanche slopes under difficult conditions'. They had broken the golden rule which lays down the necessity for at least one member of the party to carry a map and compass. But, he concluded, '. . . to expect ski runners to observe every safety precaution all the time is, I suppose, too much.'

In 1975 one of his last articles in *The Field* speaks of Hillary, a man who stood on the summit of Everest and who also stood at the South Pole. Bentley's own achievements some 20 or 30 years earlier in the Himalaya and British Columbia were no less remarkable.

Beauman died on 26 July 1989. The Presidents of both the Alpine Club and the Alpine Ski Club, the latter himself a distinguished aviator, attended the funeral service at St Michael's, Chester Square. They heard his son Christopher read an aviation story and then an extract from his father's favourite written work, 'A night in the Matterhorn Couloir'. Some weeks later this essay (published in the *National Review*, March 1930) was read again in the more relaxed atmosphere of the Alpine Club where its self-deprecating, dry humour roused much laughter.

Such was the man, mountaineer, writer and aviator who lived through most of the twentieth century. I am sure that we would all wish to thank him for the part that he played.

D le R Bird

Marjorie Heys-Jones d 1989

Marjorie was already a member of the Pinnacle Club when she joined the Ladies' Alpine Club in 1935, and she was on the second Pinnacle Club Alpine meet in 1930. She climbed often and to a good standard in Britain, Switzerland, France, Corsica, the Dolomites, Austria and the High Tatra. After the Second World War she had a particularly good season in 1947 in the Bregaglia and Bernina, and she was again climbing in 1948 and 1949. She climbed with Joseph Georges, and guideless with Jo Marples.

After 1949 she gave most of her time and energy to an exacting job as headmistress of a new school. My only close contact with her was on the LAC Turkish expedition in 1963, when she had hoped to make a climbing comeback after her retirement. The trip was a disappointment for her as she found (not surprisingly after such a long gap) that she could no longer rock-climb, though she was still a strong walker.

Marjorie was Hon Auditor of the LAC from 1950 until 1975, when the AC and LAC amalgamated, and she served on the LAC committee. For several years she was the Pinnacle Club representative on the BMC in its early days. She was active in the negotiations with the University Women's Club (of which she was a member) when the LAC migrated there from the National Book League.

Soon after the AC/LAC amalgamation Marjorie moved to a nursing home – up to that time she had been alert and competent and always good company, and that is the impression I have of her. But she soon lost contact with the Club, and I don't think she ever came to an AC meeting or dinner, though she remained a member until she died – an inactive spell almost as long as her active years in the mountains.

Margaret Darvall

Julian Vincent Anthoine 1939–1989

It was an unusually bright, clear day in North Wales when Julian (Mo) Anthoine was buried in Nant Peris cemetery. The little stone church, across the road from the house he had built and lived in for most of his life, was packed with 350 or so of Mo's friends and family. Outside, lining the path from the church to the grave, were over a hundred more. Most of them were weeping.

As the coffin was lowered into the ground, a lonely figure could be seen with his arms above his head outlined against the clear blue sky near the top of Y Garn. It could almost have been Mo, wondering what all these climbers were doing in the bottom of the valley on a day when they should have been climbing on the crags. But it wasn't Mo: that extraordinary personality of the British climbing world had died of a brain tumour the previous weekend.

Mo had lived a life of freedom – free to travel, to climb, to carouse, to adventure, to bring up a family and to behave just as he liked. He ran a business making climbing helmets, ice-axes and outdoor clothing, but this seemed to have more to do with dissatisfaction with the quality and performance of existing gear than with a drive to make money. Despite all the hard work he put into these enterprises, he never seemed to allow them to interfere with or limit his freedom to go on 'trips', as he called them.

The first time I came across Mo was in 1961 when Jim Swallow and I heard that some instructors from Ogwen Cottage had spent several days putting up a new, hard route on Llech Ddu in North Wales. At the time we believed anyone from 'Og Cot' earned their meagre keep pulling beginners up easy slabs. But the next day we made what was probably the second ascent of the route, and realized that the guy with the French-sounding name, with his pal Cam, were a climbing force to be reckoned with. He had an epic three-year trip, raising hell across the Far East with his boxing pal Fox, ending up by having to be rescued from some dreadful asbestos mine in Australia. The stories of this 'trip' alone would have been worth a book but Mo, one of the great humorist raconteurs, was too keen on planning his next adventure and recounting stories of the last one over pints of beer to settle down to the tedium of writing.

During the sixties his climbing was mainly in the Alps, where one well-documented adventure on the N face of the Cima Grande di Lavaredo showed his capacity for survival. Leave late, under-equipped, ignore weather forecasts, bivouac half-way up in a storm inadequately clad, survive the night half-frozen with your companion half-dead, climb to the summit and emerge triumphant. The impact this had on Al Alvarez, who was with him, was the cornerstone story of Mo's biography that Al wrote. The seventies saw the start of Mo's expeditions. El Toro, Fitzroy, Trango Tower, Gasherbrum IV, Brammah II and the Ogre where, with Clive Rowland, he accomplished an incredible rescue of Doug Scott, who had broken his legs just below the summit, and Chris Bonington who smashed his ribs on the descent. Mo, typically, took no credit for this epic.

All of these were small expeditions where Mo took a major role in leading and organizing. His outspokenness, with a few well-chosen words and a scornful smile, could deflate and discredit the inflation and exaggeration that were synonymous with the large, well-financed Himalayan expeditions of that time. Mo's non-conformity and outrageous behaviour were simply unacceptable to conformist expedition leaders, and these attitudes probably reached an all-time low when he was blackballed from the Climbers' Club during one of its more intolerant and parochial periods. To Mo's delight he was made a member of the Alpine Club in 1969 and he remained a member for the rest of his life.

The eighties saw even more expeditions which gave a better insight into Mo's character. His stubborn determination showed when he attempted to climb Thalay Sagar in the Garhwal during four consecutive years; and his firm belief that climbing a mountain was never worth the sacrifice of a human life – however much effort and expense had been put into the attempt – was demonstrated when he turned back just below the summit rather than risk an accident induced by exhaustion. As he put it: 'when Joe fell off and didn't know why, I became safety conscious.' He climbed Mt Kenya and Mt McKinley and made two attempts on Everest, the last one after having the first operation on the tumour which killed him. He will be remembered by many for his hospitality, and by even more for his waspish repartee. He firmly believed that his constant climbing partner Joe Brown had invented the handjam. Whenever they climbed together on some gritstone outcrop, Mo's fun was to try to extract royalties from anyone using a handjam within sight of the Master.

As a friend he was more generous than anyone I have met in giving real help and caring when most needed. With him as a climbing companion you knew you were totally safe wherever you were, and he seemed to have the magic of being able to fix protection above his head before he did any hard move. To go out with Mo for an evening was full of unpredictable consequences. If there was fighting, it always seemed to be others doing it, but somehow you had the idea that in some mysterious way Mo had triggered it off. His verbal assaults were against the pompous, the bullshitters, and his weapon was humour wielded like a deadly rapier. As a family man he was fortunate in finding and marrying Jackie Philippe, who has endured and enjoyed his eccentric lifestyle for many years. He was proud of his two children and, when one of them couldn't read at the age of two, he said: 'he is so backward that all he can look forward to is being the head of an outdoor pursuits centre' – several of these, of course, being amongst his best friends.

And so, finally, amongst the sad slate tombstones of Nant Peris his friends and family came to mourn him. A climber who valued the traditions of climbing, who set an example of what can be done if the energy, the love and the enthusiasm are there. A rich, generous and unpredictable character. We all miss him.

Ian McNaught-Davis

(Shortened version of an obituary in *Mountain 130*. Reprinted by permission.)

Soli Mehta 1927–1989

I came to know Soli Mehta rather late in his life. It was in 1978 that Jagdish Nanavati quietly broached the subject of my helping with the *Himalayan*

Journal as Soli, editor for the past eight issues, was leaving for Nigeria. I had no editorial experience – not even on a college magazine. My reaction was, of course, to say no, but Jagdish knows his job and I was persuaded. I was assured that R E Hawkins would lend a keen eye to it.

When I first met Soli and Hawkins, their expertise and experience were evident. After explaining the current issue (the Golden Jubilee issue, Vol 35) over a few meetings, Soli handed over files and left for Nigeria, leaving his beloved 'baby' in my care. We kept in regular touch – great correspondent as he was.

For seven years Hawkins and I edited the journal, bringing out seven issues. During all these years we kept in contact with Soli in Nigeria. He procured articles with his contacts, suggested subjects and enquired. Once there was a poem on the mountaineer's world at high altitude (*HJ36*), called 'Ballad of Bethertoli'. It naturally included four-letter words which mountaineers use at high altitude. I was at a loss whether to include these in the journal or not; Jagdish Nanavati strongly objected to such 'filth' in our respected journal. Hawkins came with *Oxford Dictionary* to analyse each word, to determine whether it could be classified as 'dirty'. He eventually 'cleared' all except two words. Finally all the material was forwarded to Soli in Nigeria for a final verdict. 'Keep every word of it. We don't want to be left behind in these days of permissiveness' – came a curt telex that settled it.

Soli returned to India in 1985 and I was glad to hand over his 'baby' to him. Policies of editing remained the same, but the modes changed totally. Now you go to Soli's house, there is always *pakora* and tea, side-tracking to various subjects and lots of laughter. Soli's Parsee humour regaled all of us. He liked to laugh at everything, including himself. He once passed me a letter from a Polish climber, Voytek Kurtyka, at a meeting. Soli had asked him for an article which had already been printed in a past *Himalayan Journal*. Kurtyka wrote: 'Don't you read your own *Journal*?' Soli added with a grin: 'Look, I messed up.' Every time I would ring him up there would be a strong welcoming voice: '*Bol Dikra*' ('Yes, son') and we started shooting. Exchanging editorial notes in the margins was also fun with Soli. Once, after striking out an utter nonsense, he wrote: 'Shit.' I wrote there: 'Soli, be careful, we preserve these papers on file for posterity, and people will refer to them after many years.' Papers came back with Soli's curt writing below mine: 'Sorry, in that case I'll use stronger words next time.' He was irrepressible.

From 1964 to 1979 Soli produced 12 issues of the *Himalayan Club Newsletter* which painstakingly covered all the details. He was editor of the *Himalayan Journal* from 1967 to 1978. His achievement was phenomenal, in face of extinct finances, with absolutely no one to help him and no organization of any kind. He left for Nigeria in 1979 and on his return he resumed the editorship from 1985 until he died, producing three issues. All this puts him in the ranks of the senior editors of the mountaineering world. Only the great Kenneth Mason, the first editor of the *Himalayan Journal*, has produced more than Soli.

Soli had a long and distinguished association with the Himalayan Club. He was a Life Member from 1955, and served on the Managing Committee from 1964 to 1973; he was Vice-President of the Club in 1974, and again from 1986 to 1989; he also acted as the Hon Secretary in 1970. Earlier, he was Hon Local Secretary for Bombay from 1962, when he took over from R E Hawkins. In fact, in 1970 he was instrumental in shifting the Club to Bombay with him. He became a member of the Alpine Club in 1974.

Apart from editing, Soli was an excellent pianist and cellist, who regularly played in the Bombay Chamber Orchestra. He worked for ICI (India) from 1950 to 1985, when he retired, serving in various senior positions in Bombay, London, Rishra (Bengal), Sudan and Nigeria. He had a degree from the University of Cambridge. He travelled a lot and met many editors, trekkers and mountaineers, world over. Also he trekked regularly in the Himalaya and talked about it with excellent slides.

In 1988 The Himalayan Club celebrated its Diamond Jubilee. To commemorate the event it was proposed to publish *Exploring the Hidden Himalaya* (Hodder and Stoughton), jointly written by Soli and myself. At once Soli flung himself into the project with great energy. We collected slides and material and wrote all the chapters. It was great fun, with Soli's lunches and humour. Alas, he will not be around to see the book. He looked forward to retired life, enjoying music, editing, writing further books and producing *HJ*s. Death came suddenly: a heart attack snatched him away on 4 November 1989. He leaves behind his wife Meheru and daughters Naushad and Yasmen.

When the name of the famous hill-station Simla was changed to Shimla, and this was mentioned in an article in the *Himalayan Journal*, Soli, not to be outdone, added a footnote: 'There is no truth in the rumour that the editor is about to change the spelling of his name to Sholi. Beware, when you are requested by the *Survey of India* spelling experts to sit. – *Ed*'.

Many of us will miss his assuring presence, devotion to mountaineering and humour. Rest In Peace, Sholi.

Harish Kapadia

Alison Barton d 1989

Alison Barton joined the Ladies' Alpine Club in 1956. She was the wife of Dr Arthur Barton AC, who died in 1976.

Until 1975 Alison and her husband climbed extensively in the Alps, almost exclusively in Switzerland. Dr Barton was a headmaster, so they were able to take advantage of long school holidays. Many Alpine Club members will remember seeing their party, which usually included two or three young climbers – nephews whom they were introducing to the mountains.

For many years, Alison and Arthur attended the Easter Meets of the ABMSAC in Scotland and Wales, and took a full part in all the climbing. Alison was a very lively person and added greatly to the social enjoyment of any party of which she was a member.

Mary Starkey

John Baptist Lucien Noel 1890–1989

(Captain John Noel was the third son of Lieut-Col the Hon Edward Noel, and a grandson of the second Earl of Gainsborough. He was educated in Switzerland and at the Royal Military College, Sandhurst, whence in 1908 he was commissioned into the East Yorkshire Regiment. While serving with his regiment in India in 1913, he took local leave to visit the Mount Everest region and to come within 40 miles of the mountain. After serving throughout the First World War, he resigned his commission in 1922, prior to joining the Everest expedition of that year. He was elected to the Alpine Club in the same year, being proposed by Dr T G Longstaff and seconded by George Leigh-Mallory, but he resigned his membership in 1925. The following is the text of the address delivered at the Requiem Mass held for him in St Mary's Church, Cadogan Street, on 24 April 1989; it is reproduced here with the approval of his daughter Miss Sandra Noel, and of his cousin the Earl of Gainsborough, who arranged the service.)

We remember today John Noel – soldier and revolver expert, mountaineer and photographer, author, lecturer, artist and master craftsman. We cannot mourn his passing as we would the passing of a younger man, for our sadness is tempered by gladness for the fullness of his years and of his achievements. As a pioneer to the region in 1913 and as expedition photographer in 1922 and 1924, he will ever be associated with Mount Everest, as of course are his friends George Leigh-Mallory and Andrew Irvine, who from the 1924 expedition did not return. John Noel was the last living participant in those imperishable enterprises, so beautifully enshrined in the films and slides that he had widely shown. Sir Francis Younghusband wrote of him that 'he was a man of deep intensity of nature and of fine feeling for mountain beauty', and of his part on the expeditions he went on to say that, whatever the occasion, 'when most wanted Noel would be there. Every member . . . said on his return that Noel worked harder than anyone.' A fine tribute indeed from a former President of the Royal Geographical Society.

Some of you joined in the quiet dignity of his funeral service at Charing and may remember that the Irish priest referred to John Noel grappling with high and lonely places; he said that there 'he may have touched the face of God'. It was indeed in this sense, more than in a formal sense, that John Noel appeared to me as a religious man. The priest's words echoed those written about Captain Scott: '*Quaesivit arcana poli, videt dei*,' freely translated as: 'He sought the secrets of the Pole, he sees the hidden face of God.' For 'the Pole' we can read 'Everest'. And it is interesting here to recall that Scott's photographer, Herbert Ponting, was the close friend and mentor of John Noel, thus linking two of the most epic and moving stories in the history of exploration.

It was John Noel's particular pride that he had – as he put it – come through unscathed from fighting the greatest army in the world, and had then gone on to tackle the highest mountain in the world. In the horrors of the retreat from Mons and later in the trenches, as an officer in the East Yorkshire

Regiment and with the Machine Gun Corps, he knew war as few men living knew it. Yet he did not lose his faith in humanity; rather the faith was strengthened of one who could later write: 'This world is owned by man. Man has infinite capacity within himself.'

Thus he saw the Kingdom of Heaven on Earth, but beyond that he saw in 'mysteries' – a favourite word – or 'as through a glass darkly' the glimmer of what might lie beyond. Take the 'mystery' of Mallory and Irvine. Firm in his belief in the survival of the spirit, he convinced himself – he knew – by no ordinary means that they had reached the summit of Everest – and so to the ultimate heights where all was well with them, among the very brave, the very true.

The members of these early expeditions to Everest were greatly encouraged in the field by messages of goodwill and blessing from His Holiness Pope Pius XI, himself a distinguished alpinist who could write of the view from the summit of a mountain that it 'raises the spirit to the Divine Author and Sovereign of Nature'. This association of His Holiness leads me on to the next thing I want to say.

The religious side of John Noel was shown in his absorption with the 'mystery' of St Bernadette, who as a girl saw visions of the Virgin Mary in the grotto at Lourdes. In 1933 he was present at her canonization by the same Pope Pius XI in St Peter's, Rome; by reason of his uncle's service as Chamberlain to the three previous Popes, he was privileged to sit near the High Altar. For the long service he provisioned himself with two – as it turned out – lightly boiled eggs, secreted in his coat-tails, but they were sat on and squashed as he took his pew. From there, equipped with a miniature camera disguised as a prayer-book, he secured the only photographs taken of the service. He later lectured widely on St Bernadette's story, and there can be no doubt that he saw in her experience a Divine revelation.

Other 'mysteries' absorbed him. When I saw him for the last time on his 99th birthday, he was in excellent form – full of anecdotes from his unclouded memories of the past. Then his mind turned to the 'mystery' of the Universe and the vast distances of interstellar space, measured in light-years. 'It is all beyond our imagination,' he said, and I sensed his accord with the words of the beautiful 18th-century hymn by Joseph Addison:

> The spacious firmament on high,
> And all the blue ethereal sky,
> And spangled heavens, a shining frame,
> Their Great original proclaim . . .

And it goes on and ends:

> The hand that made us is Divine.

John Noel was a man of vision but also – and in rare combination – an intensely practical and inventive man. He was as superbly capable in the restoration of an ancient Kentish house or the reconditioning of an old clock, as in the technicalities of expedition photography. His clear insight into practical problems was wonderfully demonstrated in signal but barely recognized service to his country in the Second World War.

As an officer in Military Intelligence, it was *he* who prescribed the best supply route from India to the Allied armies in Burma – he as might none other, for it was based on his own detailed ground observations of the region before the war. His exact route was later chosen and called for a few months the 'Noel Road', but was later and unfairly known by another name. This was an oversight of which he never spoke – at least, not to me. He preferred to show his pride as a soldier in letters of greeting from his Colonel-in-Chief, Queen Elizabeth the Queen Mother, the second letter – shortly before he died – expressing Her Majesty's pleasure in receiving a reprint of his Everest book, first published in 1927.

In remembering John Noel, we think especially of his Edwardian charm, courtesy and sense of values, his gentle humour, his keen interest in the younger generation and his love of animals. He outlived two very happy marriages, as he outlived nearly all his contemporaries. Our sympathy goes out to his devoted daughter Sandra, proud in the memory of her illustrious father and consoled perhaps by the knowledge of our esteem and affection for him shown by our presence here this evening. *Requiescat in pace*. May the earth rest lightly on the bones of a soldier.

Geoffrey Hattersley-Smith

Marco Pallis 1894–1988

Although Marco Pallis was born in Liverpool of Greek parents, it was perhaps Indian influences that first shaped his imagination. For his father Alexander combined business life in the largely eastern trading firm of Ralli Brothers with scholarship and poetry, and the family home contained a variety of oriental artefacts.

Marco survived Harrow with musical and botanical interests intact and, accompanied by his brother and sister, did ambulance work in the Balkan War of 1912–13. In the First World War he joined the Grenadier Guards and, after he was wounded in France, good use was found in censorship for his unusual command of languages.

It was after a period at Liverpool University that the three major strands of his life started to reveal themselves – music, mountaineering and metaphysics. Pre-war visits to Vevey and admiration for the work of Wagner had kindled his interest in music. This was now to develop into active enthusiasm for Bach which in turn led to participation in the revival of early music. He became a pupil of Arnold Dolmetsch in 1925 and met Richard Nicholson, thereafter his devoted and lifelong friend, when the latter was still at Oxford University. Together they studied the viola da gamba and harpsichord and collected a group of players around them – it was the brother of one of these musicians who introduced Marco to mountaineering which was to result in contact with Tibetans and with Buddhism.

Musical and mountaineering projects became more adventurous as time passed, and in the 1930s the English Consort of Viols was formed in Liverpool.

There were visits to the Alps, and in 1933 and 1936 Marco organized two expeditions to the Himalaya. During this period he fell under the spell of

Gandhi and also absorbed the teachings of René Guenon; these helped to prepare his mind for the first-hand meeting with Tibetan Buddhism, which he adopted himself in 1936.

Experiences and thoughts on these travels are recorded in *Peaks and Lamas* (1939), a travel book which combines a lucid exposition of leading aspects of Tibetan Buddhism with graphic descriptions of the mountaineering expeditions themselves. It is not too fanciful to suggest that it was at this time in Marco's life that the impulse to climb started to focus at a higher and more spiritual level. But mysticism (a word that he seldom used and perhaps disliked), as with Meister Eckhart, was always tempered with realism and practicality so that, for example, in the Second World War he devoted himself to social work in Liverpool and to study of the Tibetan language.

By the end of the war he was fully prepared for the return to Sikkim in 1947, with permission to visit Gyantse and Shigatse in Tibet. This trip was undertaken with Richard Nicholson alone, and was followed by a prolonged stay in India, during which Marco continued to make contact with Tibetans and even wrote a book in the Tibetan tongue describing the dangers soon to beset their culture and their religion.

After the invasion of Tibet by China he returned to England. The English Consort of Viols was reconstituted in London and continued to rediscover and perform relatively unknown sixteenth- and seventeenth-century English chamber music.

Musical composition and performance now went hand-in-hand with essays on metaphysics and with practical assistance to Tibetan refugees in Great Britain. That Marco became not only their friend but also adviser is acknowledged today by Lamas both here and along the length of the Himalaya.

Music from this period included a set of part-songs, pieces for viola da gamba, a cantata-like work for solo baritone and orchestra, a string quartet and many essays published in the form of books – *The Way and the Mountain* and *A Buddhist Spectrum* – as well as in collections of essays such as *Studies in Comparative Religion* and *The Sword of Gnosis*, the latter edited by Jacob Needleman. His last years were devoted to writing a full-length opera about the Tibetan sage Mila Repa.

Finally I risk a brief comment: that he was and remains a great teacher – one might also say a prophet – who made sense of life and of the life to come; in whose presence insuperable difficulties became less daunting; who took endless trouble to help those who brought their problems to him; someone to whom the spiritual quest in prayer was the one thing needful, who by his own life demonstrated the validity and truth of traditional teachings and showed that, however emasculated by modernism, these remain the only valid criteria for those who, as he would put it, have ears to hear. His life was a celebration of 'The Marriage of Wisdom and Method'; it is the title of one of his essays.

Peter Talbot

Charles Warren writes:

Marco Pallis, the well-known mountaineer, Himalayan traveller and Tibetan scholar, was a member of the Alpine Club from 1936 to 1939. In *Peaks and Lamas* he wrote one of the most fascinating books on Himalayan travel there has ever been, with its deeply considered observations on Tibetan life, religion and culture. From the mountaineering point of view, his pioneering expedition to the Gangotri region of Garhwal in 1933 should be recalled as one of the earlier 'alpine-style' expeditions in the Himalaya. It was then that we all did our own carrying on the mountains in the old Longstaff manner.

Marco was a man of varied talents. He was a musician and a student of old music which he and his fellow-musicians, of the same ilk, used to play at the Wigmore Hall in London, on contemporary instruments like the harpsichord and the viols. But perhaps Marco will be missed most of all for his Tibetan studies and contacts. These were so important both to him and to us in 1933 when we made the first ascent of Leo Pargial together. Well-known throughout the mountaineering world in the thirties, Marco Pallis, with his first ascent of Mickledore Grooves with Colin Kirkus and Ivan Waller, and other pioneering climbs at home and abroad, deserves to be remembered. He was one of the nicest and gentlest of men. I shall think of him always as 'a verray parfit gentil knight'.

Alpine Club Notes

OFFICE BEARERS AND COMMITTEE FOR 1990

President	Lt Col H R A Streather OBE
Vice Presidents	P J Nunn
	The Rt Hon the Earl of Limerick
Honorary Secretary	Dr M J Esten
Honorary Treasurer	R A Coatsworth
Committee: Elective Members	Miss M Agrawal
	M E B Banks
	C M Gravina
	P N Herold
	G D Hughes
	H R Lloyd
	Mrs J Merz
	R Payne
	S M W Venables
ACG Co-opted Members	M A Fowler
	R A Ruddle
Honorary Librarian	R Lawford
Honorary Archivist	E H J Smyth FRCS
Assistant Archivists	Miss M Darvall
	V S Risoe MBE
Honorary Keeper of the Club's Pictures	D J Lovatt
Honorary Editor of the Club's Journal	Professor E H Sondheimer
Assistant Editors	Mrs J Merz
	A V Saunders
	G W Templeman
Honorary Guidebooks Editor	G L Swindin
Chairman of the House Committee	G W Templeman
Chairman of the Library Council	M H Westmacott
Assistant Honorary Secretaries	
Annual Winter Dinner	Mrs J Merz
Candidates	A N Husbands
Lectures	S M W Venables
Meets	M Pinney

GENERAL MEETINGS OF THE ALPINE CLUB 1989

10 January	Kurt Diemberger, *K2 from both sides*
14 February	Alan Hinkes, *The Biggest Walls*
14 March	Jon Tinker, *K2 in Winter,* and *With the Mujahedin in Afghanistan*
11 April	Cecilia Nevill, *Across Tibet and Sinkiang by Bicycle*
9 May	Jim Curran, *A Slimmer's Guide to the Himalaya and other places*
12 September	Mike Banks, *Jaonli 1989*
10 October	John Harding, *The Pyrenees from Atlantic to Mediterranean*
14 November	Rob Collister, *Over the Hills and Far Away*
28 November	Guilia Zanoni, *The Italian Side of Mont Blanc* (extra meeting)
4 December	Annual General Meeting: *Valedictory Address by the President*

CLIMBING MEETINGS 1989

11–12 February	ACG Winter Meet, Glencoe
11–12 March	North Wales. Informal dinner with lecture by Dave Walsh, *Cho Oyu*
22 July–12 August	Courmayeur. Joint Meet with Climbers' Club and ABMSAC
24 July–6 August	Cornwall. CC hut, Bosigran. Family meet held jointly with Climbers' Club
30 September–1 October	Lake District. Informal dinner with lecture by Walt Unsworth, *Lost Cities*

ALPINE CLUB SYMPOSIUM 1989: THE INDIAN HIMALAYA

This expedition symposium, again organized by the Club at Plas y Brenin, was held on 25 November 1989. 160 people attended, accommodated in the excellent new lecture hall at the National Mountaineering Centre.

The President, George Band, opened the meeting. Charles Clarke gave a brief overview of the geography and history of climbing in the principal ascents in (British) imperial times before 1947, and later discussed the problems of access and the role of the Indian Mountaineering Foundation.

The speakers took us on a fascinating series of mountain journeys and ascents, indicating the variety of the terrain and the scope for future climbs in all the areas covered. Meena Agrawal described the Indian expedition to Kamet, portraying in colour the views many of us have seen only in monochrome in Frank Smythe's *Kamet Conquered.* Rob Collister guided the audience on a characteristic lightweight journey through Zanskar – ending alone with one mule after a happy and successful series of climbs. Stephen Venables, fresh from Cenotaph Corner that morning and off to Antarctica the next week, talked about Kishtwar and the ascent of Kishtwar Shivling. Alan Hinkes described his climbs in Kulu, including the S face of White Sail. Steven Berry, a director of Himalayan Kingdoms, spoke on his travels in Bhutan, with entrancing slides of the mountains of Lunana. Though His Majesty the King has, apparently, closed the nation to climbing, there is every reason to believe this will not last for ever. Doug Scott, whose first visits to the Greater Ranges were over 20 years ago, described joint expeditions with Indian climbers, including the first ascent of Changabang and a recent expedition to Rimo in the Indian Karakoram.

The meeting, masterminded by Sheila Harrison, our Assistant Secretary, drew together a wealth of information and climbers young and old. With Britain's peculiar historical connection with India, our common language, the Alpine Club's Himalayan Index, the continued support of the Mount Everest Foundation and the British Mountaineering Council – not to mention the co-operation of the Indian Mountaineering Foundation – British climbers are ideally placed to visit India, and we can expect to see many more fine climbs in the future.

Our thanks to Plas y Brenin for having us once again, to the speakers, to Victor Saunders for planning and to John Cleare for the loan of slides.

Charles Clarke

THE CLUB ARCHIVES AND THE MOVE TO EATON SQUARE

The move from South Audley Street – itself a fragment of history – has presented the Club with a rare opportunity to unearth, sort out and to some extent weed out its collection of archives. Everything has had to be exhumed from the dusty basement room which has housed them for the past half-century, including a sizeable amount of unsorted material whose existence had long been unsuspected or forgotten. All the 'no-go' cupboards and shelves are empty, but the space available at Eaton Square cannot accommodate all their contents.

We have therefore divided the archives into what must be stored away until we reach a permanent home and what we can take with us. The latter material has been selected under three particular headings: (i) items of special interest or value known from past experience to demand frequent enquiry and reference (these will include our collection of original Führerbücher, diaries and letters of famous past mountaineers, material relating to Mount Everest and presidential papers); (ii) unsorted documents which can be worked upon and indexed during the interim period; and (iii) certain Club records, including the Committee minute-books for the last 10 years. (The latter are confidential documents which may only be consulted by express permission of the Honorary Secretary acting on behalf of the Committee.)

Turning now to the content of the collection, it is to be noted that the archives remain catalogued according to the system devised by our former archivist, N R Rice, as explained and set down in his article in *AJ78*, 71–77, 1973. But although Rice's index has continued to be the main means of identification and reference, the collection itself has become greatly enlarged over the ensuing years. The broad working principle, introduced by Rice and adhered to ever since, has been to retain groupings of material as separate entities under appropriate headings – either because of derivation from a common source, as for instance presidential papers, or because of belonging to a clearly defined category such as diaries or Führerbücher. The collections of correspondence belonging to eminent climbers may be said to be covered by both these criteria.

Additions are constantly coming in. Not only is some account of the Club's day-to-day activities and transactions necessary to augment the record, but items relating to earlier times continue to arrive from the bequests or families of deceased members, as well as from other sources. Fortunately, not all the material received is of sufficient relevance or importance to be worth keeping, so that some weeding can be undertaken – a difficult but essential task if our collections are not to become unmanageable.

Amongst documents recently sorted and indexed may be mentioned the presidential papers of Lord Tangley, a meticulously kept record of his terms of office, first as Honorary Secretary and later as President. Correspondence covering the presidencies of Lord Schuster, Colonel Strutt and Captain Farrar, also indexed during the past two years, forms a useful record of their times, though one that is far from complete. We have also received the papers of Emlyn Jones and Peter Lloyd, both of them Past-Presidents in eventful times, and the task of sorting these will be one of the first on the list at our new quarters. Other acquisitions include a collection of papers from Lord Hunt which has been sorted and catalogued by V S Risoe, and some correspondence from our late members Noel Odell and Dorothy Pilley/Richards. Lastly, but most important amongst recent work, the whole collection of documents – correspondence, diaries, qualification papers, minute-books – belonging to the Ladies' Alpine Club has been sorted and put into order by Margaret Darvall during the past year. Included amongst these is a beautifully written, annotated and illustrated diary of a former member, Elaine Huth, who climbed during the early part of the century, which may well merit early publications.

The different ways in which the Club's Officers, particularly its Presidents and Honorary Secretaries, keep their correspondence provide an interesting study for the archivist. 'No names, no pack-drill,' but may I respectfully remind present and future holders of these offices that almost every letter they receive or write on the Club's behalf becomes part of its history. Initialled, carbon copies of their replies to letters are especially useful in reconstructing an incident or chapter of events, but are all too seldom available.

At Eaton Square some of our main goals will be to try to arrange the archival material, as far as space permits, in a form more easily accessible for reference purposes, to index as many unsorted papers as time allows and to improve the existing card index – at present scrappy and incomplete – of named mountaineers of former days. I hope that at some stage it may become possible to compile for issue to members an abridged index of the whole collection of our Archives. But, with present resources, that is some way in the future.

Edward Smyth

THE ALPINE CLUB LIBRARY

Moving house is a tedious, time-consuming, costly and worrying operation, but it has at least the advantage of concentrating the mind. We have long been aware that some of our possessions have little if anything to do with mountains, mountaineering or mountaineers. Now most of the irrelevant material has been disposed of, and in the process we have learned something about the more useful parts of the collection.

At time of writing (December 1989), arrangements for moving a 'working library' to the Club's temporary home at 118 Eaton Square are well in hand. Its contents have been segregated, and three months' experience confirms that it comprises the most frequently consulted journals and books (as well as maps and expedition reports). Some 75 per cent of the collection will have to go into storage until new permanent premises are available. It will be possible to get at the stored volumes, but inconvenient and expensive, so some historical research may be frustrated. There will, however, be a proportion of the archives (letters, diaries etc) readily available, as well as many volumes of miscellaneous printed matter which are in process of being catalogued. The aim is 'business as usual' as far as possible, for both Club members and the general public.

Preparations for the move, in addition to day-to-day tasks, have put heavy pressure on all concerned, but particularly on Bob Lawford, Peter Ledeboer and Jon Mellor. We are most grateful to them for shouldering the burden. Thanks also to a number of other members who have been most helpful, as well as to those who continue to support the Library financially or with gifts of books.

Michael Westmacott

THE GRAHAM BROWN CORRESPONDENCE

Professor T Graham Brown, who bequeathed his climbing books and papers to the National Library of Scotland, had conducted a large correspondence with fellow-climbers. So among the folders of letters in the Library in Edinburgh there is much to interest the Alpine historian. Any future historian of the Alpine

Club would strike a rich seam: in the collections of the 1930s, for example (when Graham Brown was on the AC Committee) there are many letters from T G Longstaff, John Waller, C F Meade, C G Crawford, E L Strutt and others, referring to the Mount Everest expeditions of 1933 and 1936; and later ones contain correspondence about the *Alpine Journal* which Graham Brown edited from 1949 to 1953.

Janet Adam Smith

ERRATA

The following errors in *AJ94* have been noted:
Reverse of title page, last line: for 0-09-173659-5 read 0-09-173770-2.
pix, line 1: for '150 and 151' read '214 and 215'. (Note: Colour Plates 56–68 are between Plates 95 and 96.)
p40, line 22: Chapman fought in Malaya, not Burma.
p93, Reference 8: the title of Fleming's book is *News from Tartary.*
p208, line 15: for 'Zemul glacier' read 'Zemu glacier'.
p292, line 8: for 'Kopiada' read 'Kapadia'.
Plates 56 and 57 (opposite p214): the captions should be interchanged.
Plate 94 (px and opposite p199): for '1862' read '1868'.
Plate 96 (opposite p262): the picture should be turned through 90°, with the left-hand side at the bottom.

EDITOR'S NOTES AND ACKNOWLEDGEMENTS

In January 1990 the Alpine Club moved from 74 South Audley Street, which had been its home since 1937, and the future role and policy of the Club are under active discussion. The issues are fully described in the Past President's Valedictory Address, reprinted at the beginning of this volume. The recommendations of the Club's Study Group include an invitation to the Editor of the *Alpine Journal* to consider commissioning articles grouped round the great issues of the day. The Editor is fully convinced that the journal should make its contribution to the debate on the many problems facing the world of mountains and mountaineering today, and articles on current issues and controversies are hereby invited (some, indeed, appear in this volume). The only caveat arises from pressure on available space in the journal: gratifyingly, we continue to receive more good contributions than can be accommodated, and there are fairly strict limits on the space which can be allocated to any one topic without unduly narrowing the wide range of the journal.

Many people, too many to be listed individually, have again given help, with practical assistance, advice and moral support. I thank them all – without the helpers the job would not be possible. I express particular thanks on this occasion to the Assistant Editors: Victor Saunders, who manages to combine his work for the journal with an incredible number of other activities, including an epic climb on Kangchuntse as recounted elsewhere in this volume; Geof

Templeman, continuing with quiet competence, as he has done for many years, to look after the book reviews and obituaries; and Johanna Merz who, with exemplary energy and efficiency, has added to her editorial responsibilities the major task of organizing the illustrations for the journal. Grateful thanks also go to Frank Solari for photographic help, to Ingeborga Doubrawa-Cochlin for her translation work and her moving tribute to Jerzy Kukuczka, and to Paul Sidey and the staff of Century Hutchinson for producing such a handsome volume last year.

Above all, thanks are due to the journal's authors. George Band, in the Valedictory Address, said that the Alpine Club lives or dies by its members. Similarly, the *Alpine Journal* lives or dies by its contributors. I am grateful to them all for the enthusiasm put into their writing as well as their climbing, and for the patience and good humour with which they – well, most of the time – endure their Editor's quibbling, nagging and cajoling.

Ernst Sondheimer

Contributors

RICHARD ANDERSON is an ex-soldier who now teaches at St Edward's School, Oxford. He tries to get to the hills as often as family and school commitments permit.

GEORGE BAND climbed in the UK and the Alps, on Everest and Kangchenjunga, in Peru and the Caucasus, before commencing a career with Shell in oil and gas exploration and development in seven countries. He was AC President, 1987–89.

MIKE BANKS is an Arctic explorer (Polar Medallist), Himalayan climber (Rakaposhi), and author. He has made the first ascent of some 35 mountains, most of them in the Canadian Arctic and Greenland, few of them worth repeating.

HAMISH BROWN is a travel writer based in Scotland, when not wandering worldwide or making extended visits to Morocco. Recent books include *Climbing the Corbetts, Hamish Brown's Scotland, The Great Walking Adventure*, and the anthology *Speak to the Hills*.

MIKE BURNS teaches biology in Wisbech. He has worked as a plant ecologist in Kashmir, Nepal, Algeria, Iceland and Greenland. He has also climbed in the Alps, Pyrenees, Corsica and Ecuador.

DAVE COMINS is a mathematics teacher who has led schoolboy expeditions to Peru and Kashmir. He was elected a Churchill Fellow for the Peru trip.

INGEBORGA DOUBRAWA-COCHLIN was born in Poland and lives in London. She has climbed extensively in the Tatra and Caucasus, up to Grade 5. She writes and translates for the *AJ* and *AAJ*, and visits the Alps and Snowdonia every year.

MAL DUFF was born, of Scottish parents, below Mt Kenya, and his adaptation to risk and altitude was instilled at the age of two. His expeditions include the NE ridge of Everest, the Muztagh Tower, Lhotse Shar and Ben Nevis.

GEORGE DVORSKY, born in Czechoslovakia, has lived in Australia since 1983 and is now a schoolteacher in Melbourne. He has climbed in the High

Tatra and on Australian rock, and has published many climbing articles, mainly in Japan.

EVELIO ECHEVARRÍA was born in Santiago, Chile, and teaches Hispanic Literature at Colorado State University. He has climbed in North and South America, and has contributed numerous articles to Andean, North American and European journals.

GERRIE FELLOWS is a poet who has been variously employed and unemployed. She has climbed in Scotland, where she lives, in England, and in the Alps and Dolomites. A first collection of poetry, *Technologies*, is published by Polygon (1990).

JERZY GAJEWSKI, born in Cracow, belongs to the Mountain Tourism Committee of the Polish Tourist Association. He has written several books and many articles in tourist journals, and has wandered through mountains in Eastern Europe, the Alps and in Wales.

TERRY GIFFORD organizes the Festival of Mountaineering Literature at Bretton Hall College of Higher Education. His collection of poems, *The Stone Spiral*, was published in 1987 by Giant Steps.

DENNIS GRAY recently retired from the post of General Secretary of the British Mountaineering Council. He has climbed extensively in the Himalaya, Japan, Korea, Africa and the Andes. His new autobiography is to be published at the end of 1990.

ASHLEY GREENWOOD OBE, MC, was born in 1912. He is an ex-President of the CUMC, the Mountain Club of Uganda and the Alpine Ski Club, and was an instructor for wartime mountain schools. He has climbed extensively in many countries.

ANDREW GREIG is a full-time writer and part-time mountaineer who climbed on the Muztagh Tower (1984), Everest NE ridge (1985) and Lhotse Shar (1986) expeditions. His books include *Men on Ice*, *Summit Fever* and *Kingdoms of Experience.*

LINDSAY GRIFFIN, after a lengthy alpine apprenticeship, has concentrated on remote ascents in the greater ranges, including 33 Himalayan peaks. He intends to continue until increasing age, unfitness and a long-suffering wife call a halt to this exploration.

JOHN HARDING is a solicitor, but was formerly in the Colonial Service in South Arabia. He has climbed extensively in Europe, Asia, Africa and Australasia.

SHEILA HARRISON is the Assistant Secretary of the Alpine Club.

COLONEL IVAR HELLBERG OBE started rock-climbing in the Lake District. He has had many alpine seasons and has participated in five Himalayan expeditions, including Everest (1976) when he reached 8200m. He is an army mountaineering and arctic warfare instructor.

JOHN A JACKSON is retired and leads photographic treks. His climbs in the Alps, Greenland and the Himalaya include first ascents in Kashmir, Ladakh, Garhwal and Nepal, and membership of the British expedition which made the first ascent of Kangchenjunga.

WENDELL JONES is a chartered accountant in Oxford, married with two sons and a daughter. He started climbing in 1952. He has had about 12 seasons in the Alps, and has also climbed in the Pyrenees, Greece and Morocco.

HARISH KAPADIA is a cloth merchant by profession. He has climbed and trekked in the Himalaya since 1960, with ascents up to 6800m. He is Honorary Assistant Editor of the *Himalayan Journal*, and compiler of the *HC Newsletter*.

NICK KEKUS lives in Cumbria. He has an enthusiasm for all aspects of climbing in Britain, but is increasingly drawn back to the greater ranges. His 10 expeditions include Shivling, Ganesh II, Everest and Rimo II.

TIM KING is a keen gardener who has climbed in the UK, the Alps, the Nepal Himalaya and the Arctic. The E coast of Greenland fascinates him.

JERZY (JUREK) KUKUCZKA died on the S face of Lhotse on 24 October 1989. A tribute appears in this volume (pp32–34).

PETER LEEMING has just left his teaching job to concentrate on photography, writing and environmental work. He has led two successful expeditions to Peru and one to Pakistan.

JANUSZ MAJER lives in Katowice, Poland. He has climbed extensively in the Tatra. The Polish expeditions he has led to the Himalaya and Karakoram include the one which made the first ascent of the SSW pillar of K2 in 1986.

JOHANNA MERZ is a photographer specializing in audio-visual presentations. She has climbed in the Pennine Alps, the Mont Blanc chain, the Brenta Dolomites, Bernina, Ortler, Dauphiné and Apennines.

EDUARD MYSLOVSKI is President of the Mountaineering and Rock-climbing Federation of the USSR. He climbed Everest in 1982 and was the leader of the Soviet 1989 Kangchenjunga Expedition.

HAMISH NICOL, a Warwickshire general practitioner, has been climbing for 40 years in Great Britain, the Alps, the Himalaya, Kenya and New Zealand. He advocated the admission of women to the Climbers' Club during his Presidency – a victory for commonsense.

PAUL NUNN PhD is principal lecturer in economic history at Sheffield City Polytechnic. His numerous climbs include first ascents of the British Route on Pik Shchurovsky and the SW Pillar of Asgard. He has been on eleven Himalayan expeditions.

PETER PAYNE has been an alpine climber for 20 years and is currently working in Nairobi.

SIR EDWARD PECK was in the Diplomatic Service until 1975, when he retired to Tomintoul. He has climbed in the Alps, Turkey, Kulu, Borneo and East Africa. His object when serving abroad was generally to reach the highest point available.

JONATHAN PRESTON studied geography and geology at Sheffield University before becoming a goat farmer in the south of France. He has made first ascents in the Garhwal Himalaya and Peruvian Andes, and is currently working in Scotland instructing outdoor activities.

STEPHEN REID is a police officer stationed in Cumbria. The few Alpine peaks he has struggled up are quite ordinary by today's standards, though they seemed hard enough to him at the time.

KEV REYNOLDS has climbed in the Atlas, the Alps and extensively in the Pyrenees. For many years a Youth Hostel Warden, he is now a freelance writer and lecturer.

JORGE RUIZ was born in Bogotá, Colombia, and is Programme Assistant of the Social Sciences Division of the International Development Research Centre. He has climbed in Colombia, Ecuador and Great Britain.

C A RUSSELL, who works with a City bank, devotes much of his spare time to mountaineering and related activities. He has climbed in many regions of the Alps, in the Pyrenees and in East Africa.

A V SAUNDERS, an architect by profession, was taken up by alpinism at the age of 27, and remembers that Marco Pallis began in his thirties, and that Andrzej Zawada led his first Himalayan expedition when he was 40.

ANNE SAUVY is a university lecturer at the Paris Sorbonne. She has climbed a lot in the Alps, mostly on ice, and is a French writer of mountaineering fiction. Her husband is John Wilkinson AC, ACG.

DOUG SCOTT is one of the world's leading high-altitude and big-wall climbers, who has pioneered new routes on many of the world's most difficult mountains. He is firmly committed to the concept of light-weight, alpine-style expeditions.

JANET ADAM SMITH (JANET CARLETON) was President of the Ladies' Alpine Club 1961–64. Her working life has been in writing, editing, broadcasting and translation. Among her books are *Mountain Holidays*, among her translations (with Nea Morin) *Annapurna* and *Gervasutti's Climbs*.

HENRY TODD is a keen climber who will try to climb anything, anywhere, anyhow, anytime. Expeditions in the Himalaya include Ama Dablam, Annapurna and Everest.

IVAN WALLER is a successful student of survival. He fell 15m from the Flake Crack on Scafell Central Buttress, got his parachute wrapped round the tail of a stricken flying-boat, and continues to climb in his old age.

MICHAEL WARD is a consultant surgeon who has combined exploration on Everest, the Bhutan Himal, Kun Lun and Tibet with high-altitude research – the mountaineer, *nolens volens*, being a model for sea-level patients with chronic heart and lung disease.

CHARLES WARREN is a consultant children's physician (retired). As a member of Marco Pallis's Gangotri expedition 1933, and of the Everest expeditions 1935–36–38, he made several first ascents, and he has climbed on Mount Kenya, Kilimanjaro and Table Mountain.

TED WHALLEY is a research chemist who works for the National Research Council of Canada. His extensive climbing experience includes many first ascents on Baffin Island and Ellesmere Island. He was President of the ACC, 1980–84.

ANDREW WIELOCHOWSKI is a past instructor for the Joint Services, with first ascents in Scotland, the Alps, Himalaya, Norway and East Africa. Publications include a guidebook to East Africa, where he has climbed and explored extensively; he currently guides there.

EDWARD WILLIAMS, Professor Emeritus of Nuclear Medicine (London), is now in Holy Orders. He has climbed in the greater ranges and has led, or been a member of, a series of mountain physiology expeditions, resulting in many scientific papers.

GUIDANCE FOR CONTRIBUTORS

The *Alpine Journal* has been published regularly since 1863 as 'A Record of Mountain Adventure and Scientific Observation'. The *Journal* has always been a record of all aspects of mountains and mountaineering and, although its main function is to record mountain adventure, articles on mountain art, literature, anthropology, geology, medicine, equipment etc are all suitable. Articles should be informative, and a good literary style is important. Scientific or medical papers should be of the general style and technical level of *Scientific American*.

Articles Articles for the *Journal* should normally not exceed 3000 words (longer articles can be considered in exceptional cases. Please indicate the number of words when submitting your article). Papers should normally be written in English. Translation is usually possible from French, German and Italian, but papers requiring translation should be submitted at least three months before the editorial deadline.

Articles submitted to the *Journal* should not have been published in substantially the same form by any other publication. Authors are not paid for articles published in the *Journal*, but they do receive a copy of the issue in which their article appears. Please send articles direct to the Editor at 51 Cholmeley Crescent, London N6 5EX.

Typescript The complete typescript including the text of the paper, list of references and captions to illustrations should be typed on one side of A4 paper, at *double spacing* and with 20–30mm margins. Authors should keep a spare copy. Authors are asked, as far as possible, to adopt the *Journal's* house style for proper names, abbreviations, mountain features, etc (for which recent copies of the *Journal* should be consulted). The Editor will advise if necessary, and he reserves the right to edit or shorten articles at his discretion.

Illustrations The number of colour photographs which can be printed is very limited and only top-quality photographs will be accepted. Prints should preferably be black-and-white, between 150 × 200mm and 220 × 300mm in size, and printed on glossy paper. Colour transparencies should be at least 35mm format and should be originals (not copies). A portfolio of up to 10 photographs should be provided. Maps and line drawings should be of a similar size to the prints and be finished ready for printing. Place-names appearing in the text, where relevant, should be marked on the maps also.

Each photograph should be clearly labelled with title, author and any copyright. This information should be typed on a separate sheet of paper attached to the photograph and not written on the back of the photograph itself. Routes of climbs should be marked on separate sheets of transparent paper.

Always take special care in sending prints through the post. Do include adequate stiffening to prevent folding and clearly label the cover: 'Photographs: Please Do Not Bend'. Do not include paper-clips or pins which could damage prints.

References Many articles do not require references. If other publications are referred to in the text, details should be given in a separate list at the end of the article (not as footnotes), and should be set out as in the following examples:

BOOKS 3 G B Schaller, *Mountain Monarchs*. Univ. Chicago Press, 1977, pp15–25 or: London (W S Orr), 1932.

JOURNAL ARTICLES 2 B C Osborne, 'Ladakh'. *Oryx 17*, 182–189, 1983. For *AJ* references, give volume number, first and last page of article, year: *AJ 90*, 201–207, 1985.

Units Metric (SI) units should be used throughout except when quoting original material which uses other units.

Biographies For the 'Contributors' section of the *Journal* authors are asked to provide a 'potted biography', in not more than 40 words, and without using abbreviated style, listing what they consider to be the most noteworthy items in their career.

Deadline Copy must be with the Editor by 1 January of the year of publication. Space in the *Journal* is strictly limited, and early submission improves the chances of acceptance. Articles for which there is no space may be considered for publication in a subsequent year.

Index

1990/91 Vol 95 Compiled by Marian Elmes